ULTIMATE Food & Drink AUSTRALIA

Ultimate Food & Drink Australia

BEN GROUNDWATER

Hardie Grant

EXPLORE

CONTENTS

Introduction	vi
Gourmet regions Australia	viii
How to visit a winery	x
Glossary of terms	xii
How to taste beer	xiv
Types of beer	xiv
Beginners' guide to Australian spirits	xvi
Australia's foodie boom	xviii
Seasonal planner	xx

NEW SOUTH WALES & ACT	**xxii**
Hunter Valley	2
Orange	16
Mudgee	26
Canberra	34
Southern Highlands	46
Best of the rest	52

VICTORIA	**58**
Yarra Valley	60
Mornington Peninsula	72
Geelong and the Bellarine Peninsula	86
Macedon Ranges and Sunbury	96
Gippsland	106
Heathcote and the Goulburn Valley	114
High Country	126
Best of the rest	140

iv

SOUTH AUSTRALIA — 150
Barossa Valley — 152
McLaren Vale — 166
Adelaide Hills — 178
Clare Valley — 188
Best of the rest — 198

WESTERN AUSTRALIA — 206
The Swan Valley and the Perth Hills — 208
Margaret River — 214
Pemberton and Manjimup — 226
Great Southern — 234

NORTHERN TERRITORY — 244
Darwin and Alice Springs — 246

QUEENSLAND — 252
The Granite Belt — 254
Sunshine Coast — 262
South Burnett — 270

TASMANIA — 276
The Tamar Valley and Pipers Brook — 278
East Coast — 290
The Derwent Valley and Hobart — 300
Coal River Valley — 310
The Huon Valley and Bruny Island — 318

Index — 330

About the author and Acknowledgements — 336

INTRODUCTION

Australia is obsessed. That's the only way to look at it. This is a nation whose culinary greatness once stretched little further than lamingtons and meat pies, but in recent years Australia has undergone a culinary revolution, transforming itself into a country of passionate gourmands. This is now a nation home to a burgeoning cast of hugely talented chefs, producers, winemakers, distillers and brewers peddling their wares in facilities that range from the rustic to the high class, from the modest to the magnificent. Australians love to eat, and they love to drink. And now we have the home-grown products and the venues serving them to prove it.

And I, for one, have been enjoying them all. I'm a travel and food writer who has been touring this country - and indeed the whole world - on my stomach for the last two decades or so. I love to eat. I love to drink. And I have thoroughly enjoyed watching as the passion that other countries have for these noble pursuits has flowered in Australia, as the scene here has gone from quirky curiosity to world power. I've seen Australia develop a cuisine of its own, a style of eating that has taken influence from the many different cultures that can now be found on these fair shores, food that's local, food that's seasonal, food that tells you something about the place you're in and the person who has prepared it. We have continued developing our own style of wine, too, which can hold its own with the Old-World legends. We have tinkered with beer and gin and whisky that is now winning slews of international awards.

Australia has arrived on the world scene, and it's an absolute pleasure to enjoy the fruits of so many labours.

Of course, if you want to eat well in Australia you could always stick to the cities. You could enjoy experiences in the nation's urban hubs at some of our most highly-respected eateries, as well as dive into the country's most exciting, most authentic foreign food scenes. Or, you could head to the source.

Australia's gourmet food and wine regions are many and varied - we're talking 50 that are covered in this book alone, and there are more - and each represents something great about the Australian scene, something authentic, something real. Each is also an ideal holiday destination, somewhere that is invariably beautiful and charming and packed with character. Yes, you will find wine in these areas, but that industry has also changed the face of regional Australian centres completely in the last decade or so, encouraging a boom in all things gastronomic, with craft breweries, artisanal distilleries, ciderhouses, and of course incredible eateries popping up in the sort of regional and rural centres you would previously have least expected them.

Three Tails Brewery, NSW

There are some seriously big-hitters in Australian wine regions, including household names such as the Barossa Valley, Margaret River, Yarra Valley and Mornington Peninsula. And those places are well worth exploring if you enjoy the good things in life. However, there's so much more to the food and wine (and beer, and whisky, and gin, and cider) scene than those obvious candidates.

In this book, I've delved into regions in every state and territory - including the great craft beer scene in the NT - to provide travellers with an in-depth look at Australia's finest destinations for gourmet travel. I've profiled many, many venues - from established wineries to lo-fi upstarts, well-known fine-dining restaurants to classic country bakeries, modern breweries and distilleries to outfits that are barely more than a homemade still in a backyard - and included a few places to stay, too.

For each region I've chosen my 'Perfect Day', the absolute winners if you only have a short amount of time to spend. I don't expect many people will actually stick to these perfect day itineraries - but what I'm really trying to do is highlight my absolute favourite destinations.

Keep this book with you next time you visit a gourmet food or wine region, next time you indulge in an increasingly popular passion. Throw it in the glovebox. Keep it in your hand luggage. And be prepared to eat, and drink, and join the obsession.

BEN GROUNDWATER

Introduction

Gourmet Regions Australia

Venue symbols

 CIDERHOUSE

 FOOD

 BREWERY

 WINERY

 DISTILLERY

 ACCOMMODATION

 FAMILY-FRIENDLY

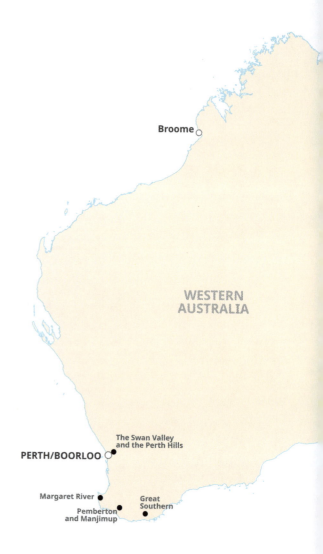

Gourmet regions Australia

HOW TO VISIT A WINERY
(And look like you know what you're doing)

Wineries can be intimidating places, even in Australia. All of that swirling and sniffing, all that black cherry and tanned leather and forest floor, all that sipping and pondering. It's easy to feel like you're the only one who doesn't know what you're doing (though trust me, you aren't).

In the world of cellar doors, it can pay to at least be able to fake it till you make it, to say just the right things and act in just the right way to impress the winemakers and find yourself being steered towards the premium tastings that only go to those who appear to know what they're doing. Fortunately, for that, help is at hand.

Know the tasting process

There's a standard progression for tasting any wine, anywhere. Pick up the glass and hold it up to a light source, a window or a light bulb. Pretend to study the wine's colour for a while. Next, stick your nose right into the glass and take a big whiff. Then, remove your nose from the glass, and give it a vigorous swirl (the glass that is, not your nose). Stick your nose in it again and take another good nostril-full. Give the glass another little swirl, then take a sip of wine. Rinse and repeat, and insert knowledgeable comments – *see* below – in between any step.

Figure out how to describe the style of wine you like

Once you know what you like, it's handy to be able to express it to the people offering tastings of their product to help them steer you in the right direction. Saying, 'Um … red wine?' is not all that helpful. So ask yourself these questions:

- Do I like dry wine, or semi-dry, or even sweet?
- Do I tend to drink wines that are kept cold, or more those at room temperature?
- Do I like light, easy-drinking wines, like gamay, or tend towards something more robust and complex, like shiraz?
- Do I favour certain grapes, and if so why?
- Do I like wine to go with spicy food? Or wine to go with, say, Italian or French food? Or just something to smash while I'm out on the patio on a hot day?
- Do I stick to traditional, well-known wines, or am I keen to experiment with low-intervention, natural styles?
- Do I like something with a lot of acid, or something with a rounder finish?
- And maybe most important of all: how much do I generally like to spend on a bottle?

These are all legitimate and helpful ways to describe your preferences.

Learn a few key wine words or phrases

I once found myself at a wine industry champagne-tasting event, where all of France's best champagne houses were pouring their finest drops for sommeliers and other professionals. I, clearly, was an imposter. However, a knowledgeable friend taught me a couple of things to ask about to cover my ignorance: 'dosage', and 'cepage'. Dosage is the amount of sugar added to the champagne; cepage is the varieties of grapes used. The winemakers lapped it up.

If you want to sound like you know what you're talking about at Australian wineries – and thus find yourself treated to tastings of the premium drops – you just need a few similar words and phrases. Talk about the nose instead of the smell. Mention something about the long finish. Ask if they use a basket press. Easy.

Don't throw out any descriptors if you're not sure about them

Saying things like, 'wow, lots of black cherry', or 'smells like leather and wood, right?' is only going to make you look knowledgeable if you're right. If you're wrong, and you're just throwing words out there to see what sticks, you're going to look like you have no idea what you're talking about (because, you don't). So, rein in the chat. There's no need for that stuff – the person pouring the wine will probably tell you about it anyway. All you have to do is smile and nod and say 'oh yeah, totally …'.

Don't ever say you don't like a certain grape

It's fine to have preferences when it comes to wine (*see* the descriptors above). But to say, flat out, 'I don't drink chardonnay', or, 'I hate cab sav', could be taken as fairly ridiculous. No grape is that much different to all of the others, and you can certainly stomach a sample to see if you like this winemaker's treatment of it. If you still don't enjoy it, no worries. Tip it into the spittoon. Move on. But as soon as anyone hears you shut down an entire varietal without even tasting anything, they won't take you seriously.

Be complimentary

Winemakers are usually intensely proud of their product – this is a year's worth of tinkering and toil in a bottle. So, feel free to gush with as much praise as you feel is necessary. Say it's beautiful, say you love it, say it's the best thing you've drunk in months. Your flattery will probably take you all the way to the premium tastings.

Understand that wine is like art

Though it certainly helps to appear to know what you're talking about when you visit a cellar door, and to be open to trying new things and give them the proper amount of consideration, by far the most important thing to decide is this: what you actually like. Wine is entirely subjective, and you should never feel ashamed of your tastes or your choices – whatever it is you decide you like, it was made by the winemaker in front of you, and they will be proud of it. So, go in with confidence, not fear. As long as you're open and inquisitive, what you like and don't like is up to you. People will respect that.

Be prepared to pay (and book ahead)

The wine-tasting experience has changed markedly since the enforced shut-downs and increased regulations during the COVID-19 pandemic. It used to be that you could just turn up at a winery unannounced, walk up to the bar and have someone pour you a whole lot of samples for free. That isn't the case anymore, and you shouldn't expect it. Paid tastings are the norm in pretty much every region and every winery in Australia now – these fees will range from as little as $5 to anywhere into the hundreds, some will be redeemable if you buy a few bottles, some will not, but the fact remains that you will have to stump up. That's just how it is.

You will also have to book ahead – most tastings are seated now, to comply with density limits and provide visitors with a more personal experience. If you don't book, there's a good chance you won't get in. Do the right thing by everyone, and let people know you're coming – and more importantly, let them know if you're not.

People who are serious about wine (or even just properly interested) visit wineries with the intention to buy wine. Some will buy whole cases, others will only buy a bottle or two, and it's pretty easy for the people doing the pouring to tell if their customers are genuinely interested in making a purchase, or genuinely interested in getting boozed on tastings.

Bottom ChaLou Wines, NSW

Designate a driver

This isn't for looks – it's for everyone's safety. This book is filled with amazing wineries, not to mention breweries and distilleries and restaurants, and if you want to enjoy them to their fullest and ensure you get home safely, you need someone else to do the driving. So, either agree that someone in your party will abstain, or look into other options in the local area. There could be mini-vans with drivers available, limousines for hire, or dedicated winery tours to join.

Relax

Remember: this is supposed to be fun. Whether you're super-serious about wine or you just like to have a drink every now and then, visiting a winery is meant to be enjoyable. So relax, and have a good time. Do the tasting ritual, ask the right questions, try to say the right things. Have a meal in a beautiful setting. Enjoy some local produce. Hang out with family or friends. And above all else, just have fun. Wine can attract its fair share of painful wannabes and difficult customers. You'll instantly put yourself in the good books if you're just there to enjoy.

Moffatdale Ridge, Qld

GLOSSARY OF TERMS

Back vintage

A wine's 'vintage' is the year the grapes were grown and harvested, and will be displayed on the label. Generally, wineries will release their most recent vintage as soon as it's deemed ready to drink, say, in the year the grapes were grown, or maybe the year after. Sometimes, however, wineries will release a 'back vintage': a wine they've been holding onto for several years, allowing it to age.

Fining

This is a winemaking technique in which wine is clarified and stabilised using one of a variety of different agents, most of which are animal-based, such as egg whites or milk casein. Wines that are fined are then filtered to remove any solids that gather during this process.

Lo-fi

Slang for 'natural wine', which itself is a nebulous term without a set definition. Any wine classed in these pages as lo-fi will probably use organic grapes, with fermentation from wild yeast rather than something artificially introduced, with possibly no fining or filtration, and minimal sulphur added at the end. *See* the natural wine boxed text on p.8 for more information.

Methode traditionelle

The method employed in the Champagne region of France – among other places – to produce sparkling wine. *See* p.286 for a more detailed explanation.

Minimal intervention
Wine in which a minimum of intervention by the winemaker is applied. *See* 'lo-fi', 'natural', and p.8 – it's all essentially the same.

Natural wine
As mentioned, for the full rundown on natural wine, *see* p.8. This is a style that is growing in popularity, in which winemakers take a hands-off approach, though it's notoriously difficult to define and categorise.

Sessionable
Something easy-drinking – the sort of beverage you could drink for a whole session.

Signature blend
This denotes the standard blend of grape varietals – say, cabernet sauvignon, merlot and petit verdot – that a winery is known for, and will attempt to repeat each vintage. For makers of spirits, for example whisky or rum, a signature blend would be the blend of spirits used to create their standard product.

Single-block
This is even more refined than 'single-vineyard' (*see* below): a wine made from grapes harvested from a single block of vines within a vineyard. These wines tend to be more expensive and sought-after.

Single-vineyard
A lot of wines, particularly those on the lower end of the price scale, will be created using grapes from a variety of locations, blended to create a product that will taste very similar year after year. A single-vineyard wine, meanwhile, uses grapes from just one location, which means more vintage variation, and wine that is more reflective of the 'terroir' (*see* below).

Skin-contact
This is how all red wine is made, with the grapes pressed and the juice then left to ferment with the pressed skins, which impart colour, some flavour, and 'tannins' (*see* below). There's a growing popularity, however, for white wines that are made in this same way, with the juice of the grapes given extended contact with the skins, giving the wine much more colour, body and texture, and changing the flavour. These wines are sometimes known as 'orange' or 'amber' wines, though we're working on a sliding scale here – the juice can be left on skins for anywhere from a few hours to a few months, meaning the effect can be subtle, or powerful.

Tannins
A natural compound found in grape skins, seeds and stems, which, when present in wine, creates a drying sensation in your mouth. Drink a cup of strong tea, and notice the way your mouth feels. That's the effect of tannins – you'll know it, now, when you sip a glass of strongly tannic red wine.

Terroir
Fancy French wine term for every environmental factor that contributes to the growing of grapes: the landscape, the soil, the temperature, the rainfall, the hours of sunlight, the drainage and aspect. Most winemakers are attempting to capture and display that terroir in their product – they're usually pretty passionate about their patch of earth – while also coaxing out the best results possible from the terroir they're dealing with.

HOW TO TASTE BEER

Wait, what? How to taste beer? Don't you just open your mouth and tip it in? And yeah, that is a reasonable way to drink beer, particularly if you're smashing schooners of a big-brand lager that you've tried a million times before. However, the beer in this book is a little different to that. We're talking artisanal, small-batch beer, beer that has had love and thought put into it, beer that is like fine-dining food, with its high-quality ingredients and deep complexity.

When you go to visit an Australian micro-brewery and you're presented with a paddle of beer samples, don't just pick up the glasses and tip them towards your face. Here's how to properly taste beer, to critique and appreciate it. And still drink it.

Look at it

As with wine, the appearance of beer – the way it looks – is important, and will tell you a lot about what you're going to taste. Grab your glass and hold it up to a light source, notice whether it's clear or cloudy, if it's light or dark, red or brown or black or golden in colour. Check out the head, too, whether it's thick or thin, bubbly or creamy. All of these are intentional characteristics that will affect the overall experience of the beer.

Sniff it

More flashbacks to wine tasting, but this is how it's done. You can't swirl your glass because it's probably full – though if there's room in the glass, definitely try this – but you can bring the whole thing up to your nose and breathe in a deep lungful. What you're now smelling is a huge part of the flavour of the beer. Depending on the style of beer and the type of hops used, you will be able to pick up all sorts from this process, from tropical fruits, even banana, to caramel, herbs, spices, and floral aromas.

Sip it

Time for the good stuff. Take a sip – not a huge mouthful – and allow the beer to cross your lips, hit your tongue, and then swirl it around your mouth to let it hit every flavour receptor and get everything you can out of it. Swallow, and repeat. Look for bitterness from hops, sweetness from malt, acidity from the brewing process, or even added fruits. Depending on the style of beer you're tasting, you might find chocolaty, toffee-like flavours, herbal flavours, fruity flavours or spice.

Sip it again

Go in for a good third sip, and this time pay attention to the beer's texture: is it fizzy, or flat? That will make a big difference to the overall experience. Is it a lager-type beer, or a British-style real ale? Is it thin, like a lager or pale ale, or full and round, like a stout or porter? Does it dry your mouth out or leave you feeling satisfied? These are all things to notice and comment on, and to think about how they affect your enjoyment of this particular beer – and to help decide if you like it.

Smash it

Job done, friend. Head back to your table with a schooner and just enjoy.

TYPES OF BEER

The following are the types of beer you're likely to find being poured at your average Aussie micro-brewery (and even the good ones), and what to look out for when you're trying them.

Lager

Think of this as the classic Aussie beer – XXXX, Toohey's and the like. Lager is usually pale in colour and subtle in flavour, easy-drinking, on the lower end of the alcohol scale, and frankly looked upon with scorn by craft beer nerds everywhere.

Pilsner

Hailing from the Czech city of Pilsen, in old Bavaria, Pilsner is basically a lager when you don't want to say it's a lager. It's also pale, easy-drinking, and low on flavour.

Pale Ale

An ale is different to a lager: it's brewed using a warm fermentation process, rather than cold, with ale yeast and pale malts, and it tends to have more flavour. There are plenty of variations on pale ale, some of which are listed below, though there's also just standard pale ale, which tends to still be fairly easy-drinking, but can also be quite bitter, depending on the hops used.

Golden Ale

This is a popular name for what is also known as a blonde ale. In Australia a golden ale is likely to be light-bodied and easy-drinking, definitely not too bitter, low on alcohol, and built for sessions in the sun.

India Pale Ale (IPA)

India Pale Ale (IPA) is the king for most craft brewers, the style they're obsessed with, the one they want to get right. IPAs tend to have big hop aromatics, floral and citrus notes that will hit you immediately, as well as high levels of bitterness. These will be more challenging than pale or golden ales, often higher in alcohol and big on flavour. Look out for variations such as Double IPA, with higher alcohol and bigger flavours, and even Triples, which turn the volume up on everything. On the flip side, a 'session IPA' will be more like a pale ale.

Extra Pale Ale (XPA)

This is a style of beer that has become very popular in Australia in the last few years, though it's still quite difficult to nail down a defined style for it. XPA means 'extra pale ale', and flavour-wise it falls somewhere between a pale ale and an IPA, with more hoppiness and bitterness than a pale, but also more sessionable than an IPA. Every brewery, however, will have a slightly different interpretation – the only thing you can rely on is that it will be worth a taste.

New England India Pale Ale (NEIPA)

New England India Pale Ale (NEIPA) is another popular variation of the IPA, and one that deserves its own entry. NEIPAs are usually hazy in colour, have big tropical flavours and aromas, and tend to be less bitter than a standard IPA. Trust me: if you see one on tap, give it a whirl.

Wheat beer

This is a style popular in southern Germany and Belgium – see Franziskaner or Weihenstephaner for great examples – beer brewed with more wheat than barley, which tends to be low on bitterness, higher on sweetness, and often with banana or even bubble gum aromas.

Sour

Here's a style of beer only just beginning to become popular in Australia: beer that is tart or sour, aping Belgian styles such as lambic, gueuze or Flanders red ale, aged in barrels and full of flavour. Sour beers in Australia often tend to have fruit added, such as blueberries, watermelon or even blood orange, depending on what's in season.

Stout

Stout is a big, thick, meal of a beer. It's dark, usually black, full-bodied, full-flavoured, and high in alcohol. Guinness is a stout. Murphy's is a stout. This is the perfect beer for a cold winter's day – low on fizz, big on chocolaty or coffee-y flavours, and delicious.

Zero alcohol

You might not have believed it just a few short years ago, but beer without any alcohol is legit popular in Australia now, and it's a perfectly delicious option for those hoping to keep a clear head. There are a few dedicated zero-alcohol breweries around – Heaps Normal (heapsnormal.com) is probably the leader, though Gold Coast-based, Aboriginal-owned Sobah (sobah.com.au), which incorporates native Australian ingredients, is also a good one – and a few of the breweries reviewed in this book do a zero-alcohol option. These beers are often lagers, but can also be XPAs or pilsners. If you're the designated driver for the day, this is very good news.

Cold beers at Three Tails Brewery, NSW

BEGINNERS' GUIDE TO AUSTRALIAN SPIRITS

The Australian distilling scene is going nuts. Though there's a long history of making booze in this country, stretching back to when rum was used as currency back in the convict era, small-pot distilling was actually banned in Tasmania in 1838, while a similar law was enacted in Victoria in 1862, and boutique, small-batch distilleries were outlawed nationwide upon Federation in 1901. So for a long time, the spirits industry in Australia was restricted to just the big players, the likes of Bundaberg Rum and Corio Distillery, which is now closed.

However, in 1990, something huge happened: a Tasmanian by the name of Bill Lark managed to get the hated 1901 Distillation Act overturned, paving the way not just for his own whisky distillery, Lark, but for a boom in artisanal Australian distillers, who now make not just whisky but gin and vodka and a whole range of boutique spirits to sell to a discerning clientele. You will find many of these distilleries in Australia's wine regions, and when you visit, you'll want to know what you're tasting.

Gin

This is probably the most popular small-batch spirit in Australia, not just among drinkers, who can't get enough of the stuff, but distillers too, given the relatively quick process involved to get gin on the shelf (we're talking a few weeks or even days, as opposed to a few years for something like whisky).

Gin is made using a neutral spirit, such as ethanol, which is then flavoured with 'botanicals', though the predominant flavour has to be juniper for the spirit to be called gin. From there, however, the gin world is your oyster, and plenty of Australian distillers use native ingredients such as lemon myrtle and pepperberry to give their gin a local spin.

Whisky

The whisky industry in Australia is booming, particularly in Tasmania and southern Victoria, where conditions are perfect for making and aging.

Whisky is a distilled beverage made from fermented grain mash – usually barley, corn, rye or wheat. If the grain is malted, or treated with water to make it sprout, then you have malted whisky. If it's made with one type of grain in one distillery, it's a single-malt whisky. If it has smoke from burnt peat added, it can be called a peated whisky. If it's made primarily from corn, it's bourbon whisky.

All are aged in wooden barrels, or casks, for as little as a year and up to several decades, and are often 'finished' in casks that have previously been used to age Spanish sherry, or Caribbean rum, or even wine, to impart more flavour.

Vodka

Like gin, vodka is made from a base of neutral spirit, such as ethanol. This spirit is distilled from any starch- or sugar-rich plant matter, such as corn, rye, wheat, potato, or even rice or soybeans. The spirit is distilled numerous times to remove undesirable flavours and chemical compounds, and this pure spirit is then usually mixed with water before bottling. Though vodka is nowhere near as popular among Australian distillers as gin, plenty of producers of the latter also do a small range of the former.

Rum

Rum in Australia used to just mean Bundy; however, those days are fortunately past. There is now a healthy smattering of small-batch rum producers here, who are fermenting and then distilling sugarcane molasses and aging the spirit in oak barrels to gift to the world this delicious beverage. Most of Australia's rum production tends to be in Queensland, where all the sugar is grown; however, you will find small-batch artisans producing rum in South Australia too, in McLaren Vale and Riverlands (*see* p.166).

Brandy

To make brandy, you distil wine. Or, you distil the marc – the solids remaining after pressing grapes to make wine – or you could even distil other fruits, such as apples, pears or plums. Grappa, the Italian spirit, is a type of brandy. Cognac is brandy. Armagnac is brandy. There aren't that many producers of brandy in Australia – certainly not in comparison to gin – though there are some big hitters in South Australia, including Renmark's 23rd Street Distillery (*see* p.204). There's grappa being made here too, though it's not easy to find – try Stefano Lubiana in the Derwent Valley in Tasmania (*see* p.307).

Opposite Tasting charcuterie at Domaine Naturaliste, WA

Liqueur

At its most basic, liqueur is a drink composed of spirits flavoured with sugar, fruit, herbs and spices. Well-known examples include the likes of Kahlua, Cointreau, Sambuca, Amaro, and Jagermeister. The flavours can vary wildly, depending on the ingredients, and some have cream added, some don't. You will find that most distilleries listed in this book produce a liqueur or two, usually as an experiment or a passion project. There's a great example at Killara Distillery (*see* p.313) in Richmond in Tasmania: a 'Bush Liqueur' made with foraged Tasmanian pepperberries. Delicious.

Native ingredients

Thoughout this book, you will notice plenty of artisans – mostly gin producers, though also a few chefs and even brewers – making use of Australia's native plants and animals to make something delicious. There are a few ingredients in particular you're likely to see a lot of in the spirits world: lemon myrtle, with its distinctive earthy, citric flavour profile; and Tasmanian pepperberry, which is similar to regular pepper. There are others, however. Look out for Kakadu plums, with a mild stone-fruit flavour; finger lime, a local citrus with tiny, caviar-like droplets; and wattleseed, with a coffee and chocolate taste.

Several high-profile chefs in Australia have also begun incorporating native ingredients into their cuisine. This cohort is probably being led by Nornie Bero, a Torres Strait Islander and Melbourne restaurateur, whose menus at Mabu Mabu include the likes of saltbush, karkalla, lemon aspen, Warrigal greens, desert lime and quandongs. Famed Melbourne chef Ben Shewry, who runs three-hatted Attica, is also leading the way by incorporating the likes of wallaby and kangaroo meat, paperbark, lemon aspen, desert lime, saltbush and more into his fine-dining cuisine.

AUSTRALIA'S FOODIE BOOM

Though it's gone global now, and morphed into something different entirely, France's famed Michelin food guide began as a free pamphlet for drivers. Two brothers, Edouard and Andre Michelin, wanted to increase the desire to drive cars in France, and hence for people to buy tyres from their fledgling manufacturing business, so they hit on the idea of giving their customers a list of the best restaurants to visit in regional France, the eateries worth the drive, the places you would make an effort to visit purely for their gastronomic excellence alone. The idea was a hit. The rest, as they say, is history.

Of course, back in 1900, the Michelin brothers would never have thought to create such a guide for Australia. Maybe not even in 2000. This country hasn't always been known for the quality of cuisine in regional and rural areas. Unless you count a vanilla slice as gourmet - and sure, we could have that discussion - food outside of Australia's major cities has typically been below par, particularly if you were after a formal, gourmet dining experience, and certainly you wouldn't drive somewhere just to eat.

But all that has changed. Thanks to pioneers such as chef Dan Hunter, whose incredible three-hatted restaurant Brae, in Birregurra (*see* p.89), in regional Victoria, has been true destination-dining now for a decade, regional cuisine in Australia is a big deal. You would now travel to the countryside just to eat and drink. And thanks to the proliferation and changing nature of Australia's wine regions, the desire to encourage tourists to visit and dine and drink and stay in these areas, the food scene in this country has completely flipped. In fact, this entire book is dedicated to the concept pioneered by the Michelin brothers: food (and drink) you would travel for, gastronomic attractions that are destinations in their own right, entire regions that tempt visitors not just for scenery or for beaches or for anything else, but food, glorious food.

Brae remains something of an outlier. It's not in a wine region (though it's close enough to the Geelong wine region to be included in that chapter). The bulk of our best rural and regional restaurants can these days be found in Australia's designated wine regions, areas that people who live for the joy of flavour would naturally flock to. I've included a wide range of eateries in this book that I think sum up the gastronomic attractions in our favourite wine regions. There are fine-diners here, for sure, the likes of Hentley Farm in the Barossa (*see* p.159), Laura at Pt. Leo Estate in the Mornington Peninsula (*see* p.79), and the Agrarian Kitchen in the Derwent Valley (*see* p.302) that would easily find their way into the haute cuisine-loving Michelin guides.

The Source at MONA, Tas

But there's far more to the Australian regional dining scene than that: in this book you will find more casual restaurants, places that go low on pretension but high on quality. You'll find gourmet food shops too, the sort of local wonderlands where you can pick up artisanal produce to take back to your cottage or apartment and create something beautiful of your own. I've even included a few bakeries, country classics, cherished local institutions where you always know you'll be able to get an excellent pie or sausage roll, or a vanilla slice, if all the gourmet offerings of the wine set start to become too much.

The food scene is booming in rural and regional Australia, and there's a real air of excitement to it, as chefs both big-name and emerging move out from their traditional bases in the cities and harness the best of local produce straight from the source, to create cuisine that is truly representative of place. These eateries are endlessly interesting, and indicative of everything the Australian scene can be, and is becoming. And, of course, they're worth the drive.

SEASONAL PLANNER

The good people of Australia's wine regions love a festival. There is a full calendar of events happening around the country year after year, everything from food festivals to wine expos to craft beer celebrations to region-wide events dedicated to all of the above. Exact dates will change slightly each year, and it's good to check ahead to ensure events are happening – especially at the time of the pandemic – but if you want to build your wine-region holiday around a major gastronomic event, this is a handy guide.

JAN

- **Cape Jaffa Seafood and Wine Festival**
  Cape Jaffa, SA
  mountgambierpoint.com.au

FEB

- **Festivale Launceston**
  Launceston, Tasmania
  festivale.com.au

- **Stanthorpe Apple and Grape Harvest Festival**
  Stanthorpe, Queensland
  appleandgrape.org

- **Taste the Limestone Coast Festival**
  Naracoote, SA
  mountgambierpoint.com.au

MARCH

- **Bendigo Craft Beer and Wine Festival**
  Bendigo, Victoria
  bendigocraftbeerfestival.com.au

- **Canberra Good Food Month**
  Canberra, ACT
  goodfoodmonth.com

- **Cellar Door Fest**
  Adelaide, ACT
  cellardoorfestival.com

- **Food and Drink Trail Mudgee**
  Mudgee, NSW
  visitmudgeeregion.com.au

- **Porongurup Festival**
  Porongurup, WA
  porongurup.asn.au

- **Tastes of Rutherglen**
  Rutherglen, Victoria
  explorerutherglen.com.au

APRIL

- **Albany Food & Wine Festival**
  Albany, WA
  wineandfood.com.au

- **Barossa Vintage Festival**
  Barossa Valley, SA
  barossavintagefestival.com.au

- **Bendigo Winemakers Festival**
  Bendigo, Victoria
  bendigoregion.com.au

- **Capital Food & Wine Festival**
  Canberra, ACT
  capitalfoodwine.com.au

- **Orange F.O.O.D. Week**
  Orange, NSW
  orangefoodweek.com.au

- **Tinamba Food and Wine Festival**
  Tinamba, Victoria
  visitgippsland.com.au

MAY

- **Chardonnay May**
  Adelaide Hills, SA
  adelaidehillswine.com.au

- **Clare Valley Gourmet Weekend**
  Clare Valley, SA
  clarevalley.com.au

- **Grampians Grape Escape**
  Halls Gap, Victoria
  grampiansgrapeescape.com.au

- **Grazing the Granite Belt**
  Stanthorpe, Queensland
  granitebeltwinecountry.com.au

- **Taste Great Southern**
  Great Southern region, WA
  wineandfood.com.au

- **Toast to the Coast**
  Geelong, Victoria
  winegeelong.com.au

Bottom Hops at Eden Brewery, NSW

JUNE

- **Heathcote on Show**
  Heathcote, Victoria
  heathcoteonshow.com.au

- **Hunter Valley Wine Festival**
  Pokolbin, NSW
  huntervalleywinefestival.com

- **Mornington Peninsula Winter Wine Weekend**
  Mornington Peninsula, Victoria
  moringtonpeninsulawine.com.au

- **Noosa Eat & Drink Festival**
  Noosa, Queensland
  noosaeatdrink.com.au

- **Rutherglen Winery Walkabout**
  Rutherglen, Victoria
  winerywalkabout.com.au

- **Truffle Kerfuffle**
  Manjimup, WA
  trufflekerfuffle.com.au

JULY

- **Barrel Tasting Weekend Bendigo**
  Bendigo, Victoria
  bendigoregion.com.au

- **Cabin Fever Festival**
  Margaret River, WA
  cabinfeverfest.com.au

- **Huon Valley Mid-Winter Festival**
  Huon Valley, Tasmania
  huonvalleymidwinterfest.com.au

- **Winter Reds Weekends**
  Adelaide Hills, SA
  adelaidehillswine.com.au

AUG

- **A Little More Barossa**
  Barossa Valley, SA
  barossa.com

- **Cellar Treasures Weekend**
  Langhorne Creek, SA
  langhornecreek.com

- **The Curated Plate**
  Sunshine Coast, Queensland
  thecuratedplate.com.au

- **Tasmanian Whisky Week**
  Hobart, Tasmania
  taswhiskyweek.com

SEPT

- **Barossa Gourmet Weekend**
  Barossa Valley, SA
  barossa.com

- **Flavours of Mudgee**
  Mudgee, NSW
  flavoursofmudgee.com.au

- **Great Eastern Wine Week**
  East Coast, Tasmania
  eastcoasttasmania.com

- **South Coast Food and Wine Festival**
  Huskisson, NSW
  southcoastfoodandwinefestival.com.au

OCT

- **Coonawarra Cabernet Celebrations**
  Coonawarra, SA
  coonawarra.org

- **Entwined in the Valley**
  Swan Valley, WA
  entwinedinthevalley.com.au

- **Murrumbateman Moving Feast**
  Murrumbateman, ACT
  makersofmurrumbateman.org.au

- **The Orange Wine Festival**
  Orange, NSW
  orange360.com.au

NOV

- **Bicheno Food & Wine Festival**
  Bicheno, Tasmania
  bichenofestivals.com.au

- **Budburst Food & Wine Festival**
  Macedon Ranges, Victoria
  macedonrangeswineandfoodfest.com.au

- **La Dolce Vita Festival**
  King Valley, Victoria
  winesofthekingvalley.com.au

- **Margaret River Gourmet Escape**
  Margaret River, WA
  gourmetescape.com.au

- **Mudgee Wine + Food Month**
  Mudgee, NSW
  visitmudgeeregion.com.au

DEC

- **Tasmania's Taste of Summer**
  Hobart, Tasmania
  tasteofsummer.com.au

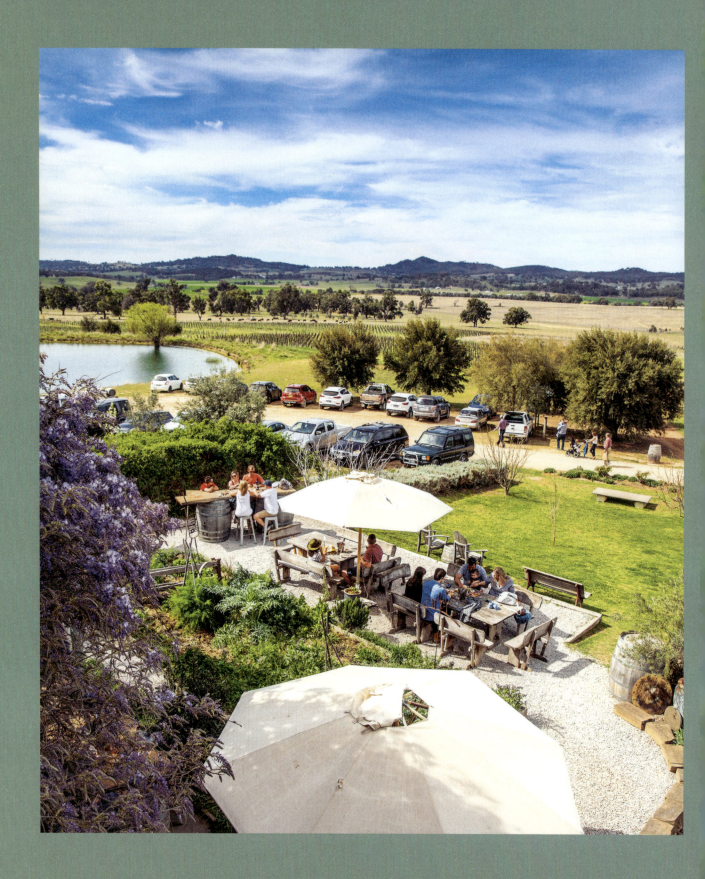

New South Wales & ACT

Offering a blend of tradition and innovation, the wine regions of NSW and the ACT are packed with high-quality cellar doors, dynamic restaurants, laidback breweries and more.

HUNTER VALLEY
WONNARUA COUNTRY

The Hunter Valley is an odd wine region in some ways, a sprawling group of vineyards and wineries with no central point, and no town or village with which to centre yourself during a stay here (though the small cluster of hotels and amenities in Pokolbin would lay claim to this). It makes getting your bearings a little tricky.

However, once you do that – and once you narrow down your accommodation from the hundreds of options of varying quality in this region – the Hunter is an enjoyable spot with some seriously good wine, particularly if you're into its signature varietals, semillon and shiraz. Though the Hunter lacks the prestige of, say, the Barossa or the Yarra Valley, this is actually the oldest wine region in Australia, with vines having been planted as early as 1825, and some of the most celebrated names in the country's winemaking fraternity, the likes of George Wyndham and Maurice O'Shea, made their reputations here.

Many of the Hunter's modern-day wineries retain that traditional feel, though there are a few young guns – the likes of Angus Vinden (*see* p.13) and Usher Tinkler (*see* p.12) – pushing the local scene forward.

Given this region is only a 2hr drive up the highway from Sydney/Warrang, it's the perfect place for a long weekend of slurping and sampling.

Scenic sunset over vineyards near Mount View
Previous Lowe Family Wine Co., Mudgee

AUDREY WILKINSON
HISTORIC WINERY HAS PICNIC HAMPERS AND VIEWS TO SWOON OVER.

One hundred and fifty years: that's serious business. The Audrey Wilkinson vineyard was the first planted in Pokolbin, way back in 1866, and it understandably commands some of the finest terroir, as well as the loveliest views, in the Hunter Valley. The cellar door here sits on top of a foothill in the Brokenback mountain range, with a vista of vines and treetops. Settle in for the long-haul, if you have time, for a 'Picnic among the vines' experience that includes a wine masterclass. Otherwise, just do a simple tasting of AW's standard or premium drops, and soak up those views.

audreywilkinson.com.au

BROKENWOOD
DIG INTO THE SOIL AND TASTE AN ICON AT THIS HUGELY POPULAR CELLAR DOOR.

Brokenwood is a Hunter Valley trailblazer that makes some of the region's best wine, though it doesn't come cheap. Fortunately there's a large range to choose from here, and you can always snarfle a few premium tastings if you sweet-talk the staff at the cellar door. Experiences range from the standard sip-and-sniff tasting, to food-matching classes, or a VIP Soil to Cellar experience that includes a sample of Brokenwood's iconic Graveyard Vineyard Shiraz, and costs more than $1000 a pop. There's a casual restaurant on-site here, doing the likes of steaks, wood-fired pizzas and pastas, and plenty of lawn space for kids to tear about and amuse themselves.

brokenwood.com.au

Top Brokenwood Wines

COMYNS & CO. (4)

ENJOY FINE WINE SERVED WITH A SMILE AT THIS LAIDBACK BUT IMPRESSIVE CELLAR DOOR.

Comyns has to be one of the friendliest and most relaxed cellar doors in the Hunter, thanks in no small part to the ever-smiling Missy Comyns, cellar door manager and wife of winemaker Scott Comyns. Though Scott has a serious pedigree, having plied his trade with local legends Thomas Wines (see p.11) and Pepper Tree Wines (see p.11), his wines are approachable and made to be enjoyed now, rather than squirreled away in a cellar for decades. Call past the lovely cellar door space, just outside Pokolbin, to sample his shiraz, semillon and more interesting blends, chat to Missy, and relax.

comynsandco.com.au

CASA LA VIÑA (3)

A LITTLE SLICE OF THE MEXICAN GOOD LIFE, SET IN THE HEART OF POKOLBIN.

If you've ever wanted to stay in a little Mexican casita – and hey, who hasn't – during your time in the Hunter, this is the spot for you. Casa La Viña is a group of villas near central Pokolbin, and built to look like traditional Mexican Adobe dwellings, though with mod-cons like gas fireplaces, flatscreen TVs and king-sized beds. Breakfast hampers are supplied, and plenty of top wineries are accessible from here, via a 5 or 10min drive. Perfect.

casalavina.com.au

CROWNE PLAZA HUNTER VALLEY (5)

PLENTY OF ACTIVITIES FOR KIDS – YOUNG AND OLD – AT THIS SPRAWLING RESORT.

The Crowne bills itself as a 'luxury resort destination' but really, it's a lot more accessible than that makes it sound. This is actually an ideal hotel for anyone travelling with kids, given there are two- and three-bedroom villas available, plus on-site facilities like a water park, a family-friendly bistro, and even a carousel. For larger children, there's a golf course at the Crowne, and a micro-brewery, called Sydney Brewery. A little something for everyone, and plenty of wineries, distilleries and breweries close by.

crowneplazahuntervalley.com.au

Top **Comyns & Co.** *Opposite* **EXP.**

DE IULIIS (6)

THE CELLAR DOOR IS LOW-KEY, BUT THE WINE IS SERIOUSLY HIGH-QUALITY.

There's nothing too fancy about De Iuliis, an underrated winery and cellar door a grape's throw from the main Pokolbin settlement. The tasting room is set inside the winery, right next to the fermentation tanks – it's all pretty low-key, which makes it even more of a surprise when you sample Michael De Iuliis' wines, particularly his semillons and shirazes, and realise they're exceptionally good. Duck next door after your tasting for a quick, casual bite at the Hunter Belle Cheese Room, or stay the night at The Winemaker's House, a beautiful four-bedroom abode on-site.

dewine.com.au

DIRT CANDY (7)

SOME OF AUSTRALIA'S BEST PET NATS SERVED UP BY A UNIQUE WINEMAKER.

Daniel Payne is an interesting character: a winemaker without a winery; a viticulturalist without a vineyard. Payne is the ultimate free spirit, someone who has no land or facilities of his own, but just buys various packages of fruit each year – from whomever, wherever – and makes wine in whichever way he pleases, though it's often experimental and usually low-fi. Under his label, Dirt Candy, Payne has been turning out some of Australia's best pet nats, as well as award-winning blends and unique takes on well-known varietals. About the only thing normal for Dirt Candy is that it has a cellar door, just south of Pokolbin, and it's unsurprisingly laidback and friendly. There's a good chance Payne will be doing the pouring, too.

dirtcandy.com.au

EXP. (8)

THE FRIENDLY BUT FANCY RESTAURANT YOU WISH YOU HAD AT THE END OF YOUR STREET.

Here's your Hunter date night, sorted. EXP. – yes, it's stylised EXP., not Exp, or even just EXP – is a friendly restaurant with sensational food, the sort of place you wish was your local go-to restaurant. Food here is served degustation style, with set menus of around 10 or 11 dishes to work your way through over the course of a relaxed and enjoyable evening. Chef Frank Fawkner, born and bred in the Hunter, creates innovative, delicious dishes using mostly local and seasonal ingredients – XO risotto with egg yolk; Tokyo turnip with pork neck and shishito – paired with a wine list featuring plenty of local heroes.

exprestaurant.com.au

What the hell is natural wine?

That's a great question. I mean, all wine is natural, right? It's just grape juice, treated to a little fermentation. And that's *sort of* right. But wine these days, particularly wine produced in large quantities by major producers, is also tinkered with in a variety of ways designed to ensure stability and consistency of the product you're drinking. The wine will be inoculated with a particular yeast strain to begin the fermentation; then, before bottling, it will be 'fined', a process that usually involves egg whites or some other animal-based protein being added to ensure the wine isn't hazy, or too astringent. It will also be filtered, to remove any suspended particles; and it will have a chemical preservative added, usually sulphur dioxide or a similar acid, to ensure its shelf-life.

There's now, however, a growing band of winemakers who are removing some or all of those processes in an attempt to make wine as close to its 'natural' state as possible, in doing so creating something that can vary from being just a little different to being wildly altered to the wine you're used to drinking. To make these wines, the crushed grapes - which should be farmed either organically or biodynamically (*see* p.183 for more info on that process) - can be left in open tanks to ferment naturally with wild yeast already in the air. Later, there might be no fining - which means wines could be cloudy or hazy, but on the flipside also vegan - and perhaps no filtration, and maybe no preservatives added.

Some winemakers, for example Jauma in the Adelaide Hills (*see* p.180), will go the whole hog and do everything here: wild ferment, no fining or filtering, no sulphur, just wine as it is, unstable and funky and weird. Others will flirt around the edges: they'll add sulphur, but only 'minimal sulphur'. They might fine their wine, but not filter it - or vice versa. Or only fine some of their wine. They might use wild ferment, but then fine and filter and add sulphur at the end. The 'natural' aspect of wine can be subtle and delicate, or it can be an absolute punch in the face.

The idea across the board, if you talk to these winemakers, is to create a product that is a better representative of their 'terroir', the land and the climate and the grapes themselves, one that is wine, essentially, as it should be. More traditional winemakers, meanwhile, might say some of these products are unstable and unpredictable, and lacking in finesse.

For drinkers, natural wines could be cloudy, funky, and maybe faulty, or just plain bad. They can also, however, be beautiful and real and even better because of their perceived imperfections.

This style might appear to be a new thing, a fad embraced by a cohort of young winemakers and young drinkers, but the reality is that this is ancient winemaking, the way it was always done over thousands of years before modern technology smoothed out the process. It's also fair to say that there is no set definition for 'natural wine': it's not an official term, and plenty of people doing it abhor the expression and want nothing to do with it. Some might cop to being 'minimal intervention', or even 'lo-fi', and others will just say they're just making wine. No biggie.

Given there are no rules here, drinkers should have no expectations (though if you're not a fan of natural wine and you're presented with a long restaurant wine list, definitely say so). This is an exciting branch of the wine industry, something that's endlessly interesting, sometimes brilliant and sometimes a total disaster. But always worth giving a whirl.

IRONBARK HILL BREWHOUSE ⑨

SPRAWLING ESTABLISHMENT HAS ALL BASES COVERED, INCLUDING ACCOMMODATION.

There's a little of everything at Ironbark Hill: a winery and cellar door, a function centre, a wedding chapel, a restaurant, boutique accommodation, and a brewery. That brewery churns out quite a lot of beer and cider, too: 12 are on tap every day, everything from approachable pale ales and XPAs to experimental fruit ales and hardy Scottish-style strong ales. The restaurant attached serves pretty passable pizzas and other snacks, making this the ideal lunchtime stopover for those not too keen to throw down a few hundred bucks (and a few hours) on one of the fancier options.

ironbarkhill.com

KEITH TULLOCH WINE ⑩

FAMOUS HUNTER NAME NOW BLAZING A TRAIL OF HIS OWN.

The Tulloch name is well known in the Hunter: the family has been making wine here for 125 years, and though the family label still exists – simply named Tulloch Wines – it's Keith Tulloch, operating a label under his own name, who is now blazing the trail. Keith Tulloch Wines is carbon neutral, and its premium products have been picking up a swag of awards. The cellar door is set in a beautiful building with views from its wide balcony over the vines; tastings range from standard sets of up to eight wines, to premium selections, to private tours of the Field of Mars vineyard with one of the winemaking team. You can also dine here at chef Troy Rhoades-Brown's 'little French bistro', Muse Kitchen (*see also Muse, p. 10*).

keithtullochwine.com.au

LAKE'S FOLLY ⑪

INCREDIBLY GOOD HIGH-END, BOUTIQUE WINERY – BUT TIME IT RIGHT SO YOU DON'T MISS IT.

You could make a case for this being the most charming cellar door in the entire valley. It's set in a beautiful old whitewashed building with views of vine-covered hills as far as the eye can see. The wine at Lake's Folly is also incredibly good. The only downside is that this is a boutique outfit with a limited amount of product – Lake's Folly only makes one cabernet blend and one chardonnay – and when they sell out each year, they just close the cellar door until next vintage. So, you know, call ahead, on (02) 4998 7507. Get the timing right and you'll enjoy a sample of what are undoubtedly two of the Hunter's finest wines.

lakesfolly.wine

Top Keith Tulloch Wine

MARGAN ⑫

GO FOR BROKE – AHEM – WITH THIS ACCLAIMED WINERY AND RESTAURANT.

In the town of Broke, about half an hour west of Pokolbin, Margan is a highly rated winery with an excellent restaurant, and a welcoming cellar door, with both indoor and outdoor spaces. Tasting experiences range from a standard set of six entry-level wines, to reserve and aged-release wines, or experiences that include snack platters, or behind-the-scenes tours of the winery with winemakers Andrew and Lisa Margan. The restaurant here is worthy of a visit alone, with much of its produce grown on the estate, used to create a Garden to Plate menu, featuring the likes of garden tomatoes with whipped ricotta, and fennel parfait with green olive and preserved lemon.

margan.com.au

MOUNT PLEASANT ⑬

LOCAL LEGEND HAS UNDERGONE A REVAMP, ADDING A SMART NEW RESTAURANT.

Mount Pleasant has always been just that: pleasant. Recently, however, this Hunter stalwart has undergone a major facelift, with a beautiful new cellar door and an onsite restaurant helmed by star chefs Justin North and Kyle Whitbourne. The only thing that hasn't changed is that the team continues to produce some of the region's best wine – James Halliday named Mount Pleasant his Australian Winery of the Year in 2017 – in particular the single-vineyard shirazes, which are legendary (if fairly pricey), though the winery's entry-level blends are great value. Come in for a quick sample, or stay for a long lunch. Either way, you will love this place.

mountpleasantwines.com.au

Bottom Muse

MUSE ⑭

THE ATMOSPHERE IS FORMAL BUT THE FOOD IS FINE AT THIS FANCY EATERY.

It's all quite adult and serious at Muse, at Hungerford Hill Winery – children are discouraged, chefs throw around words like 'restraint' and 'respect' – but the result is an insanely high-quality dining experience that would be right at home a few hours down the highway in central Sydney. In fact, maybe it wouldn't, because there you wouldn't have the same sense of place as you have at Muse, where chef/owner Troy Rhoades-Brown creates menus that feature predominantly local produce cooked with flair. It's Mod-Oz food with a slightly Japanese bent: Hiramasa kingfish with citrus kosho; smoked tomato and Koshihikari risotto; wood-fired kangaroo with black garlic. Formal, yes, and serious, but also very, very good. If you're keen on something a little less stuffy, meanwhile, try Muse Kitchen over at Keith Tulloch Wine (*see* p.9).

musedining.com.au

PEPPER TREE WINES (15)

HUNTER VALLEY CLASSIC OFFERS A RANGE OF EXPERIENCES IN SWOON-WORTHY SURROUNDS.

Pepper Tree oozes class. The setting here is beautiful, all gum trees and gardens filled with native plants, surrounding the sort of old wooden buildings that you just want to move your stuff into straight away and never leave. It helps, too, that renowned winemaker Gwyn Olsen is consistently turning out some of the Valley's best drops – with grapes sourced locally, as well as from Orange and even Coonawarra – at price points that most people will be able to get on board with. Tastings here range from standard cellar-door experiences, to specialised 'vertical' tastings of various vintages of the same wine, as well as picnics of sandwiches, fruits and cheeses, with a cheeky bottle of Pepper Tree wine. Like I said: class.

peppertreewines.com.au

POKOLBIN DISTILLERY (16)

A LITTLE POLISH HERITAGE GOES A LONG WAY WHEN IT COMES TO ARTISANAL SPIRITS.

It's easy to spot this chic venue as you drive along Broke Rd into the heart of the Hunter, nestled as it is among the trees between Vamp by Lisa McGuigan, a striking cellar door, and Blaxland Inn, an approachable, friendly restaurant. At the distillery, all of the product is made on-site, including the base spirit used to make the company's gins, vodkas and liqueurs. Owner and distiller Joe Slupik leans on his Polish heritage here – a country well known for its vodka – so you can expect high quality when you book a tasting, an experience that will take you through the full breadth of the artisanal spirits on offer.

pokolbindistillery.com.au

RESTAURANT BOTANICA (17)

SETTLE IN FOR A CLASSY MEAL WITH THE HUNTER'S WINES ALL IN ONE PLACE.

The food is fantastic at Restaurant Botanica: it's art on a plate, creatively presented, just begging to be photographed and uploaded to your Instagram feed. Dishes like cured ocean trout with pickled mussels and crème fraîche that perch elegantly in a perfect circle in the middle of your plate. But still, that's not the best reason to have lunch at Botanica. The best reason to have lunch at Botanica is the wine list, an intensely local collection featuring all of the wine you should be drinking in the Hunter Valley, including back vintages stretching five, 10, 15 years into the past from some of the Hunter's iconic producers. There are stars from across Australia too, so it's every wine nerd's dream. Spicers Retreat hotel is also on-site.

restaurantbotanica.com.au

THOMAS WINES (18)

SERIOUS WINE FROM A SERIOUS WINEMAKER, SHOWCASING THE BEST OF THE HUNTER.

Andrew Thomas has something of an obsession with purity. One of the Hunter's best winemakers only dabbles in two varietals, those he believes the Hunter does better than anyone else: semillon and shiraz. Within these two grapes he produces a series of single-vineyard wines, with the idea to showcase the Hunter's varying terroir. It's different to your average, in a region where most winemakers experiment with all sorts of grapes, and it results in top-shelf wine created with obvious passion. Thomas has an airy, monochrome cellar door in a small complex with a couple of restaurants, and it should be on the list for anyone serious about understanding Hunter wine.

thomaswines.com.au

TYRRELL'S (19)

DRINK IN THE VIEWS, THE HISTORY, AND THE WINE AT A HUNTER ICON.

Tyrrell's is a Hunter Valley icon, and with good reason: the brand has been family owned since 1858, it commands some of the best plots of land in the region, and its wine is truly some of the best around. The tasting experience at Tyrrell's is sensational, too. Talk the talk and you'll be taken through the full gamut of the winery's offerings, from approachable, entry-level shiraz and semillion to signature blends and single-vineyard wines that go for more than $100 a bottle. And all this is all done in the Tyrrell's beautiful, historic cellar door, which commands views of rolling, vine-covered hills, which look even better over the rim of a wine glass.

tyrrells.com.au

USHER TINKLER (20)

ONE OF THE HUNTER'S NEW KIDS ON THE BLOCK IS PUSHING THE HUNTER VALLEY SCENE FORWARD.

Usher Tinkler is the under-the-radar winery that everyone will be talking about over the next few years. So, book in now while you can. It's run by a winemaker of the same name, who's turning out what he calls 'authentic yet adventurous' wines. Visit his cellar door, set in the original Pokolbin church, to try Usher Tinkler's 'Nose to Tail' series – putting a new spin on well-known varietals – as well as the seriously good (and just plain serious) Reserve Chardonnay and Reserve Shiraz. Pair your tastings with a salumi platter, which is frankly enormous, and you'll be all set here for a perfect afternoon.

ushertinklerwines.com

VINDEN WINES (21)

HUNTER WINE IS TURNED ON ITS HEAD BY ONE OF THE REGION'S BEST YOUNG WINEMAKERS.

Angus Vinden – that's the guy in the hat, whose face is on the wine bottle – is a young, second-generation Hunter winemaker, who just happens to be creating some of the best, and definitely the most interesting, wines in the Valley. Through his Headcase sub-label, he's taking some of the Hunter Valley favourites and doing amazing things to them. Check out his chunky, textural semillon, and his juicy, light shiraz (called, in honour of its Beaujolais inspiration, Shiraz Nouveau). Vinden can usually be found wandering the rooms in this airy, charming cellar door, chatting to tasters and lapping up praise. He deserves it. If you're looking for Hunter wine that makes your heart sing, you will find it here.

vindenwines.com.au

THE WINE HOUSE (22)

A COLLECTIVE OF SMALL-BATCH WINERIES MEANS YOU CAN SAMPLE VARIOUS STYLES AND VARIETALS.

This cellar door, right in the thick of things in central Pokolbin, represents a collective of small-batch wineries in the Hunter that mostly don't have their own facilities, and as such is a great one-stop shop. Grab a seat at the bar and sample Italian-style reds and whites from Little Wine Co, classic semillons from Margan and First Creek, organic wines from Mercer, and high-quality reserve wines from David Hook. Alternatively, save up your cash for the real star: the chardonnay and shiraz made by Liz Silkman from Silkman Wines. Seriously, seriously good.

winehousehuntervalley.com.au

YELLOW BILLY (23)

WINE NERDS AND FOOD NERDS ARE ALL CATERED FOR AT THIS WOOD-FIRED LEGEND.

Ask pretty much any local in the Hunter Valley where you should go to eat and they'll tell you: Yellow Billy, set next to the Piggs Peak cellar door on Hermitage Rd in Pokolbin. It's not just the wood-fired cuisine that brings them here, though that's definitely a hit – the likes of barbecued Cornish game hen, flank steak with chimichurri, fire-grilled mahi-mahi and so on and so on – but the wine list here is also outstanding. Sommelier Pat Hester has put together a collection of sought-after local labels, as well as cult wines from France, Germany, Lebanon and even Georgia. Wine nerds and food nerds: you're all covered.

yellowbillyrestaurant.com

Bottom Vinden Wines *Opposite* Usher Tinkler

The Perfect Day
HUNTER VALLEY

10AM TYRRELL'S

Best to make breakfast at your accommodation before heading up the road to Tyrrell's (*see* p.12), for a relaxed early tasting and some lovely views of the Hunter terroir.

11.30AM AUDREY WILKINSON

Indulge yourself with a wine tasting and then a Picnic Among the Vines experience at this classic vineyard (*see* p.5) that commands Instagram-friendly views everywhere you turn.

2PM THE WINE HOUSE

Take a whirlwind tour of the entire region at this combined cellar door (*see* p.13), which represents a collective of small-batch producers from across the Hunter.

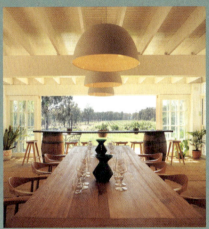

3.30PM VINDEN WINES

The Hunter Valley's best cellar door? It has to be up there. Angus Vinden (*see* p.13) is making seriously good wine, and the venue is chef's kiss perfect.

8PM MUSE

This is a serious restaurant serving serious food - the best for miles - and it's well worth making the effort to secure a booking (*see* p.10).

ORANGE
WIRADJURI COUNTRY

You're going to love Orange. This is the small regional city that could, the agricultural centre, about a 3.5hr drive from Sydney/Warrang, with charm to burn and a reputation for great food and wine.

Orange is in the Central Tablelands region and surrounded on all sides by rolling, vine-covered hills, punctuated by Mount Canobolas, the highest point – as locals never seem to tire of telling people – between here and Madagascar. It makes a powerful and ever-present backdrop to many of the cool-climate wineries that sit among its foothills.

Orange is an agricultural hub that has reinvented itself as a gastronomic hotspot in the last decade or so, with a slew of eateries that are destinations in their own right, as well as a broad range of wineries, breweries and even a cider house producing high-quality drops and providing friendly, enjoyable experiences for visitors. What's not to like?

Top Parrot Distilling Co

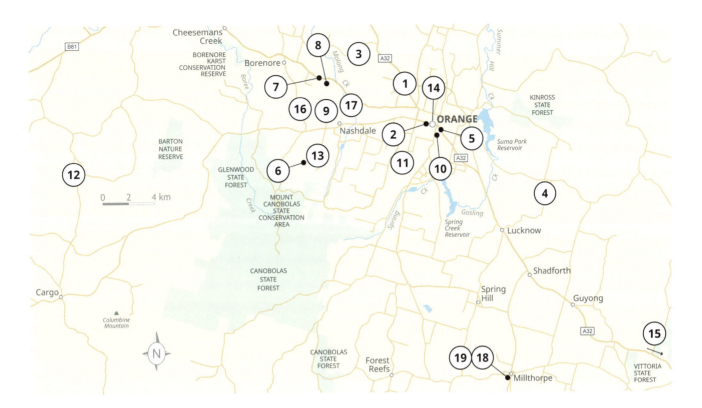

BADLANDS BREWERY

HEAD TO THE WILD WEST (OF ORANGE) TO SAMPLE A FEW TASTY BREWS.

Beer, glorious beer. Yep, you've drunk a lot of wine during your time in Orange, but now it's time to kick back with a refreshing ale, and Badlands has you covered with its cellar door in the Agrestic Grocer building on the western outskirts of town. The Badlands' range runs from the easy-drinking likes of a pilsner and a session ale, to more serious (and boozy) drops like their NEIPA and West Coast IPA. There's a restaurant on-site at the Agrestic Grocer for breakfast and lunch, as well as an excellent cheese shop, and Badlands hosts regular live music.

badlandsbrewery.com.au

BIRDIE NOSHERY

AFFORDABLE, APPROACHABLE WINE BAR AND CAFE HAS FINE-DINING IN ITS DNA.

Birdie is the casual, laidback cousin of Lolli Redini, a fine-dining institution in Orange for more than 20 years now. The 'girls from Lollis' – sommelier Leah Morphett, chef Simonn Hawke, and interior designer Georgie Hawke – have created a welcoming space with vintage posters and eclectic wallpaper, with a focus on excellent drinks, running from cocktails to craft beer to wine, and approachable, affordable food, beginning with a strong brunch offering, and running through to small plates of Italian- and Spanish-inspired cuisine.

birdienosherydrinkingest.com

BLOODWOOD ③

SETTLE IN FOR AN INTIMATE EXPERIENCE AT ORANGE'S ORIGINAL WINERY.

It's a truly personal experience when you go to meet Orange winemaking legends Stephen and Rhonda Doyle at Bloodwood Winery. The pair only take one group at a time for cellar door visits, which means Stephen himself is likely to be taking you around the winery, while Rhonda will be pouring tastings out on the deck of the family home, overlooking the vines. The Doyles established the first winery in Orange in 1983, and Bloodwood is still a boutique, hands-on operation with all sorts of charm to it. The wine is sensational too, particularly Stephen's chardonnay, his riesling, and a red blend called Maurice.

bloodwood.biz

CHALOU WINES ④

YOUNG WINEMAKERS DOING VERY GOOD THINGS AT THIS NEW ESTABLISHMENT.

ChaLou is the talk of the town in Orange, a new winery featuring two stars of the local industry: Nadja Wallington, former winemaker at Philip Shaw, and Steve Mobbs, who was in charge at Nadja's family estate, Wallington Wines in nearby Canowindra. Together they are now making premium cool-climate wines under three different labels: ChaLou, The Somm & the Winemaker, and Dreaded Friend (check out Steve's hair for an explanation). The cellar door at ChaLou still has that new car smell – though actually it's more like a nose of lime and stone fruit and red berries – as it only opened in 2021. Nadja and Steve offer intimate tasting experiences usually hosted by one or both of them, and do a standard sampling of the wine, or take you on a full tour of the vineyard and winery.

chalouwines.com.au

Bottom **ChaLou Wines**
Opposite **Cheese platter at Heifer Station Wines**

CHARRED KITCHEN BAR & RESTAURANT ⑤

HIGH-QUALITY EATERY THAT WOULDN'T BE OUT OF PLACE IN SURRY HILLS OR FITZROY.

Ask for the wine list when you sit down at Charred, and prepare yourself. Award-winning sommelier David Collins has created a stunning list that runs more than 90 pages, featuring rare back-vintages from well-known wineries not just in Orange – though that's a focus – but across Australia and even into the likes of France and Italy. Those wines all go beautifully with the seasonal, local produce that's utilised to create an inventive and ever-changing set menu of wood-fired, smoke-kissed, fine-dining dishes at Charred. The restaurant is housed in what looks to be a revamped steak 'n' ribs type joint, but somehow it works. Every visit to Orange should include a night out here.

charred.com.au

DE SALIS (6)

FAMILY WINERY DOING LOW-INTERVENTION FRENCH VARIETALS WITH STYLE.

Here's a winery that began in a garage, and has been moving on to bigger and better things ever since. Charlie Svenson teamed up with a few like-minded friends back in 1999 to begin making wine on Sydney's Northern Beaches, with fruit sourced from Orange vineyard Canobolas-Smith. It was a hit, so much so that Svenson and his family moved out to the source, purchasing Lofty Vineyard, about 10min outside of Orange, in 2009, and establishing De Salis proper. Svenson and his team, including his wife Loretta, and son Mitch, take a low-intervention approach to winemaking, and they do a fine, fine job of it. Make an appointment at the rustic cellar door, overlooking the Lofty vines, for a sample of De Salis' all-French varietals, the likes of chardonnay, fume blanc, pinot noir and syrah.

desaliswines.com.au

HEIFER STATION WINES (7)

PREMIUM WINES TO TASTE, AND CUTE FARM ANIMALS TO FEED.

Good news: Heifer Station lives up to its name. There are real live heifers on what should have been a cattle station, given owners Phillip and Michelle Stevens bought the property with the intention of running cattle, until they realised the site's ideal elevation and sunshine. Still, the pair have something of a hobby farm on top of a burgeoning wine business, which means kids can pet and feed all sorts of cute animals, while the adults taste wine at the bucolic farmyard cellar door. Great for families, and great for people who love premium cool-climate wines.

heiferstation.com

HOOSEGG (8)

PHILIP SHAW'S NEW WINERY TAKES ITS PRODUCT SERIOUSLY – BUT NOT ITS LABELS.

Hoosegg is different. Very different. Take the name, which is gobbledegook essentially, a blend of the word 'who', misspelled (because people don't know who the winemaker is), and 'egg', because something new is being hatched, and an 's', because owner and renowned winemaker Philip Shaw (*see* his original venture, p.20) says 'it just makes it into a word'. So, make of that what you will. This is Shaw's passion project, the kind of thing you get to do when no one can tell you not to anymore. He's making very expensive wine: a tasting here will set you back about $50, but you will get to sample some of Orange's best wine, made by a master at the top of his game. Tastings are private, by appointment only, and Philip himself is likely to be doing the pouring. Keep an eye out for the labels on his 'Hoo' range of wines, which are risqué to say the least, and again demonstrate the fact that Philip is really doing whatever he wants here.

hoosegg.com

NASHDALE LANE WINES (9)

GLAMPING TENTS AND A WELL-RESPECTED WINERY – WHAT'S NOT TO LOVE?

Nashdale has plenty going for it, not least its excellent range of wines, but also its on-site accommodation, which is pretty unusual in Orange. There are two beautiful glamping tents here, each with hardwood floors, four-poster queen-sized beds, outdoor lounges, barbecue facilities, and wood-fires for those chilly High Country evenings. Wake up, and you're already at your first tasting. Nashdale is known for its shiraz, its pinot noir and its riesling – there's a good chance there will be a few bottles making their way back to your tent with you.

nashdalelane.com

PARROT DISTILLING CO (10)

COME FOR THE CLASSIC AND SEASONAL GINS; STAY FOR THE WOOD-FIRED PIZZAS.

Gin infused with chilli and lemongrass? They're doing it at Parrot Distilling Co – and it works. It really works. The Oriental Gin is just one of Parrot's extensive range that's up for tasting at The Aviary, the company's standalone bar in a warehouse space near Orange's train station. A 'Beginner' tasting paddle includes a sample of classic and seasonal gins, which can be drunk neat, over ice, or mixed with a little tonic. The Aviary also does a good range of wood-fired pizzas, making this a popular stop-off for people on wine tours who are keen to take a break from all the serious supping.

parrotdistillingco.com.au

PHILIP SHAW (11)

BEAUTIFUL WINE IN A MODERN SETTING AT ONE OF ORANGE'S FINEST.

Philip Shaw the man is an Orange icon, and Philip Shaw the label is just as well respected. The man doesn't work at the winery anymore: he's handed the reins to his son Daniel, and now tinkers away on his own label, Hoosegg (*see* p.19). His eponymous winery continues to go strong under Daniel's guidance, and the cellar door experience is one of Orange's best. Set in a building that's part historic bluestone and part bold modern architecture, the cellar door offers tasting flights either with or without a local cheese and charcuterie board. Keep an eye out in your tasting flight for the chardonnay and shiraz, both of which are award-winning and seriously good.

philipshaw.com.au

PIONEER BREWING (12)

IT'S ALL LOCAL AND SUSTAINABLE AT THIS BOUTIQUE BREWERY ON AN OLD FARM.

Though it's a bit of a mission to get here – Pioneer is set up in a big shed out on the family farm about half an hour west of Orange – it's well worth the effort. Brewer Peter Gerber and his partner Tamara are turning out the best beer in the region (or probably any region for that matter), and it's served up in friendly surrounds. They run tours of the brewery and farm – where they even grow their own barley, wheat and rye – and pour tastings and larger glasses of their fine product at the bar. The Vienna Lager and Amber Ale are award winners, but save room for seasonal releases like the Double Chocolate Milk Stout, and the Summer Wheat Beer. Oh, and don't forget a home-made pie from the warmer.

Pioneerbrewing.com.au

PRINTHIE WINES (13)

GRAB A DOZEN OYSTERS AND A BOTTLE OF SPARKLING AT THIS BEAUTIFUL CELLAR DOOR.

The Swift brothers, Ed and Dave, are winemakers with vision. They've taken the ball – in this case the family winery, Printhie – and run with it, setting up a huge new cellar door and restaurant in 2022, atop a hill overlooking a lush valley, producing a whole new line of specialty sparkling wines under their own Swift label. They've even set up an oyster tank on-site to hold live oysters from Batemans Bay, which visitors can pair with their bubbles. It's all really impressive, and well worth experiencing. Book a table for a long lunch at the restaurant, or just grab a spot outside in the late afternoon with a dozen oysters and work your way through the sparkling wines on the list.

printhiewines.com.au

RACINE BAKERY (14)

INCREDIBLY GOOD CROISSANTS IN A SUPERMARKET CARPARK? IT'S REAL.

A small shout-out here for a bakery that has no place existing in a shabby carpark at a shopping centre in downtown Orange. And yet there is Racine, churning out some of the best pastries you'll have this side of Paris. Grab a croissant, or a pain au chocolat, or a kouign-amann, and a takeaway coffee and you've started your day off right.

racinerestaurant.com.au

Top Pastries at Racine Bakery *Opposite* Philip Shaw wines

Orange

SMALL ACRES CYDER [16]

TAKE A BREAK FROM ALL THAT WINE WITH SOME HIGH-QUALITY CIDER.

Two pieces of great news here: one, that someone is making artisanal cider (or cyder, as it's spelled in older English, which should tell you something of the tradition here) in an area that is not at all known for it; and two, that that artisanal cider is actually really, really good. Small Acres sells a range of ciders and perries (pear ciders) from its modest headquarters, essentially a shed with tables, about 15min west of Orange. These range from the simple and approachable likes of the Poire and Pomme, to the Cat's Pajamas, a barrel-aged cider that has all sorts of funk to it, and will challenge everything you think you know about fermented apple juice.

smallacrescyder.com.au

SWINGING BRIDGE [17]

INVENTIVE WINES PAIRED WITH KILLER VIEWS AT THIS FRIENDLY CELLAR DOOR.

You want views? Swinging Bridge has got views. On a sunny day there's pretty much nowhere better than the patio out the front of the Swinging Bridge cellar door, with its views across grape vines and rolling green hills as far as the eye can see. Pull up a chair and prepare to work through a tasting of winemaker Tom Ward's excellent product, which ranges from the traditional – single-vineyard chardonnays that will blow your mind – to the more experimental, like a blend of tempranillo and pinot that Ward calls Tempinot. It's generally six wines per tasting, but if you ask nicely there's a good chance of a few more to sip while you enjoy those views.

swingingbridge.com.au

RENZAGLIA WINES [15]

FATHER AND SON'S INNOVATIVE DIFFERENCES MAKE FOR SOME VERY GOOD WINE.

Father-and-son winemaking team Mark and Sam have some very different ideas about winemaking – though both extremely good – which serves to create a label with plenty of diversity. There's loads here to offer both fans of traditional winemaking, and those chasing something a little different. The Renzaglia cellar door is actually well outside Orange, closer to Bathurst, though it's worth making time to visit here, either on your way in or out of town. Try the standard Renzaglia range for traditional winemaking, and the 'di Renzo' label for something a little different.

renzagliawines.com.au

Top **Crates of apples at Small Acres Cyder**
Opposite **Dessert at Tonic**

TAMBURLAINE (18)
THE SWEETEST CELLAR DOOR YOU EVER DID SEE, IN MILLTHORPE.

Tamburlaine makes award-winning organic wines, and it pours them out for tastings at its charming cellar door on the main street in Millthorpe, a village about 20min south of Orange. The venue offers standard wine-tasting experiences during the day – which can include platters of gourmet local produce – but on Friday and Saturday nights morphs into Sam's Bar, serving cocktails with a side of live music.

tamburlaine.com.au

TONIC (19)
COUNTRY DINING DOESN'T GET MUCH BETTER THAN THIS CHERISHED MILLTHORPE EATERY.

Tonic is a country classic, a Millthorpe restaurant that has been around for almost 20 years, and it's well worth making the short drive from Orange to experience it. Chef Tony Worland's tasting menu makes the most of local produce, with dishes that provide a welcome sense of place, served in a dining room with plenty of exposed-brick walls and picture windows looking out over the Millthorpe milieu.

tonicmillthorpe.com.au

The Perfect Day
ORANGE

9AM RACINE BAKERY

Begin with coffee and a pastry at this amazing bakery (*see* p.21), set in a supermarket carpark in downtown Orange.

10.30AM BLOODWOOD

Book in for a private tour of Orange's original winery, Bloodwood (*see* p.18), with its welcoming owners, Stephen and Rhonda Doyle.

12.30PM PRINTHIE WINES

Cross to the other side of town for lunch with a few samples of the product at Printhie Wines (*see* p.21); alternatively, grab a dozen oysters to pair with a bottle of sparkling.

2.30PM SWINGING BRIDGE

After lunch, ease yourself over to Swinging Bridge (see p.22), just 10min away from Printhie, for a relaxed tasting out on the patio.

4PM PHILIP SHAW

Finish off the day of wine-tasting nearby at Philip Shaw (see p.20), one of Orange's best-known wineries, and one that puts on an excellent cellar-door experience.

8PM CHARRED KITCHEN BAR & RESTAURANT

Treat yourself to a small lie-down after Philip Shaw, before getting dressed up and heading out to Orange's best restaurant, Charred (see p.18).

Lowe Family Wine Co.

MUDGEE
WIRADJURI COUNTRY

There are two Mudgees, as you will discover over a few days here. There's old-school Mudgee, agricultural Mudgee, where the pubs are full of blokes in high-vis and the wine choices are red or white. And then there's the new Mudgee, the gentrified Mudgee, the Mudgee of seriously good wineries and hipster-friendly craft breweries, of wine bars and uber-cool cafes, of whisky distillers and brisket smokers and the like. You can take your pick of Mudgees, though this chapter is dedicated to the latter, because … that's what we're here for, right?

Spend a long weekend here – Mudgee is about a 3.5hr drive from Sydney/Warrang in the Central West – and you have everything from the town's 19th-century streetscapes, to local art galleries, to fashion boutiques and more to explore.

On the food and drink front, you can move from the masters, such as Robert Stein, to the young guns, such as Gilbert, and drink beer, sample gin, eat Texas-style barbecue, and live the Mudgee dream.

BAKER WILLIAMS DISTILLERY (1)

TAKE A BREAK FROM THE MUDGEE WINE SCENE WITH SOME ARTISANAL GIN.

Mudgee has a serious wine culture these days, but it's always a pleasure to try something a little different, which is where Baker Williams comes into play. Tucked behind Vinifera winery, this is a distillery with a wide range of spirits on offer, and it only costs $5 to work your way through a significant number of them. Chat to the friendly staff behind the bar and sample the Baker Williams' gin, alongside more experimental numbers, such as a lemon myrtle liqueur, a vert jus, orancello, schnapps and more.

bakerwilliams.com.au

ELTONS BAR + BITES (2)

EASYGOING WINE BAR IS THE PERFECT DESTINATION AFTER A DAY OF TOURING.

Small bar culture is alive and well in Mudgee thanks to Eltons, a classic of the local scene. The bar does a great mix of small plates and other American-influenced food, the likes of barbecue pork sliders, tacos and quesadillas, and there's plenty for vegans and vegetarians. As you'd expect, there's also a wide-ranging drinks' selection, including six draught beers from small brewers Australia-wide, plus wines from the Mudgee region, and spirits from around the world. The crowd here is young and friendly, and you'll easily settle in for the long haul.

eltons.com.au

GILBERT FAMILY WINES ③
OLD-SCHOOL WINEMAKERS BRING A NEW-SCHOOL SENSIBILITY TO THE LOCAL SCENE.

This winery is easily up there with Mudgee's best. The Gilbert family are old-school winemakers from the Barossa who have made their home – and their name – in Mudgee. Simon Gilbert is a fifth-gen winemaker, his son Will the sixth, and together they are making some truly sensational wine. If you like your wines crisp and fresh, with minimal intervention and maximal skill, then you're going to enjoy the Gilbert product, which runs the gamut from pet nat to traditional sparkling, chardonnay to riesling, shiraz to pinot noir. Sample them all at The Cellar by Gilbert, a cellar door on the edge of town, where a fee of $10 buys you all the tasting you desire. And trust me, you will desire a lot.

gilbertfamilywines.com.au

HUNTINGTON ESTATE ④
THESE WINES ARE MADE TO CELLAR – BUT THAT DOESN'T MEAN YOU CAN'T ENJOY THEM NOW.

Huntington Estate makes serious wine, the sort of stuff that's designed to be laid down in a musty cellar for a decade or two until it really hits its peak. Don't have access to a musty cellar? Don't have the patience even if you did? No dramas – this is still one of Mudgee's most enjoyable cellar doors, and it's not as if the Huntington wines are bad if you drink them now; they're just designed to be even better later. Still, book in for a tasting at one of several spaces throughout the property, and $25 will get you access to all of the premium drops, for a little taste of the high life. On weekends, Huntington also has the Buckaroo Bar, which serves burgers, craft beers, cider and cocktails.

huntingtonestate.com.au

LOGAN WINES ⑤
MUDGEE'S MOST INSTA-FRIENDLY CELLAR DOOR ALSO POURS A RANGE OF EXCELLENT WINE.

If you've seen any photos of Mudgee cellar doors, then you're probably already familiar with Logan Wines. The tasting room here is an impressive architectural feat, encased in glass, jutting out from the hillside above the vines, with views across Apple Tree Flat. The wine, fortunately, is also delicious: Logan produces a large range, some classic and approachable, others leaning more towards the natural side, though all made with skill using grapes from Mudgee and Orange. Tastings here can include cheese platters or local pastries. Make sure you book ahead.

loganwines.com.au

LOWE FAMILY WINE CO. ⑥
ENJOY ORGANIC, BIODYNAMIC WINE AND SEASONAL FOOD GROWN LOCALLY AND ON-SITE.

David Lowe and Kim Currie are a formidable team: he's been making organic, biodynamic wine in Mudgee for more than 20 years, some of the region's finest small-batch drops; she's a dedicated foodie, setting up the Mudgee Farmers' Market, as well as the Zin House, the on-site restaurant and events space at the Lowe winery. The result of this teamwork is the ideal experience for visitors to the region, the chance to enter the cellar door for a standard or premium tasting, pair it with a platter of local food, and head over to the Zin House later for a long lunch or dinner of Mod-Oz cuisine served in a beautiful, airy dining room. Kim's expertise is on full display in the set menus here, with plenty of ingredients from the Lowe garden used in dishes such as tomatoes with smoked goat's curd and olive crumb, and roasted pumpkin gnocchi with slow-cooked egg and pecorino. Afterwards, stroll the gorgeous grounds, with views of the majestic Mudgee countryside.

lowefamilywineco.com.au

MUDGEE BREWING COMPANY (7)

THE GOING IS EASY AT THIS STALWART BREWPUB IN THE CITY CENTRE.

It's not as if the cellar doors in Mudgee are exactly stuffy – this is a pretty friendly, laidback place to tour a few wineries. Still, it's nice to switch off for a while, and that's where Mudgee Brewing Company comes in. This is the ideal spot to grab a few beers, maybe a pizza, and just kick back with a crowd of like-minded souls enjoying the atmosphere in this 100-year-old red-brick former wool store. If you're visiting in the cooler months, be sure to try the brewery's signature beer, Mudgee Mud, named in honour of the town's original brewery, which, way back in the early 1900s, used to produce a beer of dubious cleanliness that went by the same nickname.

mudgeebrewing.com.au

PERRY STREET HOTEL (8)

EVERYTHING OLD IS NEW AGAIN AT THIS CENTRAL HOTEL IN A HISTORIC BUILDING.

There are a few hotels among the vines in Mudgee (*see* Rosby Wines, p.31), but the bulk of the accommodation options are in town, and this might just be the best of them: Perry Street Hotel, a luxury, boutique property, only a block or two from the main drag. The hotel is housed in an 1860s building made new, with contemporary furnishings and plenty of mod-cons. The town's best restaurants and bars are walking distance away.

perrystreethotel.com.au

ROBERT STEIN (9)

A MUDGEE ORIGINAL STILL OFFERING SOME OF THE REGION'S BEST WINE AND FINE FOOD.

Don't be fooled by the modest exterior of the Robert Stein cellar door. It's true there are no grand architectural flourishes here, no crowd-pleasing outdoor spaces with rolling-hill views – but you're here for the wine, and the wine is very, very good. The Robert Stein winery has been up and running since the 1970s, and it's still comfortably among Mudgee's best, producing a seriously high-quality range of rieslings in particular, though there's also excellent chardonnay, shiraz and cabernet sauvignon to be sampled. None come cheap – but then, wine of this quality rarely does. There's a restaurant on-site too, called Pipeclay Pumphouse, a fine-diner doing locavore food: six-course set menus that will help you pass a lazy afternoon or evening in style.

robertstein.com.au

Pipeclay Pumphouse at Robert Stein
Opposite Three Tails Brewery

ROSBY WINES (10)

WAKE UP TO VIEWS OF VINES IN THE COUNTRY HOME OF YOUR DREAMS.

Rosby offers one of the few 'among the vines' accommodation options in the Mudgee region: a gorgeous guesthouse and studio with the sort of idyllic rural outlook over the Mudgee Valley that will have you making plans for a tree change in no time. This large house sleeps eight, with a separate, private studio to sleep two more, and it's the epitome of countryside delight. While you're staying, tour the farm and say hello to the chickens, try the excellent Rosby wines at the cellar door, and check out the sculpture garden, set up by Kay Norton-Knight, host, artist-in-residence, and wife of winemaker Gerald. This whole outfit is a family affair, borne of passion and joy – and it shows.

rosby.com.au

ROTH'S WINE BAR + CELLAR (11)

TAKE A WINERY MINI TOUR, SAMPLING DROPS FROM SOME OF THE BEST IN MUDGEE.

Maybe you don't have time to tour every winery you want to visit in Mudgee; maybe you just can't be bothered. Either way, you can find all of the region's hits in one spot at Roth's Wine Bar + Cellar, a sprawling space that's part restaurant, part live music venue, part bottle shop and part bar. It has an enviable list of local wines – drop in at the beginning of your stay and you will soon have your itinerary sorted.

rothswinebar.com.au

THREE TAILS BREWERY (12)

THE ULTIMATE AMERICAN CRAFT BREWERY EXPERIENCE, TRANSPLANTED TO MUDGEE.

Three Tails kicks arse – there's no other way to put it. This is the American craft brewery experience transplanted to downtown Mudgee, even though it's set in a classic Aussie building, even though it's … well, it's in downtown Mudgee. Three Tails has a phenomenal 18 beers on tap, most made on-site by the local team, though they always feature some greats from around the world, crafty brews from as far afield as the UK, Europe and the US. To eat, you have genuine American dude food: smoky brisket burgers, whopping racks of ribs, tacos, even bacon mac 'n' cheese. This place is the real deal – probably not what you were expecting to find in Mudgee, but more than enough reason to keep coming back.

threetailsbrewery.com.au

The Perfect Day
MUDGEE

10AM LOGAN WINES

Begin your day of perfection out to the south-east of Mudgee at Logan Wines (*see* p.29), perhaps the region's most impressive cellar door, to enjoy the views and the tasting experience.

11.30AM GILBERT FAMILY WINES

Head back through Mudgee and over to the Gilbert cellar door (*see* p.29) to sample the future of the Mudgee wine scene.

1PM ROBERT STEIN

This is a classic, no frills but all class in the wine department. It's also a great place to settle in for a long lunch at Pipeclay Pumphouse (*see* p.30).

3.30PM HUNTINGTON ESTATE

After lunch, ease on down the road to Huntington Estate (*see* p.29) for a tasting of some serious wine in gorgeous surrounds.

6PM THREE TAILS BREWERY

Dinner tonight is at the superb Three Tails Brewery (*see* p.31), which has 18 craft beers on tap, smoked brisket and ribs to dine on, and a super-friendly crowd.

9PM ROSBY WINES

Spend tonight at the Rosby Guesthouse (*see* p.31), and wake up to rural splendour.

Clonakilla

CANBERRA
NGAMBRI/NGUNNAWAL COUNTRY

Welcome to Canberra/Ngambri/Ngunnawal, the nation's capital, where the vast majority of its region's wineries are well outside city limits, and indeed outside of the entire ACT. Weird, huh? The Canberra District wine region mostly lies across the border in NSW, spread in an arc to the north of the territory, from Murrumbateman to Collector and Lake George.

This is a relatively young region and a small one too, though it punches well above its weight in terms of quality, with established icons such as Clonakilla and Helm, alongside exciting up-and-comers like Mallaluka and Contentious Character.

The vineyards of the Canberra District tend to be fairly spread out, making planning your travels here essential: it's best to group your days either around the Murrumbateman area, which has plenty to keep you occupied, or over on the Lake George side, rather than attempt to flit between the two.

Accommodation is also tricky, as there aren't a huge number of options among the vines themselves; though, with downtown Canberra only a half-hour to 45min drive from the wineries, a stay in town is definitely a possibility – plus there's some great bars and breweries in the city too.

If you have longer to spend in Canberra itself, you can soak up the many national museums, monuments and galleries, but let's face it … you're here for the food and wine.

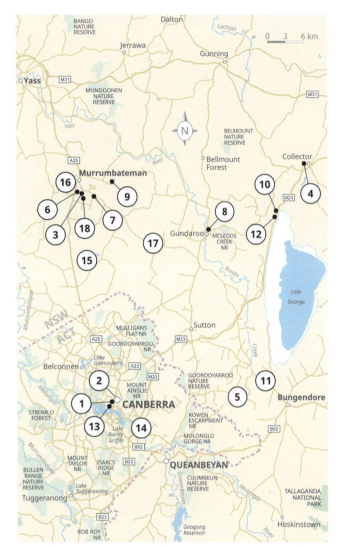

BAR ROCHFORD (1)

IMAGINATIVE SMALL-PLATES MENU MEETS A WINE LIST TO HANG AROUND FOR.

This is a bar, not a winery, and it's in the city, not among the vines – but still, Bar Rochford should be on the itinerary for any food and wine lover. Set in downtown Canberra, this is a sleek, classy establishment with a drinks' list any wine nerd would swoon over, featuring a blend of Australia's finest drops, up against sought-after wines from France, Italy, Spain and even Austria. The food is set-menus of imaginative small plates, the likes of smoked beef tongue with anchovy mayo, galette with tuna and bottarga, and white asparagus with gribiche and pangrattato.

barrochford.com

BENTSPOKE BREWING CO. (2)

BIKE-THEMED CRAFT BREWERY BRINGS A MALTY, HOPPY TOUR DE FORCE.

BentSpoke, again, is not exactly among the vines – it's in Braddon, on the northern fringe of Canberra's CBD. Still, if you're basing yourself in the city, the BentSpoke brewpub is an excellent venue to have on your itinerary, particularly if you appreciate a cold ale. The pub has a rotating selection of 18 beers and ciders on tap at any given time, plus there's top-notch food, a fairly wild mix that runs the gamut from American dude food to Italian and pan-Asian. While you're there, grab a few takeaway cans: BentSpoke is probably best known for its Crankshaft IPA, but keep an eye out for the more experimental Drifter range, which features the likes of the fruity Hop Juice IPA, and Fixie, and alcoholic ginger beer.

bentspokebrewing.com.au

Bar Rochford *Opposite* Clonakilla cellar door

CLONAKILLA (3)

TRUE CANBERRA CLASSIC OFFERS TASTINGS OF ITS MOST ICONIC WINE.

This is it: the icon of the Canberra region, producer of perhaps its single best-known wine, the Clonakilla Shiraz Viognier. Plenty of Canberra wineries are now copying this signature blend, but none are doing it so well. For this reason alone, Clonakilla should be on every Canberra wine-tasting itinerary. It helps, too, that the cellar door here is a beautiful, airy space, where the welcome is warm and the tastings are generous, including samples of that sought-after shiraz viognier. Keep an eye out, too, for Clonakilla's riesling, its chardonnay and its single-vineyard shiraz. This is a boutique business, still owned and run by the Kirk family (since 1971), and it shows.

clonakilla.com.au

COLLECTOR WINES (4)

HISTORIC COTTAGE HOUSES ONE OF THE REGION'S MOST UNLIKELY CELLAR DOORS.

Are we … in the right spot? That's a common enough question as you approach the cellar door at Collector Wines, housed in the town of Collector, population 313. There are no vines around here. Not much of anything at all. But yes, you are in the right place when you pull up to the Old Collector Inn, a brick cottage built in 1829 that today houses the Collector Wines cellar door, as well as a cracking little eatery called Some Cafe, which does classic Mod-Oz breakfasts and lunches. The wines on offer here are the pride and joy of winemaker Alex McKay, who sources grapes from around the traps, and makes excellent chardonnays, as well as lesser-known varietals such as fiano, grüner veltliner and sangiovese.

collectorwines.com.au

CONTENTIOUS CHARACTER (5)

THIS WINERY MIGHT BE CONTENTIOUS BY NAME, BUT SERIOUS BY NATURE.

As you can tell by the name, Contentious Character is all about doing things a little differently. The wines themselves are called things like Dry as a Dead Dingo's Donga Riesling, and Fifty Shades of Grape Pinot Grigio. So yeah, the idea is to get people talking. And they do. The names, however, are something of a bluff, because the winemaking here is serious business and the product is extremely good. Give it a sample on-site at the Contentious Character winery, just south of Lake George in Wamboin. The team here are friendly and knowledgeable, and there's a restaurant here too, serving up pan-Mediterranean fare with an interesting Korean flex. There are trivia nights if you're there on a Thursday.

contentiouscharacter.com.au

FOUR WINDS VINEYARD ⑦
MURRUMBATEMAN ESTABLISHMENT KEEPS THINGS COOL AND CASUAL.

Does Four Winds make the best wine in the Canberra District? No. Does it make nice wine though, and provide an enjoyable, laidback tasting experience? Most definitely. Four Winds has put plenty of work into making a visit here fun, and it shows. The setting is stunning, among vines and towering gum trees, and there's often a party atmosphere, as large groups pile in to sample the wines and smash a few pizzas. No frills, no pretenses, just good times.

fourwindsvineyard.com.au

EDEN ROAD WINES ⑥
THE PERFECT PLACE TO SAMPLE THE VARIED VARIETALS OF THE CANBERRA WINE REGION.

Eden Road's organic vineyards are spread around the local area – in Murrumbateman, over near Lake George, even as far afield as Tumbarumba in the Snowys – which makes for a varied array of varietals all chosen from the areas in which they grow best. And what that means is really, really good wine. Renowned French winemaker Celine Rousseau is in charge here, and she makes some of Canberra's best syrah, and some of Tumbarumba's best chardonnay and pinot noir. They're all on for tasting at Eden Road's base near Murrumbateman, a friendly spot that offers 30min or 1hr tasting experiences, with or without cheese platters to match.

edenroadwines.com.au

GRAZING ⑧
ENJOY MOD-OZ FINE-DINING IN A SURPRISING RURAL LOCATION.

Fine-dining restaurants aren't easy to come by once you're outside the Canberra city limits, which makes Grazing, in small-town Gundaroo in the Yass Valley, all the more welcome. Accessible from pretty much anywhere within the wine region, Grazing serves up two- or three-course lunches and dinners in the historic and thoroughly charming 1865 Royal Hotel building. The food here is modern Australian, featuring local ingredients, with a lean towards the flavours of the Mediterranean. The wine list is compact but well chosen, with plenty of local stars making an appearance. Gundaroo itself is National Trust–classified, with 19th-century heritage buildings and slab huts, so a walk around town is a worthy pre- or post-meal activity.

grazing.com.au

Top Eden Road Wines *Opposite* Winemaker Ken Helm, Helm Wines

HELM WINES
THERE'S A STORY IN EVERY GLASS AT THIS CLASSIC, CASUAL CELLAR DOOR.

Come for the wine, stay for the chat. Winemaker Ken Helm is the consummate host at this quirky little cellar door, housed in a historic building that was once, as Helm likes to tell people, a public schoolhouse used by the Temperance League for its meetings. No doubt the attendees would have disapproved of its current use, which is allowing visitors to sample Helm's incredibly good wine, made with great care and minimal intervention at the winery on-site. Helm is a former CSIRO scientist turned winemaking prodigy, and he's a proper character. You'll have plenty of time to draw a few stories out of him while sampling Helm's award-winning rieslings and cabernet sauvignons.

helmwines.com.au

LAKE GEORGE WINERY
ENJOY A GLASS OF WINE, A BITE TO EAT, AND A PLACE TO STAY, ALL UNDER ONE ROOF.

There's a lot going on at Lake George Winery, one of the original Canberra District wineries. Vines were first planted here by a legend of the local scene, Edgar Riek, in 1971. They're still going strong, and the winery's current owners produce top-quality riesling and chardonnay – among others. But anyway, like I said, a lot going on: Lake George Winery has a cellar door, a restaurant, spaces for weddings and events, and accommodation in the form of two cosy 'tiny homes'. There's even a 'dining dome' for your exclusive use. Owner Sarah McDougall also runs Vine to Wine tours, going from vineyard to winery to cellar door.

lakegeorgewinery.com.au

LARK HILL WINERY (11)

LARK HILL IS ALL ABOUT TIME WELL SPENT, SO CHILL OUT AND ENJOY THIS BIODYNAMIC WINERY.

The idea at the Lark Hill cellar door is to take your time and just relax. There are flights of wines to try, or you can grab a whole glass and a cheese platter and enjoy the surrounds either in the leafy courtyard, or inside the stone-walled original winery. Lark Hill is a certified biodynamic winery that specialises in pinot noir and riesling, though there's also excellent chardonnay here, grown nearby on an old Ravensworth site, and there's syrah. There's a restaurant, too: D&K Kitchen, which does modern Australian cuisine – barramundi in Thai green curry sauce; slow-cooked lamb shoulder on potato gnocchi – in a dining room overlooking the vines.

larkhill.wine

LERIDA ESTATE (12)

SOAK UP STUNNING VALLEY VIEWS AT THIS SPECTACULAR CELLAR DOOR AND CAFE.

This is a relatively new winery – under its current ownership – with a frankly kick-ass cellar door and cafe, a sprawling modern space overlooking vines and hilltops out to Lake George. It's also just off the Federal Highway, so you can't (and shouldn't) miss it if you're driving from Sydney to Canberra, or vice versa. The focus here is supposed to be pinot noir, though Lerida now produces award-winning shiraz, excellent riesling, and a whole range of easy-drinking rosés. The cafe serves a compact and tasty menu, with all tables and tasting positions enjoying sweeping views out across the valley.

leridaestate.com.au

MALLALUKA

SUPER-TALENTED WINEMAKER IS SET TO OPEN THE DOORS FOR VISITORS.

Just a quick shout-out, really, for Mallaluka Wines, near Yass. It's a shout-out because the wines being made by up-and-comer Sam Leyshon are seriously good: these are low-fi natural drops with plenty of texture and crunch, influenced by some of the best experimental winemakers in the world. It's a quick shout-out, because at the time of writing Mallaluka didn't have a cellar door, though with plans to open one in 2022, it's worth checking in to see if they're now taking visitors.

mallaluka.com.au

OVOLO NISHI (13)

DESIGN-HEAVY HOTEL MAKES THE PERFECT BASE IN THE NATION'S CAPITAL.

This is without a doubt Canberra's most stylish hotel, and with accommodation options limited around the wineries themselves, this is the perfect place to base yourself during a weekend (or week) of capital wine-tasting. From the moment you step into the lobby here, with walls of wooden beams set out like mosaics, to the time you sling your bags onto the floor in your unique and creatively designed room, you will be impressed. Try to make it back to the hotel each day in time for 'social hour', when complimentary sundowner drinks are served to all guests.

ovolohotels.com

PIALLIGO ESTATE (14)

PLAN TO SPEND THE DAY AT THIS MULTI-FACETED WINERY – THERE'S A LOT TO DO HERE.

Pialligo is a bit of a beast, but in a good way: there's something here for everyone, from standard wine-tasting experiences at the cellar door, to seasonal and organic fine-dining at Pavilion, fresh produce at the Pialligo Market Grocer, a Farm Shop Cafe serving food utilising that produce, and a smokehouse that produces its own bacon and smoked salmon. The kids will be kept happy at the Kids Academy with its sensory playground, plus there's a wedding and events space, and they do cooking and art classes at the Pialligo Estate Academy. Phew. You could make a whole day of it here and still not do everything.

thepialligoestate.com.au

Top Lerida Estate *Opposite* Vines at Mallaluka

POACHERS PANTRY SMOKEHOUSE (15)

SUMPTUOUS BRUNCHES AND GOURMET PICNICS IN IDYLLIC RURAL SURROUNDS.

Brunch fans, set your GPS for Poachers Pantry. This beautiful, rustic eatery, just south of Murrumbateman, is famous for its two-course brunches, which begin with a choice of pastries, scones or fruit, and then ramp things up significantly with options such as a full Smokehouse Breakfast (bacon, sausage, tomatoes, eggs, potato rosti, sourdough), or eggs Benedict with 63-degree eggs. If you're arriving later in the day, the Pantry also does a lunch menu, or picnic hampers stuffed with gourmet produce, perfect for pairing with a Poachers wine, produced nearby. The setting here is rural beauty at its finest and you'll never want to leave.

poacherspantry.com.au

RAVENSWORTH

THE WINE HERE IS SENSATIONAL BUT THE ONLY CHALLENGE IS GETTING IN.

Ravensworth has a lot going for it: excellent pedigree, with winemakers coming across from Clonakilla; great product, with a highly rated riesling and shiraz viogner; and a beautiful spot in the Murrumbateman area. About the only thing Ravensworth doesn't have – at time of writing, at least – is a cellar door. I've included it here, however, because there are always rumours of guests being welcomed soon, and the wine is sensational, so it's worth checking the website and hoping.

ravensworthwines.com.au

SHAW WINES (16)

PREPARE TO TAKE FLIGHT AT ONE OF CANBERRA'S MOST STYLISH CELLAR DOORS.

Shaw Wines is a pretty schmick operation, set in the sort of building most architects dream of designing, all sharp lines and striking glass walls. The building is reflective of the product, too: Shaw is one of the largest producers in the Canberra district, a family-owned outfit that makes very good wine. There are all sorts of ways of experiencing that wine too, from a standard tasting flight at the cellar door, to premium wine-and-chocolate tastings. For something a little more luxe, there are chartered light-plane flights from Sydney to Canberra with a three-course lunch and access to the Shaw private cellar. Fancy.

shawwines.com.au

Top **Poachers Pantry Smokehouse**
Opposite **The Vintner's Daughter**

TALLANGANDRA HILL (17)
BED DOWN FOR A NIGHT AMONG THE VINES, OR JUST CALL IN FOR A TASTING.

Here's something you won't find too often in the Canberra region: a winery with on-site accommodation, in this case a selection of three cottages, each self-contained and sleeping two adults, with kitchen, lounge area and deck, overlooking Tallangandra Hill Winery. The cottages are only for adults, but kids are catered for if you're just calling in to the cellar door, with a playground on-site. The wines on offer here are all approachable and affordable, and there are platter-style lunches served on weekends.

tallangandrahill.com.au

THE VINTNER'S DAUGHTER (18)
FAMILY TRADITION IS KEPT ALIVE BY A WINEMAKER CARVING HER OWN NICHE.

The titular vintner here is Ken Helm, the charismatic winemaker at Helm Wines (*see* p.39). The vintner's daughter, meanwhile, is Stephanie Helm, who has inherited her father's skill at the alchemical creation of delicious beverages, as well as his knack for telling a good story. Stephanie, together with her partner and vineyard manager Benjamin Osborne, is turning out wine to be seriously proud of, on an estate nestled between Clonakilla and Eden Road near Murrumbateman. Keep an eye out for the award-winning rieslings when you drop in for a tasting here, and if it's a warm day ask for a spot on the deck for the perfect experience.

thevintnersdaughter.com.au

The Perfect Day
CANBERRA

9AM POACHERS PANTRY SMOKEHOUSE

Time to load up for a big day ahead with a two-course brunch at Poachers Pantry (*see* p.42). And once you're done, grab a generous gourmet hamper for lunch on the go.

11AM HELM WINES

Begin the day's wine tasting with a relaxed experience in the old school house at Helm Wines (*see* p.39). The riesling and cabernet are top-notch, and winemaker Ken Helm's company is always a pleasure.

1PM CLONAKILLA

Nearby to Helm, you'll find what is probably Canberra's best-known winery, Clonakilla (*see* p.37), producing its best-known wine: the shiraz-viognier blend. It's on for tasting here too, despite the high price tag.

3PM THE VINTNER'S DAUGHTER

You've barely fastened your seatbelt before arriving at the Vintner's Daughter (see p.43), where a spot out on the verandah with a flight of tastings should see you through the rest of the afternoon.

7PM BENTSPOKE BREWING CO.

Time to head back into the city and begin your evening with a beer at BentSpoke Brewing Co. (see p.36), just north of the Canberra CBD.

8PM BAR ROCHFORD

Spend a long evening working your way through the menu of small plates at Bar Rochford (see p.36), paired with wines from around the world. And then ... a cab home.

SOUTHERN HIGHLANDS
DHARAWAL AND GUNDUNGURRA COUNTRY

It's easy to miss the Southern Highlands wine region – in fact many no doubt have as they've made their way along the Hume Highway from Sydney/Warrang south to Canberra/Ngambri/Ngunnawal and beyond. However, it's worth slowing down around Bowral, Mittagong and Moss Vale to sample the produce of a region that, though modest in reputation, has been growing grapes and producing wine as far back as the 1870s.

These days, the Southern Highlands is home to a smattering of well-respected wineries producing excellent high-altitude chardonnays, cabernet sauvignons and shiraz, plus these country towns are now home to an increasing number of laidback microbreweries, and distilleries that take their craft very seriously. And, perhaps weirdly, you will also find one of Australia's best Thai restaurants here. Score.

Mittagong makes a good base for Southern Highlands exploration: it's a compact though lovely town that offers easy access to most of the wineries and other food and drink attractions included here, as well as being very close to Bowral, a much larger population base. Mittagong is also home to that aforementioned Thai restaurant Paste (*see* p.49).

ARTEMIS ①

ALL BASES ARE COVERED HERE, FROM WINE TO GIN AND WOOD-FIRED PIZZA.

Give yourself a good couple of hours to visit Artemis, a charming winery, distillery and cellar door just off the highway near Mittagong. To begin with, there's plenty here to sample: cool-climate wines such as Artemis' signature pinot noir, plus highly rated riesling and other aromatic whites; a huge range of spirits, from gin to eau de vie to baijiu; plus, during the week, charcuterie boards to pick over, and wood-fired pizzas on weekends. Best of all, the Artemis cellar door is set next to a rolling green lawn, perfect for long afternoons in the sun as the kids enjoy the chance to run wild. In winter, there's always a fire going inside.

artemiswines.com.au

BENDOOLEY ESTATE ②

GET COMFY, GET BOOZY, EVEN GET MARRIED AT THIS SPRAWLING ESTATE.

The wines at Bendooley Estate are probably not going to change the world – but then, that's not why you're here. You're here for a full experience, a place to stay, a place to eat, a place to drink, a place, maybe, to even get married – and for all that, Bendooley has you well and truly covered. This is a gorgeous, sprawling estate that mixes old and new, with its cafe and bookstore, Berkelouw Book Barn, housed in a beautiful, classic building, its cellar door (which morphs into a restaurant at night) set in a stunning, modern space nearby overlooking the vines, and luxurious cottages spread throughout the estate's grounds, with views of lakes, gardens and valleys beyond. You could spend your entire Southern Highlands getaway here and leave satisfied.

bendooleyestate.com.au

Artemis *Opposite* Centennial Vineyards

Southern Highlands

BURRAWANG VILLAGE HOTEL ③

ENJOY BEER AND AUSSIE PUB GRUB AT THEIR FINEST.

You have to love a classic country pub, and Burrawang Village Hotel, 15min east of Moss Vale, is about as classic as they come. There's indoor dining and drinking here, or if the weather is warm, grab your schooner and head outside to the patio areas or the extensive beer garden. The food is standard pub fare – burgers, schnitties, steaks, though prepared with skill and care. There's also accommodation on-site.

burrawangvillagehotel.com.au

CENTENNIAL VINEYARDS ④

EMBRACE THE OLD-WORLD VIBES OF THIS QUAINT AND LOVELY WINERY.

There's some serious charm to Centennial Vineyards, which has the feel of an English manor, with its manicured gardens and stately drive. That feeling is only compounded at the on-site restaurant, which offers lovely high teas, either with or without sparkling wine or rosé. And, of course, there's Devonshire tea, too. If you're after wine, the cellar door offers samples of the Centennial product, single-vineyard reds, whites and sparkling wines that are reflective of the cool-climate terroir. There are options to focus your tasting experience on either pinot noir or sparkling.

centennial.net.au

Top Centennial Vineyards *Opposite* Eden Brewery

EDEN BREWERY (5)

GOOD VIBES, GIVING BACK AND BEING SUSTAINABLE ARE THE ORDER OF THE DAY HERE.

Don't be fooled by the laidback look of the Eden Brewery team: these guys are serious about their beer, and serious about the way they run the company that produces it. Eden is all about staying local but thinking globally. Ten per cent of the brewery's profits are donated to Oxfam, and their beer is produced using 100 per cent renewable energy. The brewhouse is an open, welcoming space where the local community is encouraged to wander down and have a chat over a frothy brew. It works, too: the beer is high-quality and the crowd is friendly. Well worth calling past for a guilt-free brew.

edenbrewery.beer

JOADJA DISTILLERY (6)

HISTORY REPEATS IN AN OLD SCOTTISH-RUN MINING TOWN-TURNED-DISTILLERY.

There's plenty of history in Joadja. This is both a distillery and a whole town, a historic settlement near Mittagong that is all but in ruins these days, though once was a thriving base for oil shale mining. Many of those miners back in the day were Scots, which goes some way to explaining the establishment of Joadja Distillery, an outfit that makes whisky, among other spirits. It's run by the Jimenez family, who lead tours of the old town as well as the distillery itself, and who make single-malt whisky, gin, rum, brandy, and Pedro Ximenez-style sherry on-site. Call in for a free tasting on the weekend, or by appointment during the week.

joadjadistillery.com.au

PASTE (7)

MICHELIN-STARRED THAI CUISINE THAT'S WORTH TRAVELLING TO MITTAGONG FOR.

One of Australia's best Thai restaurants, and it's in … the country town of Mittagong? It's true, this does seem an odd location to find a restaurant of Paste's quality, but Michelin-starred Thai chef Bee Satongun liked what she saw in the Southern Highlands, and chose this spot to set up a second outpost of her celebrated eatery, Paste Bangkok. Satongun has a serious pedigree, having been named Asia's Best Female Chef by 50 Best (plus awarded that Michelin star) and she brings her flair for high-end Thai cuisine to Mittagong, utilising local ingredients to create a unique and frankly exquisite menu. Here you're likely to find, say, Phuket-style yellow curry with swimmer crab, or slipper lobster noodles with shellfish bisque. Any major city in Australia, or in fact the world, would be very happy to call Paste its own. As it stands, you'll have to go to the Southern Highlands.

pasteaustralia.com

SOUTHERN HIGHLANDS BREWING AND TAPHOUSE ⑧

LOCAL FAVOURITE HAS GREAT BEER, GREAT FOOD, AND A GREAT CROWD.

The Southern Highlands Taphouse is all about having a good time – no airs, no graces, just great beer and tasty food in comfortable surrounds. Set right on the main street in downtown Moss Vale, this is the perfect community gathering point, a venue set up by good friends Cameron James and Ben Twomey, after their pet brewery project started gaining some serious popularity. The beer ranges from easy-drinking lager and pale ale to a bulkier red ale and porter, while the food is pizzas, steaks and other grilled meats. The crowd is mostly locals, which has to be a good sign.

southernhighlandsbrewing.com.au

STATION LANE DISTILLERY

ENJOY WHISKY FOR THE AGES AT THIS FLEDGLING DISTILLERY.

Back in 2016, Mark Coburn had a dream: by the time he was 70, he wanted to be able to drink his own 20-year-old single-malt whisky. That meant he had to get cracking: he had just turned 49, and he still didn't have any spirit in barrel. So, he set about creating Coburns Distillery, now called Station Lane, a small-batch outfit that makes the most of local Highlands' ingredients to produce whiskies of distinction and class. He's well on his way to his goal. At the time of writing, Coburn hadn't yet set up a cellar door to offer tastings of his product, though plans were afoot to open up a space in Burrawang. Their five-year-old first-release single-malt whisky is due out in early 2023.

coburnsdistillery.com.au

TERTINI ⑨

COOL-CLIMATE WINE SPECIALISTS PROVIDE A WARM HIGHLANDS WELCOME.

If you're travelling to the Southern Highlands purely because you love wine, then Tertini should be at the top of your list. This is a high-quality winery that specialises in cool-climate classics, such as pinot noir, riesling, chardonnay and cabernet sauvignon, created with minimal intervention both in the vineyard and the winemaking process. Grapes here are sourced not just from the Southern Highlands but also a vineyard in Tasmania, which means you have the best of two cool-climate worlds. The cellar door is great too, a warm, welcoming space with a log fire crackling in the colder months, where guests can sample the full range of Tertini product. And it's only an hour and a half from Sydney.

tertiniwines.com.au

Top Tertini

The Perfect Day
SOUTHERN HIGHLANDS

12PM

4PM

2.30PM

7PM

11AM TERTINI

Make a leisurely start to your day with a tasting of the excellent cool-climate wines at Tertini (see p.50), just north of Mittagong.

12PM ARTEMIS

Next up, head over to Artemis (see p.47), just 10min away from Tertini, for a sample of the many wines on offer, and then grab a wood-fired pizza or two to enjoy on the lawn.

2.30PM CENTENNIAL VINEYARDS

Time for more wine-tasting, this time at Centennial Vineyards (see p.48), a short drive away in Bowral. If you're still peckish, take time out for a more-English-than-the-English high tea in the dining room.

4PM EDEN BREWERY

Back in Mittagong, finish off the day's tasting with a cleansing ale among a friendly crowd at Eden Brewery (see p.49).

7PM PASTE

Dinner tonight is at one of Australia's best Thai restaurants, Paste (see p.49), run by Michelin-starred, Bangkok-based chef Bee Satongun.

BEST OF THE REST

Though NSW isn't known for its wine in the same way as, say, Victoria or South Australia, this huge state still has an incredible 16 distinct wine regions (the whole of Italy, in comparison, has 20), spread throughout its area. In other words, there are far too many to do justice to in this book.

As a way to make up for that, this section features the best venues from some of NSW's lesser-known wine regions, places where you may not have even realised wine is produced. If you find yourself in the vicinity, they're well worth visiting.

TUMBARUMBA

WIRADJURI COUNTRY

Situated in the foothills of the Snowy Mountains, about 3hr south-west of Canberra, Tumbarumba is an exciting and relatively new region where you'll find some seriously good white wine in particular. People who consider their wine preferences to be 'ABC' - Anything But Chardonnay - need not apply.

COURABYRA WINES

GET SET FOR SOME OF THE BEST CHARDONNAY AROUND – AND MAYBE A CHOPPER FLIGHT.

Chardonnay fans, get yourself over to the Courabyra cellar door and prepare to be impressed: the two chardonnays on offer here, the 805 and the 1-11, are shockingly good. You'll be wondering how you never heard of this place before. There's more on offer at Courabyra too, including a very tasty grüner veltliner and some high-quality pinot noir, all of which are up for tasting or pairing with the Italian and pan-Asian food at the on-site restaurant. For a truly baller experience, Courabyra can organise a helicopter winery tour, which will include a tasting at nearby Obsession wines, and lunch at Courabyra.

courabyrawines.com

TUMUT RIVER BREWING CO.

HEAD RIVERSIDE FOR SOME OF THE TASTIEST BREWS IN THIS PART OF THE WORLD.

Tumut is actually about an hour north of Tumbarumba, but still worth including in your itinerary, not just for the town's access to outdoor activities on the Tumut River and in Tumut State Forest, but the chance to call in to the excellent Tumut River Brewing Co. The team here brew a huge range of beers – from standard pale ales and IPAs, to seasonal, experimental NEIPAs, fruit sours and ginger ales – which should appeal to pretty much every drinker. They serve food here too, breakfast, lunch and dinner, so you really can't go wrong.

trbc.com.au

Courabyra Wines

NEW ENGLAND

NGANYAYWANA AND KAMILAROI COUNTRY

This is one of Australia's newest wine regions, a mostly high-altitude area that runs along the Great Dividing Range from Tamworth, up through Uralla, to Armidale, Glen Innes and Tenterfield. Despite its youth, there are already a few well-respected wineries in the region, and a heap of excellent microbreweries.

DOBSON'S DISTILLERY

ENJOY HIGH-QUALITY WHISKY IN A MOST UNLIKELY LOCATION.

For a distiller of fine whisky, there are worse places in the world to be based than Kentucky. Only thing is, this is Kentucky, NSW, in the high country just south of Uralla. The whisky here, made by master distiller Stephen Dobson, is also more Scotch than bourbon – in fact there are three styles that mimic the smoky, heavily peated drams of the Scottish Hebrides, the softer style of traditional Highland whisky, and the triple-distilled Irish style. Dobson is a fascinating character, having left behind the cinematic world to follow his passion for spirits and craft beer, and his whiskies, gins and liqueurs have been picking up bags of awards. Taste them at the Dobson's 'Speakeasy' on-site, where there's also cocktails, craft beer and food. There's a winery here, too.

dobsonsdistillery.com

GREAT HOPS BREWERY

MICROBREWERY AND TAPHOUSE IS COMING ON IN LEAPS AND BOUNDS.

You get it, right? Great 'hops' – the stuff that goes into beer, and the thing the local kangaroos are always doing? It's a fun name for a great operation on the outskirts of Armidale, a microbrewery and taphouse in what is essentially an aircraft hangar, a long shed where there's live music, burgers, tacos and bar snacks – and of course plenty of beer. Local brewer and University of New England science graduate, Sam Martin makes a pretty approachable range of IPAs, XPAs and seasonal brews, most of which are available to drink on-site or take away in can form.

greathops.com.au

MERILBA ESTATE WINES

SEE THE 'NOSE TO TAIL' OF WINEMAKING AT THIS IMPRESSIVE ESTATE.

The team at Merilba Estate, out to the west of Uralla, do everything themselves – from growing to picking, fermenting to ageing to bottling. That makes a visit to this winery a comprehensive experience, with all facets of the process visible. Even if your passion is more for drinking than learning, call past the big shed with its floor-to-ceiling windows and Merilba will sort you out with a flight of tastings of their cool-climate sauvignon blanc, chardonnay, cabernet sauvignon and shiraz, matched with share platters of delicious treats. Kids' meals are also available.

merilbaestatewines.com.au

NEW ENGLAND BREWING

OLD-WORLD AND NEW-WORLD CRAFT BEERS IN A BREWPUB FOR THE COMMUNITY TO GATHER IN.

Back in 2003, Ben Rylands and Mirela Suciu had one of those 'penny-dropping' moments. The pair were sitting in a small-town bar in Suciu's home country, Germany, watching as locals came in to chat, catch up, and appreciate the product of their town's brewery. Why, the pair thought, can't we do this in a small town in Australia? And so, New England Brewing was born, a now-much-loved institution in small-town Uralla. Here Rylands and Suciu brew a top-quality array of old-world and new-world craft beers, from barrel-aged stouts to citrus sours to West Coast IPAs. Everything is done in small batches by hand, and it shows. The real attraction, however, is the community gathering space Rylands and Suciu have created – the perfect homage to that small bar in the German countryside.

newenglandbrewing.com.au

PETERSONS WINES

STAY THE NIGHT, TRY THE WINE – IT'S A WIN WIN.

Petersons has something of a mini empire in NSW, with vineyards and cellar doors in the Hunter Valley, in Mudgee, and here just outside Armidale. This is more than just a cellar door though, with a full guesthouse with seven rooms, each with antique furniture and an ensuite bathroom. It's the ideal place to base yourself for a weekend, with wine tasting on-site – work your way through the full Petersons range from across their NSW vineyards. Meals are served for guests. And in your downtime, beautiful common areas and gardens mean you can relax.

petersonswines.com.au

WELDER'S DOG BREWERY

IT'S ALL BIG SMILES AND TASTY BREWS AT THIS ARMIDALE STALWART.

How's this for a *raison d'être*: 'At the core of everything we do is a love of our local community, and a desire to see everyone around us smiling'. That's the approach to running a brewery for Dan Emery, Tom Croft and Phil Stevens, who say they're friends first, brewers second. The Welder's Dog is all about community, bringing people together over a frothy brew. The guys use barley from local farmers to produce a range of beers that's unique and distinctively 'Armidale', including IPAs, stouts, pale ales and sours. They're served up at the Welder's Dog bar in the town's north, with platters of snacks available, and BYO food also an option. Have a look around at the crowd: there's a good chance everyone will be smiling.

theweldersdog.com.au

Welder's Dog Brewery *Opposite* Cupitt's Estate

SHOALHAVEN COAST

DHARAWAL AND YUIN COUNTRY

As the name suggests, Shoalhaven is far better known for its beaches and classic coastal activities than its wineries. This is a very small wine-producing region that stretches from Kiama in the north - about 2hr south of Sydney - to Milton in the south, and west to Kangaroo Valley, known mostly for varietals such as chardonnay, chambourcin and shiraz.

CUPITT'S ESTATE

ENJOY WINE, CHEESE, BEER AND MORE, ALL TAKEN WITH A SEA BREEZE.

Here's the thing about Cupitt's: the winery is in Ulladulla, on the gorgeous NSW South Coast, but most of the grapes come from elsewhere: from the Canberra district, from Hilltops, from Orange and from Tumbarumba. That gives visitors the best of both worlds, the beauty of the South Coast with the high-quality wine of some of NSW's best regions. Visit Cupitt's to taste the full range, to eat at either the fine-dining restaurant or in the more casual outdoor space, to sample beer from the on-site brewery, or cheese from the on-site cheese-making operation. You can even stay in one of Cupitt's luxury one-bedroom 'pods', which each have beautiful views over rolling hinterland. And the beach is just a 5min drive away.

cupittsestate.com.au

RIVERINA

WIRADJURI COUNTRY

Think of the Riverina, in NSW's south-west, as the engine room of the state's winemaking enterprise. This region isn't particularly famous or prestigious, and yet there's a huge amount of fruit grown here by some of the largest producers in the country, and much of it goes into making some of Australia's best-known and biggest-selling wines. For visitors, the Riverina - with the town of Griffith, with its heavy Italian influence, at its heart - is a pleasure to visit, with several big-name cellar doors to call into and work your way through a mammoth tasting.

CALABRIA FAMILY WINES

EMBRACE THE HERITAGE OF ONE OF THE RIVERINA'S BIGGEST LABELS.

This winery is an absolute classic of the Riverina, with a rich Italian heritage and a history stretching back 75 years. Calabria now owns vineyards not just in Riverina but also in the Barossa and Eden valleys in South Australia, King Valley in Victoria, and Hilltops in NSW, which means a tasting here is a tour through all five regions. Some of Calabria's best include their Riverina semillon, Eden Valley riesling, and Barossa grenache shiraz mataro, all available for tasting in the 45min session at the Tuscan-style cellar door. Numerous specialist experiences, such as a 90min tasting of durif back vintages, hosted in a private cellar, are available.

calabriawines.com.au

Calabria Family Wines *Opposite* De Bortoli Wines

DE BORTOLI WINES
SEE WHERE IT ALL BEGAN FOR ONE OF AUSTRALIA'S BEST-KNOWN WINE FAMILIES.

This is another classic producer with a long history in Australia, as well as a growing list of locations: there are De Bortoli cellar doors in the Yarra Valley, the Hunter Valley, Rutherglen, and here in the Riverina. This is where De Bortoli's most famous wine is produced, Noble One, a sweet semillon with a relatively low price-tag for such a well-known drop. This is also where it all began for the De Bortoli family, when Vittorio and Giuseppina De Bortoli began a small winery way back in 1928, so it's lovely to head into the cellar door and enjoy either a standard tasting of up to eight wines for only $5, or match it with a cheese platter for $20.

debortoli.com.au

MCWILLIAM'S WINES
FORTIFIED-WINE SPECIALISTS STILL GOING STRONG FOR OVER 100 YEARS.

Here's another huge name in Australian winemaking, one of the country's 'First Families of Wine', an operation that has been around more than 100 years, known mostly for its fortified wines, muscat and tawny and the like. McWilliam's owns vineyards in Hilltops, the Yarra Valley, Tumbarumba and Margaret River, so again, you're in for a nationwide tour when you do a tasting here. The cellar door was closed for a while during the COVID-19 pandemic, so be sure to call ahead if you'd like to visit.

mcwilliams.com.au

Victoria

From the Yarra to Mornington, Beechworth to Bendigo, the Garden State has an embarrassment of gastronomic riches, with high-quality wine regions offering everything a gourmand could ever want.

YARRA VALLEY
WURUNDJERI COUNTRY

Sigh, if only every city was like Melbourne/Naarm – an urban base that luxuriates in its proximity to an absolute smorgasbord of bona fide brilliant wine country. This is a bustling state capital that is enveloped in a boozy hug by the Mornington Peninsula on one side, the Bellarine on the other, and the Yarra Valley not far from the suburban limits. Take your pick for a daytrip from the city – these regions are all little over an hour away. And those world-class areas are just the merest gateway to Victoria's embarrassment of fermented riches. This relatively compact state features 22 separate and distinct wine regions, areas that are producing some of the country's – and indeed some of the world's – finest drops.

But anyway, we're here, in this section at least, to talk about the Yarra Valley, which is surely up there with the Barossa in South Australia as Australia's absolute best wine region. And when it comes to the quality of experiences on offer, there's a very real argument for the Yarra being the winner. It's just an hour from the Melbourne CBD to the town of Healesville, and here you're in the heart of the valley, a place of spectacular and classically Australian scenery, all stringy barks appearing from the morning mist, where vines cling to rolling hills and higher peaks dominate the horizon.

The Yarra is famous for its traditionally produced pinot noir and chardonnay, though there are a band of young winemakers now trying new varieties and tinkering with styles. This area is also rife with producers of excellent beer, cider, whisky and gin. To top it all off, it's home to restaurants with stacks of hats; and there are so, so many beautiful places to stay. It's all good, and it's all right on Melbourne's doorstep.

Four Pillars Gin *Previous* TarraWarra Estate

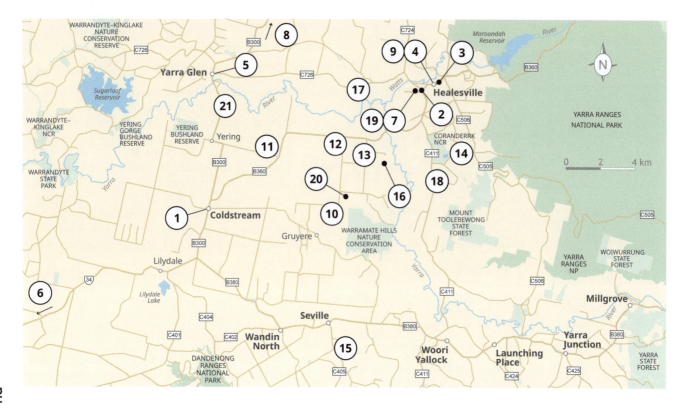

COLDSTREAM BREWERY ①

THE NOW ICONIC 'SHIVERING MAN' MARKS THE SPOT FOR GREAT CRAFT BEER.

Old school mates Rohan Peters and Mike Basset spent their 20s bumming around Europe, as you do, and it was there that they were inspired by local beer cultures to bring something similar to Australia. So, way back in 2005, the pair went in with a few more mates, bought a brewing kit, rented a space in a building that was once a tannery – then a general store, then a Chinese restaurant – and Coldstream Brewery was born. It's been hugely popular, too, which is why it's still going more than 15 years later, and why visitors to the Yarra Valley often call in for a freshly poured beer or a cider, as well as a massive pub meal of a chicken parma or a pizza, and a chat to the team. Look for the distinctive 'shivering man', as you drive into Coldstream.

coldstreambrewery.com.au

FOUR PILLARS GIN ②

LOCAL SUCCESS STORY SERVES UP A RANGE OF EXPERIENCES TO THE MASSES.

Four Pillars can barely be described as a craft gin maker. 'Craft' implies a small operation, and these days Four Pillars is anything but: you'll find their products on the shelf at your local Dan Murphy's, plus, if you live in Sydney, you can visit their northern outpost 'Laboratory' for a gin workshop or a cocktail. This is clearly a success story, and it began in Healesville, where Four Pillars still has its distillery, and still hosts guests for tastings, or G&Ts, plus a range of masterclasses on gin-making and cocktail creation. There's a huge range of gin here to try, from standard dry gin to gin matured in wine casks, or flavoured with olive leaves, or macerated on shiraz grapes. Despite Four Pillars' success, this is still a warm, friendly spot, and the ideal place to dive into the local distillation industry.

fourpillarsgin.com

GIANT STEPS ③

RELATIVE NEWCOMER HAS TAKEN – AHEM – GIANT STEPS TOWARDS YARRA DOMINATION.

Here's another Yarra Valley success story, a winery that has only been around since the late 1990s – very much a newcomer for the Yarra – and yet is already up there with the region's finest, turning out wines of style and grace, served up to adoring punters in a compact cellar door on the outskirts of Healesville. It's just near the headquarters of a few of its affiliated businesses: Innocent Bystander wines, once a sub-label of Giant Steps, and Matilda Bay Brewery, co-founded by Giant Steps owner Phil Sexton. Back to Giant Steps though, which produces the sort of single-vineyard chardonnay and pinot noir that you'll want to fill the back of your car with, particularly given the prices are pretty reasonable for wine of this quality. Still, best bring the credit cards.

giantstepswine.com.au

HEALESVILLE GRAND HOTEL ④

STALWART HAS BEEN RESTORED TO ITS FORMER GLORY, WITH GREAT FOOD TOO.

This is the sort of country pub Victoria seems to do so well, a cosy space where there's always a fire roaring in winter, a friendly place to grab a beer or a glass of wine and settle down to some seriously good food in easygoing surrounds. The Healesville Hotel has been renovated recently, sensitive to its proud history, it's a rambling venue with dining options at the bar, in the dining room and on the sunlit balcony, and stylish accommodation – smart though welcoming rooms to base yourself in the middle of the action (such as it is in Healesville).

healesvillegrandhotel.com.au

Top Coldstream Brewery

Yarra Valley

HEARTSWOOD (5)

FROM HEART-STARTERS TO HEALTH-CONSCIOUS, THIS IS BRUNCH DONE PROPERLY.

This is Australia, so you probably want to find somewhere to have brunch. And in the Yarra Valley, that's Heartswood, in Yarra Glen, run by chef Matt Binney and his partner Bianca. Heartswood's brunch menu kicks arse, frankly, a classy affair featuring favourites like waffles, fritters, scrambles, and 'obligatory avo', moving up to hangover-smashing dishes such as schnitties and a pulled wagyu burger. The menu is seasonal and locally sourced, of course. Plus, as you'd expect, there's coffee, juices and soft drinks. Good for what ails ya.

heartswood.com.au

JAMSHEED (6)

ONE OF THE YARRA INNOVATORS HAS ALMOST ACHIEVED LEGEND STATUS.

According to Persian legend, King Jamshid – sometimes spelled Jamsheed – the fourth shah of a mythological kingdom, used to store grapes in jars, where they would spontaneously ferment and become regarded as poison. One day, a desperate woman, having been banned from the king's harem, drank the poison and discovered … that it was delicious. And thus, wine was born. Is the story true? No. But it does make for a nice introduction to Jamsheed the wine label, one of the real leaders of natural wine in the Yarra, helmed by Gary Mills, a Yarra Valley innovator whose products are quickly becoming the stuff of legend too. Gary creates a mix of traditional cold-climate wines, with most grapes sourced from the Yarra Valley, though some further afield, as well as lighter, juicier, more experimental drops under the Apricity sub-label (plus some seriously funky, lo-fi stuff on the Park sub-label). It's all on for tasting at Jamsheed's 'urban winery', a cellar door and restaurant that is actually in Melbourne – Preston, to be exact, on the way out towards the Yarra. Make it your first stop.

jamsheed.com.au

JAYDEN ONG (7)

FORMER SOMMELIER IS DOING EVERYTHING RIGHT IN THE NATURAL-WINE WORLD.

Jayden Ong is one impressive character: here is a former Melbourne-based sommelier who took the leap into the winemaking world less than a decade ago, and he already has four distinct labels, looks after multiple vineyards, and runs a cellar door and restaurant in Healesville. The wine is making a serious splash, lo-fi drops with plenty of character and a sense of place, some with skin contact, others light and easy drinking. Everything is thoughtfully and skillfully done. On the food side of things, it helps to know that Ong's business partner is celebrated Melbourne restaurateur Andrew McConnell – of Cumulus Inc fame – which goes some way to explaining the popularity of their shared venture. All of Ong's wine is on to taste here in Healesville, plus a selection of cult local and international favourites, paired with sensational food. Go. Now.

jaydenong.com

KINGLAKE WHISKY (8)

DISTILLATION NEWCOMERS DOING GREAT THINGS, THANKS TO A SPRING.

When Chantal Daniels and Sam Lowe moved back to Australia from the UK and set up camp on Chantal's family property in Kinglake, they made a fortuitous discovery: a spring, a fountain of pure, natural water that was erupting from the earth. From there, an idea coalesced, to use that water and the wild yeasts and local grains to make whisky; whisky that would be able to hold its own with the finest in Australia. They're getting there, too, despite this being a relatively young operation, and one that does whisky and whisky only, not wishing to be sidetracked by other projects. Chantal and Sam only open their rustic distillery on certain days, and if you're in the area at the right time this is definitely a great place to call past.

kinglakedistillery.com.au

KITCHEN & BUTCHER (9)

HEALESVILLE CLASSIC STOCKS THE BEST IN LOCAL AND INTERNATIONAL PRODUCE.

If you love delicious things – and you do, right? – then get yourself directly to K&B, on Healesville's main street, and bring a big shopping bag. This place was once just a butcher, though has morphed now into a gourmet food shop stocking all sorts of goodness, from a huge range of local and international cheeses, to small-batch jams, relishes, pickles and other preserves, to locally produced small goods, pre-made meals and more. This is a Healesville institution, and you'll soon see why.

kitchenandbutcher.com.au

MEDHURST (10)

STUNNING VIEWS AND EXCELLENT WINE ROUND OUT THIS TOP-NOTCH EXPERIENCE.

You would visit Medhurst, about 10min east of Coldstream, purely to see the cellar door, a work of architectural beauty that combines floor-to-ceiling windows with vast concrete walls to focus visitors' attention where it should be: out onto the vines and the beautiful Yarra countryside, as well as on the glass in your hand. The experience here is expert from the second you walk in, from the flights of tastings poured by knowledgeable staff, to the superb wines themselves, to the restaurant, Palo Alto, which serves beautiful food, either as a degustation-style Grazing Menu, or a more casual Grazing Box, a series of pick-and-eat smallgoods that work perfectly with a few glasses of Medhurst's chardonnay or pinot noir.

medhurstwines.com.au

NAPOLEONE CIDER (11)

SIT AMONG THE APPLE TREES AND ENJOY THE FRUITS OF THE LOCALS' LABOUR.

When it comes to drinks, the Napoleone crew have taken the humble apple, and made something beautiful. And when it comes to drinking venues, they've taken the humble shipping container and done the same thing. Napoleone's Orchard Bar is a shipping container set up among apple trees, with ample space around it for sitting and drinking the fine products on offer – which include ciders from around the world, plus a few apple-based spirits. These guys make cider with no added sugar or any other nasties, vegan-friendly booze that uses traditional European methods to coax complex flavours from local fruits. And it works.

napoleone.com.au

Opposite **Jayden Ong**

OAKRIDGE WINES (12)

COLDSTREAM CLASSIC COMBINES BEAUTIFUL ARCHITECTURE WITH SERIOUSLY GOOD WINE.

The most important thing you need to know is this: Oakridge makes extremely good wine. The team here makes a lot of wine – three tiers of ascending quality, with multiple releases dedicated to single blocks of vines – and it's all very, very good. Okay, now that that's out of the way, you can concentrate on the experience here at the Coldstream winery, which is a standout for the Yarra Valley. Book in for one of three different tasting options, running from a simple introduction to the Oakridge range ($10), to a flight of the premium '864' range ($25), to a chardonnay masterclass that's still only $25 per person. There's also a restaurant on-site in a beautifully designed building, where set menus draw on local produce and veggies from the Oakridge garden to further increase your sense of place. Impressive stuff.

oakridgewines.com.au

PIMPERNEL VINEYARDS (13)

LOW-TECH OPERATION MAKES WINE THE WAY IT SHOULD BE DONE.

Pimpernel is an old-school outfit, seemingly uninterested in awards or glory, concentrating instead on making really good wine employing traditional, low-tech methods. Grapes are still stomped by foot here. Fermented juice is run through a basket press. There's nothing big or fancy about Pimpernel, and that's exactly the way it should be. Drop into the cellar door and you'll invariably meet the people involved with those processes. This is a low-key space where the focus is on chardonnay, chenin blanc, pinot noir and syrah. Again, as it should be.

pimpernelvineyards.com.au

ST. RONAN'S CIDER (14)

TRADITIONAL METHODS BRING THE BEST OUT OF LOCAL APPLES AT THIS BOUTIQUE PRODUCER.

There's a way to make sparkling wine in France, known as 'methode traditionelle', which is slavishly adhered to in the Champagne region in particular. Grapes are fermented and the wine goes into bottles, where it then undergoes another fermentation, and the lees, or dead yeast cells, are left in the bottle, usually for years, to help develop flavour, before being 'disgorged' before drinking. That's how you make great Champagne, and it's also how you make great apple and pear cider – and it's the method used at St. Ronan's, a ciderhouse with a cellar door just outside Healesville. Cider here is serious business, coming in cork-sealed 750ml bottles, and it's complex and delicious. You need to taste this, maybe with a platter of local produce, to see.

stronanscider.com.au

Top Oakridge gardens *Opposite* Seville Estate

SEVILLE ESTATE

GAMBLE HAS PAID OFF FOR SHIRAZ PIONEERS IN THE SOUTHERN YARRA.

The McMahon family were pioneers when they decided to plant vines around Seville, at the southern end of the Yarra Valley, way back in 1972, and concentrate on shiraz, which wasn't really the done thing at the time. Still, it was a hit, and the winery has since gone on to bigger and better things, with third-gen winemaker Dylan now at the helm, producing a large suite of wines. Give them a try at the laidback cellar door – or, better still, while you're staying on-site at the vineyard. Seville Estate has the luxury, four-bed Seville Homestead, plus three self-contained Vineyard Apartments, which each sleep two people. All have gorgeous views of the lake and vines, and plenty of places to sit and drink a glass (or bottle) of shiraz.

sevilleestate.com.au

SOUMAH OF YARRA VALLEY

LONG LUNCHES ARE THE ORDER OF THE DAY AT THIS STYLISH WINERY.

Soumah sounds quite exotic until you find out the provenance of the name: it's a portmanteau of 'South of Maroondah Highway'. Still, don't let that put you off, because this is a legitimately excellent winery offering a whole swag of experiences at their Gruyere vineyard. Begin with a tasting flight, either standard or premium, running through Soumah's top-notch chardonnays, cabernet sauvignons and nebbiolos, then head next door to Ai Fiori trattoria for an Italian-style lunch; if you're there later in the afternoon, the restaurant is also open for 'merenda', the snacky Italian meal designed to fill the gap between lunch and dinner. There's accommodation here, too: Villa Sophia is a gorgeous three-bedroom homestead nestled among the vines, close to a host of Gruyere wineries.

soumah.com.au

THICK AS THIEVES [18]
THE YARRA'S LO-FI LEADER WELCOMES VISITORS TO HIS CELLAR DOOR.

There's a small, underground movement of lo-fi winemakers beginning to make their names in the Yarra Valley, though most don't have permanent facilities or cellar doors. Thick as Thieves is one of the exceptions: winemaker Syd Bradford bought a vineyard back in 2012, and now does tastings on-site, just south of Healesville. Be warned, however: it's by appointment only, and there's a $100 minimum spend for your group, given all wines are opened fresh. There's a good chance you will run that money up pretty quickly though, after tasting the fruits of Bradford's labour, wines that are mostly wild-fermented, whole-bunch-pressed, with minimal sulphur added and no fining or filtration. What that means, to the uninitiated, is wine that's as close to its 'natural' state as possible, true expressions of land and fruit. Oh, and really tasty.

tatwines.com.au

TARRAWARRA ESTATE [17]
FAMED ART COLLECTION AND FINE-DINING RESTAURANT CONTINUE TO DRAW THE CROWDS.

It's not so much 'come for the wine, stay for the art collection' at TarraWarra, but more, 'come for the art collection, stay for the wine'. TarraWarra is a Yarra Valley icon, a hugely important winery that has been around since the early 1980s; however, these days it's actually known more for the TarraWarra Museum of Art, featuring the private collection of TarraWarra owners Eva and Marc Besen, as well as an ever-changing list of exhibitions and events in a building that's an attraction in itself. The permanent collection features artworks by Charles Blackman, Joy Hester, Daniel Boyd and more. Of course, there's also a cellar door, a similarly beautiful spot offering tasting flights and bottle purchases, and a hatted restaurant serving beautiful set-menu, Mod-Oz cuisine.

tarrawarra.com.au

WATTS RIVER BREWING [19]
BEER-LOVING DUO MAKE SURE HEALESVILLE STILL HAS CRAFT BREWS.

This much-loved brewpub is the work of two mates, Ben Hamilton and Aaron Malmborg, who were out of a job when the White Rabbit brewery was shifted out of Healesville back in 2014, and decided to fill that gap – both for themselves and the town – by starting up their own operation. Watts River Brewing is still going strong, doing a tasty core range of approachable brews, ranging from a hoppy IPA to a gutsy stout, to the more easy-drinking likes of a blonde and a session pale ale. Give them a try at the brewery, surrounded by tanks and barrels, with seasonal beers usually available.

wattsriverbrewery.com.au

Top TarraWarra Estate *Opposite* Yering Station

YARRA YERING (20)
LOCAL SUPERSTAR KEEPS ITS TRADITIONS ALIVE – INCLUDING MAKING AMAZING WINE.

Yarra Yering is an absolute superstar of the region, one of the oldest wineries in the Yarra Valley, and still one of its finest. These guys are old-school, as you'll see immediately from the labels: Yarra Yering's flagship Bordeaux-style and Rhone-style blends, made by celebrated winemaker Sarah Crowe, are still known as Dry Red No.1 and Dry Red No.2. It's a nice nod to the winery's history, though Yarra Yering also now has a range of more recognisable and slightly cheaper wines under its Warramate sub-label. Drop in for a tasting and you have three options, none of which are exactly cheap, but we're talking about samples of some of the Yarra's best wine here: there's a Current Release flight for $40, a Carrodus Premium flight for $45, and an Icons flight, which includes those fabled dry reds, both current and museum releases, for $50 per person. Easily worth it to sample Yarra Valley history. Yarra Yering has a homestead too, a five-bedroom house available for short stays.

yarrayering.com

YERING STATION (21)
BOLDLY MODERNIST BUILDINGS WILL SURPRISE AT VICTORIA'S OLDEST VINEYARD.

Victoria's first vineyard: that's some claim to fame. There were vines planted at Yering Station in 1838, and this has been a vineyard and cattle farm ever since. You can feel the history as you wander the grounds here, even though the restaurant is set in a building so boldly modernist this feels as much like the future as it does the past. This place is an Instagrammer's paradise, all bold, curvy lines and reflecty pools. The wine is lovely, too: classic Yarra fodder like chardonnay, shiraz and pinot noir, available to taste in the original winery building, dating back to 1859, with standard or premium flights to choose from. The restaurant does two- or three-course lunches, or simple cheese boards out on the deck, there's an art gallery and sculpture garden on-site, and the whole outfit sits right next door to Chateau Yering, a classic, luxury accommodation, restaurant and cafe.

yering.com

The Perfect Day
YARRA VALLEY

Victoria

10.30AM FOUR PILLARS GIN

Begin your adventure today in Healesville, at Four Pillars Gin (*see* p.62), for either a masterclass or a tasting of the ample product on offer.

11.30AM JAYDEN ONG

It's just a 1min skip now from Four Pillars Gin over to Jayden Ong's winery and cellar bar (*see* p.64), where you can try a few lo-fi beauties, as well as grab some excellent snacks.

12.30PM GIANT STEPS

Staying in Healesville, Giant Steps (*see* p.63) offers easygoing tastings of some extremely high-quality wine that you will no doubt want to purchase.

1.30PM YERING STATION

It's lunchtime, so make your way west to historic Yering Station (*see* p.69) for a multi-course lunch in beautiful surrounds, matched by some fancy wine.

3.30PM OAKRIDGE WINES

Head back to the east now, 10min from Yering to Oakridge Wines (*see* p.66), which is doing some of the most reliably delicious wine in the valley.

6PM COLDSTREAM BREWERY

It's been a big day: finish up in Coldstream, at the laidback brewery of the same name (*see* p.62) for a few cleansing ales and a no-frills meal.

Polperro

MORNINGTON PENINSULA
BOON WURRUNG COUNTRY

You can't help but swoon over the Mornington Peninsula. It's just so perfect. So lovely. Here is an outcrop of land just south of Melbourne/Naarm, so well connected by highways that there's barely a single set of traffic lights between the airport at Tullamarine and the heart of wine country in Red Hill. It has an incredible amount going for it. Rolling green hills covered with forests and vines. Village-style settlements either up on the hills or down hugging the coast. Sheltered bays. Gorgeous beaches. Endless views. And just about every venue a lover of good food and drink could ever ask for: wineries, restaurants, cafes, breweries, distilleries, everything high-quality, everything thoughtfully and beautifully done.

The Mornington Peninsula is a wine region that screams 'premium'. It's not cheap to own a vineyard here, and to try to produce wine, which means it's mostly well-established players, big-name labels, big-name stars. There's not a whole lot of room to experiment when you have to compete on the peninsula, to produce pinot noir and chardonnay of a standard that will be noticed among such revered company. Still, the region is an absolute pleasure to visit, whether as a daytrip from Melbourne or a weekend or week in gastronomic paradise.

The breweries here are some of the best in Australia, too; the distillers are coming on strong. And the food, grown and created by an embarrassment of talent, is up there with the nation's finest. Swoon-worthy? You betcha.

AVANI

ONE OF MORNINGTON'S MOST EXCITING TALENTS HAS A STORY TO TELL.

I've just gone and told you that the Mornington Peninsula has little room for small players, for emerging names, and yet here's Shashi Singh, an absolute powerhouse of a winemaker who came to this industry with no experience and no vines, but who has made a name for herself here. Shashi and her husband Devendra moved to Melbourne from India in the early '80s and immediately got into the hospitality business, running restaurants in the city, and then in Frankston, before eventually shifting down the peninsula. Shashi had always liked wine, so in 1998 the couple bought a Red Hill vineyard and Shashi, already a qualified chemist, did a viticulture and oenology degree and started making wine. And boom, Avani was born. It's been a raging success. Shashi is now known for her delicate, perfumed syrah, as well as a series of textural whites on her Amrit label. Give them all a try – for $10 per person – at Shashi's Red Hill vineyard and cellar door.

avanisyrah.com.au

CRITTENDEN ESTATE

MORNINGTON PENINSULA PIONEER IS STILL DOING THINGS A LITTLE DIFFERENTLY.

Garry Crittenden was one of the Mornington Peninsula pioneers, a former horticulturalist who bought a plot of land up the hill from Dromana and chucked some vines in back in 1982, when no one else was really doing it. It was the start of something big, not just for Garry but the whole region. Crittenden Estate is still going strong, producing some of the best wines in the region, classics like chardonnay and pinot noir, but also an eclectic range of Spanish, Italian and rare French varietals. Want to try a tempranillo, a prosecco and a savagnin? This is the cellar door for you. Tastings are all seated, and personalised experiences. Stillwater Restaurant is here too, offering two- or three-course Mod-Oz lunches and dinners, plus there's a group of beautiful lakeside villas to spend a few nights in.

crittendenwines.com.au

FOXEYS HANGOUT

GORGEOUS VIEWS AND GREAT FOOD KEEP THE CROWDS FLOCKING BACK.

Hangout is such a perfect word for Foxeys: this is a place you will want to hang out at for hours and hours, for the whole afternoon. The cellar door looks out over a gorgeous stretch of undulating, vine-covered terrain, hemmed in by native bushland, with a big wooden deck to sit on or a lawn to really stretch out. The food is prepared by co-owner Tony Lee, an experienced chef who puts together a menu of small plates that keep you coming back for more; Mod-Oz cuisine that lets the ingredients do the talking. The wine, made by Tony and his brother Michael, is similarly beautiful: biodynamic, savoury, textural drops with minimal intervention. The crowd here is friendly, the atmosphere welcoming. Come in. Hang out. You won't want to leave.

foxeys-hangout.com.au

JACKALOPE

LUXE HOTEL HAS TWO FINE-DINING RESTAURANTS AND PLENTY OF INSTA-WORTHY VISTAS.

If you're looking to spoil yourself with a stay on the Mornington Peninsula, look no further. Jackalope Hotel is five-star all the way, from the swish rooms with stylish furnishings and beautiful views, to the two-hatted restaurants, to the spa facilities, to the art gallery and installations spread around the grounds. It's not cheap, obviously, but this is splash-out, spoil yourself territory. Even if you're not staying, it's worth booking in for lunch or dinner, either at Doot Doot Doot, a fine-diner of set-menu cuisine with the option of extras, like caviar served with honey truffle crumpets; or at Rare Hare, a more affordable though still hatted bistro, serving what is essentially a modern take on rustic country fare, most of which is cooked in the wood oven. Afterwards, stroll the grounds, and bring your camera.

jackalopehotels.com

HABITAT ARTISAN PRECINCT, DROMANA

This is probably not where you would expect to find a group of the Mornington Peninsula's best artisans and producers: the Dromana Industrial Estate, a rough-and-ready area on the eastern fringe of town, just off the Mornington Peninsula Freeway, that's filled with utes and trucks parked outside storage facilities and garden centres. And yet, explore the streets here and you will find a loose collective of creators, boutique producers of tasty things, in what is known as the Habitat Artisan Precinct. This area is home to everyone from gin distillers to coffee roasters to gluten-free brewers to vegan cheesemakers. Here are some of the venues you should definitely visit.

BASS & FLINDERS DISTILLERY ⑤

TAKE A MASTERCLASS AND DESIGN YOUR OWN GIN OR BRANDY.

Bass & Flinders was the first distillery set up on the Mornington Peninsula (established in 2009) and it's still a leading producer of artisanal gin, brandy and liqueurs, a family business these days run by second-gen distiller Holly Klintworth. The distillery is probably best known for its masterclasses, in either gin or brandy, where visitors are taken through the entire distillation process, and then given the chance to design their own gin or spiced brandy – and take home a unique bottle of the end result. These classes are justifiably popular, and you'll have to book ahead.

bassandflindersdistillery.com

JETTY ROAD BREWERY ⑥

HAS ALL THE INGREDIENTS – INCLUDING GREAT FOOD – FOR A LONG AFTERNOON.

Just near Bass & Flinders, Jetty Road is an easygoing sort of place with an easy-drinking set of beers, nothing too boozy, nothing too challenging – just the sort of tasty drinks you want to take with you to a seat in the old carpark, under an umbrella, and while away an afternoon with friends. There's plenty of food too, from fried snacks and salads to vego-friendly small plates and bigger meaty dishes, like twice-cooked lamb shoulder, or barbecued swordfish. Pair them with a schooner of pale ale, IPA, or New England Hazy, and you're on your way.

jettyroad.com.au

Top JimmyRum Distillery

JIMMYRUM DISTILLERY (7)

RUM SPECIALIST PUTS THE FUN BACK INTO A MALIGNED BEVERAGE

The guys from JimmyRum believe in the three 'Rs': rum, respect, and rambunctiousness. The rum is obvious – this is Victoria's first craft rum distillery, and still a rarity in these parts; the respect is for community, and their product; and the rambunctiousness is all about having a bit of fun, and not taking life so seriously. Something we can all get behind, surely. JimmyRum's Dromana distillery is a hugely popular spot to grab a cocktail or a standard drink, maybe some food, and hang out in the Rum Garden. Forget everything you think you know about rum in Australia – this stuff is classy, it's tasty, and it's respectable.

jimmyrum.com.au

TWØBAYS BREWING CO (8)

GLUTEN-FREE, VEGAN-FRIENDLY BREWERY IS DOING EVERYTHING RIGHT

TWØBAYS is a massively popular craft brewery for one important reason: it produces a large range of beer that is entirely gluten-free and vegan-friendly. This is a whole gluten-free, vegan brewery, in fact. There's lager, pale ale, XPA, IPA, session ale and more, all without a skerrik of gluten involved. Get down to the taproom to give them a try, and be pleasantly amazed by how good gluten-free beer can be.

twobays.beer

BEST OF THE REST

Little Rebel Coffee Roastery

Cracking coffee – either drink on-site or take the beans away. *littlerebel.com.au*

Millers Bread Kitchen

Baker on the northern fringe of the industrial estate does great bread and pastries. *millersbread.squarespace.com*

Mr Little Cider

High-quality cider dished out in seriously low-key surrounds. *mrlittlecider.com.au*

Rhino Tiger Bear Wines

Friendly, rustic cellar door pours Rhiannon Goodwin's excellent wine. *rhinotigerbear.com.au*

Peninsula Fresh Seafood

Does what it says on the tin: fresh seafood to take home and devour. *peninsulafreshseafood.com.au*

The Vegan Dairy

Specialist vegan cheesemaker will easily convert the sceptical. *thevegandairy.com*

LE BOUCHON (9)

FRIENDLY BISTRO TAKES THE STUFFINESS OUT OF FINE FRENCH CUISINE.

A 'bouchon' in France can mean many things: it can be a plug or stopper, most notably a wine cork; it's a word for a traffic jam; and in Lyon, it's also a style of restaurant, a convivial, casual place where the focus is on good, hearty food and fine wine. You can guess which definition Le Bouchon, a bistro in Balnarring, takes its inspiration from. This is a passionately French venue that is also at pains to dismiss any feelings of stuffiness or pretension: it's supposed to be casual and friendly, with the focus on simple, delicious food. Sound familiar? On the menu you'll find duck liver paté, snails in garlic butter, steak tartare, duck confit, steak frites, cassoulet and more. These bistro staples are matched with wines from the peninsula, and from France, all thoughtfully chosen and well priced. C'est magnifique.

lebouchon.com.au

MAIN RIDGE ESTATE (10)

THE FIRST IS STILL ONE OF THE FINEST – AND GREAT VALUE FOR MONEY.

It's nice to find that the first commercially licensed winery on the Mornington Peninsula is still a family affair, still an intimate spot where you can call past for a tasting or a casual drink or even a whole lunch. Main Ridge was founded back in 1975, and its chardonnay and pinot noir are still legendary. The cellar door is small and friendly, offering tastings of four wines for $10 per person, while the restaurant does set-menu lunches for $60, including the wine-tasting fee, and there are casual drinks and tapas on the verandah from 3pm until 5pm.

mre.com.au

MONTALTO (11)

MULTI-FACETED VENUE OFFERS EVERYTHING YOU NEED FOR A FULL DAY'S ADVENTURING.

You would travel down from Melbourne for the day and just go to Montalto. This place is the full package, a destination in itself where there's a restaurant, a cellar door, a 'piazza', or casual eatery, a picnic spot, a wedding venue, and a sculpture garden. Much of the produce for the restaurant meals and piazza bites comes from the estate gardens, and is served in a beautiful dining room with views over the hills. The 'sculpture trail' is a 1km track winding past more than 30 works of sculptural art. And then there's the wine, which focuses on the region's classics: pinot noir, shiraz and chardonnay, and is truly beautiful. The cellar door has a whole range of tasting experiences, from a standard run-through, to museum releases, to longer experiences, such as behind-the-scenes winery tours and a Pinot Lovers Road Trip that includes lunch, a tour, and a six-bottle take-home wine pack for $2000 per couple. But you don't need to splurge to have a great day out here.

montalto.com.au

Montalto *Opposite* Pt. Leo Estate

MOOROODUC ESTATE
LOW-KEY WINERY FOCUSES ON WHAT REALLY MATTERS: MAKING GREAT WINE.

You almost have to chuckle at the Moorooduc cellar door, which lies down the end of a long dirt road, a small and unimposing space that doesn't tell you anything at all about the wonders that lie inside. Moorooduc may be small and it may be tucked away from the grand estates of the Mornington Peninsula, but it's still doing some very good wine – chardonnay and pinot – and it's a super-friendly place to spend some time just tasting and learning about the winery. There's no restaurant, no cafe, no sculpture garden, no playground, no accommodation. Just great wine.

moorooducestate.com.au

OCEAN EIGHT
MOVIE-STAR GOOD LOOKS AREN'T THE ONLY ATTRACTIONS AT THIS CLASSY CELLAR DOOR.

Annoyingly for Ocean Eight – you assume – this winery was around well before the film *Ocean's Eight* was released, so you could say Hollywood copied the Mornington Peninsula, rather than the other way around. Anyway, you're not here for film references, you're here for wine, and Ocean Eight does that extremely well. The winery is probably best known for its pinot gris, though winemaker Mike Aylward also makes great chardonnay and pinot noir. Be sure to bring the camera when you visit the cellar door, too: it's housed in a beautiful New England–style home at the end of a long, tree-lined drive that is just begging to be posed in – like you're a movie star.

oceaneight.com.au

PT. LEO ESTATE
SWISH CELLAR DOOR AND RESTAURANT OFFERS THE CHANCE TO SPLASH OUT.

Pt. Leo Estate is one of those Mornington Peninsula wineries, like Port Phillip Estate (*see* p.80), with a cellar door you will never forget. It's all sexy curves and architectural flair, poured-concrete walls that somehow complement the manicured lawns and rolling countryside, brutalist design for the modern age. Like Port Phillip – as well as Montalto (*see* p.78), and Ten Minutes by Tractor (*see* p.83) – Pt. Leo is also designed as a full destination, a place to spend your entire day, to dine and taste and stroll and photograph. The cellar door offers standard and premium tastings; the fine-dining restaurant, Laura, has two chef's hats from the *Good Food Guide*, and offers either four- or eight-course set menus; there's also a la carte dining at the one-hatted Pt. Leo Estate Restaurant, and casual dining on the Wine Terrace. There's an extensive sculpture park as well, because of course there is, plus occasional exhibitions of vintage cars. The full package.

ptleoestate.com.au

POLPERRO (15)

SURPRISING WINERY NEAR RED HILL HAS A LITTLE SOMETHING FOR EVERYONE.

Polperro is seriously underrated. This winery isn't one of the big guns, certainly not a household name even among wine nuts. And yet you arrive here and find one impressive operation, with plenty of options for drinkers and diners in beautiful surrounds. Set just outside Red Hill, the Polperro cellar door has been thoughtfully designed to encompass sweeping views of vines and hillside, the terroir that makes the wines here what they are. Visitors can have a tasting at the classy cellar door, or head out on the lawn on a nice day for an outdoor tasting and wine platter. Those keen to hang around a little longer can have lunch at the restaurant on the sublime terrace overlooking the vineyard, dining on four-course menus that feature the likes of crayfish caviar, kingfish with lemon aspen, native marron, and dry-aged duck with blood plums. The wine here – single-vineyard pinot noirs and chardonnays – is also superb. And a final surprise: there's accommodation including four luxury villas and a three-bed farmhouse.

polperrowines.com.au

PORTSEA HOTEL (16)

SEASIDE PUB DOES ALL OF THE CLASSICS, JUST THE WAY YOU WOULD WANT THEM.

Portsea, the idyllic coastal town at the far end of the peninsula, is not exactly known for its lack of class, so it should come as no surprise to find that the local pub, the historic (1876) but renovated Portsea Hotel, is an absolute stunner of a venue that you really want to pay a visit to. You can do the usual pub thing and prop up at the bar with a schooner of beer and a chicken parma, if you really want. What's even better, however, is to take a seat out on the deck, at a wooden table overlooking the entrance to Port Phillip Bay, order a bottle of Amrit pinot gris and a plate of oysters and then get ready to go to town on a beautiful menu of pub staples – pizza, pasta, steak, seafood – done to perfection. Stay the night if you want, too, at one of the chic rooms upstairs.

portseahotel.com.au

PORT PHILLIP ESTATE/ KOOYONG (17)

TWO WINE LABELS, A RESTAURANT, AND ONE OF THE MOST IMPRESSIVE BUILDINGS IN THE REGION.

This place is a jaw-dropper, from start to finish. First you have the building itself, an architectural gem just out of Red Hill, a place of poured concrete in flowing lines that draws the eye to the surrounding forests and vines, with a spacious interior that again pushes your gaze out to the beautiful surroundings. Gorgeous. And then you have the wine: not one but two distinct labels, Port Phillip Estate and Kooyong; same owners, same winemaker, but differing philosophies. Kooyong is traditional and high-end, Port Phillip is a little more accessible, a little more experimental. Both are bloody great. There's food here, sophisticated cuisine served in refined surroundings, open for dinner on Fridays and Saturdays, which you don't always find at wineries. There's accommodation, too, six luxury suites with views of the vineyard and coast. Stunning.

portphillipestate.com.au

QUEALY WINEMAKERS
OLD STYLES MEET NEW AT THIS INTIMATE CELLAR-DOOR EXPERIENCE.

At Quealy Winemakers, you have the best of the peninsula's old world and new: Kathleen Quealy has been making wine here for decades, and her pinot grigios and pinot noirs are widely respected and sought after. Meanwhile, her partner Kevin McCarthy and son Tom have a thing for friulano, an Italian grape variety that is traditionally made with plenty of skin contact, a style that's popular now with the natural wine crowd. At the Quealy cellar door you can taste them all and decide on your favourite: set among the barrels and clay amphorae used to make the wine, the tasting area is intimate and the welcome friendly, with plenty of wine to swirl and sip and discuss.

quealy.com.au

Top Red Hill Brewery *Opposite* Polperro

RED HILL BREWERY
THE PENINSULA'S ORIGINAL BREWERS ARE STILL GOING STRONG IN A BEAUTIFUL LOCATION.

Karen and David Golding were into craft beer way before it was cool. The pair established their own brewery back in 2005, in a beautiful wooden brewhouse in Red Hill where they still grow their own hops and lovingly craft their own suite of beers. Red Hill Brewery is known for its core range, which is all easy-drinking, sessionable (brewer chat for 'could drink about a million of them') beers, like kolsch, pilsner and wheat beer, supplemented by an experimental range of seasonal brews that could be matured in oak barrels, or make use of local produce like cherries, honey and even truffles. The brewpub opens to the public from Thursday to Sunday and serves beer plus casual pub-grub food. This is a laidback, friendly joint that's the perfect antidote to the swish wineries of the region. There's accommodation, too, at the three-bedroom Brewer's Cottage.

redhillbrewery.com.au

SCORPO WINES (21)

KEEP AN EYE ON THE CALENDAR, BECAUSE SCORPO IS WORTH THE WAIT.

The Scorpo Wines cellar door is a seriously pared-back affair, with none of the flash of some of its local competitors. It's rarely even open: winemaker Paul Scorpo welcomes visitors on the first weekend of each month, or by prior appointment. It's worth making the effort though, because Scorpo is quietly producing some of the best wines on the peninsula, using old-world techniques to harness new-world flavours, working with pinot noir, chardonnay, pinot gris and shiraz.

scorpowines.com

ST ANDREWS BEACH BREWERY (20)

FORMER RACETRACK AND STABLES IS NOW ONE OF THE REGION'S BEST BREWERIES.

It's quite amazing to see an aerial view of the St Andrews Beach Brewery site, to see the old horse stables in front of what looks distinctly like a horse-racing track – only, this one is covered in crops. This is a brewery with history, a place that was once called Markdel, the headquarters of the Freedman horse-racing team in the early 2000s, a stables and track where champions such as Makybe Diva, Mummify and Alinghi were trained. Back in 2015, Andrew and Jane Purchase bought it and went about turning it into a serious brewing facility, complete with a brewpub in the old stables – dining booths are in individual stalls, with the names of horses that once inhabited them. There's also a 'Birdcage', or casual bar in the old parade ground, and a retail store in the old barn. And fruit and veg are grown on the old track. The beer is great too, approachable, easy-drinkers perfect for a day at the races.

standrewsbeachbrewery.com.au

TEDESCA OSTERIA (22)

THE COUNTRY ITALIAN RESTAURANT OF YOUR DREAMS EXISTS ON THE MORNINGTON PENINSULA.

Warning: if you want to visit Tedesca Osteria, you will have to book well ahead. Like, months in advance. And trust me, you want to visit Tedesca Osteria. This is the platonic ideal of a countryside Italian restaurant, only it's just outside Red Hill. Chef and owner Brigitte Hafner has created something truly special here, an intimate space that brings together the joy in so many of the good things in life, from art to music to wine to nature and the company of good friends. The food is set-menu, hyper local, featuring antipasti, handmade pasta, and seafood and meat often cooked with skill in the wood-oven. No foams or squeezy-bottle sauces or other artifice: just very, very good food. You want to visit. Hafner and her partner, architect Patrick Ness, also offer accommodation in the beautifully restored, three-bedroom Graceburn House, as well as the studio-style Glasshouse.

tedesca.com.au

Top St Andrews Beach Brewery *Opposite* Ten Minutes by Tractor

TEN MINUTES BY TRACTOR (23)

FLASH RESTAURANT OFFERS THE CHANCE TO SAMPLE SOME SERIOUSLY AMAZING WINE.

You could visit the Mornington Peninsula and only go to Ten Min by Tractor, and it would not be a wasted journey. This is just such a lovely place, with amazing food, beautiful wine, friendly people, and a stunning hillside location. 10X – as it's sometimes abbreviated – was founded when Martin and Karen Spedding bought three vineyards, each 10min from the other by tractor, in 1999, and began producing chardonnay, pinot noir, pinot gris and sauvignon blanc. They still do that, though tastings are now served in an urbane cellar door space, plus there's now a restaurant doing five- and eight-course menus of serious haute cuisine, with dishes like Bundarra pork belly with foie gras and black pudding, green-lip abalone with dashi and confit potato, and some outrageously beautiful snacks. The wine list at the restaurant is sensational too, featuring all of the 10X products, as well as an extensive range of imports. There are several wine pairing options, in fact, from The Alternatives, for $145 per person, to Rare Finds, for $550 a head. If you want to sample some truly life-changing wine, the sort of stuff you will rarely have the chance to enjoy again, this is the place to do it. Time and money well spent.

tenmintuesbytractor.com.au

WOWEE ZOWEE (24)

AMERICAN-STYLE DUDE FOOD IS SERVED TILL LATE IN RELAXED SURROUNDS.

There are so many fancy, serious dining venues on the Mornington Peninsula, many of which have been mentioned on these pages (hi there Pt. Leo, Montalto, 10X, Tedesca, et al). So it's something of a relief to get to talk about Wowee Zowee, a pub essentially, with a '70s vibe, a raucous place that serves straight-up American-style dude food, the likes of buffalo wings, buttermilk chicken burgers and mac-and-cheese burgers, served up till late at night with cheap beer, cider and wine.

woweezowee.com.au

YABBY LAKE (25)

PLEASANT CELLAR DOOR IS ONE OF THE FIRST YOU'LL HIT ON A TRIP OUT FROM MELBOURNE.

You've barely even hit the Mornington Peninsula, just south of Frankston, and already you've found one of the region's best wineries: Yabby Lake. This place is 50min from downtown Melbourne on a good day, and yet it is also a world away from the urban bustle, a pleasant cellar door and restaurant amid gently sloping, vine-covered plains, with, of course, views of a lake – though the presence of yabbies hasn't been confirmed. The wine here is all about the region's classics, pinot noir and chardonnay, with a sub-label, Red Claw, providing a more accessible avenue into top-quality vino, with most bottles coming in at under $30. The restaurant is open for lunch daily, doing two- or three-course set menus of Italian-leaning Mod-Oz cuisine.

yabbylake.com

The Perfect Day
MORNINGTON PENINSULA

Victoria

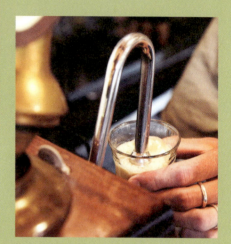

11AM AVANI
I'm not going to lie: today is a long and crazy day that could easily be separated into two days and you'd be just fine. Anyway, begin with a tasting of Shashi Singh's beautiful syrah at Avani (see p.75).

12PM TEDESCA OSTERIA
Next up it's lunchtime, so head 5min down the road from Avani to Tedesca Osteria (see p.82) for a truly memorable lunch of modern Italian-style cuisine.

2PM RED HILL BREWERY
Time to hit the road, just another 5min from lunch to Red Hill Brewery (see p.81), where you can call in for a quick cleansing ale and a chat with the friendly team.

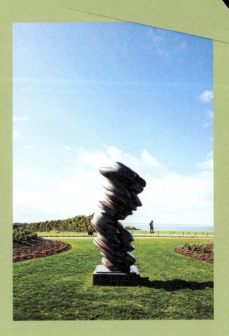

3PM PORT PHILLIP ESTATE

Staying in the Red Hill area, it's only another 5min from the brewery north to Port Phillip Estate (see p.80), where there's a huge range of both Port Phillip and Kooyong wines to try, and views to appreciate.

4PM FOXEYS HANGOUT

There's still time to make a stop at Foxeys Hangout (see p.75), one of the most amiable cellar doors in the region, for a quick glass of wine on the deck and a snack or two.

7PM PT. LEO ESTATE

Take a little break - you've earned it - and prepare for dinner, which tonight will be a multi-course extravaganza of haute cuisine at one of the peninsula's best restaurants, Laura at Pt. Leo Estate (see p.79).

GEELONG AND THE BELLARINE PENINSULA
WATHAURONG COUNTRY

Every Australian, and probably almost every visitor to this great land, knows about the Great Ocean Road. This is one of Australia's premier tourist attractions, a 240km stretch of highway that takes in truly spectacular coastline, lined with sheer cliffs and towering limestone stacks pummeled by cold Antarctic waters, punctuated by quiet bays and pumping surf beaches, backed by windswept hinterland and densely forested hills. And here's another thing too: the beginning of the Great Ocean Road, from Torquay down to Anglesea, is also part of one of Australia's great designated wine regions, Geelong.

The name of this wine region is actually simply 'Geelong', which is a little misleading, and no doubt something of an annoyance to residents, because this is a broad area that goes far beyond the titular city (both geographically and culturally). Geelong the wine region takes in all of the Bellarine Peninsula, from Portarlington to Queenscliff to Barwon Heads, but also goes up north almost to the outskirts of Melbourne/Naarm, then north-west to Mount Mercer and Shelford – and, of course, south along the Surf Coast and south-west along the Great Ocean Road.

The Geelong wine region deserves to be known as much for its gastronomic attractions as its natural wonders. This area is strewn with wineries that are perfectly set up for tourism, with friendly cellar doors and high-quality restaurants making the best of the local produce. The Bellarine Peninsula, in particular, is perfect for cellar-door touring, with winery after winery within touching distance, offering great views across vineyards and waterways, and all a little more laidback than on the fancier Mornington Peninsula across Port Phillip Bay.

The region has also quickly spawned a host of great microbreweries, particularly along the Surf Coast around Torquay and Anglesea, with a few classic pubs thrown into the mix. Though there are a heap of great microbreweries in Geelong city that I unfortunately didn't have space to cover in this book, you can check out Great Ocean Road Brewing, Bellarine Brewing Company, White Rabbit, Little Creatures and Valhalla if you're going to be there.

Pack your wetsuit when you come down here, and maybe your surfboard too. And get ready to eat and drink with maximum pleasure.

BAIE WINES ①

FAMILY BUSINESS MAKES THE MOST OF ITS PRIME LOCATION.

The Kuc family do everything at Baie Wines: Nadine Kuc manages the business, Simon Kuc looks after the wine, Peter and Anne Kuc do the weddings, and the kids help out where they can. This is a family business, in case you couldn't tell, and it's one where you feel you've been welcomed into that family, even if only for an hour or so, when you call into Baie's cellar door near Curlewis on the Bellarine Peninsula. Baie produces lovely cool-climate wines, sauvignon blanc, shiraz and the like, and pours them at their laidback cellar door, where you can easily catch a whiff of bay breeze. You can see why the family stays here.

baiewines.com.au

Opposite The Whiskery

BANNOCKBURN VINEYARDS ②

ONE OF THE REGION'S ORIGINALS IS STILL MAKING SOME OF ITS BEST WINE.

It's handy, when you're one of the first winemakers to arrive in a new region, to have the pick of the best locations. And Bannockburn chose the best locations. This was one of the Geelong area's first wineries, established in 1974, dedicated to making chardonnay and pinot noir in the style of France's famed Burgundy region, though with some shiraz and riesling now thrown in for good measure. So yeah, the wine here is incredibly good. It's also reasonably good value for an outfit of this prestige, with bottles starting at $30, though heading up north of $100 once you get into the really good stuff. The cellar door is only open by appointment, but if you're lucky enough to secure a spot you will be treated to a generous tasting of some of the region's finest.

bannockburnvineyards.com

BARWON HEADS WINESTORE ③

PASSIONATE WINE FANS SERVE UP THE BEST OF THE REGION'S SCENE.

Here's your chance to deep-dive into the Geelong wine scene without even getting into the car. Barwon Heads Winestore, run by passionate wine nuts Richard and Erena Crowley, stocks a whole heap of highly sought-after wine from the region, as well as a few enticing imports from around Australia and the world. There are artisanal spirits for sale too, many produced locally, plus a few non-alcoholic wines, and a pantry with gourmet deliciousness to take home. Perhaps the most valuable aspect of a visit, however, is chatting to Richard and Erena and learning about the area.

barwonheadswinestore.com.au

BASILS FARM ④

FAMILY-FRIENDLY BELLARINE WINERY HAS PLENTY TO OFFER IN RELAXED SURROUNDS.

Wine is really just a small part of the Basils Farm experience. In fact, don't even think of this as a winery – it's more a place to come, relax, enjoy the views, stroll the gardens, eat some nice food and drink some good wine. It just so happens that the wine is made on-site. Basils Farm sits right on the coast at Swan Bay, on the Bellarine Peninsula, with gorgeous views across the water to Queenscliff and Swan Island. There's a cafe here that makes the most of that maritime outlook, serving up lunches inside or alfresco, easy-breezy Mod-Oz food that isn't trying to do too much, and there's a new event space too. At the cellar door, tasting flights of Basils Farm's minimal-intervention reds and whites are offered. Keep an eye out for the farm animals too, including llamas and sheep, that kids are allowed to hand-feed, and the permaculture garden that the cafe staff pluck ingredients from.

basilsfarm.com.au

BELLARINE DISTILLERY/ THE WHISKERY ⑤

GRAB A G&T AND RELAX IN THE GARDEN AT THIS BELLARINE PENINSULA INSTITUTION.

Imagine you had a couple of friends who had a nice house by the coast, a place with a garden and lots of chairs under the trees, plus these friends just happened to distil their own gin and whisky. That, essentially, is Bellarine Distillery. Meet your new best friends, Russ Watson and Lorelle Warren, who run the distillery and are responsible for The Whiskery, the bar and bistro serving their lovingly crafted spirits (you might have seen the Teddy & the Fox label around) out of an old farm shed in the Bellarine countryside near Clifton Springs. It's fancier than it sounds, though it's still so comfortable and homely that you really do feel like you're over at a friend's house, sipping G&Ts in the backyard, enjoying a few casual snacks and whiling a sunny afternoon away. Sounds okay, right?

bellarinedistillery.com.au

BLACKMAN'S BREWERY AND PIZZA BAR ⑥

DIVE INTO A FEW BARREL-FERMENTED BREWS AT THIS TORQUAY MAINSTAY.

The smaller towns outside Geelong boast their fair share of brewers doing interesting things with small-batch beers, and Blackman's Brewery is one such establishment, a Torquay favourite set up by Renn Blackman, a local with a passion for tasty brews. There's a huge and interesting range here, from core beers like IPA and pale ale, to a suite of barrel-fermented brews with a huge depth of flavour. The bar and restaurant at the brewery is open every day for lunch and dinner, churning out pizzas and other pub classics to the hungry, thirsty masses. There's also a Blackman's Brewery & Burger Bar on the Bellarine Peninsula in Ocean Grove, and a recently opened Blackman's Brewery in Geelong too.

blackmansbrewery.com.au

BRAE ⑦

ICONIC EATERY IS FINE-DINING AT ITS GREATEST, AND DEFINITELY WORTH THE DRIVE.

This iconic restaurant – easily one of Australia's finest, and arguably its absolute best – is actually outside the Geelong wine region, a little to the west of the boundary in beautiful Birregurra in the Otways, but how could I leave it out? Brae is stunning. It's incredible. It's a rural eatery in the style of the great European countryside restaurants, destination diners like Asador Etxebarri in the Basque Country and Reale in Abruzzo that you would do anything to be able to drive deep into the countryside to experience. Like those famed European eateries, Brae is very much of its own place. The ingredients used here are mostly grown or raised at the organic farm on-site, and in the hands of chef Dan Hunter are turned into something spectacular, something transcendental. The menu changes every day, so I can't give too much away. Just trust that you will be wowed, and that your wallet will be significantly lighter for the experience (set menus are $310 per person, with an extra $190 for matching wines). Brae has accommodation on-site too, six beautiful suites reserved for those who have managed to swing a restaurant booking.

braerestaurant.com

Brae *Opposite* Basils Farm

BREWICOLO BREWING CO. (8)

EMBRACE GLORIOUS ISLAND TIME AT THIS LAIDBACK, SUNNY BREWERY.

Ocean Grove is a coastal town that only has a population of about 15,000, and yet it boasts the Blackman's Burger Bar (*see* p.89), plus even better, its own craft brewery, Brewicolo, located in the Ocean Grove industrial estate. The name is a bit of a mouthful but there's method to the madness: it's a play on co-owner and brewer Chilla Tuicolo's last name, which someone changed to 'Brewicolo' one boozy night, and it stuck. Chilla's family heritage is in Fiji, and that island nation is the inspiration for much of what you'll find at Brewicolo, from the palm trees on the label to the sense of 'island time' in the bar. The idea is to slow down, relax, have a beer, take it easy. And it's good beer, too, served in an outdoor area that's designed to work for everyone, with space for kids to play, live music and bingo nights, and plenty of cheap, tasty food on offer. Embrace the island spirit.

brewicolo.com

CLYDE PARK (9)

ONE OF THE REGION'S FINEST OFFERS A WIDE RANGE OF TASTING EXPERIENCES AND BEAUTIFUL FOOD.

Along with Bannockburn (*see* p.87) and Scotchmans Hill (*see* p.94), plus a few other big guns that don't have cellar doors – Wines By Farr the most notable – Clyde Park is hands-down making some of the best wine in the Geelong region, the sort of single-block, Burgundian-style chardonnays and pinot noirs that will knock your wine-loving socks off when you get in here for a sample. And there are so many ways to do that sampling: Clyde Park's cellar door, open daily in the north of the region, offers Premium Masterclass tastings for $20 per person, Taste Clyde Park flights for $30 a head, and Stay-a-While tastings, which include a tour of the vineyard with a glass of cracking Block F Pinot Noir in hand, for $50. Visitors can add a cheese platter to any of these experiences, or head over to the airy and atmospheric bistro overlooking volcanic plains for a pizza, a steak, or something a little fancier. Pair it with some wine: pretty much the entire Clyde Park list is available by the glass.

clydepark.com.au

CURLEWIS WINERY (10)

EUROPEAN INFLUENCES CONTRIBUTE TO ONE LOVELY PLACE TO SPEND THE DAY.

The Curlewis experience on the Bellarine Peninsula is gorgeous from start to finish, from your first stroll up the pathway to the cellar door, to your final sip of wine while looking over the vines to the bay and the You Yangs. This is a small operation, one that focuses mainly on pinot noir and chardonnay made in the style of the Burgundy region of France, as well as cool-climate shiraz influenced by the winemakers of the Rhone. To sample them, visitors can hang out in the cosy cellar door (open Saturdays and some Sundays) and take a $15 flight through six wines, including the Reserve Pinot Noir – Curlewis' top drop – or settle down for an Italian-style lunch either inside or out, with wines by the glass or bottle. Everything is so lovely, you'll never want to leave.

curlewiswinery.com.au

FISH BY MOONLITE (11)
CASUAL FISH AND CHIPS DONE RIGHT BY LOCAL FOODIE SUPERSTARS.

It's fish 'n' chips, but not as you know it at Fish by Moonlite in the Great Ocean Road gateway town of Anglesea. This casual seafood joint, run by local foodie superstars Matt Germanchis and Gemma Gange, is inspired by the portside restaurants in the Greek Islands that Matt used to love during his time living and working in Skiathos. At Fish by Moonlite, the pair source the freshest local catch and turn it into fish and chips the way it should be, treated with skill and care, though still affordable enough for pretty much everyone to tuck in. Pay them a visit – you'll never think about fish and chips the same way again.

fishbymoonlite.com.au

FLYING BRICK CIDER CO. (12)
CIDER MAKERS KEEP IT FRESH AND CLEAN, WITH LOCAL BEER AND WINE A BONUS.

There aren't too many dedicated cider makers in the Geelong region, but the team from Flying Brick, in Wallington on the Bellarine Peninsula, are definitely dedicated cider makers. These guys use local apples and pears – and only apples and pears – to make their compact core range of drinks, just two apple ciders and one pear cider, and they serve them up on-site with great food to match. There's lawn space for the kids to run around on or alfresco tables, cider is served by the glass or as part of a tasting paddle with a few of Flying Brick's more seasonal creations, plus there's local wine, craft beer and coffee if fermented apple juice isn't strictly your thing. The menu is extensive, ranging from pasta to steak to a teriyaki duck leg with creamed corn and barbecued leek. Good times guaranteed.

flyingbrickciderco.com.au

JACK RABBIT (13)
HIGH-END RESTAURANT IS A JUSTIFIABLE DRAWCARD AT THIS CHARMING WINERY.

Jack Rabbit is a winery with an acclaimed fine-dining restaurant, a casual cafe and spectacular views. The fine-diner here is a work of gastronomic art, a beautiful spot where a range of high-quality Australian produce is harnessed on a menu that draws influence from around the world. Think yuzu-cured ocean trout, smoked kangaroo loin, confit duck leg, gin-glazed kohlrabi. And all this served on a terrace with sweeping views of Port Phillip Bay? Yes. Thing is, however, you don't have to go fancy at Jack Rabbit if you don't feel like it: the winery also has a cafe, House of Jack Rabbit, that does brunches and lunch every day, and where the offerings range from breakfast burgers to fish and chips. It's all relatively inexpensive, but still made with care. Oh, and there's wine too, including great riesling and shiraz, up for tasting.

jackrabbitvineyard.com.au

Top Jack Rabbit *Opposite* Clyde Park

LETHBRIDGE WINES & HAT ROCK VINEYARD (14)

FORMER SCIENTISTS ARE STILL EXPERIMENTING WITH THEIR HIGH-QUALITY DROPS.

Maree Collis and Ray Nadeson did their research back in 1996, when these two scientists decided to start a vineyard. They scoured the entire Geelong region, checking soil types, researching weather patterns and comparing aspects, before finally settling on a site in Lethbridge, up in the north. There, they began clearing out the old shed, and discovered something interesting: an old, wooden fermentation vat. Turns out this site had been a vineyard before, planted by Swiss migrants back in the 1870s. Clearly, this is a place for making good wine, and that's exactly what Collis and Nadeson do, even 25 years later. The pair are well known now for their super high-quality chardonnay, shiraz and pinot noir, made with minimal intervention, it's textural and delicious. They release wine across four labels, allowing them the chance to experiment and diversify. Pay them a visit at one of two cellar doors: there's the original site in Lethbridge, and another venue on the Bellarine Peninsula, between Drysdale and Portarlington, at their Hat Rock Vineyard. Visitors can have a tasting flight, or just a glass of something good to go with a platter.

lethbridgewines.com

LEURA PARK ESTATE (15)

PUT A LITTLE SPARKLE IN YOUR DAY WITH A VISIT TO THIS FRIENDLY CELLAR DOOR.

Leura Park on the Bellarine Peninsula does something not many others do in Geelong: sparkling wine. They're pretty proud of their Blanc de Blancs (sparkling made with only chardonnay grapes) and Blanc de Noir (made with chardonnay and pinot noir). If you're in the mood to celebrate – or just feel like a glass of bubbles – this is your spot. There's plenty of other wine here as well, all of which should go nicely with the food at the Leura Park restaurant, which offers everything from pizzas to sandwiches to salads, served on the sunny terrace.

leuraparkestate.com.au

MINYA WINERY (16)

STUNNING BUSHLAND OUTLOOK IS ONE OF MANY REASONS TO VISIT THIS CLASSY WINERY.

The Australian bush has a distinctive charm about it, something you can't find anywhere else, something that lets you know: this is Australia. And they have that at Minya, a winery just inland from Torquay, perched in bushland that's distinctly and beautifully Australian. The cellar door here is only open by appointment, but do make the effort, even just for the view over a billabong surrounded by trees (maybe as part of a visit to on-site restaurant Moonah, *see* below). Minya is a word in the local Aboriginal language that means 'place of many birds', and you will see why. The wine, too, has a sense of that Australian terroir, the bush captured in a bottle.

theminya.com.au

MOONAH RESTAURANT (17)

SUSTAINABLE CUISINE IS GIVEN THE FINE-DINING TREATMENT AT THIS IMPRESSIVE EATERY.

Never before has sustainability looked so good, or tasted so delicious. Welcome to Moonah, the tiny, 12-seat fine-diner run by chef and gardener Tobin Kent up on the coastal fringe near Torquay. Moonah is all about sustainable, local eating, with zero waste, and plenty of the ingredients are either grown on-site or foraged from the windswept grounds nearby (reflecting Kent's time working with Dan Hunter at Brae, *see* p.89). Guests at Moonah sit in the intimate dining room, near the big picture window overlooking the billabong at Minya Winery (*see* above), under the watchful gaze of Kent himself, and are treated to an ever-changing menu of sustainable, ethical meat, seafood and vegetable delights. Moonah's sommelier, Amy Tsai, provides the perfect wines to match.

moonahrestaurant.com.au

OAKDENE VINEYARDS (18)
BOUTIQUE ESTATE HAS A HUGE AMOUNT TO OFFER VISITORS OF ALL KINDS.

Oakdene is emblematic of many of the Bellarine Peninsula wineries: a relatively boutique affair that even still has a huge amount for visitors, from wine to food to extensive grounds, and in this case, somewhere to stay. But let's start with the wine, Oakdene's raison d'être, and something that's done extremely well. Oakdene is known for its classic cool-climate wines, chardonnay, shiraz, pinot noir and riesling that have a maritime influence, thanks to the vineyard's proximity to Ocean Grove, just 5min away. Visitors don't just come here for that, though. They come for the cellar door, an iconic piece of rustic architecture that's built to look like an old cottage laid on its side (you'll understand when you see it). Tasting flights cost $10. They come to try the Oakdene olive oil; they come to eat at Mr Grubb, the Oakdene bistro, nestled in the trees by the cellar door; they come to curl up on a couch with a glass of wine at the Manor Suite Wine Bar; and they come to spend the night, either at the three-bedroom Lighthouse Cottage with views over the Bellarine, or the Guest House, a lovingly restored 1920s homestead. And they all leave happy.

oakdene.com.au

PORTARLINGTON GRAND HOTEL (19)
CLASSIC COUNTRY PUB HAS BENEFITED FROM AN EXTENSIVE RENOVATION.

You have to love a classic Victorian country pub on the coast, and Portarlington Grand is one of the best of them. This imposing property was built in 1888, and underwent a huge restoration in 2021, ensuring punters will be piling in here for many years to come. The new Portarlington Grand is a pub, a restaurant and a hotel, with multiple areas to relax and enjoy. Choose from the Atrium, an open-air dining space; the Lawn, another alfresco spot for pizzas and beers; the Front Bar, a classic drinking venue; and the Bistro, where pub grub is given a nudge into gourmet territory, with a nice wine list to match. There are rooms upstairs, 18 abodes with plenty of charm and all the mod-cons – thanks to that recent reno.

portarlingtongrandhotel.com.au

Top Oakdene Vineyards *Overleaf* Provenance

PROVENANCE 20

HISTORIC MILL PROVIDES THE PERFECT HEADQUARTERS FOR ONE CLASSY WINERY.

Prepare to swoon over the Provenance headquarters: they're bloody gorgeous. On the banks of the winding Barwon River, on the outskirts of Geelong itself, the old Fyansford Paper Mill is a series of heritage-listed bluestone buildings constructed during the 1870s, and which just happen to provide perfect cellaring conditions for Provenance's wine. This is also the ideal location for a cellar door and restaurant. Provenance makes high-quality chardonnay, pinot noir, pinot gris and shiraz, grown in vineyards spread throughout the Geelong region. They're made at the mill though and, more importantly, they're poured and drunk at the mill. Take your time when you visit here, to idle over a six- or eight-wine sample, to enjoy the locavore tasting menu at the restaurant, and to stroll around and attempt to capture the magic of this place on film (or your phone).

provenancewines.com.au

QUEENSCLIFF BREWHOUSE 21

HISTORIC PUB HAS REINVENTED ITSELF AS A CRAFT BEER WONDERLAND.

There's a good amount of history at the Queenscliff Brewhouse, having been open since 1879, but it's fair to say the pub probably didn't have quite as many craft beers on tap back in those halcyon days. The Brewhouse now bills itself as a 'craft beer haven', and with more than 400 boutique brews to try – including at least 10 or so that are brewed on-site – that's hard to argue with. There's a distillery here too, because of course there is, doing artisanal gin, and the pub puts on regular gin-blending masterclasses. Visitors to the Brewhouse will also find a tasting room for beer and spirit sampling, a dog-friendly beer garden, a restaurant, a sports bar, and an events space.

queensclifbrewhouse.com.au

SCOTCHMANS HILL 22

TOP-TIER WINERY PRODUCES A WHOLE SERIES OF DROPS THAT ARE SURPRISINGLY AFFORDABLE.

You may think you can't afford a lot of the wine at Scotchmans Hill on the Bellarine, given it's one of the top-tier producers in the Geelong region and, look, you could be right. A lot of the good stuff here is quite pricey. Fortunately, however, Scotchmans Hill has a large range of wine under multiple labels that are good-quality drops at a whole series of price points. Even better, they do generous tastings at the cellar door, so even if you can't buy a bottle, you can at least have a taste (standard five-wine flights are $10, and you can shift up to a premium tasting, with top-shelf wines and back vintages, for $15 a head). A visit here is about more than the wines though, thanks to the bistro, set in an undercover courtyard with stunning views over Port Phillip Bay. On a sunny day, there are few better places to be.

scotchmans.com.au

The Perfect Day

GEELONG AND THE BELLARINE PENINSULA

10AM

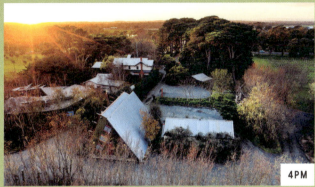
4PM

1.30PM

6PM

10AM CLYDE PARK

The day begins up in the north of the Geelong wine region, near Bannockburn, for a tasting of the high-end, Burgundian-style wines at Clyde Park (*see* p.90), one of the best wineries around.

11AM LETHBRIDGE WINES

Just a few minutes up the road from Clyde Park, you'll find another of the region's best wine producers, Lethbridge Wines (*see* p.92), where you can taste the lo-fi, cool-climate drops. It also has another cellar door, Hat Rock Vineyard, on the Bellarine Peninsula.

1.30PM JACK RABBIT

Take the 1hr drive now from Lethbridge Wines down to the Bellarine Peninsula, where your lunch stop is at Jack Rabbit (*see* p.91), home of a fine-dining restaurant or casual cafe, and some of the best views around.

4PM OAKDENE VINEYARDS

Next, call into Oakdene Vineyards (*see* p.93) - your accommodation for the night - to check in, drop off the bags, and maybe have a glass of the local vino.

6PM QUEENSCLIFF BREWHOUSE

Once evening sets in, dash down to the historic seaside town of Queenscliff for great craft beer and a relaxed dinner among friends at the impressive Queenscliff Brewhouse (*see* p.94).

MACEDON RANGES AND SUNBURY

Melbourne/Naarm, apparently not content with having the Yarra Valley, Mornington Peninsula, and the Geelong wine region within easy striking distance, also has dreamy, delicious wine being produced immediately to its north-west, in Sunbury (*see* p.97) and the Macedon Ranges (*see* p.98). You've barely put Melbourne Airport in your rear-view mirror before you find yourself surrounded by vines once again, with first Sunbury and then Macedon appearing.

These two small regions that are nonetheless home to some seriously exciting wineries, not to mention a whole host of breweries, distilleries, and places to eat good food. Stay for a few days, or just commute back to the city. These regions have what you need.

Top Mount Towrong

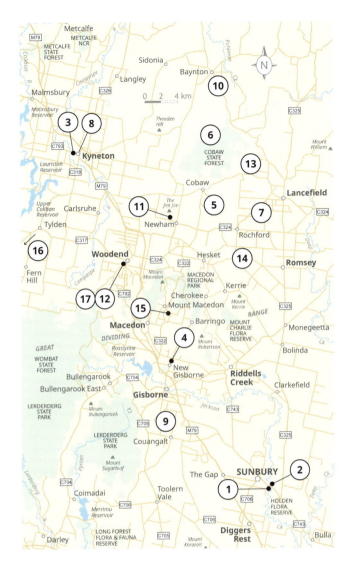

SUNBURY

WOIWURRUNG COUNTRY

There's been wine made in Sunbury since the 1850s, though the scene has never really exploded in the same way it has in somewhere like the Yarra Valley. There's still quality to be found, however, particularly if you're into shiraz.

CRAIGLEE VINEYARD (1)

THE REGION'S BEST WINERY IS WORTH PLANNING YOUR CALENDAR AROUND.

It's hard to believe you're on the outskirts of Sunbury when you arrive at the Craiglee Vineyard cellar door, just 15min from Melbourne Airport and yet an idyllic slice of rural Victorian life. To say 'cellar door' is a bit of a stretch, in fact – Pat Carmody's winery is only open to visitors on the first Sun of every month, and there isn't a huge amount of infrastructure dedicated to those guests. Still, make a plan to be one of them, because this is a beautiful, historic winery, one at which vines were first planted in 1863, and where the original bluestone winery, also built around that time, is still in use. Craiglee is famous for the quality of its shiraz, though there's also chardonnay and cabernet sauvignon to swirl and sip. This is a warm and intimate experience, worth planning around.

craigleevineyard.com

GOONA WARRA VINEYARD (2)

CLASSIC WINE MATCHES ITALIAN-STYLE FOOD AT THIS EASY-GOING ESTABLISHMENT.

Goona Warra is another historic Sunbury winery – vines were first sunk into the rocky earth here in 1863 – and it provides a similarly warm welcome as Craiglee for visitors interested in the region's viticulture. The cellar door here is open for three hours a day – 11am to 2pm – from Thursday to Sunday, providing a good chance to get in and try the semillon, chardonnay, pinot noir, shiraz and more. There's a restaurant, too, serving lovely Italian-style cuisine, a nice match for Goona Warra's classic wines.

goonawarra.com.au

Macedon Ranges and Sunbury

MACEDON RANGES

DJAB WURRUNG, TAUNGURUNG AND WOIWURRUNG COUNTRY

Drive just a tiny bit further from Sunbury and you'll hit the Macedon Ranges, a sensationally beautiful place that's these days stuffed with a whole heap of wineries doing interesting things, including a few lo-fi superstars. Plus there's friendly country towns and hipster-friendly rural hubs like Kyneton and Woodend, with high-end food and intimate bar scenes.

ANIMUS DISTILLERY

ARTISANAL GIN AND WHISKY TAKES A BACK SEAT TO THE WARMTH OF THE WELCOME.

Animus in Kyneton is supposed to be all about creating high-quality, artisanal spirits – gin and whisky predominantly – and yet all anyone can talk about when they leave the distillery door here is how nice everyone is. Sure, the drinks were great and all, but what about those lovely people? It's a good problem to have, and one you're sure to enjoy experiencing if you, too, pop in for a tasting flight or a cocktail or two. Come for the drinks, stay for the company. Animus, on downtown Piper St, really does do great booze, hand-crafted gin with locally grown botanicals, and whisky that has been painstaking in its creation, which began back in 2015 and has only just come to fruition. Drop by and give it a sample. Maybe have some food. And enjoy the warm welcome.

animusdistillery.com

BARINGO FOOD AND WINE CO

POPULAR EATERY CHANNELS THE GREATNESS OF THE MACEDON REGION.

If you want to taste the Macedon Ranges, you could very easily tour around its various wineries and distilleries and artisanal providores, sampling as you go – or, you could book in for a meal at Baringo Food and Wine Co in Gisborne. The menu here features everything that makes the region good, from local produce ultilised for breakfasts, lunches and dinners (and Sunday high teas), to more than 300 wines to choose from, many from the local area. There's a small deli, too, to pick up treats for later.

facebook.com/bfwco

BIG TREE DISTILLERY

BOUTIQUE GIN THAT'S A WORK OF ART BOTH INSIDE AND OUTSIDE THE BOTTLE.

The Big Tree gin bottles are works of art – literally. They're designed by Lauriston-based artist Sarah Gabriel, and they're quite beautiful, featuring renderings of local flora and fauna – so nice, in fact, that you'll want to keep the bottle on the shelf long after the gin has magically disappeared. Best way to sample that gin, and check out the bottles, is to visit the Big Tree distillery door out at Jack's Spring, a farm deep in the Macedon countryside near Newham. Here you're surrounded by many of the botanicals that go into making Big Tree's artisanal gins, which are such a beautiful snapshot of the region, and the passion of those behind it. There's food available too, picnic boxes and light snacks, to make a proper event of it.

bigtreedistillery.com.au

COBAW RIDGE/ JOSHUA COOPER 6
ENJOY THE BEST OF TWO GENERATIONS' APPROACH TO WINEMAKING AT THIS FAMILY CELLAR DOOR.

In Victoria, you'll find a few special cellar doors – Eastern Peake (*see* p.140) is one, too – where you get the best of two worlds: where you can sample the work of some of the pioneers of the region, while also appreciating the talents of their offspring, who are experimenting far more with lo-fi winemaking. Cobaw Ridge was founded by Alan and Nelly Cooper back in 1985, and they're still producing complex, impressive wines like chardonnay and shiraz out to the east of Kyneton. Meanwhile, their son Joshua Cooper is now working with a coterie of local growers to make a highly regarded, eponymous range of ethereal, lo-fi wines that are very difficult to get your hands on. Call into the Cobaw Ridge cellar door – only open on weekends – to try whatever is available from both outfits. Win-win.

cobawridge.com.au

CURLY FLAT 7
SIGNATURE 'WHITE PINOT' IS JUST ONE REASON TO VISIT THIS LOW-KEY WINERY.

There's a wine at Curly Flat that you may not have encountered before, but which is in high demand: white pinot, pinot noir that's essentially made in the style of a white wine, with minimal skin contact, resulting in a textural, salmon-pink drop that gives your palate all sorts of fresh red-berry flavours. It's worth the trip to the Curly Flat cellar door, set in an 1890s home among the vines just outside Lancefield, for this alone. Though of course you'll also want to try the traditional pinot noir and the chardonnay, both of which are amazing, and poured without charge at this friendly, family establishment. It's all pretty low-key, only open three days a week, but lovely.

curlyflat.com

Bottom Curly Flat

DHABA AT THE MILL (8)
CHERISHED LOCAL INSTITUTION DOES HOME-STYLE INDIAN FOOD WITH FLAIR.

You probably didn't come to Kyneton with the intention of eating home-style Indian food in an old flour mill, but work with me here. A 'dhaba' in the Indian subcontinent is a small roadside diner, a cheap, no-frills place where people can gather and eat and chat and be on their merry way. Indian chef Amar Singh was inspired by those dhabas when he set up his Kyneton restaurant, a homely, friendly place that's now a stalwart on the local food scene, having spawned two Dhaba food trucks that can also be found at various locations around the Macedon region. At the old flour mill, Amar serves classic curries and Indian sweets to an appreciative crowd of regulars and passersby. There's nothing lo-fi or locavore or any of those other buzzwords about Dhaba – it's just good. That's all you need to know.

dhaba.com.au

GISBORNE PEAK WINERY (9)
IDIOSYNCRATIC WINERY IS STILL DOING THINGS ITS OWN WAY – AND SUCCEEDING.

Gisborne Peak is old-school: Bob Nixon first planted vines here 'to see how they would go' in 1978, and it turns out they went well indeed. Still, the experience of visiting Gisborne Peak is one that recalls plenty of the winery's history. It's all laidback and no-frills here, with wine tastings seven days a week (for the curious price of $10.50 a head), a restaurant doing pizzas and platters, and even accommodation in the form of four self-contained cottages – for adults only – each overlooking vines and water, with wine-tasting experiences and breakfast included. And it's only 45min from Melbourne.

gisbornepeakwines.com.au

Bottom Granite Hills *Opposite* Hanging Rock

GRANITE HILLS (10)
TRAILBLAZER IS STILL GOING STRONG, THANKS TO SOME VERY GOOD SHIRAZ.

Back in 1970, when Llew Knight set up his vineyard atop the peaks of the Great Dividing Range, the coolest region on mainland Australia, no one thought you could make shiraz there. No one except Llew. Turns out he was right, too, given there are now plenty of shiraz vines throughout the region, and Granite Hills is still making an excellent version. Some 50 years later, Llew is making all sorts of wines, from riesling to grüner veltliner to chardonnay to pinot noir, and they're all highly regarded and delicious. His cellar door here is open daily, and visitors are encouraged to BYO a picnic and get comfortable somewhere with a gorgeous view over the Macedon Ranges, and just appreciate this amazing place. Which, it turns out, is good for shiraz.

granitehills.com.au

HANGING ROCK
FAMOUS GEOLOGICAL FEATURE PROVIDES THE BACKDROP FOR THIS HIGH-QUALITY WINERY.

The best-known natural feature of the Macedon Ranges, and in fact one of the most famous in Victoria, is Hanging Rock. Also known as Mount Diogenes, this is a sacred place for local First Nations People, as well as being the infamous setting for the novel and book, *Picnic at Hanging Rock*, and, it turns out, a good place to grow grapes and make wine. Hanging Rock Winery is a 5min drive from the geological formation, and it's a 40-year-old operation that was one of the Macedon pioneers, known for its sparkling wines as well as a huge range of whites and reds. The property is also a beef farm and cattle stud, which means after a visit to the cellar door, you'll likely walk away with not just wine, but a few cuts of beef, as well as in-house smallgoods like pastrami and bresaola. Some of those meats end up on the deli platters too, available to drinkers looking to extend a very pleasant experience.

hangingrock.com.au

HOLGATE BREWHOUSE
LOCAL STALWART IS STILL CHURNING OUT GREAT BREWS – AND CLASSIC PUB MEALS.

Small-town Woodend has a few big-time drawcards, and Holgate Brewhouse is one of them (*see* p.103 for the wine store which is another reason to visit). Holgate is a stalwart of the craft beer scene, having been around more than 20 years, and an independent, family-owned business set in a historic hotel. The bar has 12 taps pouring beer that's all made on-site, Euro-inspired brews such as wheat beers and British ales, as well as the American-leaning likes of IPAs and session ales. There's so much to do on a visit here: take a tour of the brewery, grab a tasting paddle of beers, sit down to a meal of pub classics, or spend the night in the hotel, with spacious, modern rooms available above the restaurant.

holgatebrewhouse.com

LYONS WILL (13)

WINEMAKING PAIR ATTEMPT TO DIVIDE AND CONQUER, WITH ADMIRABLE RESULTS.

Oliver Rapson and Renata Morella say they craft their wines together, but that isn't strictly true. The pair might run Lyons Will, near Lancefield, as a partnership, but they each handle their wines solo: Oliver is in charge of the pinot noir and chardonnay, and Renata takes the reins for the riesling and gamay. Whose style is best? You'll have to decide for yourself with a tasting at the cellar door, which is set within the winery at Lyons Will, in the centre of the vineyard. This is a beautiful spot where you're always welcomed with a smile; tastings are $15 per person, or you can buy wine by the glass to enjoy with a local produce platter. And you'll no doubt agree that when it comes to winemaking, there are no losers here.

lyonswillestate.com.au

MOUNT MONUMENT (14)

CELEBRATED ARCHITECT TURNS HIS ATTENTION TO BUILDING THE PERFECT WINERY.

You probably know Nonda Katsalidis, even if you think you don't. Been to MONA, the Museum of Old and New Art in Hobart, that impressive, stunning subterranean warren? Nonda Katsalidis is the architect who designed it. Seen the Australia 108 skyscraper, with its inset gold star, in Melbourne? Again, Katsalidis' work. This is one of Australia's most celebrated current architects, and now, he has a winery. In 2008, Katsalidis bought a little-known vineyard near small-town Romsey and began to do something amazing with it, turning it into a premium producer, with wine now made by rising star Ben Ranken. At the time of writing, Katsalidis was in the process of building a cellar door and restaurant on this spectacular site, which you can absolutely guarantee is going to be a thing of architectural wonder, very much in keeping with the estate pinot noir and chardonnay.

mountmonument.com.au

MOUNT TOWRONG (15)

LO-FI WINE AND HIGH-QUALITY FOOD COMBINE TO MAKE ONE WONDERFUL EXPERIENCE.

Mount Towrong is one of the stars of Macedon's lo-fi winemaking world, a friendly, family-owned outfit that takes a lot of care to sustainably produce wines with minimum sulphur added, and very little winemaking trickery involved. The Cremasco family's wine is a snapshot of place, countryside in a bottle, and it's all the better for it. Turn up at the Mount Towrong cellar door on a weekend and you'll not only be treated to gorgeous views of that rolling countryside, but also have the chance to try the wines, which are made using Italian varietals that are rare in these parts: whites like ribolla gialla and vermentino, and reds such as nebbiolo and negro amaro. The home-style Italian food served at the cellar door matches these drops perfectly: your little slice of northern Italy nestled in the Macedon Ranges.

mounttowrong.com.au

PASSING CLOUDS
STYLISH CELLAR DOOR AND RESTAURANT ENJOYS A PRIME POSITION NEAR DAYLESFORD.

Passing Clouds has a lot going for it. For starters, this is the closest cellar door to Daylesford, every Melburnian's favourite weekend spa retreat. The winery also has its own train station, essentially, with the tiny platform at Musk just a 10min walk away. The restaurant and cellar door here both have great views, over lake and vines. And, of course, there's the fact they serve Passing Clouds' wine: beautiful Macedon chardonnay, shiraz and pinot noir. Lunch is served from Thursday to Monday, with fixed menus of family-style cuisine, with pretty much everything cooked over the charcoal fire-pit. More than enough reason to come by.

passingclouds.com.au

Top Pouring wine at Mount Towrong
Opposite Overhead Mount Towrong

WOODEND WINE STORE
FRIENDLY NEIGHBOURHOOD BOTTLE SHOP STOCKS A HUGE RANGE OF MACEDON FAVOURITES.

Maybe you're just passing through the Macedon Ranges. Perhaps you don't have time to visit wineries and breweries and while away easy afternoons on the drink. No worries. Plan a stop at Woodend Wine Store, a super-friendly little joint owned and run by sommelier Caroline Bailey, who has a deep passion for the wine and produce of the Macedon area, as well as an equal desire to share that knowledge and the tasty, boozy treasures of the region. Bailey's store features a huge and expertly curated range of Macedon wines – plenty from outfits that don't even have cellar doors – as well as sought-after wines from around the world, plus small-batch spirits, craft beers and artisanal local produce. If you want to know about wine, or food, or Woodend, or pretty much anything else really, call in for a chat.

woodendwinestore.au

The Perfect Day
MACEDON RANGES AND SUNBURY

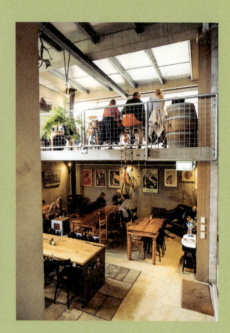

11AM COBAW RIDGE/ JOSHUA COOPER

Begin your day out to the west of Kyneton at Cobaw Ridge (*see* p.99), where you can taste wines by both the old school and new from the Macedon Ranges.

12PM ANIMUS DISTILLERY

Head back into Kyneton for a quick sample of the product at Animus (*see* p.98), an uber-friendly little distillery with excellent whisky and gin.

1PM MOUNT TOWRONG

It's time for lunch, which you're having at Mount Towrong (*see* p.102), a lo-fi winery that also does beautiful, home-style Italian food served with an incredible view.

3PM MOUNT MONUMENT

Continue up the road to Mount Monument (see p.102) for a sample of the wines at one of the most exciting ventures in the region.

4PM WOODEND WINE STORE

Head to friendly Woodend now, where you probably don't need any more wine to drink, but it's still worth calling in to Woodend Wine Store (see p.103) to pick up a few bottles for future enjoyment.

6PM HOLGATE BREWHOUSE

Finish up tonight with a pub meal at Holgate Brewhouse (see p.101), washed down with a pot of the in-house beer. And spend the night at the hotel upstairs.

GIPPSLAND

BOON WURRUNG, WOIWURRUNG, GUNAIKURNAI AND BIDAWAL COUNTRY

The Gippsland region is an interesting one, because what should be a weakness here is actually a strength. Gippsland doesn't have a lot of ingrained tradition as an area for winemaking, it's not a major player with obvious expectations of its finest products, it's still an up-and-comer, still an underdog. That lack of recognition, however, frees up the winemakers here to take a few chances, to experiment, to be unafraid to do exactly what they want and produce exactly what they desire. It allows newcomers to get a look-in. And it also means that you, the traveller and the drinker, need not have any deeply set expectations of this region. Just get out there and discover.

About the only thing you are certain to find on your journeys through Gippsland is one spectacularly beautiful part of the world. This region is a vast one, despite only being home to 50 or so wineries, and takes in a wide array of landscapes, from ruggedly handsome coast to gently rolling foothills to the majesty of the Great Dividing Range. Gippsland begins just outside Melbourne/Naarm, at Wonthaggi, and stretches all the way along the south-east coast, past Wilsons Promontory, past 90 Mile Beach and up the east coast to the NSW border; its north-western reaches go to the edge of the High Country.

There's plenty of foodie heritage here though, particularly in country towns such as Maffra, Traralgon and Inverloch, where much of the produce served in fancy Melburnian restaurants originates. And now, there's wine, and even beer as well. No expectations. Just passionate people doing their thing.

Cannibal Creek *Opposite* Lightfoot and Sons

CANNIBAL CREEK ①

THE WELCOME IS RELIABLY WARM HERE FOR A WINERY WITH 'CANNIBAL' IN THE NAME.

That's a punchy name. You have to be pretty sure of yourself before you go whacking the word 'cannibal' on your label, but you get the feeling Patrick and Kirsten Hardiker are pretty comfortable with who they are and what they do. The pair fell into winemaking after acquiring a property on the very western edge of Gippsland, only an hour from downtown Melbourne, and having to learn the ropes on the go. Their wines these days are works of natural beauty, all high-quality and low-intervention, and they're on for tasting at the airy cellar door and award-winning restaurant at the foot of Mount Cannibal. Kids are welcome, and dogs are too. This is a family affair, and everyone's invited.

cannibalcreek.com.au

Gippsland

DIRTY THREE WINES

INVERLOCH CELLAR DOOR SERVES UP SOME OF THE REGION'S FINEST.

You have to love the way Lisa Sartori and Marcus Satchell describe their products: 'We make wines with soul,' they say, 'that sing of the dirt in which they're grown'. Beautiful. Poetic. Much like the wine. The Dirty Three in question here are the 'three dirts', the three types of soil found in Sartori and Satchell's vineyards in West Gippsland. Those varying terroirs go into making a beautiful suite of wines that focus on pinot noir, but include chardonnay, riesling and rosé. The Dirty Three cellar door and wine bar is found in the coastal town of Inverloch, only a short drive from Melbourne. Here, the team do tasting flights for $15 per person, or full glasses to pair with a range of local snacks at the wine bar.

dirtythreewines.com.au

Top Dirty Three Wines *Opposite* Gurneys Cider

GRAND RIDGE BREWERY ③

VICTORIA'S FIRST CRAFT BREWERY RETAINS MUCH OF ITS DOWN-HOME CHARM.

Grand Ridge was Victoria's first craft brewery, and one of the first in Australia, having roared into business way back in 1989 when Eric Walters converted an old butter factory in Mirboo North. The brewpub and restaurant here is seriously old-school, with carpeted floors and the sort of decor that you last saw in your local RSL. That's all part of the charm though, and it makes the fact the beer is so good just that little bit more surprising. Try the pilsner, the pale ale, or some gutsy numbers like the Moonshine – a dark ale weighing in at 8.5% alcohol – or the Supershine, a scotch ale that nudges 11%. Serious beer. Fortunately, there's accommodation on-site: a three-bedroom 'manor' that is ideal for sleeping off any excess.

grand-ridge.com.au

GURNEYS CIDER (4)
TRADITIONAL CIDER WITH A STUNNING VIEW – WHAT MORE COULD YOU ASK FOR?

The outlook is nothing short of spectacular at the Gurneys Cider cellar door, perched on a hilltop overlooking the northern reaches of Wilsons Promontory. It's all windswept and interesting here, perfect for sitting out on a picnic table when the sun is shining, or huddling up behind floor-to-ceiling glass when it isn't. Regardless of your choice of seat, there's cider to be drunk, traditional British-style cider made by the traditional, British Gurnett family. Those ciders are made with apples grown on-site, a mixture of English, French and unique Gippsland heritage varieties that are perfect for the production of juicy, boozy beverages. Everything is done on-site, in fact, with wild yeasts, vegan-friendly, no nasties added. Gurneys does cheese boards too, plus 'vegan boards', and ploughmans platters to ease you through an enjoyable afternoon.

gurneyscider.com.au

HARMAN WINES (5)
FAMILY-RUN OUTFIT KEEPS THINGS LOCAL, WITH GREAT SUCCESS.

It's an intensely local affair at Harman Wines, from the winemaking team – which is essentially the Harmans, David and Nicole, with a little help from their children, Jenna and James – to the produce at the restaurant, taken from a range of suppliers in the immediate area. Harman Wines is in West Gippsland, close enough to Inverloch to catch the sea breeze, and it's a friendly, intimate spot where you'll always be made to feel welcome. The wines here are cool-climate drops with a little maritime influence, wild-fermented and with very few additions or other tinkering. The Harmans' restaurant serves those wines, as well as locally made beers and ciders, plus tapas and wood-fired pizzas. Using, of course, local ingredients.

harmanwines.com.au

HOGGET KITCHEN

FOODIE TRIO UNITE AT A LOCAVORE EATERY THAT'S EVEN GREATER THAN THE SUM OF ITS PARTS.

You may have heard of the team behind Hogget Kitchen in Warragul. There's William Downie, renowned maker of lo-fi Victoria pinot noir; Trevor Perkins, long-time Warragul cheffing star; and Pat Sullivan, a well-known lo-fi Gippsland winemaker. Together, the trio have been running Hogget, a country restaurant that could itself be described as lo-fi, where the focus is on high-quality ingredients, utilised at the right time of year and allowed to speak for themselves – and where everything is done by hand, in-house. That results in a locavore menu that's big on creativity and respect for produce, where you'll find the likes of pasta with grilled quail, braised lamb shanks with 'belly croquette', or Alpine trout consommé with roe and dumplings. The dishes are served in a bright, beautiful dining room overlooking the vines at Wild Dog Winery, just outside Warragul.

hogget.com.au

LIGHTFOOT AND SONS

IT'S THE SON DOING THE HEAVY LIFTING THESE DAYS AT THIS EXCEPTIONAL FAMILY WINERY.

The name here should more correctly be 'Lightfoot and Father', given it's the son, Tom, who these days is in charge of winemaking at his dad Brian's vineyard. He's doing a fine job too, producing mostly shiraz and chardonnay that says a lot about Gippsland's possibilities. Under those premium releases, the Lightfoots also do a range of more experimental drops, most of which fall under the lo-fi banner, from juicy reds to textural whites. Choose your favourites at the cellar door, out in East Gippsland near Lakes Entrance, where there are both indoor and outdoor spaces in which to settle, take a flight of six wines and pair them with a platter of produce from local purveyors. There's Gippsland craft beer available, too, for those who aren't so keen on the vino.

lightfootwines.com

NARKOOJEE

FATHER AND SON TURNING OUT AN IMPRESSIVELY ECLECTIC RANGE OF WINES.

The father-and-son teams seem particularly successful in Gippsland, and here's another example: Harry and Axel Friend, who have been coaxing deliciousness from the soil near the Strzelecki Ranges, in the Traralgon area, for more than 40 years now. Narkoojee has a beautiful cellar door and restaurant, where they do tasting flights of their wines – which are released across three premium ranges – as well as food that ranges in influence from India to Thailand to Italy. There's plenty of seating outside, too, to make the most of warm, sunny days.

narkoojee.com

Top Narkoojee *Opposite* Nicholson River Winery

NICHOLSON RIVER WINERY (9)

GIPPSLAND PIONEER SERVES UP EURO-STYLE WINES WITH GORGEOUS RIVER VIEWS.

Back in the day, when Gippsland as a winemaking region was little more than a wild idea, there were three pioneering outfits planting vines and coaxing juice out of them: Lulgra, Golvinda, and Nicholson River. Of those three trailblazers only one remains, way up near Lakes Entrance on the banks of its eponymous body of water. Though Nicholson River Winery was up for sale at time of writing, until now it has always been in the hands of Ken Eckersley, who's still making European-style wines more than 40 years on. The cellar door has a stunning view over the Nicholson River, the perfect spot to relax and sample, and toast hardworking people with good ideas.

nicholsonriverwinery.com.au

RIPPLEBROOK WINERY (10)

ITALIAN WARMTH RUNS THROUGH THIS FRIENDLY, RELAXED RESTAURANT AND CELLAR DOOR.

You have to love a winery with Italian heritage – you know you're going to be looked after. And that's absolutely the case at Ripplebrook Winery, in West Gippsland, the passion project for winemaker Catena Raffaele, whose parents moved to Australia from the Aeolian Islands, near Sicily, and set about raising three daughters with Italian fire in their veins. The Ripplebrook cellar door and restaurant, Giuseppe's, is named after Catena's father, and it's built to recreate the warmth of the Raffaele family home, a place where you can grab a wood-fired pizza and a glass of good wine and feel at ease. The wine is great, too, single-vineyard, organic chardonnay, pinot noir, shiraz and more. And only a 1.5hr drive from Melbourne CBD.

ripplebrookwinery.com.au

SAILORS GRAVE BREWING (11)

DEDICATED SEAFARERS MAKING BEER THAT CAPTURES THE ESSENCE OF THE OCEAN.

Gab and Chris Moore are seafarers at heart, who love diving for abalone and sea urchin, and who say they've always been interested in creating 'ocean beers'. Their farmhouse brews, made up in the far-east of Gippsland in an old butter factory near the coast, are made using the likes of seaweed and sea salt, as well as other local, native ingredients to give a deep sense of place – the 'terroir' that you usually hear winemakers talk about. It's all small-batch, done on-site, done with skill. Definitely worth checking out. The brewpub is a pretty casual space, on the banks of the Snowy River in Orbost, where most seating is outside and dogs are welcome. Everyone is welcome, in fact, to taste the region in a glass.

sailorsgravebrewing.com

TOM'S CAP VINEYARD (12)

ACCOMMODATION OPTIONS, RESTAURANT AND CELLAR DOOR OFFER PLENTY OF NATURAL BEAUTY.

You may remember the name Marcus Satchell from Dirty Three Wines (see p.108), and he's also making wine here, at Tom's Cap Vineyard, which is a self-contained attraction and the perfect base from which to explore the wonders of Gippsland. There's a one-bedroom retreat to rent here, a two-bedroom cottage or a four-bed lodge, all of which provide access to Tom's Cap restaurant and cellar door, where there are beautiful spaces to drink and dine both indoors and out. More importantly, however, they allow access to the surrounding area, to 90 Mile Beach, to Tarra Bulga National Park, to the Strzelecki Ranges and much more. This is what makes this area so attractive. Satchell's wine is just a bonus.

tomscapvineyard.com.au

Top Sailors Grave Brewing

THE WINE FARM (13)

A LITTLE SLICE OF STELLENBOSCH-STYLE CHARM TRANSPORTED TO GIPPSLAND.

If you've spent any time in South Africa, particularly around the Stellenbosch area, you will know about the excellent wine produced in that part of the world, and you might also know of the custom to call a vineyard there a 'wine farm'. Hence, it will come as no surprise to find that winemaker Neil Hawkins hails from South Africa, and that his West Gippsland winery produces some seriously tasty pinot noir, riesling and the like. Call into the cellar door and give them a try: it's a family-friendly, low-key space where the focus is on enjoying the wine, with flights for $25 per person. There's accommodation too, a three-bedroom worker's cottage with everything you need for a short stay.

thewinefarm.com.au

The Perfect Day
GIPPSLAND

12PM

3.30PM

2.30PM

6PM

11AM RIPPLEBROOK WINERY

Today's itinerary focuses on West Gippsland, though you could just as easily focus on the region's east on a different day. Begin at Ripplebrook (see p.111), which is really just a short drive from Melbourne, for a tasting among friends.

12PM HOGGET KITCHEN

Time for lunch, and fortunately Gippsland's best locavore restaurant, Hogget Kitchen (see p.110), is just around the corner from Ripplebrook. Leave plenty of time here to feast.

2.30PM DIRTY THREE WINES

Head down to the coast now, to Inverloch, where there's time to call into the Dirty Three Wines (see p.108) cellar door on the outskirts of town for a tasting of some truly excellent wines.

3.30PM GURNEYS CIDER

Enjoy a lovely drive over to Foster for a sample of the tasty brews served up with a view at Gurneys Cider (see p.109).

6PM GRAND RIDGE BREWERY

Finish up today's adventuring with a counter meal and a pint of Victoria's oldest craft beer at Grand Ridge Brewery (see p.108) in Mirboo North - and, you can stay the night.

HEATHCOTE AND THE GOULBURN VALLEY

The wine regions of Heathcote (*see* p.120) and the Goulburn Valley (*see* p.115), in central and northern Victoria, are essentially neighbours, separated in the south by a large military zone, and in the north by a thin sliver of land where no wine is produced. Both are still handily close to Melbourne/Naarm, in the grand scheme of things: it's a 1.5hr drive from the Victorian capital to either the town of Heathcote or Nagambie, which are the hearts of their respective regions.

It's also very easy to treat these two regions as a package, dedicating a day to one area and then skipping over to the other, with very little hassle. And in both places you will be seriously well looked after.

THE GOULBURN VALLEY

TAUNGURUNG COUNTRY

Let's begin in the Goulburn Valley, a place of shimmering lakes and burbling creeks, rolling hills covered in grape vines, and a cherished part of Australia's wine history. That's thanks to Tahbilk (see p.118), the winery that has been going strong since 1860. It's since been joined by a series of wineries, breweries and eateries that run the gamut from traditional to boundary-pushing, though all utilising the natural gifts of the valley to make something delicious.

Further south-east is the Upper Goulburn (see p.149), with a few cracking venues near Mansfield.

Tahbilk *Opposite* Fowles Wine

BRAVE GOOSE VINEYARD

PARTNERS IN LIFE AND WINE ARE PRODUCING SOME TRULY BEAUTIFUL DROPS.

This is a love story, in so many ways. Love for wine, love for place, love for each other. Nina Stocker and John Day are partners in marriage as well as business, dual owners of Brave Goose Vineyard, having been handed the reins by Nina's parents in the early 2000s. Now, Nina is the winemaker, responsible for coaxing flavour from the estate's shiraz, viognier, cabernet, merlot and gamay grapes. John, meanwhile, is the grower, responsible for the care and nurture of that fruit, gifting Nina with the best ingredients possible. It's a perfect match, and the result is some truly beautiful wine (as well as a couple of kids). Brave Goose – named after the sole survivor of a flock put into the vineyard to repel cockatoos and foxes – doesn't have a permanent cellar door, but opens the winery to visitors on 'pop-up' days, which are announced through its mailing list. Be sure you're on it, and share the love.

bravegoosevineyard.com.au

EIGHTEEN SIXTY

PASSIONATE LOCAVORES SOURCE ALL OF THEIR WINES FROM WITHIN A 50KM RADIUS.

There are more than 50 wines on the list at Eighteen Sixty, an intimate, friendly Italian eatery and wine bar in Nagambie, and pretty much all of them are made within a 50km radius. That should tell you all you need to know about the desire to take the best of the Goulburn Valley – as well as a little of Heathcote and the Strathbogie Ranges – and turn it into something even more beautiful. The food at Eighteen Sixty is local too: antipasti, pasta and serious meat dishes that allow chef Adele Aitken to utilise seasonal produce in the way Italians so often do. And the wine list represents the best of the region, with an ever-changing by-the-glass offering designed to highlight local producers and interesting styles. You'll find everything here from Tahbilk classics to hard-to-source drops from cult locals like Trust Wines. The best of the region in every way.

eighteensixty.com.au

FOWLES WINE

EXTENSIVE WINERY IS ON TARGET WITH A FEW OF ITS EDGIER LABEL CHOICES.

You know Fowles Wine, even if you don't realise it. Think back to your last trip to Dan Murphy's, trawling through the wine aisles, and see if you can picture a few bottles memorably titled Ladies Who Shoot Their Lunch. Fowles Wine makes the Ladies Who Shoot Their Lunch range, a series of wines, complete with a woman holding a shotgun on the label, that are designed to complement the textures and flavours of wild food (as well as grab the attention of shoppers at Danny's, no doubt). That's not all they do at this Goulburn Valley stalwart, which has been around since 1968: there's the Farm to Table range, the Are You Game? range, the Stone Dwellers – and more. Far too many, in fact, to explain in this short paragraph, which means you'll have to call into the Avenel cellar door and give them a sample. Fowles does generous tastings for $10 per person, plus there's a restaurant next door, serving breakfast and lunch, if you feel like settling down for a while.

fowleswine.com

MITCHELTON WINES (4)

HISTORIC WINERY DESTINATION OFFERS TASTINGS, A SPA, AN ART GALLERY AND AN AIRSTREAM TO STAY IN.

Mitchelton, on the banks of the Goulburn River in Nagambie, is a stunning achievement. It's everything you could want in a winery and then about 20 other things on top of that. It's a destination in itself, a place you would drive to from Melbourne and spend a few nights and never feel you had to leave. To begin with: yes, this is at its heart a winery, one that has been in operation since 1969, a producer of fine wines from estates in both the Goulburn Valley and Heathcote, known for its shiraz, as well as Rhone varietals, such as roussanne, marsanne and grenache. Taste them at the cellar door, beneath Mitchelton's iconic wooden tower, where flights include wines from both the Mitchelton and Preece labels. But then, as they say, there's more. There's a restaurant, The Muse, offering rustic yet refined cuisine utilising Goulburn produce. There's a hotel, stylish and modern, filled with luxurious touches. There's the Airstream Hotel, a luxury caravan stay among the vines. There's a day spa, offering 'holistic nourishment'. There's an art gallery, a wedding venue, a conference facility, a place for outdoor concerts … and probably, by now, more.

mitchelton.com.au

MONICHINO WINES (5)

OLD-SCHOOL FAMILY WINERY STILL WEARS ITS ITALIAN HEART ON ITS SLEEVE.

Here's another Goulburn Valley classic, founded in the far north of the region by Italian migrant Carlo Monichino in 1962. This is a winery that has stayed true to its Italian roots: many of the grape varietals are native to that country, most notably pinot grigio and barbera. Given its heritage, it's no surprise to find that this is one friendly winery that's all about family, food and wine, with tastings at the wood-panelled cellar door five days a week, or outside on the lawn on nice days, and meals served at the restaurant on weekends.

monichino.com.au

MOON (6)

GOULBURN'S LO-FI STAR MAKES NATURAL WINE THAT IS ENDLESSLY INTERESTING, AND DELICIOUS.

Moon is very much a leader of the Goulburn Valley new-school, an organic and biodynamic operation that proudly calls itself a 'natural' winemaker – and yet, the techniques it uses are actually ancient. Essentially, very little is added or subtracted in the winemaking process at Moon. No added yeast – it's all wild. No fining or filtering to remove anything unwanted at the end. It's basic winemaking that results in textural, savoury, delicious wines: chardonnay, marsanne, shiraz and cabernet sauvignon that are endlessly interesting and beautiful. They're not always easy to get your hands on, though: Moon has a cellar door in downtown Nagambie, but it's only open every now and then (join the mailing list to be notified), or by appointment if you ask nicely. It's worth the effort.

moonwine.com.au

Top Mitchelton Wines *Opposite* Fowles Wine

MURCHISON WINES ⑦
THE ITALIAN INFLUENCE IS STRONG AT THIS INTIMATE VENUE.

Things are kept personal at Murchison Wines, along with its sister label Longleat. Here on the banks of the Goulburn River, near the town of Murchison itself, owners and winemakers Guido and Sandra Vazzoler like to welcome guests themselves, take them through a tasting, and serve a platter of local food, including the pair's house-made cheese. It's the best way to get to know the area, and the winery. The wines tend to be Italian in style, particularly the Ragazzone, a bold, rich wine that's produced in the style of Italian Amarone, where grapes are sun-dried before being pressed, enhancing the flavours and intensity of colour. Let Guido and Sandra talk you through it – they know best.

murchisonwines.com.au

NAGAMBIE BREWERY AND DISTILLERY ⑧
LAKESIDE RESTAURANT AND TAPHOUSE OFFERS A LITTLE SOMETHING FOR EVERYONE.

There's surely something for everyone at Nagambie Brewery and Distillery, set on the shores of Lake Nagambie. As the name suggests, there's beer made here: a hand-crafted range of easy drinkers, nothing too heavily boozy, nothing too bitter or overly hoppy. Just good, solid beer. And then there are spirits, too, artisanal gins and a rye vodka. Food comes in the form of burgers and pizzas and other Mod-Oz favourites that go just nicely with a beer or a G&T. And finally, there's the location, whether you're sitting inside or out, looking over the lake and the beauty of the Goulburn Valley. Brilliant. If you're in town early, drop into the brewery's casual cafe off-shoot, Ma Forbes, for an egg-and-bacon roll and a coffee.

nagambiebrewery.com.au

Bottom **Nagambie Brewery**

TAHBILK ⑨
HISTORIC ICON OFFERS AN EXCITING LOOK INTO BOTH THE PAST AND THE FUTURE.

This might be a case of saving the best till last: Tahbilk is the original, one of the oldest wineries in Australia, let alone the Goulburn Valley, an icon that is fully deserving of the status. Family owned for five generations, Tahbilk oozes history, and you can't miss it as you wander around the estate by the Goulburn River. The cellar door is set in the original winery, built in 1860 from handmade bricks and mudstone quarried nearby; and visitors can still explore the underground cellars, built in 1862, and see the 'new cellar', built by James Purbrick in 1875. Though it has a heap of history, Tahbilk is also forward thinking, a carbon-neutral winery that has a renewed focus on sustainability. Its wines are icons too, particularly the shiraz made from the estate's original vines, though the Rhone-style roussanne-marsanne is also delicious. There's a restaurant on-site, too. Famed wine reviewer James Halliday says Tahbilk, 'should be visited at least once by every wine-conscious Australian'. I can't argue with that.

tahbilk.com.au

The Perfect Day
THE GOULBURN VALLEY

11AM

3PM

12.30PM

7PM

11AM FOWLES WINE
Begin a relaxed day with a tasting at Fowles Wine (see p.116), just off the highway in Avenel.

12.30PM MITCHELTON WINES
Next, head to the west to the sprawling Mitchelton complex (see p.117), your accommodation for the night, and the perfect place to have lunch, and try some wine, before checking in.

3PM TAHBILK
Skip over now to historic Tahbilk (see p.118), and while away the rest of the afternoon exploring the old cellars and tasting some wine.

7PM EIGHTEEN SIXTY
Dinner tonight is at Eighteen Sixty (see p.116), a friendly Italian-style wine bar in Nagambie that puts the focus on local ingredients, and local wine.

HEATHCOTE

DJA DJA WURRUNG AND TAUNGURUNG COUNTRY

In Heathcote you have Victoria's answer to the Barossa Valley, where the welcome is warm and the shiraz could feed a small family. This area isn't just about punchy reds, however: it's a hub for talented, creative brewers and distillers, as well as winemakers unafraid to take a few chances and mess with the accepted style.

BARFOLD ESTATE

WINEMAKING HERE IS SERIOUS BUSINESS – DRINKING, HOWEVER, IS ANYTHING BUT.

They make great wine at Barfold Estate – but they don't take it too seriously. 'Good wines are for good times,' is the motto. This is a small, family-run operation in the south-west corner of the Heathcote region, just a little over an hour from downtown Melbourne. The fruit here is seriously high-quality, and the Barfold way isn't to tinker too much with it: the fermentation is natural, the grapes are hand-plunged, basket-pressed, and then put in barrel or bottle without too much else going on. The result is the sort of wine you might not be used to tasting in Heathcote, but that there should be more of. Barfold is open to visitors most days, though call ahead to make sure someone will be around.

barfoldestate.com.au

THE CELLARS AT HEATHCOTE II

SELF-CONTAINED VILLAS EACH FEATURE A FULLY-STOCKED WINE CELLAR.

Okay, this is not a wine cellar. Or more accurately, it's not just a wine cellar. It's actually a set of luxury villas overlooking the vineyards and the olive grove at Heathcote II, a local winery. The villas each sleep two and are fully self-contained, with king-sized beds, fireplaces, and decks with barbecues perched above the vines. And within each villa lies a small cellar, featuring wines selected by Heathcote II winemaker Pedar Rosdal, a mix of local stars and hard-to-find imports, predominantly from France. There's a focus on the Burgundy region in the whites, and the Rhone in the reds – more than enough to keep any wine nut happy for a good few nights. In emergencies, however, the Heathcote II cellar door is just nearby.

thecellars.heathcote2.com

Top Peregrine Ridge

CHAUNCY (12)

THE PERFECT EURO-STYLE BISTRO EXISTS – AND EVERYONE WANTS IT AS THEIR LOCAL.

Argh, Chauncy, why don't you exist in my home town? Everyone deserves the chance to go to this French bistro on the reg, to be treated to Tess Murray's wine knowledge and Louis Naepels' cooking skills whenever we like. Alas, that just can't happen, so instead you will have to go to Heathcote and make a booking at Chauncy. Tess and Louis are something of a foodie power couple: she ran wine at Supernormal and Cutler & Co in Melbourne; he was head chef at Grossi Florentino (and, as an aside, also at one of my favourite little neighbourhood restaurants in the world, a place called Maitenia in the French Basque town of Ciboure). Now, the pair run an intimate diner in the Heathcote High Street, taking on French, Basque and Italian influences to create truly beautiful and ever-changing dishes, from ingredients sourced from the best local suppliers, paired with wine from around the world. It's a shame we can't all have a Chauncy – but at least we can visit Heathcote to experience it.

chauncy.com.au

GAFFNEY'S BAKERY (13)

IF YOU'RE UP FOR A GOOD PIE, THIS COUNTRY BAKERY IS A STANDOUT.

You have to love a country bakery, and more than that, you have to love a country bakery that does a good pie. Trust me, friends: Gaffney's Bakery in Heathcote does a very good pie. This isn't exactly haute cuisine, it's not the kind of thing that's served with flower petals and foams and designed to be photographed and sent straight to your Instagram feed. It's just pies, in flavours like triple-chilli braised beef, chicken parma, beef bacon and cheese, and beef and shiraz. They do a mean vanilla slice here, too. Get in.

gaffneysbakery.com.au

HEATHCOTE JUNIPER LOUNGE (14)

DOWNTOWN BAR DEDICATED TO A RANGE OF DISTINCTLY 'HEATHCOTE' GINS.

Distiller Clare Voitin says she was drawn to Heathcote by the soil: 500-million-year-old Cambrian soils, to be precise, perfect for growing and nurturing the botanicals needed to make high-quality gin. And that's what she does, utilising a whole suite of ingredients, both native and imported, to make a range of gins that are distinctly grown and made here. Give them a sample, maybe in a cocktail, at Heathcote Juniper Lounge, a gin bar in downtown Heathcote that exclusively serves Voitin's pride and joy.

theheathcotegin.com.au

JASPER HILL (15)

WILDLY POPULAR WINES HERE ARE DELICIOUS, BUT TIME YOUR VISIT SO YOU DON'T MISS OUT.

The Jasper Hill wines are seriously popular, so much so that they sell out regularly, and can be difficult to get your hands on. And if the product is gone, there's nothing to sample at the winery, hence tastings here are done by appointment only, and you'll have to hope to be lucky to get in. Ron Laughton and his daughter, Emily McNally make classic Heathcote wines, the likes of bold shiraz and elegant nebbiolo. There's a whole lot of love and skill that goes into making them, so make sure to grab a few if you can. The Jasper Hill wines are generally released every August, so around that time is your best bet for a visit.

jasperhill.com.au

M CHAPOUTIER (16)

FAMED RHONE-BASED FRENCHMAN ALSO HAS A BIODYNAMIC OPERATION IN AUSTRALIA.

Michel Chapoutier, as you may have gathered, is French, and a famed biodynamic producer from the Cotes-du-Rhone, a maker of very good grenache-syrah blends, as well as other classics of the region. Happily for Australians, Michel also operates a business in our homeland, with vineyards spread across Victoria and a cellar door in downtown Heathcote. Here you can taste Chapoutier's wines from both France and Australia, though with a focus on the latter. Michel produces several labels in Australia in varying styles and price points, enough to keep interested drinkers sipping and swirling for a good few hours.

mchapoutier.com.au

PALLING BROS BREWERY (17)

LOCAL CRAFT BREWER IS IN FINE COMPANY ON HEATHCOTE'S HIGH STREET.

There's a host of attractions set along Heathcote's main drag – Chauncy (*see* p.121), Gaffney's (*see* p.121) and the Juniper Lounge (*see* p.121) among them – which make perfect company for Palling Bros, the Heathcote craft brewery that is a long-time favourite of the local crowd. Palling Bros does a huge range of beer that's all reliably tasty, from easy-breezy ales and lager to the more flavour-packed likes of NEIPA, 'Ice Cream IPA', and a dark German wheat beer. There's food served at the brewhouse: pub favourites like schnitties, tacos and burgers that will always work well with a cold beer. You can either dine in the brewery, where there's usually live music, or head out to the beer garden on sunny days.

pallingbros.beer

PEREGRINE RIDGE (18)

CELLAR DOOR SERVES STUNNING SHIRAZ AND MAKES THE MOST OF HEATHCOTE'S BEST VIEWS.

You would visit the Peregrine Ridge cellar door just for the views. The building here, with its floor-to-ceiling windows, is perched almost 300m above sea level, the highest vineyard in the Mount Camel Range, and it commands incredible views across the valley floor – beautiful on sunny days, even more spectacular when there's rain rolling in. The wine here is delicious too, and it's all shiraz, from classic Heathcote style, to a few different sparkling versions. Call in on weekends, perch up near the windows with some wine and a produce platter, and enjoy the experience.

peregrineridge.com.au

SANGUINE ESTATE (19)

CLASSIC SHIRAZ IS SERVED IN BUCOLIC SURROUNDS AT THIS FRIENDLY FAMILY WINERY.

As with so many wineries in the Heathcote region, Sanguine Estate is all about shiraz: bold, flavourful shiraz, punchy wines topping out at 15% alcohol, full of fruit and warmth and deliciousness. The wine is all made on-site by the Hunter family, from estate-grown grapes, and it's a pleasure to roll up on a weekend and sample them in good company. It's a personal experience here, with someone involved in the winemaking process usually doing the pouring, and all backed by beautiful rural views.

sanguinewines.com.au

TELLURIAN WINES (20)

HEATHCOTE STALWART MIXES THINGS UP WITH A SOLID SELECTION OF WHITE WINES – AND VIEWS TOO.

Of course, you will find shiraz in the Tellurian line-up. This is the grape upon which the winery has made its name, and it does a fine line in these bold reds, as well as grenache, nero d'avola and mourvedre. What's more interesting, however, is that Tellurian also does excellent white wine, in particular marsanne, but also fiano and even riesling. That makes for a great tasting experience at the cellar door, which is open on weekends, or mid-week by appointment. This is a relaxed space with pleasant views out on the covered deck to vines and rolling countryside; sometimes they have oysters on too, which go nicely with some of those whites.

tellurianwines.com.au

VINEA MARSON (21)

ITALIAN VARIETALS STAR AT THIS WINERY WITH A PROUDLY MEDITERRANEAN INFLUENCE.

You'll notice a theme that appears in this book: where a winery has strong Italian heritage, there's almost always a warm welcome, a sense of easy hospitality that visitors immediately fall for. And Vinea Marson is no exception. This boutique winery in the Mount Camel Range is run by Mario Marson, the son of Italian migrants who planted vines in their Melbourne backyard and made wine for the Marsons to drink over dinner. Fair to say that Mario's products these days are a little more refined, though they still owe a lot to that Italian heritage, with classic Heathcote shiraz complemented by Mediterranean varietals like nebbiolo, sangiovese and friulano. The highlight, however, is the warmth of the welcome at the cellar door, with tastings done at the family table, paired with locally made antipasti. Stop by on a weekend and see for yourself.

vineamarson.com

THE WINE HUB (22)

BOTTLE SHOP DOES TASTINGS OF LOCAL DROPS, PLUS IS OPEN WHEN THE CELLAR DOORS ARE NOT.

If you're calling through Heathcote during the week, you'll find plenty of the cellar doors closed; however, help is at hand at The Wine Hub. This Heathcote bottle shop stocks only locally grown and locally made wines, and the owners are passionate about supporting and promoting the work of their fellow residents. There's local beer and cider for sale too, and produce from local artisans. The Wine Hub does regular tastings, for a small fee that is waived if you decide to buy a bottle. And let's face it, you will.

heathcotewinehub.com.au

Top Tellurian Wines

The Perfect Day
HEATHCOTE

Victoria

8AM THE CELLARS AT HEATHCOTE II

Wake up in your accommodation at Heathcote II (*see* p.120), and tuck into the hearty breakfast that's supplied - maybe out on the verandah to enjoy the view.

10AM TELLURIAN WINES

It's just a short drive this morning from Heathcote II over to Tellurian Wines (*see* p.123), where you can kick off the day with a tasting flight, and maybe even a few oysters, if you so desire.

12PM PEREGRINE RIDGE

It's a very short journey from Tellurian up to Peregrine Ridge (*see* p.122), where there's time to try the product while also marvelling at the cellar door's incredible view.

1.30PM GAFFNEY'S BAKERY

Time to head down to Heathcote town, where you have to call into Gaffney's Bakery (*see* p.121) to grab a pie - there's a flavour to please every palate and diet.

2.30PM VINEA MARSON

Make your way now to Vinea Marson (*see* p.123), one of the friendliest little joints around, for a run through the Italian varietals.

7PM CHAUNCY

Prepare yourself tonight for some Mediterranean splendour: food inspired by the French, Italians and Basques, cooked with skill and served with care at the amazing Chauncy (*see* p.121).

Pizzini

HIGH COUNTRY

There's a long history in Victoria's High Country, though not always of wine. There are First Nations' stories here dating back millennia. This is former bushranger territory too, the home – and prison – of Australia's favourite anti-hero, Ned Kelly. There's been a gold rush in Beechworth; cattlemen roaming *Man From Snowy River* territory below; migrants from the Mediterranean bringing their food and traditions. It's seen a lot, this area that encompasses Rutherglen, Beechworth, Glenrowan, Yackandandah, Bright and more. And it's an amazing place for a weekend or a week.

Thing is though, the High Country is not actually one wine region. This area of north-eastern Victoria, beginning about a 3hr drive north of Melbourne/Naarm, is made up of five distinct, officially recognised wine regions: the Alpine Valleys, Beechworth, Glenrowan, Rutherglen and the King Valley. I've chosen to group them together in this chapter for a number of reasons, most notably because I just can't dedicate 22 sections of this book to all of Victoria's wine-producing areas, and also because most of the High Country is quite compact, which means you could conceivably base yourself in, say, Beechworth, and spend a day in King Valley, or in Rutherglen, or even Bright. You wouldn't want to flit from region to region within the same day, but one base here for gastronomic exploration is a real possibility. You'll need plenty of time to experience all of the options, and it will most definitely be worth it.

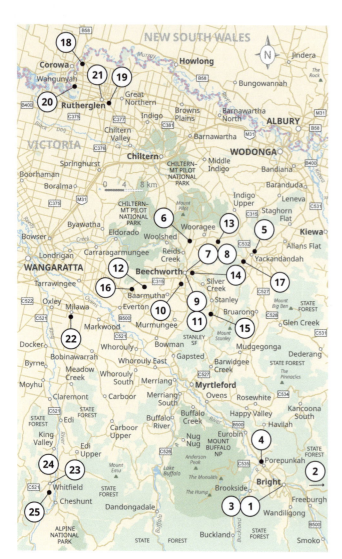

ALPINE VALLEYS

WAVEROO AND YAITHMATHANG COUNTRY

This wine region, centred around the town of Bright and taking in everywhere from Myrtleford to Mount Beauty, is only a small one in terms of volume produced, though in terms of charm and allure it's right up there with the best. The Alpine Valleys is a cool-climate region, home to a few really exciting producers, as well as a high-quality craft beer and spirits scene, with some excellent food thrown in as well.

BILLY BUTTON WINES

WELCOME TO YOUR ONE-STOP SHOP FOR ALPINE REGION GOODNESS.

Call into the Billy Button cellar door, a shared space with a number of other small-batch local wineries, and you will have the chance to taste a wide range of wines that will be different every time you visit. Winemaker Jo Marsh releases her numerous single-varietal wines whenever they're ready, so you might find cold-climate fiano, albariño, chardonnay, friulano, pinot blanc, grüner veltliner, aglianico, barbera, refosco, saperavi or so much more. Phew. You may not know a lot about those varieties when you arrive, but you'll be all over them by the time you leave. There are actually two Billy Button cellar doors, one in Bright and the other in Myrtleford, both shared with Bush Track wines, and featuring products from Mayford Wines, Bike and Barrel, and Dalbosco Wines – plus local cheese boards and charcuterie. In other words, this is your one-stop shop for Alpine Valleys' boutique goodness, and it should be on every itinerary.

billybuttonwines.com.au

CRANK HANDLE BREWERY ②

MOUNT BEAUTY ESTABLISHMENT MAKES PERFECT BEER FOR THE COLD WEATHER.

If a cold day puts you in the mood for a good, strong beer, then Crank Handle Brewery, in small-town Mount Beauty, has you covered with its English Special Bitter, a classic ale that's brewed with chilly weather in mind. That's not all there is to drink here, as you sit in the foothills of Mount Bogong and Falls Creek and enjoy the views, with plenty of easy-drinkers like an Alpine Ale and an American pale ale, plus a nice, chewy porter. Crank Handle does food, too: beer-friendly snacks and share platters of cheese and charcuterie. Plus, there's toasties for more sustenance on those cold days.

crankhandlebrewery.com.au

REED & CO DISTILLERY ③
FRIENDLY PURVEYORS OF LOCAL GIN ALSO MAKE SOME OF BRIGHT'S BEST AND BRIGHTEST FOOD.

Hamish Nugent and Rachel Reed have a problem: they opened Reed & Co Distillery as a way to step back from their lives as chefs, to get out of the kitchen and concentrate on making great gin, while also bringing up a family. Trouble is, the food the pair are making at their distillery door, an old mechanic's workshop in central Bright, is just so good that as many people are turning up for the meals as the booze. If you want to stay out of the kitchen, guys, stop making such amazing food. That might be a problem for Hamish and Rachel but it won't be for you, as the Japanese izakaya-style snacks here are worthy of their own restaurant: dishes like pickled kingfish with fennel and yuzu, and venison tataki with kombu and dashi that take a standard distillery experience and push it to the next level. Or, several levels. The gin is lovely too, using wild and locally grown botanicals, and the crowd is always friendly. But seriously, that food ...

reedandcodistillery.com

RINGER REEF ④
FOR LOVERS OF DELICIOUS COLD-CLIMATE WINE, THIS REALLY IS A GOLD MINE.

Not that sort of reef. Ringer Reef was once the site of a gold mine – the 'reef' here being a vein of quartz that contains gold – and was later turned into a vineyard, a project of passion if not exactly a gold mine for the Holm family. You're likely to meet one of the Holms, in fact, if you visit the cellar door for a friendly guided tasting, which can easily be extended into a picnic on the lawn with gorgeous alpine views. There are tables outside on the deck, too, where you can order a glass or a bottle of your favourite wine, a cheese or charcuterie platter, and just enjoy.

ringerreef.com.au

Top Ringer Reef

BEECHWORTH

WAVEROO COUNTRY

Beechworth is going absolutely gangbusters on the wine front, a region producing some of Australia's best chardonnay, thanks to Giaconda (a fabled winery that doesn't feature in these pages, because they won't let anyone in to visit), as well as numerous other high-quality drops. The country town that was previously most famous for the jail that housed Ned Kelly, and its eponymous bakery's top-notch 'bee stings', is now firmly wine, beer and spirits country, with a few high-quality restaurants, boutique stores and reliable country hospitality. Even if you can only manage a weekend away from Melbourne (3.5hr) or Canberra (4hr), head to Beechworth.

BACKWOODS DISTILLING CO ⑤

YACKANDANDAH CLASSIC DISTILLS A TRUE TASTE OF THE HIGH COUNTRY.

There's something in the water in Yackandandah – probably literally – because this tiny hamlet just outside Beechworth has become a hub for high-quality artisanal spirits (Yack Creek is also here; Barking Owl is close by). Backwoods is all about keeping things local, distilling a taste of the Victorian High Country, whether that's through the water and the artisanal malt that goes into its excellent whisky, or the mountain botanicals in the gin. Leigh and Bree Attwood grew up in north-eastern Victoria, and their passion for the region is pretty easy to see. Call in to see them at their new distillery space in Yackandandah, where they do tastings, cocktails and other drinks right near the big copper stills.

backwoodsdistilling.com.au

BARKING OWL DISTILLING CO ⑥

CHARACTER-FILLED STILLHOUSE IS JUST ONE REASON TO HEAD OUT TO WOORAGEE.

You'll fall instantly for the Barking Owl stillhouse. It's set in an old tin shearing shed, built in the 1950s in rural Wooragee, and it absolutely oozes High Country charm. You couldn't be anywhere else. (Even the name has a sense of place, thanks to the frequent avian visitors to the stillhouse.) The gin at Barking Owl is also reflective of the area, using local botanicals such as lemon myrtle, pepper berry and even fresh pine. Try one in a cocktail: at the Barking Owl stillhouse they do a mean negroni and espresso martini, as well as offering the usual tasting experiences. Take note of your drinking vessel, too, as the ceramics are produced on-site, and available to purchase.

barkingowldistillery.com

Top Barking Owl Distilliing Co

BILLSON'S BREWERY (7)

HISTORIC ESTABLISHMENT HAS BEEN RESTORED TO ITS FORMER GLORY.

You want history? Billson's Brewery was established in 1865, and it's still housed in a beautiful Victorian-era 'tower brewery', built in 1872, that is set in what is now essentially downtown Beechworth. The brewery was actually known as Murray Breweries for much of the 20th century, and was in a state of serious disrepair – though still trading as a producer of cordial – in 2017, when Melburnian Nathan Cowen swooped in and bought the whole operation, promising to restore the brewery to its former glory. And he has. These days Billson's makes beer, gin, and cordials using the original recipe, making use of the natural spring below the brewery. The venue is now one of Beechworth's most popular spots, the ideal place to grab a few drinks, eat some tasty snacks, and soak up the history.

billsons.com.au

BRIDGE ROAD BREWERS (8)

LOCAL FAVOURITE STILL GOING STRONG WITH CRAFT BEERS AND PIZZAS.

Bridge Road is a stalwart of the Beechworth scene, and indeed of the Australian craft beer scene in general: the brewery has been around since 2005, when local Ben Kraus, having been inspired by a trip to Austria, decided to bring small-batch beer to Australia. It's been a raging success, clearly, given Kraus and his partner, Maria began their operation in a shed on his dad's property, and these days the pair have a 340-seat taproom, pizzeria and brewhouse in an 1850s coach house on Beechworth's main street. You'll find out why when you visit and taste the brews – pale ale, XPA, IPA, sour, saison – polish off a pizza or two and listen to the locals wax lyrical about their favourite place to hang out: it's here, in case you didn't guess.

bridgeroadbrewers.com.au

ELDORADO ROAD (9)

ENJOY THE FRUIT OF SOMEONE ELSE'S LABOUR AT THIS COSY DOWNTOWN SPOT.

The Eldorado Road vineyard is a long way out of Beechworth, halfway down the highway to Wangaratta. It was planted way back in the 1890s, and was in an absolute state when winemakers Paul Dahlenburg and Lauretta Schulz leased it and began the back-breaking work of clearing debris and getting the vines to once again produce fruit. It gives you an idea of why their flagship shiraz is called 'Perseverance Old Vine Shiraz', and should also give you renewed appreciation for the product when you visit the cellar door and cantina in downtown Beechworth, to give it a sample. Eldorado Road does a series of wines, all of which are on for tasting, plus there's great snacky food to pair with it.

eldoradoroad.com.au

PENNYWEIGHT WINERY (10)

ONE OF THE BEECHWORTH PIONEERS DOES SOME OF ITS BEST BIODYNAMIC WINE.

Take a look outside when you visit the Pennyweight cellar door and see if you recognise the view: those tree trunks framed by the window feature on the Pennyweight labels, which serve as a nice sense of place when you're back at home cracking a bottle. And you will have plenty of bottles to crack. Pennyweight is one of the Beechworth pioneers, a small winery run by the highly respected Morris family, who produce biodynamic wines that range from classic Beechworth chardonnay and pinot noir, to a highly sought-after, small-batch gamay (seriously, if they have any, grab me a few bottles), to the best range of Spanish-style aperas (that is, sherries) you will find this side of Xerez. The cellar door is a pretty simple affair, friendly and laidback, and just on the edge of town, making it well worth including on your itinerary.

pennyweight.com.au

High Country 131

PROVENANCE

CHEF MICHAEL RYAN'S TWO-HATTED JAPANESE EATERY IS TRUE DESTINATION DINING.

There aren't many country towns in Australia where you can sit down to a high-end, two-hatted meal of Japanese wonder, but Beechworth is one of them, thanks to chef Michael Ryan. His restaurant, Provenance, is destination dining, a place plenty of Melburnians would be happy to drive over 3hr up the highway just to sample (or 6hr down the highway if you're based in Sydney). Ryan's food is clearly Japanese – mushroom tofu with katsuobushi, braised daikon with miso, grilled beef with smoked miso butter – though making use of the best local ingredients. His restaurant is housed in Beechworth's old Bank of Australasia headquarters, built during the gold rush in 1856, and there's accommodation on-site, both in the converted stables out the back, and upstairs in what's called the Manager's Residence. The Provenance wine list is also sensational, and if you're hoping to try a wine from Giaconda, which is rare even in these parts, this is the place to do it.

theprovenance.com.au

SAVATERRE

ONE OF BEECHWORTH'S FRIENDLIEST SPOTS ALSO MAKES SOME OF ITS BEST WINE.

The Savaterre vineyard is directly across the road from the Giaconda holdings, where some of Australia's best chardonnay is made, so you know this is a good location, and the wines are going to be similarly impressive. And they are. Keppell Smith makes chardonnay that is up there with Beechworth's finest, as well as excellent pinot noir and cold-climate shiraz. There's not much of a cellar door here, more just a space in the shed where wines can be poured with views of the vines, but this is a seriously friendly outfit, where the welcome is warm and the pours are generous. You should definitely take the time to make an appointment to call in.

savaterre.com

STAR LANE

WINE-LOVING COUPLE TAKE A LOW-KEY APPROACH AT ONE SPECTACULAR SPOT.

Star Lane is about as local and as low-key as you can get. Brett Barnes tends the vineyard, Liz Barnes makes the wine, and there's a good chance you will meet one or both of them if you drop into their spectacularly picturesque winery, up near Yackandandah, for a sample of the products. Star Lane is all about red wine, from shiraz to nebbiolo, sangiovese and merlot, and it's all done extremely well. Call ahead before visiting, as cellar door hours can be a little unpredictable.

starlanewinery.com.au

Provenance

TRAVIARTI AND NATURE OF THE BEAST (14)

SAMPLE THE SKILLS OF TWO GENERATIONS AT THIS UNDERRATED CELLAR DOOR.

Beechworth is a little too young, as a region, for there to be many second-generation winemakers taking over from their parents, and that's not quite what's happening at Traviarti, either. Instead, you have a cellar door here for two family wine labels: Traviarti, the passion project of Simon Grant and Helen Murray, who love nebbiolo and produce some of Australia's finest, as well as chardonnay; and Nature of the Beast, the fledgling label for Phoebe Grant, daughter of Simon and Helen, who is only in her early 20s, and yet is already producing a seriously impressive range of lo-fi wines from locally sourced grapes. Give them all a sample at the cellar door on the outskirts of Beechworth, open by appointment only.

traviarti.com; natureofthebeastwine.com

VIGNERONS SCHMOLZER AND BROWN (15)

NEWCOMERS PUTTING THEIR STAMP ON THE REGION WITH LO-FI BRILLIANCE.

There's so much to love about this newcomer to the Beechworth scene, a project by super-talented winemaker Tessa Brown and her architect partner Jeremy Schmolzer. The pair only planted their vineyard in 2014, so it's still coming to full maturity – in the meantime, Schmolzer and Brown are making powerful riesling from a King Valley vineyard, beautiful pinot and chardonnay from a tiny block next door in Beechworth, plus a series of easy-drinking blends called Pret-a-Blanc, Pret-a-Rose and Pret-a-Rouge. Everything is done with minimal intervention and maximum care. There's not really a cellar door here, but call ahead and make an appointment, and Tessa and Jeremy will be happy to have you in for a taste and a chat.

vsandb.com.au

WEATHERCRAFT (16)

ONE-WOMAN TEAM PROVIDES AN INTIMATE, FRIENDLY CELLAR DOOR EXPERIENCE

It's personal at Weathercraft: the winemaking is hands-on, made by one maker, and the wine-tasting experience is similarly exclusive. Visit the purpose-built cellar door here, just outside Beechworth, and you will be met by winemaker Raquel Jones, to be guided through a taste of her amazing products, which range from shiraz to tempranillo to chardonnay and pinot gris. There are several of these personal experiences to choose from, from a straightforward tasting with Raquel, to a 1.5hr 'barrel room experience' that takes in a tour of the winery and a taste of some of the new Weathercraft wines straight from the barrel. Raquel is a wonderful host and the wine is beautiful – there's little more you could ask for. Be sure to book ahead.

weathercraft.com.au

YACK CREEK DISTILLERY (17)

RIVERSIDE STILLHOUSE IS DOING AN IMPRESSIVE RANGE OF WHISKY, RUM AND GIN.

Yack Creek is positioned where you think it would be – on the banks of Yackandandah Creek, the water source for the distillery's whisky and rum, and home to a colony of Blue Murray Spiny Crayfish, the likeness of which you will find on the Yack Creek label. This distillery was born as a specialist in single-malt whisky and barrel-aged rum, though these days the team also produces a range of gins, and a vodka. The distillery is open in the afternoons, Friday to Monday, for tasting flights taken either inside or out on the lawn.

yackcreekdistillery.com.au

The Perfect Day
BEECHWORTH

Victoria

11AM PENNYWEIGHT WINERY

Begin on the edge of town at the laidback Pennyweight cellar door (*see* p.131), for a taste of the full range.

12.30PM BRIDGE ROAD BREWERS

It's time for lunch, which today you're taking in town at a Beechworth institution, Bridge Road Brewers (*see* p.131). Grab a schooner or two to go with your meal.

2.30PM SAVATERRE

Time to head out into the countryside now to taste some of Beechworth's best wine, at Savaterre (*see* p.132). Be sure to call ahead and make an appointment.

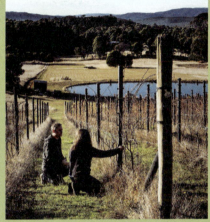

4PM VIGNERONS SCHMOLZER AND BROWN

Head over to the other side of town now to visit Tessa and Jeremy at Vignerons Schmolzer and Brown (*see* p.133), and sample the work of some of Beechworth's best new winemakers.

7PM PROVENANCE

Dinner tonight is back at your accommodation, at chef Michael Ryan's two-hatted eatery Provenance (*see* p.132). And your room is only a short meander away.

High Country

RUTHERGLEN

WAVEROO COUNTRY

Rutherglen is seriously old-school, a region that has been producing wine since 1839, and retains much of its history with an easygoing vibe that lacks the flash of some of its Victorian counterparts. This isn't a huge region, despite a boom during the gold rush years in the 1800s, but Rutherglen continues to be known for the quality of its fortified wines, which are easily up there with Australia's best. Most cellar doors here are small and friendly, with plenty of history and intergenerational winemaking to tap into.

Jones Winery *Opposite* Pfeiffer Wines

ALL SAINTS ESTATE

FORTIFIED WINES AND A FORTIFIED CELLAR DOOR ARE EQUAL ATTRACTIONS AT THIS 19TH-CENTURY CASTLE.

All Saints goes way back to 1864, when two Scottish migrants, who were only in their 30s at the time, decided to plant some vines near Wahgunyah, and soon shifted to the current All Saints site, where the pair built the now famous All Saints Castle. The edifice was based on the Castle of Mey, in the Scottish Highlands, and it still houses the All Saints Estate cellar door today, though there's also plenty of space out on the lawns for visitors on sunny days. There's a huge series of wines here to taste, including All Saints' extremely highly rated fortified wines, plus there's a restaurant, and accommodation at the three-bedroom Castleview Cottage.

allsaintswine.com.au

JONES WINERY & VINEYARD

SIXTH-GENERATION WINEMAKER IS DOING THE FAMILY PROUD AT THIS HISTORIC SPOT.

Here's another Rutherglen winery with serious history, this time dating back to 1860, and the sixth generation of the family owners – Ben Jones – is now involved with winemaking, assisting his mother, Mandy. Jones Winery is a small operation with an intimate cellar door, set in an old cottage that's a slice of history in itself, plus there's a restaurant in the same building, serving high-quality French-style cuisine that matches perfectly with the Jones range. Those wines take in the likes of shiraz, malbec, durif and fiano, as well as a series of beautiful fortified wines.

joneswinery.com.au

PFEIFFER WINES

HISTORIC FAMILY WINERY HAS SOMETHING FOR EVERYONE – INCLUDING THE KIDS.

Who are you in Rutherglen if you don't have at least 100 years of winemaking history? The Pfeiffer winery was built in 1895, and has been in the Pfeiffer family since 1984. These days, Jen Pfeiffer looks after the winemaking, and welcomes visitors to one of the most laidback cellar doors around. There are several tasting experiences available here, though the best would have to be the True Muscat Experience, which includes tastings straight from the barrels, and a class in muscat blending. For the kids, there's a turtle pond and a play area, plus the Pfeiffers can pour tasting paddles of local cordials, so everyone wins.

pfeifferwinesrutherglen.com.au

THOUSAND POUND

MELBOURNE-STYLE WINE BAR STANDS OUT ON THE RUSTIC RUTHERGLEN SCENE.

To be honest, Rutherglen doesn't have a heap of good food options. There's a great pie shop, and a couple of decent pubs, but if you're hoping to sit down to a nice dinner, the options are few. Happily, however, there's Thousand Pound, owned by the All Saints Estate team. This wine bar, on the Rutherglen main street, is a little slice of Melbourne transported to the High Country, a classy bar with an impressive wine list, and a compact but beautiful menu of locavore cuisine. This is the place you've been looking for.

thousandpound.com.au

The story of Australian prosecco

Think prosecco and you think Italy, right? You dream of an aperitivo in a bar in Bologna, Aperol spritzes on a beach in Sicily, or toasting a big day at a wine bar in Florence. And it's because of this strong association that the Italians are not entirely pleased with the fact that prosecco is being produced in Australia, mostly around the King Valley, with that famous name on its label.

See, prosecco is the name of a wine, but it was also, up until 2009 in Italy, the name of the grape used to produce this famous sparkling. In 2009, the Italians awarded the prosecco-producing regions in Veneto and Friuli-Venezia with 'DOC' classification – a mark of quality and protected origin, 'denominazione di origine controllata' – and began to refer to the wine as Prosecco, and to the grape as 'glera'. Given strict European Union rules to protect regions and their brand names, all other producers of prosecco the grape in Europe were forced to refer to their product as glera from then on.

But not in Australia. Here, those restrictions don't apply, which means you will still find prosecco the grape being produced, and the wine called as such.

Prosecco was first planted in this country in 1999 by Italian migrant Otto Dal Zotto, who grew up in traditional prosecco country in his former homeland. Dal Zotto (see p.139) is still the leader of a handful of King Valley wineries making Australian prosecco. The Italians aren't pleased, but though there are protracted and ongoing legal battles underway, as things stand, Australian prosecco is still a thing. It's delicious, too.

KING VALLEY

WAVEROO COUNTRY

It's all about la dolce vita in the King Valley, a little slice of Italy in the Victorian High Country, a place that has been hugely popular with migrants from the Mediterranean over the years, mostly Italians who brought with them a love of fresh food and fine wine. Plenty of the wineries here have a distinct Italian influence, and produce the likes of prosecco, nebbiolo and pinot grigio. Plenty of the winery restaurants also pick up that Mediterranean influence and run with it, which has to be good news.

If you're in this region, you might also want to explore the highly recommended food and wine stops of the Upper Goulburn (see p.149), around Mansfield and Alexandra.

BROWN BROTHERS

HISTORIC WINERY OFFERS GENEROUS TASTINGS AND HIGH-QUALITY CUISINE.

Anyone who has had anything to do with wine in Australia for the last century or so – from industry leaders to kids having a peek in their parents' drinks cabinet – will be familiar with the Brown Brothers name. The company began in Milawa in 1885, when John Francis Brown decided to grow some grapes, and these days is a behemoth of an operation with rootstock spread throughout Victoria. However, Milawa is where it began, and Milawa is where it's still based, and you can soak up the history here with a visit. The Brown Brothers cellar door is open daily, offering tastings of eight to 10 wines for $15 a head, or $20 for the premium drops. There's an award-winning restaurant, too, doing lunches Fri to Mon, where tables groan under the weight of set-menu share platters, featuring delicious Italian-style dishes made with local ingredients. There are a huge range of other experiences here too, from prosecco brunches to wine-blending experiences and hot-air balloon rides. The full package.

brownbrothers.com.au

DAL ZOTTO

WELCOME TO THE FAMILY, AS ITALIAN MIGRANTS BRING PROSECCO AND GREAT FOOD TO THE VALLEY.

The Dal Zotto family used to grow one very important cash crop – tobacco – until they saw the writing on the wall in the 1980s and ripped up their plants to put grape vines in. They've never looked back. Dal Zotto now specialises in prosecco – it's a grape variety, not just a wine style – though the winery also produces other Italian varietals such as barbera, nebbiolo, sangiovese and pinot grigio. A visit to Dal Zotto is all about being welcomed into the family. You sit down, taste a few wines, chat to the team, and then tackle a massive trattoria lunch, from antipasti to handmade pastas to wood-fired pizzas and more. And you quickly realise that this is a family you want to be part of.

dalzotto.com.au

KING RIVER BREWING

CZECH-STYLE BREWERY SPECIALISES IN VARIOUS EUROPEAN FAVOURITES.

King River Brewing also has an unashamedly European vibe, though this time it's more Czech than Italian – and surely, for a brewer of good beer, that's not a bad thing. There are some really interesting, authentic Czech-style brews here, including the Cisarske Pivo, an imperial pilsner that uses the traditional Budejovicky Budvar yeast strain and weighs in at 8% alcohol. Delicious. There's also a standard pilsner, as well as a punchy Belgian-style tripel, and more recognisable brews such as a porter and a mango sour. Give them a try at the King River taproom, where hearty Euro fare like cheese Kranskys with pickles – or, you know, wood-fired pizzas, because this is the King Valley after all – will help work up a beery thirst.

kingriverbrewing.com.au

PIZZINI

ITALIAN VARIETALS ARE THE STARS OF THE SHOW – ALONG WITH THE ANTIPASTI PLATTERS.

Here's another of the King Valley's Italian stalwarts, Pizzini, which also specialises in prosecco, plus does a delicious, savoury riesling, as well as a whole heap of Italian varietals you almost certainly have never heard of before, and will almost certainly love drinking. They're all on for tasting at the cellar door: flights can either be standard, for $10 per person, or Special and Rare, for $20 a head. Whatever you go for, you can pair the tasting with an antipasti platter, and while away a few hours enjoying the views and the hospitality. Stay overnight if you want, too – Pizzini has two beautiful, self-contained guesthouses.

pizzini.com.au

Top Dal Zotto

BEST OF THE REST

There's just. Too. Many. Too many great wine regions in Victoria, too many great wineries, too many breweries and too many distilleries and everything else. Sadly, I just can't cover them all. What I can do, however, is give you a brief rundown of a few more of Victoria's hits – wine regions that might not be as famous or as densely populated as the likes of the Yarra Valley or Mornington Peninsula, but which still offer amazing experiences in truly beautiful locations.

BALLARAT

WATHAURUNG COUNTRY

The Ballarat area is such an up-and-comer that it isn't even an officially designated wine region - it's just a place where a few people have planted grapes. Still, that's no reason to avoid it, because this space around the gold rush-era regional city, known mostly for the Eureka Stockade, Sovereign Hill and grandiose streetscapes, has some great venues, with a couple in particular I'm keen to highlight.

EASTERN PEAKE/ LATTA VINO

NATURAL-WINE STAR IS IN CHARGE OF TWO LABELS, WHICH OFFER THE BEST OF BOTH WORLDS.

Here is the best of two disparate worlds, traditional and youthful. First we have Eastern Peake, a winery founded by Dianne Pym and Norman Latta in the early 1980s, an estate that is now well known for its classically made syrah, pinot noir and chardonnay. And then you have Latta Vino, owned and run by Dianne and Norman's son Owen, who is one of the new darlings of the natural-wine world. At Latta Vino, Owen uses grapes sourced from across Victoria to produce a range of wines that are unique, and probably like nothing you've tried before: pinot gris that is so textural it's almost chewy; super-funky, natural-ferment chardonnay; bright, juicy cabernet franc. Get down to Eastern Peake Tues to Sat to try them all (both labels are now run by Owen), either in a four- or six-wine flight, paired with a produce board from local artisans.

easternpeake.com.au

MITCHELL HARRIS WINES

BALLARAT BAR AND EATERY HIGHLIGHTS A GENEROUS SELECTION FROM AROUND VICTORIA.

In the heart of Ballarat, in a 150-year-old workshop that's been given a fair bit of love, lies this gem, Mitchell Harris Wines. This is a cellar door, a restaurant and wine bar, and a place to come in, hang out, try a few wines and have a few bites. The house wine is the work of John Harris and his in-laws, the Mitchell family, who have teamed up to create a suite of wines using fruit sourced from vineyards in Ballarat, the Pyrenees and the Macedon Ranges. The food, meanwhile, is a tight list of snacky cuisine – empanadas, tostadas, polenta chips, tuna carpaccio – that goes well not just with the Mitchell Harris wines, but with its list of stars from around Victoria. This is the classy, friendly space you've been looking for on a night out in the Goldfields.

mitchellharris.com.au

BENDIGO

DJA DJA WURRUNG COUNTRY

As with so many of Victoria's wine regions, Bendigo has a long history with a large gap in the middle: the area was well known for wine during the gold rush-era around the 1850s, and continued to flourish until phylloxera - the vine-destroying pest that swept the world in the 1890s - destroyed everything. It took another 60 years before someone decided to give it a go again, and even now it's one of Victoria's smaller regions, in terms of winery numbers, but one that can easily hold its own in quality. This is red wine country, a region that takes in the stately city of Bendigo and the trendy tree-changer town of Castlemaine, and there's plenty to keep drinkers and diners amused.

BALGOWNIE ESTATE

TRY THE WINE AND STAY THE NIGHT AT THIS SPRAWLING VINEYARD COMPLEX.

Balgownie was the first of Bendigo's modern-era wineries, established in 1969, and it's gone gangbusters ever since (to the point where the winery has a large presence in the Yarra Valley now, too). It's quite the set-up in Bendigo, just 15min west of the town centre, with a cellar door, a restaurant, and accommodation in glamping tents, cottages, or the homestead. Wherever you are, you'll be able to soak in the beauty of the central Victorian countryside, among the gums overlooking Myer's Creek. Tastings at the cellar door are $10 a head, or $15 for the premium range, which takes in wines from across the Balgownie stable, including vineyards in the Yarra and Macedon ranges. The restaurant is a beautiful spot doing breakfast, lunch and dinner, and on a cool night, the glamping tents among the vines are perfect for cosying up.

balgownie.com

BLACKJACK WINES

POWERFUL REDS ARE THE CALLING CARD AT THIS HARCOURT VALLEY STALWART.

Blackjack is all about elegant and yet immensely powerful red wines, the sort of shiraz you could build a house with, cabernet that could prop up a car. It's impressive stuff, made since the '90s in the Harcourt Valley, formerly the Castlemaine Goldfields, just off the highway on the way up to Bendigo. The cellar door here is flung open on weekends and public holidays, the perfect opportunity to enjoy a friendly welcome at a winery that's still boutique in size, and tuck into a few of those reds.

blackjackwines.com.au

Top Balgownie Estate *Opposite* Mitchell Harris Wines

SUTTON GRANGE

GORGEOUS HOMESTEAD HOUSES ONE LAIDBACK CELLAR DOOR.

Make a plan to be around Sutton Grange on a Sunday, because that's the only day this winery is open, and you want to get in here. This is one truly beautiful spot, a winery set in a limestone homestead overlooking vines and a lake, the best of the central Victorian countryside, and some of the best of central Victorian wine. Tasting flights cost $10 per person, and take in a solid range of the Sutton offerings: skilfully made reds and whites that come in at a huge variety of price points. There's no food served, so you probably won't be hanging around – but still, make sure this place is on your itinerary.

suttongrange.com.au

BRESS

TALENTED WINEMAKERS DO A GOOD LINE OF WHITE WINES TO COMPLEMENT CLASSIC REDS.

Of course, Bress has the punchy red wines that the Bendigo region is known for. But it has more, too – much more. Arrive at the pet-friendly cellar door in the Harcourt Valley on a weekend and you'll be able to sample some beautiful, subtle pinot noir, not to mention top-quality chardonnay, rosé, and a Rhone-style blend of viognier, roussanne and marsanne that will make your palate sing. It's all pretty laidback here, despite the seriousness of the wine. There's no food on offer, but bring a picnic, hang out among the vines, and drink a glass or two of your favourite drop.

bress.com.au

WILD

LOCAVORE ICON CATERS TO CASTLEMAINE VISITORS AND TREE-CHANGERS ALIKE.

Castlemaine has been a town reborn over the last decade or more, as Melbourne tree-changers have flocked to this regional centre – that's still just an hour and a half from the city – to live a slightly quieter life. And of course with that new population comes a new wave of venues – and Wild is one of the finest. This is a restaurant and wine bar that's very much of its place, making a point to use seasonal, local ingredients to create a compact but gorgeous menu of modern cuisine. The restaurant is housed in Castlemaine's historic fire brigade headquarters, and has become a local icon for a reason.

wildfoodandwine.com

Top **Sutton Grange**

THE GRAMPIANS/ GARIWERD

DJAB WURRUNG AND JARDWADJALI COUNTRY

Your first impression of the Grampians/Gariwerd will probably be the region's sheer, rugged beauty. This is a part of the country that travellers have been flocking to for decades to enjoy its forested foothills and rocky ranges, for the chance to hike or ride through jaw-dropping terrain, to go on scenic road trips, to camp out under the stars. And, of course, to eat and drink. This mountain region is a low-key gastronomic wonderland, an area - centred around the towns of Stawell and Ararat - filled with historic wineries and destination-dining venues, a place where food and wine is grown and enjoyed without artifice or ceremony. This is a friendly region, and a beautiful region. Dig in.

BEST'S WINES

THE NAME IS A GOOD GUIDE – THIS IS SOME OF AUSTRALIA'S BEST WINE.

How is it that you don't know more about Best's Wines? Here is a winery that has been around since 1866, a producer of some of Australia's finest drops, an iconic operation set in a beautiful spot. And yet, it's not even famous. You can take advantage of that fact, however, by enjoying an intimate cellar door experience in the Great Western sub-region, just south of Stawell. Best's cellar door is housed in the property's original stables, built in 1866, with walls of local red gum, and the ideal place to feel the winery's history, particularly if you take up an offer of a tour of the old cellars, dug by local miners. Tastings are free if you're happy to settle for the standard pours; however, splash out $10 a head and you will be treated to the finest Best's has on offer, which takes in award-winning reds, whites and even sparklings. Some of Australia's best wine, and there's a good chance you'll be among only a few people here to try it.

bestswines.com

FALLEN GIANTS

EASYGOING CELLAR DOOR HAS WINE TO TASTE, AND A BARBECUE TO USE.

Fallen Giants is a great winery name. It's inspired, according to owners Rebecca and Aaron Drummond, by Dreaming stories of the Djabwurung and Jardwadjali People, and it's fitting for this area of immense beauty: a valley shaped by a fierce kick from a giant emu, fallen giants to each side. The vineyard has been here since 1969, and in Rebecca and Aaron's care since 2013 – in that time they've transformed it into one of the Grampians/Gariwerd's finest, and they're more than happy to welcome guests in to see why. This is such a classic rural cellar door, a super-friendly spot offering tasting flights of recent releases, as well as platters of local produce to enjoy on the deck with a beautiful view. You're encouraged to bring your own picnic, too, plus there's a barbecue you're free to use if you want to cook up a few snags or a steak to match a good red.

fallengiants.com.au

GRAMPIANS ALE WORKS

LOCAL SMALL-BATCH BREWERS ARE ONTO A SERIOUSLY GOOD THING.

Of course they make beer in the Grampians/Gariwerd – why wouldn't they? And Grampians Ale Works, in Stawell, makes very good beer – a welcome addition to the local scene. This is a pretty modest operation, size-wise, but Michael and Shawna Dominelli have got a good thing going, using grain and hops from local farmers to create a suite of tasty brews, both straightforward and experimental, that they serve to an appreciative crowd in the centre of town. There's food too, hefty barbecued goodness that works perfectly with a refreshing ale.

grampiansaleworks.beer

GRAMPIANS ESTATE

DRINK AND DINE AMONG THE VINES AT THIS SHIRAZ SPECIALIST.

The terrace at the Grampians Estate cellar door is set so close to the vines you could reach over and pick a bunch of grapes – don't, though, because they're needed to produce some of the region's best wine. Grampians Estate specialises in shiraz, both standard and sparkling, some of it from vines that date back to 1878. There are plenty of wines to try at the cellar door, including a tight but impressive range of whites, for $5 per person per flight. They serve food, too, simple fare like country pies and cheese platters, that will make hanging out on the terrace, keeping careful watch on those vines, a pleasure.

grampiansestate.com.au

MOUNT LANGI GHIRAN

LIKE ITS NAMESAKE, THIS WINERY STANDS TALL – EVEN IN THE GRAMPIANS/GARIWERD.

Prepare for yet more gorgeous views at Mount Langi Ghiran, easily one of the Grampians/Gariwerd's best wine producers. Based deep in the countryside about half an hour west of Ararat, Mount Langi Ghiran makes wine to write home about, or even better, wine to take with you to that home: shiraz and cabernet sauvignon in particular, though the riesling and pinot gris are also rippers. The cellar door here is open every day, with five wine flights for $10; there's also a cafe, which serves simple meals or provides picnic hampers to eat out on the lawn. This is a slick, impressive operation – you'll love it.

langi.com.au

MONTARA

THERE ARE VIEWS TO DIE FOR HERE – PLUS THE WINE IS DELICIOUS.

Come for the wine, stay for the view. In fact, just come for the view. It's breathtaking at Montara, as you stand on the deck at the cellar door and stare out over the Grampians/Gariwerd's natural splendour. You could stay here all day and just take it in. Might as well have a glass of wine while you're doing it, of course. Montara, just south of Ararat and open on weekends, offers standard tasting flights for $5 per person, or you can do a Sip & Sit, with a glass of your favourite drop paired with a platter of local produce. Go for the shiraz or the riesling – they're both sensational – then sit back and enjoy.

montarawines.com.au

PAPER SCISSORS ROCK BREW CO

SMALL-TOWN BREWERY OFFERS BIG-TIME FLAVOURS.

You could be forgiven for assuming that the Grampians/Gariwerd town of Halls Gap, population 430, would not have its own craft brewery. But you would be wrong. Because that's where you'll find Paper Scissors Rock, a kick-arse brewery with a fancy taphouse in the heart of one of Victoria's most spectacular locations. There are eight beer taps to choose from, pouring the PSR range – including the amusingly named Normal Beer, because people kept coming in saying, 'I just want a normal beer' – plus tasty, hearty food to pair it with.

paperscissorsrock.beer

Opposite Paper Scissors Rock Brew Co

POMONAL ESTATE

WHATEVER YOU'RE INTO, THIS SPRAWLING WINERY WILL HAVE YOU COVERED.

Set just outside Pomonal, about 20min from Stawell, Pomonal Estate is a winery first and foremost, though it does far more than that. Owners Adam and Pep Atchison make beer – a tight but tasty list of pale ale, pilsner and the like – plus they make cider, serve food at their cellar door and cafe, and finally, they also run Mount Cassel Villa, a three-bedroom abode within touching distance of Grampians National Park. Busy people – and yet still so friendly. Pay them a visit for a tasting, a meal, or a few nights.

pomonalestate.com.au

ROYAL MAIL HOTEL DUNKELD

TRUE DESTINATION DINING IS COMBINED WITH A CLASSY RANGE OF ACCOMMODATION OPTIONS.

There are a few regional dining experiences in Victoria – Brae (*see* p.89), for example, and Provenance (*see* p.132) – that seem almost unreasonably good, the sort of eateries that would stand out even in the city, though of course they wouldn't feel right anywhere but their own place. They're destination dining, restaurants worth several hours' driving on their own. Wickens, the two-hatted restaurant at the beautiful Royal Mail Hotel Dunkeld, is another. The food here is created by chef Robin Wickens, who serves a degustation-style menu utilising seasonal ingredients, mostly grown in the garden nearby. The wine is a highlight too, sourced from the restaurant's 30,000-bottle cellar, and served either by bottle or glass, or as part of a paired selection with food. Destination dining wouldn't be complete without spending the night, and here there's standard hotel suites with incredible views, apartments and a selection of cottages and heritage homes within the Dunkeld area. This is one of Victoria's great tourism experiences for people who like to wine and dine, and you shouldn't miss it.

royalmail.com.au

SEPPELT

A 3KM WARREN OF UNDERGROUND CELLARS IS THE HIGHLIGHT AT THIS HISTORIC SPOT.

To say Seppelt has been around for a while would be an understatement – this winery, sporting one of the most famous names in Australian viticulture, was established in 1863, and its past is filled with stories of gold rush toil and winemaking excellence. The highlight of a visit to Seppelt, in the town of Great Western, is to experience that history first-hand with a tour of 'The Drives', a 3km warren of underground cellars that can hold 3 million bottles of wine, the largest in the southern hemisphere, dug in 1868 by local gold miners. There are three tours daily – at 11am, 1pm and 3pm – which finish with a glass of sparkling shiraz. To really step things up, you can even have dinner in the Drives, though you'll need a group of at least 12 to book it. There's a standard cellar door here, too, for people just up for a quick tasting, or if you would like to stay a lot longer, there's Vine Lodge, a seven-bedroom homestead built during the gold rush.

seppelt.com.au

HENTY

GUNDITJMARA, JARDWADJALI AND DJABWURUNG COUNTRY

The Henty wine region is a sprawling area of undulating, grassy plains, and prime sheep country that takes up the bulk of western Victoria, from Warnambool in the east to the South Australian border in the west, and up to the Grampians/Gariwerd near Dunkeld. It's a fledgling wine region, though one with an exciting future, as more winemakers move in to take advantage of the good conditions and relatively low land prices. This isn't a region to just drive around hoping to find a vineyard - you'll need to plan ahead and ensure you're in the right area, though the wool-capital town of Hamilton would make a decent base.

CRAWFORD RIVER

CATTLE STATION HAS BEEN PUT TO EVEN BETTER USE BY THE THOMSON FAMILY.

The Thomson family have been making wine on a sheep and cattle station near Condah since 1975, back when no one else had thought to put vines in the ground, rather than just let animals graze. It was a good call – they're still going, among the livestock, these days with Belinda Thomson in charge, making incredibly good riesling in particular for a place still not known for wine. The cellar door is open by appointment only, which means an intimate experience with the Thomsons, and plenty of time to linger over the wine.

crawfordriverwines.com

HOCHKIRCH WINES

BOUTIQUE, BIODYNAMIC WINERY WAS DOING THE LO-FI THING BEFORE IT WAS COOL.

Hochkirch is one out of the box, a boutique, biodynamic winery in the heart of Henty, a family-run business that is quietly going about making some truly delicious wine. In keeping with the holistic approach here, that wine is made in the lo-fi style that's now fashionable around Australia, but has always been the way at Hochkirch, with natural ferments in open vats, and extended skin contact on some of the white wines for more texture and complexity. There's no filtering or fining, and minimal sulphur added. Who knew some of the original natural winemakers were out in Henty? The team here only open up by appointment, so call well ahead and see what you can arrange – it will be worth it.

hochkirchwines.com.au

PIERREPOINT ESTATE

THERE'S MUCH TO LOVE AT THIS FRIENDLY WINERY, NOT LEAST THE DOG.

Everyone loves a winery dog, and Pierrepoint Estate has a particularly lovable pooch: Bear, a border collie who loves a game of fetch or a scratch behind the ear. There's more, too: Pierrepoint Estate, just outside Hamilton, is a well-established vineyard, having been planted in 1998, and there's a big-name winemaker utilising its grapes, Owen Latta, from Eastern Peake (*see* p.140), utilising its grapes. He's doing great things here with quality fruit, so call ahead to book an appointment at the cellar door, and enjoy. There's accommodation too, a couple of bed-and-breakfast-style suites that ooze country charm.

pierrepointwines.com.au

THE PYRENEES

DJAB WURRUNG AND JARDWADJALI COUNTRY

This grand Victorian mountain range has, of course, a more famous European namesake, which divides Spain and France and hosts many a fine winery. Fortunately, the Australian version of the Pyrenees can make that same claim to fine wine, despite this being an up-and-coming region without a huge number of wineries. Those that do exist are genuine heavy-hitters, making wine worth travelling for. There are no large population bases in the Pyrenees – Avoca is probably the largest town, with just a few thousand inhabitants – so there aren't many great restaurants or even breweries here. It's all about the wine, but you could also combine it with exploring the Grampians/Gariwerd (*see* p.143) or the Bendigo region (*see* p.141).

AMHERST WINERY

HISTORIC VINEYARD HAS AN AMAZING STORY BEHIND IT.

If you're a sucker for a good story then you're going to love Amherst Winery, near the town of the same name. Amherst's shiraz vineyard is known as 'Dunn's Paddock', named in honour of a former convict who made a very circuitous journey to this area back in the 1850s. Ask for the full yarn when you make it to the Amherst cellar door (open by appointment), where the friendly team will be happy to pour you out a tasting – the shiraz from Dunn's is great, but look out for the pinot noir and cabernet sauvignon as well – and walk you through the estate's history.

amherstwinery.com

BLUE PYRENEES ESTATE

IMPRESSIVE VENTURE HAS A CELLAR DOOR, A CAFE, AND A FEW PLACES TO STAY.

Just outside Avoca, at the foot of the hills, lies Blue Pyrenees, probably the largest of the Pyrenees wineries, an impressive venture with a cellar door that's open seven days a week, and a cafe serving grazing platters, coffees and desserts. Being such a large operation, you can imagine that the wine list here is a long one, and you'll be spoiled for choice with a $10 tasting in the roomy cellar door – though if the weather is nice, head outside with your glass to the verandah or the lawn. Dogs are welcome if you're outside. You can stay the night, too: The Lakehouse is a gorgeous, airy spot that sleeps up to eight guests with the sort of scenic views the name implies; there are also three 'tiny homes' on different parts of the estate, managed by Unyoked Cabins.

bluepyrenees.com.au

DALWHINNIE

ONE OF THE PYRENEES' ORIGINALS MAKES SOME INCREDIBLY GOOD WINE.

There are a lot of big wineries in a lot of famous regions that would dearly love to be making wine that's as good as Dalwhinnie's. This is one of the Pyrenees pioneers, and its best, an almost 50-year-old venture among the foothills near Moonambel. The reds are the real winners here, the ultra-premium shiraz in particular, velvety and complex, though Dalwhinnie also makes a chardonnay that's no slouch. To try them, visit the cellar door from Friday to Monday, enjoy the stunning views over vines and mountains from the wooden deck, and sit back for a journey through some truly special wine. If there's nowhere else you need to be, grab a glass of your favourite and hang out for the afternoon.

dalwhinnie.wine

Top Blue Pyrenees Estate

DOGROCK WINERY

RARE EUROPEAN VARIETALS ARE GIVEN TOP PRIORITY AT THIS LO-FI WINERY.

Dogrock is a welcome break from the norm: yes, this winery makes shiraz, but it also specialises in European varietals you may not have quite as much experience with, from Portuguese touriga nacionale and arinto, to Spanish tempranillo, to French marsanne. There's also chardonnay and grenache in there for good measure. The wines are made in the lo-fi style that has been the norm in some parts of the Old World for centuries, with minimal additions or other tinkering. That results in a suite of elegant, balanced, and above all, delicious wines. The cellar door, just south of Landsborough, is open any time, as long as you make an appointment.

dogrock.com.au

MOUNT AVOCA

ORGANIC WINERY DOES EVERYTHING SUSTAINABLY, INCLUDING ITS LUXE ACCOMMODATION.

'Australia's most highly awarded organic winery' – that's some claim to fame, and one that's much easier to understand after a visit to the Mount Avoca cellar door, which is open daily. This is a charming, friendly space, where you're more than likely to run into winemaker and owner David Darlow, who can introduce you to the organic mindset, as well as Mount Avoca's excellent wines (highlighted by the shiraz, which has to be responsible for a whole swag of those awards). This is such a lovely place, where there's play equipment for the kids, food platters and hampers to make picnics with, bushwalking tracks and bikes for hire, and accommodation at four 'eco–luxe' lodges set among the vines. You're 2hr from Melbourne here, but another world away.

mountavoca.com

MRS BAKER'S STILL HOUSE

LOCAL WINEMAKERS ALSO DISTIL SPIRITS, AND THEY DO IT VERY WELL.

The Pyrenees has a distillery! Happy days. It's a good one, too, Mrs Baker's Still House at Wimmera Hills winery just north of Elmhurst. Winemakers Jane and Benjamin Baker also distill fine spirits, mostly gin using botanicals grown on-site, though they also do vodka and a few liqueurs as well. Pay them a visit at Wimmera and you can try three spirits for free, or go up to $15 for eight samples, plus of course there's wine to try, grazing platters to munch on, and a few walking tracks if you want to explore the beautiful Pyrenees and work off some of your lunch.

wimmerahills.com.au

TALTARNI

PYRENEES' PIONEERS OFFER GENEROUS TASTINGS WITH BEAUTIFUL VIEWS.

Taltarni is another of the Pyrenees' pioneers – started in 1969 – that is still leading the field, a polished operation that knocks out premium shiraz, cabernet sauvignon and petit verdot, among many others. The vineyard is in the region's viticultural heartland, near Moonambel, and is open to visitors Wednesday to Sunday. Those who call in are treated to lovely views, not to mention generous tasting flights either inside or on the verandah, with the chance to dine, on special occasions, in the underground cellars.

taltarni.com.au

Opposite Delatite Winery

UPPER GOULBURN

TAUNGURUNG COUNTRY

This region is the gateway to Victoria's High Country (see p.127), a visually stunning area north of Melbourne that takes in the likes of Mansfield, Alexandra, Eildon and Yarck. Unlike in the Goulburn Valley (see p.115), there aren't a huge number of wineries, restaurants or other producers here - however, this area is home to a few of my absolute favourite venues in Victoria, and this book wouldn't be complete without them.

ALEXANDRA HOTEL

RECENTLY RENOVATED PUB DOES THE BEST CHIPS YOU'VE EVER TASTED.

A quick shout-out to one of the great Victorian regional venues, a recently renovated pub, restaurant and hotel in downtown Alexandra that – I'm just going to put it out there – does the best goddamn chips you've ever tasted. All of the food at the Alex Hotel is way above what you would expect for a country pub, from trout roasted with fennel, to Milawa duck breast and smoked sweet potato – but seriously, those chips.

alexandrahotel.net.au

DELATITE WINERY

MANSFIELD FAVOURITE DOES EXCELLENT WINE AND GREAT FOOD, ALL ON ITS OWN.

You sit out on the terrace at Delatite, a cracking winery just outside Mansfield, drinking beautiful wine after beautiful wine, thoughtfully made riesling and chardonnay and Malbec and more, and you gaze at the surrounding countryside that seems to go on forever and you ask yourself: Why aren't there more wineries around here? Because if Delatite is anything to go by, this is prime winemaking country, and yet they've got it all to themselves. Where are the others? Still, that's not your problem. Your problem is deciding which of the many, many wines you'll try here, either with a $20 standard flight, or a $60 wine and food match. There's a brand-spanking new restaurant at Delatite too, a classy affair serving up beautiful food either as set menus in the dining room (chicken terrine, five-spice duck leg, grilled wild venison), or more casual à la carte on the terrace (salumi, fried whitebait, antipasto platters and more). And everywhere you go, those views, that wine, and that question to ponder.

delatitewinery.com.au

SWIFTCREST DISTILLERY

SUSTAINABILITY IS TAKEN TO A NEW LEVEL AT THIS STEAM-DRIVEN, OFF-GRID GIN PRODUCER.

Carrie and Hank Thierry don't do things by halves: when they decided to set up a sustainable, carbon-neutral distillery in the hills above Mansfield, they took it all the way. Swiftcrest Distillery is totally off-grid. It was built by hand by Hank; the whole distillery runs on steam, powered by a big old steam engine that is fueled by naturally fallen timber; the water is from a spring on the property; the gin botanicals are grown on-site; the grains are bought from a local biodynamic farmer. If this all sounds very serious, it is, though Carrie and Hank are absolutely lovely people, super laidback and friendly, and only too happy to take you for a tour and a taste, to try the vodka, gin and whisky, to see how this whole steam thing works, and to soak up the beauty of this special place.

swiftcrest.com

South Australia

The Festival State has the big-hitters of the Barossa and McLaren Vale, but you'll fall in love with smaller regions like the Clare Valley too.

BAROSSA VALLEY

PERAMANGK, KAURNA AND NGADJURI COUNTRY

This is it. The icon. The legend. Australia's most famous wine region: the Barossa Valley. Australia's best-known wines come from the Barossa Valley. Australia's most expensive wines come from the Barossa Valley. If anyone knows anything about the wine of Australia, then they have inevitably heard of the Barossa Valley. This is a beautiful region, and a historic region. Some of the grape vines here are among the oldest still producing fruit in the world. Some of the wineries – Penfolds, Wolf Blass, Yalumba, Peter Lehmann, most of which I've tended to avoid writing about here, because they're easy enough to find for yourself – are among the largest and most successful in Australia, or indeed the world.

And the good news for visitors is that despite all this prestige and sense of exclusivity, the Barossa is actually a very laidback, and very enjoyable place to spend some time. Set just an hour north-east of downtown Adelaide/Tarndanya, the Barossa has few airs and graces: people are friendly, they're keen to share their stories, to share their culture, to share their wine.

This is also one of Australia's most developed regions in terms of tourism, which means you have literally almost 100 cellar doors to choose from, everything from the sprawling estates of world-famous big-hitters, to the tiny boltholes of boutique producers.

However, there's more to the valley than wine: the food scene here is also excellent, driven by a host of talented chefs who get to work with world-class local produce. There's now a growing array of microbreweries and distilleries too, offering something different again to the standard winery experiences. In short, the Barossa is awesome. You're going to love it.

For the purposes of this book, I've combined the Barossa with its next-door neighbour, Eden Valley, which is known more for its rieslings than the bold, rich shirazes of its famous compatriot. Stay in either one of these, and you will be able to pass back and forth between them with ease.

Yalumba *Previous* Jim Barry Wines, Clare Valley

APEX BAKERY (1)
COUNTRY CLASSIC DOES THE SAUSAGE ROLL YOU'VE BEEN DREAMING ABOUT.

Apex is an absolute classic, the no-frills country bakery of your dreams. Just off the main drag in Tanunda, the wood-oven at Apex has been burning continuously since 1924, and it's still used to bake the bakery's famous bread. Call past here for a pastry, a pie or a sausage roll, and enjoy a cherished slice of Barossa history.

apexbakery.com.au

ARTISANS OF BAROSSA (2)
COMBINED CELLAR DOOR FEATURES MORE THAN 100 WINES UP FOR TASTING.

This is a slick, impressive operation, a combined cellar door featuring some of the Barossa's most sought-after winemaking names and a modern, friendly venue in which you can sample pretty much the full gamut of what the region has to offer. Artisans offers tastings of more than 100 wines, from the likes of John Duval (former head winemaker at Penfolds), Sons of Eden, Spinifex, Schwarz Co. and more. You can choose flights of four standard wines, six 'adventurous' drops, or six rarities. Artisans also offers unique, premium experiences, such as The Grenache Project, a series of six wines made by six different winemakers from the same block of vines, and Six Origins, a set of six Barossa shirazes made from different areas of the valley. There's a great restaurant on-site here, called Essen, doing thoughtful, Japanese-leaning cuisine, plus a delicatessen, and plenty of space on the lawn next to the vines in which to relax.

artisansofbarossa.com

Bottom Artisans of Barossa

BAROSSA DISTILLING CO. (3)
CONTEMPORARY DISTILLER INHABITS A HISTORIC SPACE AT PROVENANCE.

It's impossible to not be wooed by the charm of the 'distillery door' at Barossa Distilling Co. Housed in the building where Penfolds' brandy was once produced (and next to Penfolds' current Barossa cellar door), this historic space still features original stills and piping, as well as a spiral staircase leading up to a mezzanine floor. Punters can choose to do a tasting of the company's artisanal gins and other spirits, or settle in for a cocktail and a few bites of food. It's worth exploring the surrounding site here, too: called 'Provenance', it's home to a cafe, a microbrewery, a wood-fired pizza restaurant, and two cellar doors.

barossadistilling.com

BAROSSA GIN SCHOOL/ DURAND DISTILLERY ④

CREATE YOUR OWN GIN WITH LOCAL BOTANICALS – AND TAKE A BOTTLE HOME.

Your gin. Your very own, unique gin. That's what you will walk away with after a 4hr experience at Barossa Gin School, at Durand Distillery just outside Nuriootpa. Book a 'station' at the distillery and you will be set up in front of your very own copper still, given the base spirit, and then taken through a selection of classic and native botanicals to decide how to flavour your gin. There are, of course, experts on hand to advise and help select and measure, before the still is set and the amateur distillers head off to The Eatery nearby for a three-course lunch. Get back to the still, bottle up the finished product, stick your own label to it, and you're off with your very own gin.

duranddistillery.com

Fino restaurant

BROCKENCHACK WINES ⑤

CRACK OPEN A BOTTLE OF ESTATE WINE AND ENJOY THE GOOD LIFE AT THIS B&B.

There are few things better than cracking open a bottle of wine, pouring a couple of glasses, and then going outside to sit around the fire and watch the sunset from the 'Retreat B&B' at Brockenchack Wines. Set with views over the rolling hills of Eden Valley, with river red gums dotting the pastures, this is bucolic bliss. The modern, spacious Retreat is one of three accommodation options here – others include the smaller Studio B&B and the charming Vineyard B&B – and all are sensational places to base yourself during a stay in the area. The Barossa wineries are only 10 or 15min away; Eden Valley is at your doorstep. And of course, you'll do a tasting of the Brockenchack product, which has recently come under new ownership and is picking up a swag of awards. Their grenache in particular makes the perfect drop for those long evenings around the fire.

brockenchack.com.au

CIRILLO ESTATE ⑥

ENJOY THE FRUITS OF THE WORLD'S OLDEST CONTINUOUSLY PRODUCING GRENACHE VINES.

Cirillo has a seriously impressive claim to fame: the oldest continuously producing grenache vines in the world, planted in 1850 (South Australia was one of few regions in the world to escape the phylloxera outbreak of the late 19th century). The winery isn't particularly well set up for tourists – visits are by appointment only, and not always available – however, it's worth making the effort to get in, meet the affable owners and witness a piece of Barossa history. If you're lucky, you may even get to drink some of that history, too – in the form of the Cirillo 1850 Ancestor Vine Grenache.

cirilloestatewines.com.au

The history of Barossa wine

You're going to see a lot of references in this chapter to the 1850s, and there's good reason for that: it's essentially the beginning of the Barossa wine industry, of Barossa the icon, and any winery with a link to that time will be making it clear.

This area of South Australia is Peramangk, Kaurna and Ngadjuri Country. It was colonised by Europeans in 1836, when English shipping merchant George Fife Angas arrived and awarded himself more than 11,000ha of land. The famous Barossa moniker was given to it a year later, when Colonel William Light named the surrounding mountain range after a British victory over the French in the Battle of Barrosa - only, he got the spelling wrong. Anyway, by the early 1840s, more British settlers had arrived, while George Angas had also agreed to allow a group of Silesian Lutheran farmers, persecuted in their homeland, to settle on his land and grow fruit.

Things were happening. Samuel Smith, a brewer from England, landed in the Barossa in 1847, and by 1849 he had bought a parcel of land from Angas and planted grapevines at a vineyard he called Yalumba. Around the same time, one of those Lutheran farmers, Johann Gramp, had sent home for some riesling cuttings and planted them where he was living, on the banks of Jacob's Creek. Just nearby, in 1850, another Silesian, Joseph Seppelt, bought a parcel of land to farm and called it Seppeltsfield.

By the early 1850s, all of these settlers were producing wine, and many more joined them throughout the decade as they realised the suitability of the area for growing grapes. An industry, and an icon, was born.

DAVID FRANZ

NEXT-GEN WINE PRODUCER HAS MADE HIS MARK WITH AN ECLECTIC OFFERING.

David Franz Lehmann has a touch of the mad scientist about him – just check out the esoteric list of wines up for tasting at his dreamy cellar door, which run the gamut of everything from scrumpy cider to pet nats, whites, roses, reds, liqueurs and even fortified wines. On top of that, David also smokes and cures his own charcuterie, and makes a mean paté. Obviously, you should set aside at least a few hours for tasting and snacking overlooking the vines at this estate. Make sure you glance up to your left, too, just over the hill, where you'll see the tops of a few silos at the winery owned by David's dad, Peter. As in, Peter Lehmann. Yes, this is a mad scientist with a serious pedigree, and it shows in David's extremely good wine, as wildly varied as it may be. Come here to relax, to enjoy friendly, laidback service, and to sample the next generation of Barossa talent.

david-franz.com

FINO

SEPPELTSFIELD'S IN-HOUSE EATERY TAKES MOD-OZ FOOD TO THE NEXT LEVEL.

There are plenty of great places to have lunch in the Barossa, but Fino might just be the best of them. Housed in the sprawling, historic Seppeltsfield complex – home to the Seppeltsfield cellar door, plus a casual cafe, an art gallery, and even a working cooperage – Fino occupies a lovely corner surrounded by gardens and fountains. Chef Sam Smith turns out a beautiful, if pricey, menu of modern Australian fare, the likes of cured kingfish with buttermilk and radish, whole char-grilled garfish with celeriac, and wagyu brisket with confit leeks. Pair those dishes with a wine from Seppeltsfield, or one of its well-known neighbours, and you've got yourself one damn fine lunch.

fino.net.au

South Australia

GREENOCK BREWERS
THE BAROSSA'S GERMAN HERITAGE IS UTILISED IN THIS RANGE OF BEERS.

The Barossa has a proud German history stretching back to the early 1800s, and it's something the brewers at Greenock are tapping into. Here, the beer is brewed under the German Beer Purity Law, established in 1516, which stipulates that only four ingredients can be used: water, malt, hops and yeast. That still leaves the team at Greenock plenty of room to tinker, and they've produced a range of five excellent beers that are on for tasting and drinking at their brewery in their eponymous town on the fringe of the valley. It's a pretty modest set-up, but friendly, with meat and cheese platters on offer to pair with your frothy brews.

greenockbrewersbarossavalley.com.au

HARVEST KITCHEN
THE PERFECT CASUAL ALTERNATIVE TO THE BAROSSA'S FINE-DINING SCENE.

You don't always want to sit down to a formal, multi-course extravaganza of a lunch while you're in wine country – sometimes, casual and relaxed will do the job. And that's Harvest Kitchen's bag. Informal, fun, and delicious. The food here is all meant to be shared, with large platters of Mediterranean-style seasonal cuisine that's ideal for those in large groups, those with kids, or those who just want a nice lunch without all the palaver. You can sit on the restaurant's beautiful deck, and it's right next to the Calabria Family Wines cellar door, so it's easy to combine a tasting with lunch.

harvest-kitchen.com.au

Hentley Farm *Opposite* Henschke

HAYES FAMILY WINES

ORGANIC WINE IN A PERFECT LOCATION, AND MADE BY BAROSSA ROYALTY.

Chief winemaker Andrew Seppelt is under close supervision. 'Got the family watching over me,' he smiles, motioning towards a hillside over in the distance, where the Seppelt Family Mausoleum commands an impressive view. Yes, Andrew is from *those* Seppelts, the founding members of the Barossa wine industry, the legends of the valley. It's a pedigree that comes with prestige, but also pressure. If you're a Seppelt in the Barossa, you better be making good wine. And Andrew is. The Hayes Family boutique label is certified organic and sustainable, specialising in shiraz, grenache, mataro and semillon. It's all on for tasting in the winery's amiable cellar door, surrounded on all sides by established vines, with that mausoleum on the horizon. This is the perfect meeting of the Barossa's past and present. Tasty wine, too.

hayesfamilywines.com

HENSCHKE

PRODUCERS OF AN ICONIC AUSTRALIAN WINE OFFER A RANGE OF EXPERIENCES.

Few names in the Barossa are as esteemed as Henschke. This is the winery responsible for Hill of Grace, one of Australia's finest and most expensive wines, with a pedigree in the Barossa that stretches back more than 150 years. Of course, you're not going to get a sample of Henschke's iconic drop if you opt for the simple Discovery tasting at the cellar door, housed in the original 1950s woolstore just outside Keyneton, on the eastern edge of the valley. For that you will have to step up to the Hill of Grace Experience, a private tasting that includes a tour of the historic Hill of Grace vineyard, a visit to the original winery built in the 1860s, and then a taste of several premium wines, including that incredible Hill of Grace. It's a 2hr tour and it costs $300 per person, so you better be keen. Otherwise, a standard tasting here is still a memorable experience.

henschke.com.au

HENTLEY FARM

THE PINNACLE OF BAROSSA FINE-DINING IS A DESTINATION ALL OF ITS OWN.

Hentley Farm is proper destination dining, a three-hatted restaurant that's a member of the prestigious Relais et Chateaux Association – one of only three in Australia. You would visit the Barossa just to eat here. You would visit South Australia just to eat here. Head chef Clare Falzon has created something amazing at this winery and restaurant, though she started with the perfect canvas: an 1840s' stone farmhouse in the heart of Barossa wine country, surrounded by rolling, vine-covered hills. Take a seat in the atrium space, with its floor-to-ceiling glass walls, and prepare for a 3hr celebration of intensely local cuisine, paired with Hentley's beautiful wine. Most of the ingredients Falzon uses are sourced from her own garden, foraged from the surrounding countryside, or supplied by local Barossa farmers and artisans. From these bare bones she creates something magical, something memorable – and, of course, something expensive. You won't eat at Hentley Farm every day. But you should eat here once.

hentleyfarm.com.au

MICHAEL HALL WINES (14)

FORMER JEWELLERY VALUER IS NOW PRODUCING A FEW GEMS OF HIS OWN.

Michael Hall clearly has an appreciation of fine things: he was once a jewellery valuer for Sotheby's in Switzerland, and the Englishman now makes extremely good wine in the Barossa Valley. Hall shares a cellar door space with Rieslingfreak (*see* p.160), in a historic building on the outskirts of Tanunda. It's a basic set-up, but that's fine – what you're here for is the excellent wine. Keep an eye out for Hall's Sang de Pigeon range (named after the perfect colour for a ruby), as well as his sauvignon blanc, which will change the way you think about 'savvy b' forever.

michaelhallwines.com

POONAWATTA (15)

SUPERB RIESLING TO SAMPLE IN IDYLLIC SURROUNDS AT AN EDEN VALLEY LEADER.

The Poonawatta cellar door is perfection. It's the ideal antidote to all of the sprawling estates of the Barossa, all of the bustle of the big players. Set in the Eden Valley, on a hilltop with a lake on one side and a paddock filled with towering river red gums on the other, Poonawatta's cellar door is all about the casual, friendly enjoyment of wine that is clearly made with love and care. Settle in with a nice view, give the winery dogs a pat and get ready to work your way through some of the best rieslings around. Poonawatta also makes a range of reds utilising ancient vines, including shiraz from a block planted in 1880, and grenache from vines that have been producing fruit since 1858. If this winery was in the heart of the Barossa it would be packed every day. The fact it's not is yours to take advantage of.

poonawatta.com.au

REHN BIER (16)

OLD-WORLD BEER IS RECREATED WITH CARE AT THIS TANUNDA INSTITUTION.

Germans know a thing or two about brewing beer, so it would make sense that Brenton Rehn would call on his family heritage when opening his own craft operation back in 2012. It was a success, too: Rehn Bier is now a staple on the Barossa brewing scene, and a very popular stop for beer lovers calling through Tanunda. The brewhouse has 12 beers on tap, mostly traditional old-world styles (pilsner, stout, weizen, tripel) that make a nice change to the IPA obsession of your standard craft brewer, and there are pies and toasted sarnies to munch on.

rehnbier.com.au

RIESLINGFREAK (17)

ONE MAN, ONE GRAPE VARIETY – AND THE RESULT IS BRILLIANT.

When winemaker John Hughes was studying his craft at university, his fellow students nicknamed him 'riesling freak', such was his obsession with that one varietal. 'So,' he shrugs, 'the name was already there.' Hughes is now in charge of Rieslingfreak, his own label, which produces nothing but riesling. As you will quickly find, however, this is a very versatile grape, which can be dry, off-dry or sweet, even fortified as a dessert wine. Call into Hughes' cellar door in Tanunda – a shared space with Michael Hall Wines (*see* this page) – and work your way through the whole range, which is numbered (No.2, No.3, etc) for ease of navigation, given it's all riesling. Pretty soon, you will understand Hughes' obsession.

rieslingfreak.com

SEPPELTSFIELD ROAD DISTILLERS ⑱

AWARD-WINNER TAKES BAROSSA SHIRAZ GRAPES AND TURNS THEM INTO GIN.

How's this for a combination: you take the house gin from Seppeltsfield Road, created by head distiller Nicole Durdin (already an award-winner) and you pour it over tonnes and tonnes of premium Barossa shiraz grapes. Allow it to macerate for a while, and you have Seppeltsfield Road's Barossa Shiraz Gin, awarded the No.1 flavoured gin in Australia, and No.2 flavoured gin in the world at the International Wine & Spirit Competition in 2021. That's impressive stuff, and all the encouragement you need to call past this airy, modern distillery in the small town of Marananga. There's more to try here, including Durdin's excellent Native Ground Gin, made using local native aromatics, and her Barossa Dry Gin. Taste them on a paddle, first neat, then on ice, then with tonic.

seppeltsfieldroaddistillers.com.au

THE STANDISH WINE COMPANY ⑲

SMALL-BATCH WINERY DOES EVERYTHING SO WELL THAT IT OFTEN SELLS OUT.

Small problem with the Standish Wine Company: they don't have a lot of wine. This is a one-man operation, owned and run by winemaker Dan Standish, who takes care of everything in the winemaking process himself. That makes for some outstanding wine – some of the best in the Barossa Valley – but it also makes for necessarily low yields. So, while it will be a highlight of your stay in the valley if you can get in for a tasting at Standish's stylish winery and cellar door, once he runs out of product for the current vintage, he closes the doors. Book ahead, and hope to get lucky.

standishwineco.com

Bottom Seppeltsfield Road Distillers

TSCHARKE (20)
BIODYNAMIC WINERY DELIVERS A SUPERLATIVE EXPERIENCE FOR VISITORS.

Tscharke is awesome. That's it, that's the review. That's all the knowledge you need before deciding to set forth and visit this under-the-radar winery in Marananga. Of course you probably want a bit more information, so here goes. The Tscharke team have thought of everything, from the winemaking process to the experience of visiting. This is a biodynamic winery where the ageing barrels are played music from a carefully chosen playlist. There's no cellar door here, in the traditional sense. Instead, there's what the Tscharke team are calling a 'showcase', a cosy space in a German-style wooden building where all of the label's wines — current and museum releases — are available to buy by the glass or bottle, paired with a compact offering of local, seasonal cuisine. If you do a half-day winery tour, meanwhile, you will also get to experience another incredible tasting space. I won't ruin the surprise, but let's just say you walk through a warehouse and down a dark staircase and into another world. Make sure this winery is on your itinerary.

tscharke.com.au

TURKEY FLAT (21)
A BAROSSA CLASSIC STILL DELIVERS ON VALUE, AND EXPERIENCE.

Turkey Flat is one of the Barossa originals: vines were first planted here in 1847, and the Schulz family – who are still in charge today – took over the property in the 1860s. Christie Schulz is at the helm now, and under her guidance the winery is making a whole swag of wines that are high on value and relatively low on price (which is not always the case in the Barossa). The cellar door here is set in an old bluestone building that once functioned as the Schulz family butcher shop. These days it's all about the drinking, with half-hour or one-hour tasting sessions available. There's also food available, and plenty of space both outside and inside to enjoy it.

turkeyflat.com.au

VINTNERS BAR & GRILL (22)
OLD-SCHOOL RESTAURANT HAS PLENTY OF NEW-SCHOOL FLAIR ON ITS MODERN MENU.

Have a quick glance at the Japanese-inspired menu at Vintners, a lovely restaurant set among the vines on the outskirts of Angaston, and you wouldn't realise this is one of the Barossa's longest-running institutions. You'll spot the likes of fried pigs ears with barbecue sauce; salmon with ponzu, black rice and furikake; Venus Bay prawns with yuzu kosho butter and burnt lime. This is a highly modern and imaginative menu for a classic institution, and it works perfectly, particularly when matched with a local or imported wine from Vintners' extensive list. The service here is friendly but professional, and the atmosphere relaxed but sophisticated. Everything you need.

vintners.com.au

WESTERN RIDGE BREWING (23)
THIS CRUISY BREWERY OFFERS LOW-FI, SMALL-BATCH BEER AT ITS FINEST.

Here's the deal at Western Ridge, a boutique brewery in the north of Nuriootpa, just off the Sturt Highway: every beer is handmade by one of the owners on-site, using predominantly local ingredients. It's all done 'longhand', no nasty additives or dodgy extractions. This is low-fi brewing at its finest, and you can taste the care that goes into every brew: drops that can range from experimental fruit sours to pale ales, stouts and even alcoholic seltzer.

westernridgebrewing.com.au

Opposite Yalumba

YALUMBA (24)

THERE'S A WHOLE LOT GOING ON AT THIS BEAST OF A FACILITY, INCLUDING A COOPERAGE.

Yalumba is one of the Barossa icons and worth a shout-out because it's an absolute behemoth of a winery, founded in 1849 and today responsible for an incredible array of wines that begin at about $15 for an entry-level cab sav and go up to almost $400 a bottle for the really good stuff. A visit to Yalumba could take up the good part of a whole day, as there's that much to do here. Stroll the elegant grounds, with lawn games and outdoor seating, call into the Wine Room for an extensive tasting experience, even visit the cooperage to watch wine barrels being made (the only such operation in the southern hemisphere). There are plenty of package experiences offered, that go from one hour up to four for a comprehensive tour and taste.

yalumba.com

Z WINE (25)

TWO SISTERS HAVE DONE THINGS THE HARD WAY, AND SUCCEEDED SPECTACULARLY.

Sisters Janelle and Kristen Zerk have a family heritage in the Barossa that stretches back five generations – still, that doesn't mean they've done it easy. Janelle is a richly talented winemaker and Kristen an experienced wine marketer, but they've had to go it alone in the industry after the family vineyard was passed on to their brother. The sisters' independent label has been picking up bucket-loads of awards and making waves on the international stage. Their cellar door, on the main street in Tanunda, is a laidback place where you can enjoy a flight of tastings or a whole glass or two, paired with local cheeses or charcuterie.

zwine.com.au

Barossa Valley

The Perfect Day
BAROSSA VALLEY

South Australia

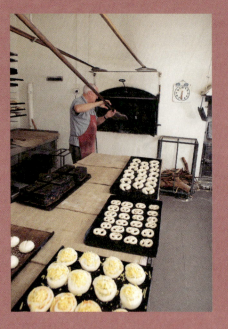

9AM APEX BAKERY

Begin the day with a quick pastry from the classic Apex Bakery in Tanunda (*see* p.155). If you need a coffee hit, try Black Bird Coffee House just down the road.

11AM TSCHARKE

Make the short drive over to Marananga and begin your day at the impressive Tscharke winery (*see* p.162). Prepare to be wowed by the wine, but also the venue.

12.30PM SEPPELTSFIELD ROAD DISTILLERS

Just up the road from Tscharke, this gin specialist is the ideal place to relax with a little pre-lunch tasting of the distillery's excellent product (*see* p.161).

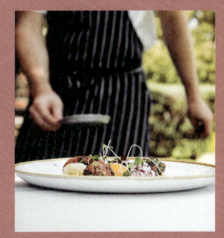

1.30PM FINO

Take your time over lunch at Fino (see p.158), a beautiful venue amid the extensive Seppeltsfield grounds. Afterwards, have a wander and check out the art gallery and cooperage.

3.30PM MICHAEL HALL WINES AND RIESLINGFREAK

Back in Tanunda, there's time to call into the shared cellar door of Michael Hall Wines (see p.160) and Rieslingfreak (see p.160), for two tastings that show the full gamut of Barossa and Eden Valley drops.

8PM VINTNERS BAR & GRILL

Finish the day with dinner at the elegant and yet friendly Vintners (see p.162), a classic of the Barossa that serves up a menu of Japanese-influenced Mod-Oz goodness.

Beckers

MCLAREN VALE
KAURNA COUNTRY

Drive south just 40min from the Adelaide/Tarndanya CBD and you're in another world. Gone are the high-rises and the city bustle, replaced by row after row of grape vines bisected by quiet country roads. Rolling hills here lead to pristine beaches. The pace of life slows considerably from Adelaide's already relatively sedate speed, and time is no longer measured in hours and minutes – but in vintages and cycles of the moon.

Welcome to McLaren Vale, one of Australia's finest wine regions, an area that falls in the shadow of the Barossa Valley in some ways, and yet is deserving of its own place in the upper echelons of the country's wine-making history. It was established as a wine region a few years before even the Barossa, with the first vines planted by British settlers Thomas Hardy and John Reynell, around 1838. Those vineyards are still in use today. While the region retains plenty of tradition, there's also an exciting band of young winemakers who are pushing the boundaries, experimenting with process and technique.

Given its proximity to Adelaide, McLaren Vale can very easily be done in a daytrip, or even as a series of afternoon explorations from the city. The wineries are all packed cheek-by-jowl – you could visit four or five and barely even need a car. With no shortage of high-quality restaurants here as well, plus a few excellent breweries, and a friendly bunch of locals, you have yourself the ideal dining-and-drinking destination.

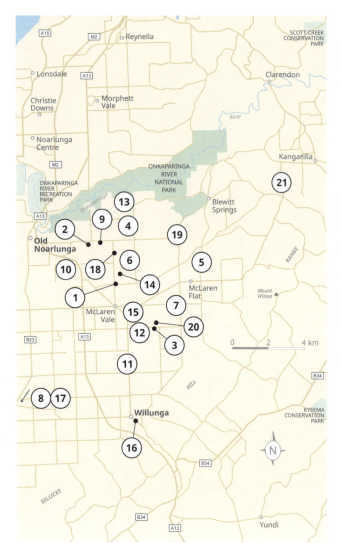

ALPHA BOX & DICE (1)

THIS IS FUN WINE, IT'S FASCINATING WINE, AND ABOVE ALL DELICIOUS WINE.

Alpha Box & Dice has a lofty goal: to create an entire Alphabet of Wine, a series of 26 different drops, each represented by a letter of the alphabet, that together will capture the essence of South Australian wine, and what the state is capable of. To do that, Sam Berketa, head winemaker, sources grapes from McLaren Vale, the Adelaide Hills and the Barossa, with a focus on Italian varietals, making wines that are innovative, interesting, and yet still pleasingly drinkable. It means that you could call into Alpha Box & Dice's ramshackle cellar door in central McLaren Vale multiple times a year, and experience a completely different tasting each time. Grab a bottle of your favourite to enjoy on the lawn with a platter of food after the tasting.

alphaboxdice.com

BEKKERS ②

SAMPLE SOME OF MCLAREN VALE'S FINEST, EVEN IF YOU CAN'T AFFORD IT.

First, the good news: Emmanuele and Toby Bekkers make sensationally good wine. Seriously delicious. The pair's aim is to make small-batch wine that will sit comfortably among the world's finest, to prove their conviction that McLaren Vale can deliver a world-class product. The bad news, if you want to look at it that way, is that the Bekkers are some way towards achieving that goal, which means their range is limited, and it isn't exactly cheap: north of $80 a bottle for anything with this esteemed label. Still, that's all the more reason to call past Bekkers' classy cellar door, in the heart of McLaren Vale, to sample the product (there's a $20 tasting fee). Winemaker Emmanuele and viticulturalist Toby are both passionate and talented wine obsessives who travel regularly to Europe to observe, to learn from friends and to benchmark their own considerable efforts. It shows.

bekkerswine.com

BONDAR ③

LO-FI SPECIALISTS DELIVER PLENTY OF SAVOURY, TEXTURAL DELICIOUSNESS.

If you've dined at any of Adelaide's fancier restaurants, you're probably already familiar with the Bondar name. This is a label that tends to find its way onto a lot of wine lists, given owners Andre Bondar and Selina Kelly's skill at producing savoury, textural low-fi wines from grapes sourced from McLaren Vale and the Adelaide Hills. (Check out their Adelaide Hills Chardonnay and McLaren Vale Shiraz for lip-smacking versions of each.) The cellar door in McLaren Vale is a space as low-key as a Bondar wine, and similarly approachable.

bondarwines.com.au

CORIOLE ④

PIONEERS OF AUSSIE SANGIOVESE ARE STILL DOING IT WELL, WITH A BEAUTIFUL RESTAURANT TOO.

You'll find the usual McLaren Vale varietals at this historic winery: shiraz, cab sav, grenache. But then you will also find some Italian grape varieties that might seem standard now, but were seriously experimental when the Coriole team first stuck them in the ground, the likes of fiano, montepulciano, negro amaro, and most importantly, sangiovese. Coriole was a pioneer of sangiovese in Australia, back in 1985, and it still makes some of the country's finest. The winery has been here since 1967, and the farmhouse that hosts the cellar door was built back in 1860. There's a swish restaurant, called Gather, which serves seasonal degustation-style lunches of modern cuisine, with ingredients sourced locally and from its own farm and kitchen garden. Arbour Bar, on-site, is a place for a glass of wine and a snack, it's only open on weekends and public holidays.

coriole.com

Top **Bekkers** *Opposite* **Alpha Box & Dice**

D'ARENBERG (6)

MCLAREN VALE'S MOST RECOGNISABLE CELLAR DOOR IS PRIME INSTA-FODDER.

If you've seen any photos of McLaren Vale, you've probably seen the d'Arenberg cellar door. This place is unashamed Instagram fodder, a four-storey glass building made to look like a giant Rubik's cube, the top two levels on a slight rotation. It rises above the grape vines of the d'Arenberg vineyard, a consciously avant-garde addition to a winery that was established back in 1912. Inside, it's just as interesting, with each level riotously and uniquely decorated, housing attractions like a 'wine sensory room' – yeah, me either – a virtual fermenter, a 360-degree video room, and, in a shocking outbreak of predictability, a tasting room and restaurant. It will probably come as a surprise to find that d'Arenberg's wines are actually quite classical in style; the winery is probably best known for its Dead Arm shiraz, but also does excellent grenache and cabernet sauvignon, as well as chardonnay.

darenberg.com.au

THE CURRANT SHED (5)

ENJOY MODERN FOOD IN HISTORIC SURROUNDS AT THIS LOCAL FAVOURITE.

The Currant Shed has been a fixture on the McLaren Vale scene for more than a century: originally the building was just that, a shed for drying currants (big business back in the early 1900s), though these days it houses a local favourite restaurant of the same name. The Currant Shed is all about good food without too many airs and graces, with a focus on enjoyment rather than a feeling of exclusivity. The dishes are seasonal, locally sourced and many ingredients are literally 'garden to plate' – plucked from the restaurant's vegetable garden. The menu is modern Australia, though with inspiration – and ingredients – from throughout Asia: from Japan to Vietnam and Thailand. The restaurant offers group menus, kids' menus, and as you would expect, has an excellent wine list. Oh, and there's a winery, Shottesbrooke, on-site.

currantshed.com.au

GOODIESON BREWERY (7)

EVERYONE IS WELCOME AT THIS LAIDBACK BUT TOP-QUALITY INSTITUTION.

Here's the perfect antidote to all of that wine sipping, glass swirling, the pressure to say something intelligent, the desire to look like you know what you're doing: Goodieson Brewery, a craft beer joint in McLaren Vale that is completely relaxed and comfortable. Jeff and Mary Goodieson have spent 10 years turning their passion for good beer and good times into a viable business, and their cellar door space is a perfect reflection of that desire. Have a seat on the big terrace overlooking the creek, pat the dog, smile at the sheep, grab a tasting paddle of Goodieson beers, tuck into a picnic – you're allowed to bring your own food, unlike many wineries here – and chill.

goodiesonbrewery.com.au

LITTLE RICKSHAW (8)

THERE'S INFLUENCE FROM ACROSS SOUTH-EAST ASIA AT THIS DECEPTIVELY HIGH-END EATERY.

The team at Little Rickshaw refer to their establishment as 'our family-run tin shed eatery', which is cute, but it also sells the restaurant a long way short. Set towards the southern end of McLaren Vale, in what is indeed a tin shed – actually a former blacksmith's workshop – Little Rickshaw is a friendly joint that serves up deceptively complex, thoughtful takes on South-east Asian cuisine. On a menu split into 'bites', 'grazing' and 'feasting', you'll find influence from Vietnam, Laos, Cambodia and Thailand, matched with a wine list of local South Australian favourites. Make sure you book ahead, because this place fills up quickly.

thelittlerickshaw.com.au

PAXTON WINES (10)

BIODYNAMIC LEADERS ARE STILL PRODUCING AN AMAZING RANGE OF REDS.

If you're looking for high-quality wine that's certified organic and biodynamically grown, look no further than Paxton, one of the largest such producers in the country. David Paxton has been tending the vines on this site, just 35min door-to-door from the Adelaide CBD, for three decades, and these days he's ably assisted by winemakers Kate Goodman and Ashleigh Seymour, to produce an amazing range of premium red wines. The Paxton cellar door is set within an old sheep farming village, housed in an 1850s shearing shed surrounded by sprawling lawns. Grab a cheeky cheese platter and a flight of wines and you're all set.

paxtonwines.com

OLIVER'S TARANGA (9)

OLD-SCHOOL WINERY AND A HERITAGE-LISTED CELLAR DOOR WITH A MODERN MAKEOVER.

In 2021, the Oliver family – early migrants to McLaren Vale from Scotland – celebrated 180 years of grape growing here in Taranga. It's easy to tap into that tradition too, with a visit to the Oliver's Taranga cellar door, set in a heritage-listed workers' cottage that was built in the 1850s, though these days with a stylish extension. Settle in to taste the range created by Corrina Wright, the sixth generation of Olivers in McLaren Vale, who makes some exceptional wine, in particular her shiraz, grenache, and cabernet sauvignon. It's all produced from grapes grown on the original Oliver's property. This is old-school McLaren Vale at its most charming.

oliverstaranga.com

Bottom d'Arenberg *Opposite* Goodieson Brewery

PENNY'S HILL

THERE'S WINE, GIN, ART, GAMES AND MORE AT THIS HISTORIC SPOT.

Just off Main Road, halfway between McLaren Vale and Willunga, Penny's Hill has the look of a French chateau at first glance, thanks to the gorgeous two-storey stone farmhouse that fronts the property. Drive around it and you arrive at a whole complex of buildings that make up the Penny's Hill experience, where there's a cellar door and tasting room, a restaurant, a gin bar, a bocce lawn, and even an art gallery. The highlight is winemaker Alexia Roberts' beautiful reds, though this is a great place to make a whole afternoon of it, to eat, to taste, to play some bocce and stroll the gallery and enjoy the historic surrounds.

pennyshill.com.au

PRIMO ESTATE

THE GRAPE VARIETIES HERE ARE ITALIAN, AND SO IS THE WARM WELCOME.

Live 'la dolce vita' for a few hours at Primo Estate, a winery that wears its Italian heart proudly on its sleeve. Founded in 1973 by Italian migrant Primo Grilli, Primo Estate specialises in Italian grape varieties – nebbiolo, sangiovese, pecorino – as well as the more expected likes of shiraz and cabernet sauvignon, served up in a classy 'piazzetta-style' cellar door and tasting room. Visitors here are served a flight of wines to taste, paired with freshly baked bread and Primo's own extra virgin olive oil; there's also a premium tasting that includes top-shelf wines and Grana Padano cheese. Antipasti-style food is available as well.

primoestate.com.au

SAMUEL'S GORGE

THE VIEWS TRULY ARE GORGEOUS HERE – AND SO IS THE WINE.

Who even are you, in McLaren Vale, if your cellar door isn't set in an 1850s farmhouse? Samuel's Gorge is in on the trend, with a beautiful tasting room set in – you guessed it – a farm shed built in 1853. This one just happens to command panoramic views over Onkaparinga River National Park, and is the ideal place to kick back on a big leather couch or out on the patio and work your way through acclaimed winemaker Justin McNamee's range of truly excellent red wines (his Rhone-style Mosaic of Dreams grenache in particular is a cracker). Though winemaking here is a serious business, the cellar door is a friendly, chill place to hang out and enjoy.

gorge.com.au

SC PANNELL (14)

ONE OF MCLAREN VALE'S TRUE LEADERS. PUT THIS PLACE ON YOUR ITINERARY.

It essentially doesn't matter what you choose to try when you front up for a wine tasting at the SC Pannell cellar door: it's all sensational. Winemaker Stephen Pannell is doing everything right, from the super-cool labelling, which runs across three disparate brands, to the outrageously good wine – everything from a crisp fiano to a fruit-forward touriga nacional to some serious shiraz and grenache – to the charm of his 'enoteca', or cellar door, which features pop-up restaurants by some of Adelaide's biggest names, as well as tastings of the kick-ass product. Trust me: you want to visit.

pannell.com.au

SERAFINO (15)

WITH FOOD, WINE AND ACCOMMODATION, THERE'S NO NEED TO LEAVE.

You can do everything at Serafino: eat, drink, sleep, play, host a conference, get married ... whatever takes your fancy. This sprawling complex is a truly beautiful, peaceful place to spend time, surrounded by towering 200-year-old gum trees, with plenty of lawn space overlooking the lake and the vines. Stroll around and you'll find a spacious tasting room with a wide verandah to sip and snack, a restaurant serving Italian-leaning cuisine, a conference centre and wedding venue, and even a 30-room four-star hotel. The team can organise a whole range of experiences, from private VIP tastings, to scenic helicopter tours, to tours of the winery, to 'wedding proposal' packages. And happily, the wine is also very good.

serafinowines.com.au

SHIFTY LIZARD BREWING CO. (16)

MCLAREN VALE'S FIRST 'BREWSTILLERY' IS THE GO-TO DESTINATION FOR BEER AND GIN LOVERS.

According to the Shifty Lizard guys – who don't take things too seriously – their Willunga venue, in the heart of McLaren Vale, is the region's first 'brewstillery'. That's because they're not only brewing excellent craft beer, but they've now got their own gin, too, called Soul Bird. The brewstillery is set up as less of a tasting venue and more of a pub-cum-gin bar, a place to hang out and have a few drinks and something to eat – only, the few drinks are hand-crafted IPAs, stouts and session ales, and the something to eat is a dude-food-heavy collection of hot dogs, loaded fries and chicken wings. Everybody wins – except, maybe, those on a diet.

shiftylizard.com

Top Serafino *Opposite* Shiraz at Samuel's Gorge

STAR OF GREECE ⑰
PORT WILLUNGA DINING INSTITUTION CONNECTS THE VINES WITH THE OCEAN.

It can be easy to forget, as you stare at the hilltops and bury your nose in a wine glass, that McLaren Vale is a coastal region, and the salty goodness of the ocean is never too far away. Star of Greece, a well-loved institution in Port Willunga, makes the most of some cracking ocean views, paired with a menu that draws plenty of its ingredients from that self-same marine expanse. You'll find King George whiting, Kangaroo Island squid, ocean trout, gulf prawns and much more here: elegant cuisine served up in a friendly coastal chic dining room that keeps most of the formalities at bay. There's a casual kiosk too, for those who'd prefer fish and chips to eat down on the beach.

starofgreece.com.au

SWELL TAPHOUSE ⑱
RIDE THE CRAFT BREWERY WAVE TO THIS EASYGOING PUB AND EATERY.

Swell is a passion project for Dan Wright, who spends most of his time growing grapes for some of South Australia's biggest wine producers, and is married to Corrina Wright, winemaker for Oliver's (*see* p.171). The pair love wine, but they also love beer, and they love to surf, which is where Swell – the brewery, and the name – comes from. Wright brews a core range of tasty, easy-drinking beers, golden ales, pale ales, lagers and an IPA. Essentially, the perfect beverage to crack after a few hours in the surf. There's food here at the brewery too: burgers, salads and light snacks, and a beautiful lawn on which to enjoy it all.

swellbeer.com.au

WIRRA WIRRA

COME FOR THE FAMOUS 'CHURCH BLOCK' RED, STAY FOR THE FRIENDLY ATMOSPHERE.

Wirra Wirra is a McLaren Vale icon, having been producing high-quality reds – and these days, also whites – since 1894. The winery is probably best known for its Church Block McLaren Vale blend, though settle in for a tasting here and you'll have a choice of more than 20 different wines made with grapes sourced both locally and in the Adelaide Hills. Despite the pedigree, most of the wines are accessibly priced, and Wirra Wirra's all-seated cellar door is a cosy, welcoming space. There's a cafe, Harry's Deli, serving casual meals in the old cellar door area, plus plenty of space outside for kids to run around.

wirrawirra.com

YANGARRA ESTATE

BRING A PICNIC AND SETTLE IN FOR SOME BEAUTIFUL RHONE-STYLE WINES.

Though the countryside around Yangarra Estate is distinctly South Australian, the style of wine produced here hails from the Southern Rhone: grenache, shiraz, mourvedre, cinsaut, roussanne, viognier. The biodynamic wines produced at Yangarra using those grapes are also top-shelf, some of the best in McLaren Vale, and indeed in all of Australia, making a visit here a very good idea if you're chasing excellent wine. Tasting flights at the cellar door range from standard, entry-level tastings, to samples of Yangarra's premium single-block range. Visitors are welcome to bring their own food, though only to consume on the lawn, rather than in the cellar door itself – the Yangarra team have picnic blankets on hand.

yangarra.com

THE VINEYARD RETREAT

SPEND YOUR NIGHTS AMONG THE VINES AT THESE SELF-CONTAINED VILLAS.

Though it's easy enough to stay in Adelaide and just commute down to McLaren Vale for the day, nothing really beats spending your nights among the vines, particularly when the accommodation is as stylish as this. The Vineyard offers six self-contained guesthouses, each with private decks overlooking the valley and vines. Those guesthouses include two studio suites, two one-bedders, and another two two-bedroom retreats. There's a concierge service so you can enjoy tours and other experiences in the region.

thevineyardmv.com.au

Top Star of Greece

The Perfect Day
MCLAREN VALE

11AM BEKKERS

Begin with a tasting of the high-quality wines at Bekkers (see p.169). If you're driving down from Adelaide, this is one of the first wineries you will hit.

12PM D'ARENBERG

Get your camera out for a stop at the famous d'Arenberg Cube (see p.170). There's time here for a tasting, a wander through the cube, then lunch at the restaurant on-site.

2PM SC PANNELL

Prepare to be blown away during a tasting of the SC Pannell (see p.173) wines at this vibey enoteca and cellar door.

3PM ALPHA BOX & DICE

Here's a McLaren Vale winemaker doing things a little differently, which makes Alpha Box & Dice (*see* p.168) the ideal venue to round out your day of wine tasting.

4PM GOODIESON BREWERY

Grab a pint or a tasting paddle of Goodieson's (*see* p.170) excellent beer and relax on the terrace, the ideal spot to while away a sunny afternoon.

6PM STAR OF GREECE

Book yourself in for an early dinner at beachside Star of Greece (*see* p.174), where you'll be able to gaze over the ocean at sunset.

ADELAIDE HILLS

PERAMANGK AND KAURNA COUNTRY

Natural-wine fans, strap on your Tevas, and head on up to the Adelaide Hills, surely Australia's spiritual home of minimal-intervention grape-squeezing. If you like your skin-contact whites, your funky pet nats and your unfiltered reds, then this is the area for you, in particular the Basket Range sub-region, home to so many of the young natchie crew making a splash across Australia.

Despite its on-trend bona fides however, the Adelaide Hills also boasts a strong culture of traditional winemaking (though still with an innovative mindset), meaning there's happily a little something for pretty much everyone here. This region begins just 20min east of the Adelaide/Tarndanya CBD, making it incredibly accessible, and yet it maintains its air of isolation, so different is the climate and the culture after you've ascended those steep hills. It's easy enough to do the Adelaide Hills as a daytrip – or even a series of daytrips – from the city, given Adelaide itself is only half an hour away. However, if you're keen to spend the night, there are some excellent options.

There's plenty to discover here too, from the German village of Hahndorf, to the hip (and hippie) vibes of Summertown, to the distinctly British charm of Stirling. The landscape ranges from dense forest to open farmlands, with vines sprawled across rolling hills. The high altitude, however, means a break from all of those punchy red wines that South Australia is mostly known for, replaced instead by the lighter likes of pinot noir, sauvignon blanc and chardonnay. Plenty of cellar doors offer high-end experiences, though there are also quite a few, in keeping with the product, offering a more personal, low-fi experience, so take your pick.

The wine is in good company with the food, too: whether it's wood-fired pizza, charcuterie or Japanese cuisine that you're after, you'll find the perfect pairing when you head for the Hills.

AMBLESIDE DISTILLERS ①

STROLL AMONG THE BOTANICALS, AND THEN TASTE THE WAY THEY'VE BEEN UTILISED.

Pay attention as you wander through the garden on your way into the Ambleside tasting bar: plenty of the botanicals growing here are used to make Ambleside's range of gin. You might spot bay leaves, cloves, rhubarb, rosemary, thyme, and even jalapeños, all of which contribute to the distinctly local feel of the product here. You can enjoy those gins, and also a few liqueurs, out on the deck overlooking the towering gum trees that surround this Hahndorf distillery. Ambleside also offers gin blending masterclasses, which include the creation of your own gin from a choice of 22 distilled botanicals – be sure to book in advance. There's food served, too: share plates of delicious produce, plus the odd sarnie.

amblesidedistillers.com

ASHTON HILLS VINEYARD ②

PINOT NOIR SPECIALISTS OFFER A TRANQUIL, FRIENDLY TASTING EXPERIENCE.

If you love pinot noir, you are going to swoon when you get to Ashton Hills, just a 20min drive up from Adelaide. This winery is well known as making the best pinot noir in the Adelaide Hills – up there with the finest in Australia – and a visit to the tranquil cellar door means the chance to sample it. At around $40, it's a bargain for a wine of this quality, though don't forget the rest of the range. Leave yourself plenty of time to hang out on the deck and enjoy the view.

ashtonhills.com.au

Opposite The Lane Vineyard

HAHNDORF HILL ③

LEARN ABOUT AUSTRIAN GRAPE VARIETIES IN THE BEST WAY POSSIBLE: BY TASTING THEM.

Hahndorf Hill specialises in a grape you may not be particularly familiar with, though will very soon come to love: grüner veltliner. This is an Austrian variety, a white grape offering plenty of minerality and complexity, which Hahndorf Hill pioneered in Australia – and they continue to make the country's finest. There's an obsession with Austrian grapes here, in fact, with blaufränkisch, zweigelt and St Laurent also planted. If that's all unfamiliar to you, fear not: visit the Hahndorf Hill cellar door, a sprawling building with beautiful views over vines and hills, and let the team familiarise you with all of these excellent wines. There's a restaurant too, so it's well worth making an afternoon of it.

hahndorfhillwinery.com.au

JAUMA ORGANIC ④

TRAILBLAZERS FOR THE LO-FI WINE SCENE KEEP THINGS SIMPLE AND NATURAL.

James Erskine and Fiona Wood are emblematic of the natural wine movement in the Adelaide Hills' Basket Range, deeply passionate lo-fi winemakers who use organically grown grapes, and only organically grown grapes – no preservatives, no additives – to make a unique set of wines. They won't be to everyone's taste, but they will make you question the winemaking process, and force you to learn more about how it's done and why there's reason to change. Visits to the Jauma farm are limited, so email well ahead (jaumawine@gmail.com) to see if you can get in. Erskine and Wood also host regular events on the farm, not to mention weekly yoga classes and seasonal retreats. If it all sounds wildly hippie, yeah, it is. But that's kind of the point.

jauma.com

KOERNER WINE ⑤

BROTHERS USE RARE GRAPE VARIETIES TO CREATE SOMETHING AMAZING.

Here's another winery that leans towards the natural side of things, though in a way that's a little more approachable and commercial than the hardcore lo-fi crew. Koerner is run by brothers Damon and Jono, and though much of the operation is based in the Clare Valley (*see* p.189), their main cellar door is in Lenswood, in the Adelaide Hills. Here you'll be able to sample the brothers' minimal intervention approach to winemaking, where everything is light and fresh and textural, from the Adelaide Hills chardonnay and pinot noir made under their LEKO label, to the predominantly Italian varietals grown in the Clare, the likes of sangiovese, mammalo and sciacarello. It's all a little different, but it's also damned tasty.

koernerwine.com.au

Hahndorf Hill *Opposite* The Lane Vineyard

THE LANE VINEYARD

INDULGE IN A UNIQUE EXPERIENCE AT ONE OF THE HILLS' MOST INNOVATIVE WINERIES.

The Lane Vineyard is all about experiences: unique, enjoyable, interesting experiences. Of course, there's wine to taste here and food to eat, but if you want to kick things up a notch and do something totally different, this is the spot to do it, particularly if you're travelling with a group. Hire out The Boatshed and have a picnic, drink some wine and whack golf balls into the lake. Learn to blend your own wine with one of the cellar door team. Dine at the Chef's Table, a special experience at The Lane's on-site restaurant. Whip out every credit card you own and fly by helicopter from Adelaide to the winery, via a stop to see lions at Monarto Zoo. Or perhaps best of all, indulge in the Panorama Picnic Experience, a private luxury meal in an incredible venue that I won't spoil by giving away too much detail. Just know this: the food and wine is truly high-end, but the view is even better.

thelane.com.au

LOBETHAL BIERHAUS

MIDDLE EASTERN FOOD MEETS MODERN BEER HALL – AND IT'S A PERFECT FIT.

There's a strong German history in the Adelaide Hills, and it's celebrated via a few frosty brews at Lobethal Bierhaus, a German-style beer hall and garden in the town of the same name. The brews here aren't strictly Teutonic, with pale ales, IPAs and stouts getting a good run, and the food at the restaurant also strays from the norm, with a distinct Middle Eastern influence and plenty of great vegetarian and vegan options – but that's a good thing. This is an independent, family-owned operation that marches to the beat of its own drum, and it's also a friendly, welcoming spot for a cleansing ale.

bierhaus.com.au

LOST IN A FOREST

PAIR BEAUTIFUL WINES FROM OCHOTA BARRELS WITH WOOD-FIRED PIZZAS IN AN OLD CHURCH.

This slightly ramshackle eatery, set in an old church in small-town Uraidla, serves two purposes: it's a restaurant, specialising in wood-fired pizzas, but it's also a cellar door for Ochota Barrels, a cult wine producer based close by. Though the pizzas here are great, as long as you don't mind a few experimental topping choices, the real attraction is the wine, which is some of the best in the Hills, and pretty hard to get hold of. Amber Ochota takes a minimal intervention approach, producing wine that is delicate, floral, textural and beautiful. And if you're a fan of punk and hardcore music, the names on the labels will be very familiar. Beer lovers, meanwhile, try a few ales from Uraidla Brewery next door, also served at Lost in a Forest.

lostinaforest.com.au

LOT.100 ⑨

SMALL-BATCH PRODUCERS MEET UNDER ONE ROOF, WITH CLASSY FOOD AS WELL.

Fans of craft beer and local spirits, this is your one-stop shop in the Adelaide Hills. Lot.100 is a collective of several small-batch operations – Hills Cider, Mismatch Brewing Co., Vinteloper wine, 78 Degrees Distillery, and Ashton Valley Fresh that makes juice – along with a paddock-to-plate restaurant, all under one roof. Make a booking here, sitting either outside in the sprawling garden space, or inside the big shed on rainy days, and you can choose your own adventure. Grab a tasting paddle of beers or spirits, eat wood-fired pizzas, or go the whole hog with a tasting menu at the restaurant, paired with a selection of drinks that covers the full gamut of the Lot.100 collective.

lot100.com.au

MURDOCH HILL ⑩

ONE OF THE HILLS' RISING STARS DELIVERS ON QUALITY IN LOW-KEY SURROUNDS.

Wine freaks, get yourself over to Murdoch Hill and prepare to be impressed. Michael Downer is a talented young winemaker who is doing amazing things on his family's Oakbank farm, producing minimal-intervention wines – wild ferment, few additives – that truly sing. The Murdoch Hill cellar door is a pretty modest affair, a small room with a pleasant balcony overlooking the vines, and the service is similarly low-key. You're here for delicious wine, and that is what you'll get. Keep an eye out for the Rocket chardonnay, which sells out quickly; otherwise, Murdoch Hill's pinot meunier and pinot noir are also sensational.

murdochhill.com.au

Right Lot.100

NGERINGA (11)

IT'S ALL ABOUT CYCLES OF THE MOON AT THIS PIONEERING BIODYNAMIC WINERY.

It's very hard to escape the feeling of goodness at Ngeringa, the beautiful wholesomeness, the idea that good people here are doing good things, and you're just privileged to be able to briefly come along for the ride. Erinn and Janet Klein are passionate winemakers who met at university way back in 2000 and soon discovered a shared love for wine, and for the world. Their winery, Ngeringa, is the product of many years of research and learning about how to grow grapes in harmony with the land. They're certified biodynamic winemakers (*see* boxed text for an explanation) and pioneers of the art in Australia. Everything they do here is organic, part of the Earth, good for the Earth. And the wine is amazing. Meet Erinn and Janet at the Ngeringa cellar door – by appointment only – and you can sample the sort of syrah, chardonnay and pinot noir (and even olive oil) that should make everyone realise the right way to do things.

ngeringa.com

PETALUMA (12)

TASTE THE BEST GRAPES FROM THE BEST REGIONS, PAIRED WITH A LITTLE CHARCUTERIE.

Petaluma is one of the Adelaide Hills' big guns, a large operation that nevertheless delivers on quality, and a tasting here will take you on a journey around South Australia: Petaluma's chardonnay is from the Adelaide Hills, its riesling from the Clare Valley, and its cabernet from Coonawarra. The best of all worlds, essentially. All wine is made on-site and available at the cellar door, in flights that can be sparkling-only, focused on various regions, or devoted entirely to Petaluma's top-tier Yellow Label wines. There are seasonal charcuterie and cheese platters too, to keep the hunger at bay, and wine can be purchased by the glass or bottle.

petaluma.com.au

What's the deal with biodynamic wine?

Biodynamic winemaking is a fascinating idea, a spiritual, ethical and ecological way of farming and creating. It's a holistic approach to winemaking in particular, that views everything in the world and indeed the universe as interconnected; the harmony of that system means using natural materials only for both farming and winemaking, no chemicals, plus planning everything around cycles of the moon.

One of the keys to biodynamic farming is the idea of different 'days'. There are four days on the biodynamic calendar, related to the position of the moon in the sky: root days, flower days, fruit days and leaf days. The way farmers and winemakers work is decided by the type of day it is: you water vines on leaf days; prune those vines on root days; harvest grapes on fruit days; and don't touch anything on flower days.

This system doesn't end at the winery, either. Biodynamic believers say your experience of drinking wine also changes depending on what sort of day it is. Fruit days are the best for drinking, when wine will taste its fullest and richest. Leaf days and flower days are both reasonably good, though wine could taste less sweet on a leaf day. Root days, however, are the worst. Don't crack that expensive bottle of biodynamic wine you've been saving up if it happens to be a root day.

The big question, of course, is does this stuff actually work? Is it real? If you're interested, buy a biodynamic calendar (and a few bottles of wine), and decide for yourself.

SHAW + SMITH (14)

ICONIC HILLS PRODUCER IS CRACKING OPEN THE TOP-SHELF DROPS.

Winery names in the Adelaide Hills don't get much bigger than Shaw + Smith – this place is an icon, and its M3 Chardonnay can lay claim to being one of Australia's finest, particularly given it comes in at around the $50 mark. Shaw + Smith produces exclusively cold-climate wines, the likes of shiraz, sauvignon blanc and pinot noir, with prices from around $30 a bottle up. Tastings at the modern, expansive cellar door are priced accordingly, beginning at $25 per person for a basic flight of five wines and going up to $45 if you're after single-vineyard drops paired with a plate of tasty artisanal treats. Worth splashing out for.

shawandsmith.com

PRANCING PONY BREWERY (13)

BEER AND FRIED FOOD – IF IT AIN'T BROKE, DON'T FIX IT.

Here's a local success story you can get behind: Prancing Pony, once a passion project that operated out of a garden shed, these days a serious craft brewery with a big restaurant and tasting room in Totness, near Mount Barker. The food, unsurprisingly, is basically 'stuff that tastes good with beer': fried chicken, schnitties, burgers, pizzas. Can't go wrong. The beer, meanwhile, is the stuff of legend, a range of lovingly crafted brews made with minimum nasties, the likes of IPAs, XPAs, amber ales, Indian red ales and more. The hardest part is choosing what to drink.

prancingponybrewery.com.au

SIMON TOLLEY WINES (15)

THIS SPRAWLING COUNTRY HOME COULD BE ALL YOURS – AT LEAST FOR A NIGHT OR TWO.

If you want to base yourself in the Hills, rather than do daytrips from Adelaide, the Lodge at Simon Tolley Wines in Woodside, in the region's east, is a standout. This newly renovated, five-bedroom home is set among 32 acres of functioning vineyard, with a full kitchen, two separate living areas, and a wooden deck overlooking the vines; the perfect place for a lazy lunch with a few bottles of wine. Source those wines – chardonnay, pinot, shiraz, sav blanc, made by a fifth-gen vigneron – from the Simon Tolley cellar door, just a grape's throw away.

simontolley.com.au

Top Shaw + Smith

THE SUMMERTOWN ARISTOLOGIST

FORWARD-THINKING EATERY OFFERS THE PERFECT GATHERING POINT FOR LOCAL WINEMAKERS.

What are the cool kids of the Adelaide Hills up to right now? Find out with a visit to the Summertown Aristologist, a restaurant, wine bar and bottle shop in arty, alternative Summertown. The Aristologist represents a collective of small-batch natural winemakers from the local area – Lucy M, Commune of Buttons, Chateau Comme Ci Comme Ca and more – whose experimental drops are matched with a compact menu of high-quality, ethically sourced food, such as parsnip with taramasalata, zucchini with sunflower miso, or pork sausage with leek and wild plum. Natural wine enthusiasts will be in heaven, of course, though there's also cider, beer and vermouth.

thesummertownaristologist.com

TAPANAPPA

TAKE THE OPPORTUNITY TO SAMPLE SOME OF SA'S FINEST, AT A REASONABLE PRICE.

There are three vineyards in the Tapanappa empire, three 'distinguished sites', according to fabled winemaker Brian Croser. These sites – The Tiers in Adelaide Hills, Foggy Hill on the Fleurieu Peninsula, and The Whalebone in Coonawarra – are utilised at Tapanappa to create a suite of high-end wines that range from chardonnay to pinot noir to cab sav. No bargains here, it's high-end wine with an appropriate price tag, but that doesn't mean you can't pop past the airy, spacious cellar door in the Piccadilly Valley, in the west of the Adelaide Hills, for a tasting flight. Experiences begin at $20 per person, which is a bargain when the wine is this good.

tapanappa.com.au

UNICO ZELO

INDULGE IN LO-FI WINE, GREAT GIN AND FANCY SNACKS, ALL IN GOOD COMPANY.

This combined cellar door, distillery and eatery is basically everything that's good about the Adelaide Hills, and all under one roof. You have a cracking range of low-fi wines: creative, experimental and, above all, extremely drinkable. You have top-quality gins that have a unique sense of place, thanks to their use of native and indigenous ingredients. You have a bar and kitchen serving cocktails, wine and fancy snacks like katsu sandos and karaage chicken bites. And you have the knowledge that this whole operation is run by two passionate locals, Brendan and Laura Carter. Can't go wrong.

unicozelo.com.au

YUKI IN THE HILLS

FROM SUSHI TO SASHIMI, GYOZA TO KARAAGE – THIS IS JAPAN ON A PLATE.

Yuki in the Hills is different. No Mod-Oz tasting menus. No dude food. No cheese platters. No artisanal charcuterie. Not that there's anything wrong with any of those things, but sometimes you need a change-up, and Yuki has you covered. This is a Japanese restaurant, as dedicated as they get, with a menu that spans all the favourites of the Land of the Rising Sun, from sushi to sashimi, gyoza to karaage, udon to ramen. If you love the food of Japan, you will find what you're looking for here. It's all served in a pleasant space with wide banquette seating in downtown Aldgate, and popular with locals and visitors alike.

yukiinthehills.com

The Perfect Day
ADELAIDE HILLS

South Australia

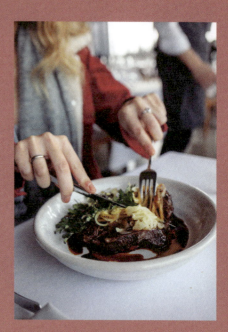

10AM MURDOCH HILL

Begin with a drive over to the west of the region to sample Michael Downer's sensational wine (see p.182), while gazing out over the vines.

11.30AM LOT.100

Make the short journey from Murdoch Hill over to Lot.100 (see p.182), where the boozy world is your oyster: taste some beer, drink some gin, have a pizza, or go the whole hog with a lunchtime tasting menu.

1.30PM THE LANE VINEYARD

Enjoy the beautiful scenery and maybe even treat yourself to a premium experience at one of the Hills' best wineries (see p.181) - oh, and grab lunch too.

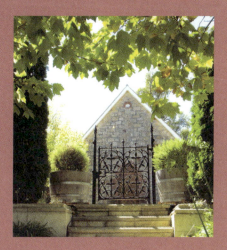

3PM SHAW + SMITH

Head on over to the Adelaide Hills classic, Shaw + Smith (see p.184), for a sample of some seriously good wine with a view.

5PM THE SUMMERTOWN ARISTOLOGIST

As the day winds towards its conclusion, head to Summertown for a few snacks at trendy Summertown Aristologist (see p.185), with a sample of the Hills' natural wine scene to pair with them.

7PM LOST IN A FOREST

Finish your day nearby at this ramshackle eatery (see p.181), with tasty wood-fired pizzas and the full list of sought-after Ochota Barrels wines there for the sampling.

Jim Barry Wines

CLARE VALLEY

NGADJURI AND KAURNA COUNTRY

Just try not to fall in love with the Clare Valley. Just try. You'll fail, I guarantee it. This is such a lovely place, with a small town (called Clare) filled with friendly people, a charming area of rolling, tree-lined hills and sweeping gullies, where life is slow and the wine glasses are full. The Clare Valley is a largely agricultural community, a typical regional centre in many ways that also happens to produce some of the best riesling – among other wines – in Australia.

The Clare is the ideal alternative for those who want to escape the big-name companies and the weekend crowds of the likes of the Barossa and McLaren Vale. It's a 2hr drive to get here from Adelaide/Tarndanya – not a lot in the grand scheme of things, but still enough to discourage many daytrippers and to ensure that those who are in the Clare really want to be in the Clare.

Most of the cellar doors are modest in size, though big on quality. There are several excellent eateries, great country pubs, a couple of breweries, and even a distillery. The Clare is also perfectly set up for cycling, with plenty of dedicated trails to ride, including the famed Riesling Trail, many of which call past the area's best cellar doors. This is a region worth making a weekend of, at the very least. Some people end up staying a lifetime.

CLARE VALLEY DISTILLERY 1

LOCAL IDENTITIES NOTICED A GAP IN THE MARKET, AND FILLED IT WITH GIN.

This boutique operation is the passion project of Guy Parkinson, owner of Seed restaurant (*see* p.194), along with a few other friends, who noticed the absence of a local gin in the Clare Valley, and decided to create their own. The result is the Clare Valley Distillery, which produces two gins under the Seed label: Seed Classic Dry Gin, and Seed Melva Riesling Gin. In keeping with the general Clare vibe, their new cellar door is a relaxed space where visitors can try the gin of their choice – either neat, on ice or with tonic – alongside a few tasty nibbles.

clarevalleydistillery.com.au

GROSSET 2

POWERHOUSE RIESLING PRODUCER FLINGS THE DOORS OPEN, BUT ONLY FOR SHORT SEASONS.

Grosset is probably the foremost producer of riesling in Australia but, still, I need to give you a warning: the cellar door here is generally only open during spring, when the latest vintage of the winery's rieslings are released. It also opens for a few weeks in autumn (around Easter) to sell chardonnay and a few red varietals. Any other time, you will find the doors here sadly closed. That said, it's an absolute joy to visit Grosset if you arrive at the right time. This is a no-frills experience that is all about the wines, particularly the four much-sought-after single-vineyard rieslings.

grosset.com.au

Opposite Jim Barry Wines

JIM BARRY WINES
FAMILY BUSINESS IS STILL GOING STRONG AT THE NORTHERN END OF THE VALLEY.

There are three generations of Barrys now who have toiled away on the family vineyard, starting from Jim back in 1959, moving to his son Peter, and finally to Peter's children, Tom and Sam. There's a good chance you'll catch the latter pair wandering around the friendly Jim Barry cellar door up at the northern end of the Clare. Here, grab a sample of some of the winery's excellent riesling, as well as Australia's first assyrtiko (a white grape native to Greece), plus a surprisingly broad – for the Clare, at least – selection of reds. True fans can opt to lay down $100 for the Collector Tasting, working through several back vintages of Jim Barry's premium shiraz in a private tasting room.

jimbarry.com

KILIKANOON
TAKE A BREAK FROM PEDDLING TO SAMPLE SOME SERIOUSLY GOOD SHIRAZ.

Kilikanoon has vineyards all the way up the Clare Valley, from Leasingham in the south to Clare in the north, which means the wine you drink here is the perfect expression of the region. The winery's cellar door, about halfway between Watervale and Sevenhill, is also very close to the 33km Riesling Trail, the Clare's most popular cycling route, making this an ideal stop-off place during a day of peddling. Call in to try some of the Clare's best wine, particularly the riesling and shiraz, though Kilikanoon's cab sav is also highly rated. There are a range of experiences to choose from at the winery, from a simple $10 tasting of four wines, to a private, premium tasting for $60, which includes a sample of Kilikanoon's Revelation shiraz, which goes for a lazy $550 a bottle.

kilikanoon.com.au

KNAPPSTEIN ENTERPRISE WINERY ⑤

HERITAGE-LISTED BUILDING NOW HOSTS ONE OF THE CLARE'S BEST CELLAR DOORS.

You don't have to travel far to visit the Knappstein cellar door: it's right in the middle of Clare town, set in the 19th-century Enterprise Brewery building, which is now heritage-listed. It's the perfect spot to grab a comfy banquette and work your way through the impressive Knappstein range, which leans heavily towards riesling and shiraz, though keep your eye out for the malbec and the rosé. Knappstein offers several focused tasting experiences, for those who know what they like: the Single Vineyard tasting, the Riesling Flight, and the Red Wine Flight.

knappstein.com.au

KOERNER WINE ⑥

VALLEY STALWART OFFERS PRIVATE TASTINGS OF ITS LO-FI PRODUCT.

Koerner is a Clare Valley brand making waves among lovers of minimal-intervention winemaking; however, the winery's main tasting room is in the Adelaide Hills, so flick to p.180 for more information. Private tastings are available here in the Clare Valley, though you will have to book ahead.

koernerwine.com.au

Knappstein Enterprise Winery *Opposite* Pikes

MOUNT HORROCKS (7)

RIESLING SPECIALIST SERVES UP TASTINGS IN AN OLD RAILWAY STATION.

Stephanie Toole doesn't make much wine. One of the Clare's best-known producers limits herself to just 2500 cases per year at Mount Horrocks, which means you're getting quality over quantity. Toole's cellar door is set in the old Auburn railway station, a beautiful venue for beautiful wine, with spots to sit both inside and out on the old platform. Stop in for samples of her organic riesling, semillon, rosé, cab sav, shiraz and nero d'avola. It's the riesling that's the real star here – even if you think you're not a fan of the varietal, there's a good chance you'll walk away with at least a few bottles. The cellar door is only open on weekends and public holidays, so be sure to plan accordingly.

mounthorrocks.com

O'LEARY WALKER WINES (8)

GREAT FOOD AND EVEN BETTER WINE AT THIS SPACIOUS, AIRY CELLAR DOOR.

This is one of the bigger cellar doors in the Clare, and as such has plenty to offer visitors, from standard wine tastings, to grazing platters to enjoy outside, and full meals at the excellent restaurant. The labels on O'Leary Walker wines tell you all you need to know about the operation: a large stripe down the middle, O'Leary on one side, Walker on the other. That's the two owners and experienced winemakers David O'Leary and Nick Walker, who each bring their own approach to the operation. Together, they come up with some very good wine. The restaurant offers perfect seasonal dishes to pair with a riesling or shiraz, with a Mod-Oz-meets-dude-food menu that takes inspiration from around the world.

olearywalkerwines.com

PIKES (9)

SETTLE IN FOR A WHOLE DAY, WITH FOOD, WINE, BEER – AND A WEDDING VENUE.

Pikes is your one-stop shop for Clare goodness. There's a winery here, plus a micro-brewery, a restaurant, and extensive grounds on which to wander and enjoy. The Pikes' cellar door offers great value for money, with plenty of the winery's best bottles coming in under $30. After a tasting, head over to the beer garden for a pilsner or pale ale, while the kids run around. Follow it up with lunch at Slate restaurant, which does a la carte or set-menus of Mod-Oz food, featuring fruits and vegetables from the Pikes' garden. There's a wedding venue here too – many a celebration has been planned over a glass of riesling at Pikes.

pikeswines.com.au

Clare Valley

SEED ⑩

FROM CASUAL TO FINE-DINING TO ARTISANAL SMALLGOODS, ALL UNDER ONE ROOF.

Being a small town, Clare doesn't have a huge number of options for those hoping for a fancy meal – however, when you've got Seed, you don't need any other choices. Seed is the sort of eatery that would sit comfortably on a busy street in Adelaide or even Melbourne; the fact it's in friendly Clare makes it even better. There's a fair bit going on here, from a deli featuring artisanal smallgoods – some local, some imported from far away – to a casual rooftop space for cocktails, beers and wood-fired pizzas, and finally a bistro, a relaxed though upmarket space serving seriously good food. If you can go past the duck paté choux bun with maraschino cherry, you're a stronger person than me.

seedclarevalley.com

SEVENHILL ⑪

FORMER JESUIT STRONGHOLD STILL PRODUCING SOME HEAVENLY WINE.

Few Australian wineries can claim the history that Sevenhill has. The winery was founded by a Jesuit priest – hence the name, in honour of Rome's seven hills – back in 1851, making it not only the oldest winery in the Clare Valley, but one of the oldest in Australia. You can take a self-guided tour here any time – cellar door staff will give you a map – calling past the old church, St Aloysius, the original underground cellar, and the old-vine vineyards. There are two tasting packages offered, basic and premium, plus platters of local smallgoods to enjoy with the wine.

sevenhill.com.au

SKILLOGALEE

TAKE A SEAT ON THE SHADY PATIO AND ENJOY SOME OF THE CLARE'S TASTIEST FOOD.

Though the Skillogalee team make some beautiful wine, it's the restaurant that tends to draw people in here, with its shady patio among the vines. The food is Italian leaning, with a few Mod-Oz touches: the likes of vitello tonnato, burrata, and pasta, alongside steak frites and barbecued spatchcock. There's morning and afternoon tea served, plus a kids' menu, which you can choose to enjoy on the old wooden verandah of an 1851 settlers' cottage, or out under the trees. Perfection. The cottage also houses the Skillogalee cellar door, where you can sample the winery's reds, whites, sparklings and fortifieds.

skillogalee.com.au

TAYLORS

FAMILY INSTITUTION OFFERS A HUGE RANGE OF WINES AND EXPERIENCES.

Taylors is a historic Clare winery, founded in the late 1960s and still family-owned. Don't take that to mean it's a small operation, however: this winery is the largest in the valley, with a portfolio of more than 20 different wines that run the full gamut of styles, varietals and price points. In other words, regardless of what you're into, you'll probably find something to suit at Taylors – they even do a great chardonnay, which is rare for this region. The cellar door offers a range of experiences, from straightforward tastings, to wine and chocolate matches, to samples of Taylors' premium wines, to space outside to hang out with a full glass of wine and a platter of local cheeses.

taylorswines.com.au

WINES BY KT

SMALL OUTFIT GOES BIG ON TASTE, WITH A FEW RARE VARIETIES IN THE MIX.

Winemaker Kerri Thompson – the eponymous KT – only opens her cellar door, on the main street in Auburn, for three days a week, which means if you call through there's a good chance you'll be chatting to Kerri herself. The whole Wines by KT operation is lo-fi and hands-on, run by a team of three, and the cellar door experience is charmingly personal. It's so relaxed, in fact, that it almost comes as a surprise to discover that KT is making some kick-ass wine, mostly riesling, but also some great Mediterranean red varietals.

winesbykt.com

Top Seed *Opposite* Overlooking Sevenhill

The Perfect Day
CLARE VALLEY

South Australia

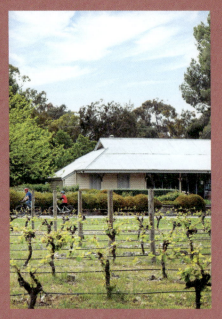
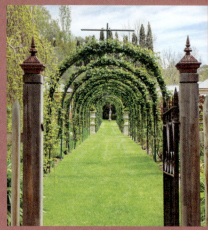

10AM MOUNT HORROCKS
Begin your day in the south of the Clare Valley, at the old Auburn railway station, which now houses the Mount Horrocks' cellar door (see p.193).

11.30AM SEVENHILL
Heading north, call into historic Sevenhill (see p.194) to tour the old cellar and check out the church, plus have a sample of the Jesuits' excellent wine.

1PM SKILLOGALEE
Lunch today is out on the shady patio at Skillogalee (see p.195), following - or followed by - another tasting at the cellar door.

3PM PIKES

Round out your wine touring close by at Pikes (see p.193), where there's also a beer garden, and plenty of outdoor space to relax.

7PM SEED

Depending on your mood, choose to eat dinner at Seed (see p.194), either at the casual rooftop bar – with wood-fired pizza – or the more upmarket bistro. Either way, begin with a G&T using Seed Gin.

BEST OF THE REST

Though the South Australian wine (and culinary) scene is best known for its heavy hitters – the big-name regions that feature in the preceding pages – there is also a host of smaller areas that are well worth a visit. You probably wouldn't plan a whole wine and food holiday around these places, though if you happen to be passing through or staying for a few days – they're pretty much all coastal and uniformly gorgeous – then you will want to make time for a little sipping and sampling.

ADELAIDE ZONE

KAURNA COUNTRY

How lucky is Adelaide/Tarndanya? Not only does the South Australian capital have an embarrassment of viticultural riches just outside its city limits, it also has wineries and cellar doors actually within its bounds. And one of those just happens to be among Australia's most famous.

PENFOLDS MAGILL ESTATE

AUSTRALIA'S MOST FAMOUS WINE HAS ITS HOME WITHIN THE ADELAIDE CITY LIMITS.

You could know almost nothing about wine in Australia and you would still have heard of Penfolds Grange. It's the wine you jokingly mention when you tell your mates you're going to pick out something fancy; it's the wine you bribe politicians with, as former NSW Premier Barry O'Farrell could attest. It's the pinnacle, in other words. And if you choose the Ultimate Penfolds Experience at Magill Estate, Penfolds Grange is on for tasting. That's just one of many incredible wine-related experiences on offer at this historic and impressive site: there are tours of the grounds and cellars, various levels of tasting experiences, casual meals at Magill Estate Kitchen, and fine-dining at Magill Estate Restaurant. This is as good as it gets, really – and it's only 8km from the Adelaide CBD.

penfolds.com

Penfolds wine *Opposite* Historic Bleasedale Vineyards

LANGHORNE CREEK

NGARRINDJERI COUNTRY

Here's another great - though small - wine region just an hour from Adelaide/Tarndanya's door: Langhorne Creek, to the south-east of the city, at the top of the Fleurieu Peninsula. It's a quiet, rural area that nevertheless has a long viticultural history and is home to a few cracking wineries, which specialise in punchy reds like cabernet sauvignon and shiraz.

BLEASDALE VINEYARDS

HISTORIC WINERY IS STILL MAKING SOME OF THE BEST REDS AROUND.

You want history? How about a 170-year-old winery, one that is still producing award-winning wines in a gorgeous location? Bleasdale is a breath of fresh air – literally, if you fill your lungs from that saline maritime breeze – with a no-frills cellar door that's open every day, offering free tastings for visitors (not many wineries left that are still doing that). Guests can take self-guided tours through the old winery, including the basket press, built in 1892; there are also guided tours of the vineyard and winery, and prestige wine flights available for those keen to get their hands on the good stuff.

bleasdale.com.au

LAKE BREEZE WINES

ICONIC WINERY ENCOURAGES VISITORS TO STAY AS LONG AS THEY LIKE – EVEN OVERNIGHT.

This Langhorne Creek winery punches well above its weight. Lake Breeze has had vineyards on the property since the 1880s, and even now is smashing it out of the park with a range of shiraz and cabernet that can compete with South Australia's finest. There's a heap to do on a visit here, including a relaxed tasting in the old limestone-shed-cum-cellar-door, as well as have lunch at the restaurant, grab a picnic to eat among the vines, or even stay over for a few nights in the bed and breakfast.

lakebreeze.com.au

SOUTHERN FLEURIEU/ KANGAROO ISLAND

KAURNA, PERAMANGK AND NGARRINDJERI COUNTRY

Here, again, is a region that's so close to Adelaide - just a little over an hour - that you could easily make a daytrip of it, if you so desired, and be back in time for dinner. However, there's plenty to encourage a few nights in the region, not least some excellent wineries and distilleries, and the chance to hop aboard the car ferry and head on over to Kangaroo Island, which is one of Australia's absolute gems. There's wildlife spotting, luxury lodge stays, great campgrounds, and beer. What more do you need?

CHARLOTTE DALTON WINES

LEADING LO-FI OUTFIT SHARES CELLAR DOOR SPACE WITH A HOST OF KINDRED SPIRITS.

Charlotte Hardy makes the sort of wines you will immediately fall in love with: unique, thoughtful wines, wines that mostly lean towards the minimal-intervention side of things, though done with skill and consideration – with some of the best label art around. Though Hardy sources her grapes mostly from the Adelaide Hills, her winery and cellar door can be found in an industrial area just outside sleepy Port Elliot on the Fleurieu Peninsula. It's a combined space with Cooke Brothers wines in an estate, called Factory 9, that also features a coffee shop, a pizzeria, a furniture designer and a few art studios. There's food available, plus local beers, and of course the excellent wine.

charlottedaltonwines.com.au

FLEURIEU DISTILLERY

NOTHING IS TAKEN TOO SERIOUSLY HERE, EXCEPT THE WHISKY.

Don't pay too much attention to the cheeky logo – Fleurieu Distillery is making serious whisky, whisky that benefits from the maritime climate of coastal Goolwa as it matures in wooden casks at the waterfront distillery. The end product is lightly peated, rich in colour and absolutely delicious. Call or email ahead to book a tasting and tour.

fleurieudistillery.com.au

THE ISLANDER ESTATE

THERE'S A FRENCH CONNECTION AT THIS HIGHLY RATED KANGAROO ISLAND WINERY.

The Islander is the best of a few different worlds: it's a Kangaroo Island winery that is very much of its place, though it's owned by Frenchman Jacques Lurton, from the famed Bordeaux region, which means you have some serious winemaking chops in a rustic Australian setting. Set in Cygnet River – an area that was hit hard by the bushfires of early 2020 – the Islander is a gorgeous spot, with a laidback cellar door offering tastings and platters of local food. If you're staying close by, the team can even organise a private tasting experience at your accommodation.

islanderestate.com

Top The Islander Estate *Opposite* Kangaroo Island Spirits

KANGAROO ISLAND SPIRITS

FAMED LOCAL DISTILLERY OFFERS A RANGE OF HANDS-ON EXPERIENCES.

A visit to KI Spirits is all about having a good time – the gin here is excellent, world-class in fact, but it's the experiences built around that gin that are the reason to put this place on your itinerary. The distillery is probably best known for its Blend Your Own Gin experience, a 2hr masterclass on coaxing the perfect flavour from juniper and botanicals. There's also a 2hr Cocktail Masterclass, in which you will be guided through the creation of three gin-based cocktails. For a less hands-on experience, simply book a table outside and work your way through a flight of gin tastings (or just have a cocktail).

kispirits.com.au

KANGAROO ISLAND BREWERY

ENJOY GOOD BREWS AND ENDLESS VIEWS AT THE PERFECT SUNNY-DAY LOCATION.

Okay, so no one is going too crazy naming their venues over on Kangaroo Island, but when you have this sort of brand recognition, why mess with it? The brewery that shares the island's name is set in a big shed near Kingscote, and it's a local favourite, with an easy-breezy food menu and some excellent brews. Call past here on a Friday night for pizzas, Saturday for burgers, or a platter during the week, and sample the team's range of ales, wheat beers and stouts. If the sun is shining, there are few better places to be.

kangarooislandbrewery.com.au

PAGO MIDDLETON

LUXE ACCOMMODATION CONNECTS GUESTS WITH LOCAL ARTISTS AND ARTISANS.

This dreamy four-room retreat in Middleton, on the Fleurieu Peninsula, is set in 1850s stables, converted with love into luxury accommodation by renowned winemaker Rose Kentish and her partner Sam Harrison. The rooms are stunning, with king beds, whitewash, natural tones and linen bedding. However, the real attraction is the opportunity to share experiences and learn from locals: the Pago team can introduce you to a First Nations Elder to learn more about the Traditional Owners of the Fleurieu region; a photographer to help you capture the area; a farmer to learn the art of organic growing; and even a knifemaker to make your own custom blade. The property is surrounded by great restaurants in Middleton and the broader region, too.

pagomiddleton.com.au

MOUNT BENSON

BUNGANDIDJ COUNTRY

This is a tiny region, really, one of a group of six strung along the Limestone Coast that have plenty to offer those soaking up the sun and sand in the region. Beyond the beaches, there's one good reason to make sure you include a stop in Mount Benson: Cape Jaffa Wines.

CAPE JAFFA WINES

FAMILY OUTFIT DOES EVERYTHING WELL, FROM WINE TO FOOD TO BEER TO HOSPITALITY.

Cape Jaffa winemakers Anna and Derek Hooper are pioneers: they were the first to set up shop in the Mount Benson region, and they were the first – and still only – to go biodynamic. Their cellar door is a friendly space filled with a mix of locals and tourists, and their kids (there's a play area), and their dogs (friendly pooches are more than welcome). Anna and Derek pour a generous selection of their wines for tasting, plus offer platters of produce from their garden and other local growers, and the pair even brew beer, under the Loophole Brewing Co label, which is available to consume. Many a long afternoon has been whiled away at Cape Jaffa – there's a good chance one of yours will be, too.

capejaffawines.com

COONAWARRA

BUNGANDIDJ COUNTRY

Proudly labelling itself Australia's 'red centre' - get it? - the Coonawarra produces some of this country's best shiraz and cabernet sauvignon, with fine wineries in a distinctly rural setting close to the Victorian border. It is about a 4hr drive from Adelaide, or a 5hr drive from Melbourne, and though the sheer number of venues pales in comparison to somewhere like the Barossa or Yarra Valley, the Coonawarra is still home to a few Aussie icons, so well worth the journey to visit.

BRAND'S LAIRA

THE COONAWARRA ORIGINAL OFFERS SOME OF THE REGION'S BEST EXPERIENCES.

The Brand's Laira vineyard boasts the oldest vines in the Coonawarra, dating back to the late 1800s, when an English sea captain decided to become one of the original 'tree changers' and plant some grapevines. And they're still producing fruit today. Some of it goes into Brand's Laira's award-winning shiraz, though the company now produces a wide range of wines, from flagship cabernet to more affordable entry-level reds, plus a healthy selection of whites and rosés. The cellar door here oozes history, though it's been recently refurbished and offers a great range of experiences, from simple tastings to tours of the vines, to a 'Blend your own wine' experience, after which you'll walk away with your own unique bottle. There's a simple menu of platters and salads available too.

brandslaira.com

RAIDIS ESTATE

SAY 'YASSOU' TO A SURPRISING LO-FI STAR IN THE HEART OF THE REGION.

Most wine in the Coonawarra is pretty classic, pretty traditional. And then, there's Raidis Estate. Steve and Emma Raidis inherited the family farm from Steve's Greek-migrant parents, they planted vines and started making distinctly modern, minimal-intervention wines, and they're smashing it out of the park. There's cabernet sauvignon and shiraz here, of course, but also chardonnay, sauvignon blanc, pinot gris and more, all treated with skill and care. Call in for the full Greek experience: a huge platter of local produce, some great wine and good people to share it with.

raidis.com.au

WYNNS COONAWARRA ESTATE

THE TRUE LEGEND OF THE COONAWARRA SCENE IS A MUST FOR VISITORS.

This is the undisputed icon of the Coonawarra wine scene: Wynns, owner of the oldest cabernet vines in the region, producer of wines you've seen on a million bottle shop shelves during your lifetime, the classic for a reason, now under the guidance of winemaker Sue Hodder. You can't miss a visit here, at the historic cellar door, to taste the wines, of course, though you can also make your own blend – using shiraz, cabernet and merlot – or try the Wynns Ultimate Experience, which includes an extensive tasting of premium wines, as well as the chance to blend your own.

wynns.com.au

YALUMBA MENZIES RETREAT

ACCOMMODATION WITH WINE IN ITS SOUL MAKES THE PERFECT PLACE TO STAY.

The Yalumba empire has its traditional home in the Barossa (*see* p.163); however, its Menzies Retreat is well worth a few nights if you're staying in the Coonawarra. There's a 'wine room' here, for intimate tastings of Yalumba's Coonawarra products, but the real attraction is the gorgeous bungalow set among the cabernet vines, ideal for families or couples, offering a genuine slice of winery life. The bungalow has a fully equipped kitchen (with wine decanter and glasses), and dinners can be delivered from nearby Soul Projects restaurant.

yalumba.com

Top Brand's Laira

RIVERLAND

MERU COUNTRY

Continue on up the highway from the Barossa Valley, about another 2hr to the north-east, and you will eventually find yourself in Riverland, which, by tonnage produced, is actually Australia's largest wine region. Interesting, huh? The Mediterranean climate here, along the banks of the mighty Murray River, is perfect for cabernet sauvignon, shiraz and chardonnay, and plenty of the biggest names in Australian wine source fruit from Riverland. As a visitor, there are a few charming, smaller-scale cellar doors that shouldn't be missed.

23RD STREET DISTILLERY

HIGH-QUALITY GIN-MAKER TAKES THE REINS IN A HISTORIC RENMARK BUILDING.

The huge building on Twentythird St in Renmark has been home to some big players in the wine industry – Hardy's, Chateau Tanunda, Berri – though these days it's all about distilled spirit, thanks to the team at 23rd St Distillery. With the use of three beautiful old pot stills, the team is producing a great range of gins, whiskies, vodkas, brandies and even a rum. Though all are high quality, it's probably the gin that makes this venue a worthy stop on your Riverland exploration – the Red Citrus Gin, in particular, is a cracker. Do a tasting, take a behind-the-scenes tour, or take a gin-blending or cocktail-making masterclass.

23rdstreetdistillery.com.au

23rd Street Distillery *Opposite* Catch of the day at 919 Wines

919 WINES

TAKE IT EASY AT THIS FRIENDLY, FAMILY-RUN WINERY AND CELLAR DOOR.

You have to love a day out at 919, hosted by owners Eric and Jenny Semmler (who have their fair share of quirk), relaxing on the lawn, letting your four-legged friends roam free, allowing your two-legged offspring to eat ice-creams and enjoy themselves, feasting on a picnic you've brought along with you, and tasting the full 919 range, from fortifieds to organic reds and whites and more. This place is all about having a good time, and it delivers.

919wines.com.au

WHISTLING KITE

RELAX ON THE BANKS OF THE MURRAY RIVER WITH SOME SERIOUSLY GOOD WINE.

If only every winery was like this. If only they all made biodynamic wine of this quality. If only you could taste those wines on the banks of the mighty Murray River, surrounded by trees and birds and wildlife, with a platter of local produce, listening to good music, enjoying the finer things in life. Whistling Kite offers this, all of this, and it's an absolute joy.

whistlingkitewines.com.au

Western Australia

This colossal state boasts one of Australia's premier wine regions in the Margaret River, plus a host of boutique producers of gourmet treats to discover and enjoy.

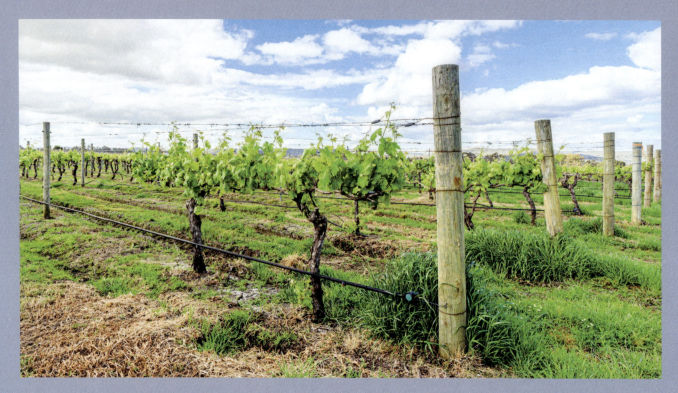

THE SWAN VALLEY AND THE PERTH HILLS

WHADJUK NOONGAR COUNTRY

You have to hope that the good people of Perth/Boorloo realise just how lucky they are. In the city's west you have perfect beach after perfect beach, these flawless patches of white sand lapped by the warm, turquoise waters of the Indian Ocean. We're talking Cottesloe, Scarborough, Trigg and Peasholm-Floreat. Some of the finest in Australia. And then you head north and east of Perth, just beyond the city limits, and you have not one but two wine regions – the gorgeous sun-bleached lands of the Swan Valley and the Perth Hills. You can reach either region in half an hour from the city centre. You can surf in the morning and have lunch at a winery by midday. Any day of the week. Amazing.

I've chosen to group these two regions together because they are so accessible, both from Perth and from each other, via a drive of about 45min through the city's east. Though geographically close, the valley and the hills are actually quite different regions for those who make wine. The Swan Valley, the oldest wine region in WA, with vines that date back to 1830, is north-east of the CBD, and enjoys a warm, Mediterranean climate that's ideal for the likes of chenin blanc, verdelho and cabernet sauvignon. In the long, languid Perth Hills region, a vast swathe of countryside to the city's east, the nights are cool, making the region more suited to chardonnay, cab sav and merlot.

The thing these two regions have in common is a passionate base of growers, makers and producers, both in terms of wine, but also beer and spirits, as well as numerous places for a sumptuous feast. It's not just grapes that grow well in the Perth Hills either – apples are another staple, and there are an increasing number of clever growers turning them into cider.

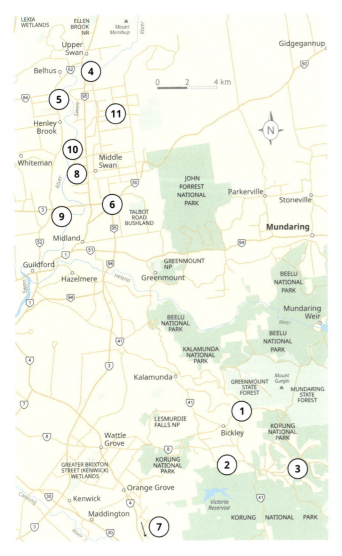

BROOKSIDE VINEYARD 1

BOUTIQUE OPERATION SERVES UP GREAT WINE AND LONG MEDITERRANEAN LUNCHES.

This cellar door in the Bickley Valley, just south-east of Kalamunda, has a rustic charm that personifies the valley: it's a boutique operation where everything is hands-on, the perfect place for everything from a quick tasting to a long lunch. The winery is probably best known for its chardonnay and cabernet sauvignon, either of which you will find a match for on the seasonal restaurant menu – a compact list of pan-Mediterranean options.

brooksidevineyard.com.au

CARMEL CIDER CO 2

FAMILY OUTFIT USES WINE-MAKING SENSIBILITY TO CREATE DELICIOUS CIDER.

The Carruthers family struck on the bright idea of turning their apples into cider and they've done a damn fine job of it too, which explains the happy crowds on weekends at the basic cellar door here, set in an old shed surrounded by apple pallets. Grab a tasting paddle to get a good introduction to the Carmel range: you'll find both apple and pear ciders produced in the Methode Traditionelle, the same process used to create the world's finest sparkling wines, and the attention to detail really shines through.

carmelcider.com.au

Opposite Swan Valley vines
Previous Domaine Naturaliste, Margaret River

The Swan Valley and The Perth Hills

CORE CIDER HOUSE ③

SERIOUS OPERATION PROVIDES SPACES AND ACTIVITIES FOR PRETTY MUCH EVERYONE.

Core is a schmick operation, a vast property deep in the east of the Perth Hills, and the perfect daytrip destination from the city. Stroll the grounds here, amid an 80-year-old orchard, and you'll find Orchard Bistro, a sit-down dining venue; Harvest Room, with its wide verandah, perfect for a cider-tasting before you tuck into some food; the Cider Garden, essentially a beer garden but for boozy apple juice, with plenty of room for kids to roam; and the Old Apple Shed, which does what it says on the box, though nowadays it also hosts live music, plus it functions as another bar space when it's raining outside. There's even accommodation, in the form of the Sundowner Cottage, a one-bedroom villa overlooking the orchard. There's a lot going on, clearly, and we haven't even mentioned the cider, which is delicious.

corecider.com.au

CORYMBIA ④

THOUGHTFUL WINES FROM A TALENTED COUPLE ARE ALL THE DRAW YOU NEED.

Take a close look at the label when you're sampling a Corymbia wine. The circular design looks a bit like a flower, and it's inspired by Marri trees – *corymbia calophylla* – an iconic WA species that grows in the Corymbia vineyards. There's more, however: each of the lines in that circular label represent actual climatic data from the vintage in the bottle, temperature and rainfall as compared to the average. All the information about that vintage, if you need it, is right there on the front of the bottle. It's a pretty natty idea, and indicative of the thoughtful, playful and skillful approach to winemaking from Genevieve Mann and her husband, Robert. The pair make sumptuous, small-batch chenin blanc, cabernet sauvignon and tempranillo, and it's well worth making an appointment to swing past the winery and give them a try.

corymbiawine.com.au

FUNK 2.0 ⑤

CIDERHOUSE OFFSHOOT BRINGS A TOUCH OF CLASS TO THE SWAN VALLEY.

Funk 2.0 is the work of Funk Cider, a ciderhouse that has its original base in Caversham, on the outer edge of Perth, but also runs this more attractive alternative in Henley Brook, in the Swan Valley. Funk 2.0 is a classy venue with plenty of space both outdoor and in, with views over grape vines, where diners can taste a range of ciders – some flavoured with other fruit, some sweet, some traditional European in style – plus try Funk's craft beer, and even find a few beer-cider hybrids. The food here ranges from tapas-sized plates of Mod-Oz cuisine, to standard individual meals, and big share platters of roast meats and trimmings. When the sun is out, there are few better venues.

funkcider.com.au

GARBIN ESTATE (6)

FAMILY-RUN WINERY KEEPS THINGS APPROACHABLE AND AFFORDABLE.

Garbin Estate has been producing wine since 1956, when Peter Garbin's parents, migrants from Croatia, bought a parcel of land in the Swan Valley and decided to try their luck with grape vines. They had some success and Peter continues that today, producing an approachable, affordable range of wines and, more importantly, a friendly, welcoming cellar door experience. For $15 you can work your way through the range of sparklings, whites and reds, plus have a cheese platter to share, and hang out for as long as you like in the big shed. There's a good chance one of the Garbins will be serving you, because that's just the sort of family place this is.

garbinestatewines.com.au

MILLBROOK WINERY (7)

THE UNDISPUTED LEADER OF PERTH HILLS' WINERIES DELIVERS AN AMAZING WINE AND DINING EXPERIENCE.

There aren't too many wineries in either of the Swan Valley or the Perth Hills producing truly high-quality wine that can hold its own against some of WA's better-known competitors – however, Millbrook is one of those places. Set in historic Jarrahdale, up in the hills, Millbrook has picked up a swag of awards in recent years not just for its wine – check out the chardonnay, viognier, and the sensational Pedro Ximenez sherry – but also for its cellar door, which is destination dining for Perth locals keen to get out for a day. Pay a visit and you'll understand why: this is a sprawling set-up in a stunning location, with a dedicated tasting room, as well as an acclaimed restaurant serving what is comfortably the best food in the Perth Hills. The ingredients are local and treated with skill, and they go perfectly with the long list of Millbrook wines, which includes a few back-vintage releases.

millbrook.wine

OAKOVER GROUNDS (8)

SPRAWLING SWAN VALLEY ESTABLISHMENT OFFERS A WHOLE DAY'S WORTH OF ATTRACTIONS.

There's all sorts going on at Oakover Grounds, in the heart of the Swan Valley – literally something to please just about everyone. First, this is a winery, obvious from all the vines, which have been here since the 1850s. There's a cellar door, offering tastings with a view, and a run through the extensive range with or without cheese to pair it with. But then go strolling around and see what takes your fancy: there's FiORi, an artisanal coffee roaster and cafe; the Smokehouse, serving smoked meats and pizzas to carry out onto the lawn by the lake; the Market Place, where there's local food to sample; Oakover Restaurant, doing breakfast and lunch on a verandah overlooking lake and vines; and the new Barrel Bar too. It's all family friendly, there are nostalgic games like totem tennis to play, water trikes you can test on the lake, and a playground, and it's all done very well.

oakovergrounds.com.au

Top Oakover Grounds *Opposite* Beer paddle from Funk 2.0

The Swan Valley and The Perth Hills

SANDALFORD WINERY (9)

ENJOY A LITTLE SLICE OF MARGARET RIVER – AS WELL AS GREAT FOOD – JUST OUTSIDE PERTH.

Admittedly, the best wines Sandalford makes don't actually come from the Swan Valley. Despite the headquarters being just outside Perth, Sandalford has extensive vineyards in Margaret River, and that's where the grapes are sourced for its ambrosial premium cabernet sauvignon, as well as its best chardonnays and shiraz. More importantly though: who cares? Good wine is good wine, and if you can drive just a few minutes outside the city, take a seat at one of the largest cellar doors in Western Australia, and enjoy a sumptuous tasting of truly top-drawer wine ... well, you're not really going to complain, are you? There's a great restaurant here, serving up a long menu featuring the state's best produce, local prawns, scallops, beef and more, either as complete dishes or turning up as ingredients atop wood-fired pizzas. Grab a bottle of wine, settle in. This place is truly great.

sandalford.com

SITTELLA WINES (10)

CHOOSE YOUR OWN ADVENTURE ON THE GORGEOUS GROUNDS OF THIS IMPRESSIVE WINERY.

Sittella has a huge range of wine made from fruit of numerous varieties grown across two regions, and frankly it all kicks arse. You won't be able to sample it all, because that's something like 30 wines – what a day that would be – but you can still pick and choose your favourites with an experience at the Swan Valley cellar door. Choose a tasting flight that focuses on sparkling wines, or any range you're particularly interested in, or even stick to certain regions or vineyards. Whatever. You'll be happy. Afterwards, stroll the lovely grounds here, take a few photos, and then settle in at the restaurant, where the classy pan-Mediterranean menu, by London-trained chef Mike Price, is a perfect foil for your choice from the Sittella wine range, much of which is available by the glass.

sittella.com.au

TYLER'S VINEYARD (11)

THERE'S A DOG, A SHEEP AND A GOOSE TO GREET YOU AT THIS FAMILY-RUN CELLAR DOOR.

This Swan Valley vineyard is all about grenache, thanks to the 100-year-old vines that are still producing beautiful fruit to this day. Tyler's Vineyard is a boutique, family-run affair offering seriously good value – where else could you find wine made from such ancient vines coming in at $25 a bottle? That's reason enough to call past the laidback cellar door here, though there's also the welcome from the vineyard dog, the goose, and the sheep that thinks it's also a dog. Oh, and there's also the Tyler family, of course, who are the consummate hosts – friendly and generous. This place has charm oozing out of its pores. You'll love it.

tylersvineyard.com.au

Sandalford Winery

The Perfect Day
THE SWAN VALLEY AND THE PERTH HILLS

6PM

11AM MILLBROOK WINERY
Begin in the far south of the Perth Hills region, at Millbrook Winery (see p.211), where you'll have time for a thorough tasting experience before heading into the restaurant for an early lunch overlooking the lake.

2.30PM CORE CIDER HOUSE
Make your way north on a pleasant drive to Core Cider (see p.210), where there's loads of time to grab a tasting paddle of the local product and relax in the sun.

4PM SITTELLA WINES
Cross now into the Swan Valley, and prepare yourself for a long and lovely tasting of Sittella's (see p.212) comprehensive range, with a little time left to explore the grounds.

6PM SANDALFORD WINERY
Round out your day with dinner at Sandalford Winery (see p.212), which has a superb menu making the best of WA's local ingredients. And it's only a 20min drive back to Perth.

Domaine Naturaliste

MARGARET RIVER
WADANDI COUNTRY

Margaret River is just ridiculous. No one region deserves all of these natural, geographical riches: some of the best beaches on Earth, whether you like surfing or strolling or simply sitting to watch the sunset over the ocean; miles of rugged, windswept coastline that's perennially enthralling; verdant pastures studded with the gnarled trunks of ancient gums; endless forests of towering karri trees; even crystal caves that open up deep below the Earth's surface. All of these riches, and then you throw in the fact that 'Margs' just happens to offer the perfect conditions for growing grapes as well, for making Bordeaux-style red wines and Burgundian whites that can hold their own with the best in the world, and you just have to shake your head in wonder. What a place. Ridiculous.

The Margaret River region is about a 3hr drive south of Perth, and it's the land of the Wadandi People, saltwater people who have been here more than 50,000 years. For a time the area was purely agricultural, and then a surfie Mecca, and then a wine region, and now you will find all of those elements, as well as a slew of micro-breweries and distilleries and world-class restaurants and even truffle producers.

Margs is a special place, where visitors can feel a genuine connection to the land, whether through boots on your feet, a surfboard under your arm, or a glass of wine in your hand. It's an idyllic spot with a huge amount going for it – all you can hope to do is drink it all in.

AMELIA PARK ①

HIGHLY RATED WINERY OFFERS AMAZING VALUE FOR THOSE HUNTING FOR A BARGAIN.

A bottle of wine for $16? In Margaret River? It pretty much doesn't happen, particularly not at any of the well-regarded wineries in this region – except, that is, for Amelia Park. This classy winery is a relative newcomer on the scene, having been co-founded in 2009 by renowned winemaker Jeremy Gordon, and it has a beautiful, boldly modern cellar door pouring a whole range of high-quality and appropriately priced wines. It also has the Trellis Collection, a group of four wines – sauvignon blanc semillon, chardonnay, rosé and cabernet merlot – that each clock in at $16 a pop. That's amazing value for Margs, and worth paying Amelia Park a visit for that alone. Of course, call in here and you can pay $10 to stand up or $20 to sit down and taste wines from throughout the range, plus find something to pair with the Mod-Oz food at the Amelia Park restaurant.

ameliaparkwines.com.au

Top **Amelia Park** *Opposite* **Cheeky Monkey Brewing Co.**

BEERFARM (2)

WORKING PROPERTY IS BIG ON SUSTAINABILITY, AND JUST AS BIG ON TASTY BEER.

You can't help but admire what they're doing at the Beerfarm. This is a working farm, hence the name, a 160-acre property on which Black Angus cattle roam, and birds sing. The idea here is to be as sustainable and responsible as possible, while still producing very good craft beer. The leftover grains from the brewing process are fed to the cattle. The cattle, in turn, wind up on the Beerfarm menu. Water usage is kept at a minimum; energy consumption is minimal. And happily, the beer is delicious. This is a friendly joint that takes its production seriously, and handles its consumption with just as much passion. In the big shed there's usually 10 different beers on tap, from lager to IPA and fruited sours, plus hearty, smashable lunches, and regular Raise the Steaks dinners on Friday nights. You'll run into plenty of locals here – Beerfarm has no shortage of admirers.

beerfarm.com.au

BLIND CORNER (3)

LO-FI LEGENDS WELCOME GUESTS TO THEIR AMIABLE, EASYGOING WINERY.

Blind Corner is one of the flag-bearers for lo-fi winemaking in a region that tends more towards old-school, hands-on methods. Ben and Naomi Gould have gone organic and biodynamic in the vineyard, and are committed to minimal additions in the winery, to produce a range that's pure and honest, with plenty of experimentation and interest. We're talking pet nats, skin-contact whites, preservative-free reds. You can sample them all on a visit to the Blind Corner cellar door, at the northern end of Margs, by appointment only, on a tour that usually includes a walk among the vines and a quick look in the winery. Much like the wine, the cellar door is pretty lo-fi, but that's all part of the charm.

blindcorner.com.au

CHEEKY MONKEY BREWING CO./CAVES ROAD BREWPUB (4)

STOP IN FOR A FEW CHEEKY BEERS IN THE HEART OF WINE COUNTRY.

The Wilyabrup area of Margaret River is prime territory for grape-growing, but it's also the place to go for a 'Cheeky' beer. This is the home of the Cheeky Monkey Brewpub, also known as Caves Road Brewpub, a sprawling and friendly facility with a little something for everyone, including a great playground for the kids to run amok while adults sip a few brews. Those brews – the Cheeky beers – range from a seriously good Oat Cream IPA, to West Coast and Hazy IPAs, Pale Ale and Sour. They all go well with food from the restaurant too: beer-loving bites like fried chicken, pizzas and burgers. For proper beer nerds, Cheeky Monkey also has its HQ Tap House within its brewery, up the road between Dunsborough and Busselton, where you can sit among all the tanks and bottling lines while sampling the product.

cheekymonkey.com.au

COLONIAL BREWING ⑤

SEE WHERE IT ALL BEGAN FOR THE LOCAL BOYS WHO WENT NATIONAL.

Think of Colonial as a 'macro' micro-brewery, a small operation that went big, an independent brewer whose products can now be found on bottle shop shelves around Australia. Though it has shifted its main production base to Melbourne now, the Colonial story began in Margaret River, and if you can get past the dodgy name – we're past celebrating colonialism – it's well worth calling in to its Bramley pub for an enjoyable afternoon. Colonial has a heap of beers and cider on tap, plus a restaurant, a playground for kids, plenty of outdoor space, and regular live music. This is a case of local boys done good, and it's nice to see where it all began.

colonialbrewingco.com.au

CULLEN WINES ⑥

ONE OF MARGARET RIVER'S ICONS, WITH A PROGRESSIVE APPROACH AND SENSATIONAL WINE.

There are a few absolute legends of the Margaret River wine scene, operations that have been in place pretty much since the beginning and which continue to dominate, and Cullen Wines is undoubtedly one of them. This Wilyabrup vineyard was established in 1971 – just a few years after the Margs' pioneer, Vasse Felix – and you can feel the history in the friendly wine room. This might be an old winery, still in family hands, with Vanya Cullen running the show, but it has some distinctly forward-thinking tendencies, being one of the first organic, biodynamic wineries in Margaret River, and the first to go carbon neutral. Make a booking for a seated tasting and you can choose between five tiers of experiences, from a basic flight right up to a $100 deep-dive into Cullen's flagship chardonnays. There's a high-end restaurant, doing four-course tasting menus, plus accommodation at the old Cullen homestead. This place is a legend for a reason.

cullenwines.com.au

DOMAINE NATURALISTE ⑦

SNARFLE THE WORKS OF A TRULY TALENTED WINEMAKER FOR A GREAT PRICE.

Bruce Dukes should be a rock star of the Margs scene. He's without doubt one of the most talented winemakers in the area, someone who lends his skills to a number of wineries around here, as well as helming his own brand, Domaine Naturaliste. And yet, he's not. He's about as down-to-earth and friendly as they come, and if you happen to run into Bruce while having a tasting at the Domaine cellar door, you'll struggle to match this guy up with the wine in your hand. Easygoing winemaker but serious wine. The Domaine Naturaliste product is also really good value, particularly for Margs, and there's every chance you'll walk out of the Wilyabrup cellar door with a case or two in hand. Bruce focuses on the Margaret River classics: cabernet sauvignon and chardonnay, at a series of price-points, and he does them really well. Charcuterie and cheese boards are also available.

domainenaturaliste.com.au

Top **Domaine Naturaliste** *Opposite* **Eagle Bay Brewing**

DORMILONA

THE LEADER OF THE LO-FI PACK IS TURNING OUT WINES OF SERIOUS QUALITY.

Here's lo-fi winemaking done right – minimal-intervention, organic and biodynamic, but also elegant, balanced, and properly delicious. This is Dormilona, the leader of Margs' nattie youngsters, the passion project of Josephine Perry, who was nicknamed 'Dormilona' – 'lazybones', or 'sleepyhead', in Spanish – during her time in Iberian wine country. You'll recognise the varieties here as Margaret River classics, the likes of cabernet, chardonnay and chenin blanc, but the texture and poise are all Perry's. Oh, and the labels are fricken rad. Obviously, you're going to want to pay Perry a visit, and you can do that by appointment on Fridays and Saturdays for a tour of the cellar and a taste of the latest releases, which are changing all the time.

dormilona.com.au

EAGLE BAY BREWING

MARGARET RIVER'S HISTORY IS ALSO ITS FUTURE, THANKS TO THREE BEER-LOVING SIBLINGS.

Eagle Bay is yet another family success story in Margaret River, a tale of three d'Espeissis siblings, third-generation local farmers, who decided to do something a little different on their inherited land, setting up a micro-brewery and restaurant, and coming out all guns blazing. People love it, too. The restaurant, which does pizzas, salads and other classics, is always heaving, set to an outlook of trees and ocean, and the perfect place to drink a few beers or even sample the Eagle Bay wine, made from vines planted by the second generation of the d'Espeissis family. Eagle Bay is the history of Margaret River, but it's also the future, and it's in good hands.

eaglebaybrewing.com.au

FERMOY ESTATE

OLD-SCHOOL WINERY OFFERS PLENTY OF VALUE, PLUS A PLACE TO STAY.

Though it doesn't have a name as recognisable as the likes of Cullen or Vasse Felix, Fermoy Estate is one of the Margaret River originals, a vineyard that has been around since 1985, and it produces some excellent wine at a much more competitive price point than some of its counterparts – we're talking highly-rated drops coming in between $20 and $30. Come here for a tasting at the beautiful old cellar door and, if you choose, stay on at the Lodge – a gorgeous four-bedroom house among the vines.

fermoy.com.au

KOOMAL DREAMING

TAP INTO THE AREA'S WADANDI AND BIBBULMAN HERITAGE WITH A HANDS-ON FISHING TRIP.

The best way to tap into Margaret River's First Nations culture, to begin to understand over 50,000 years of culture and history? Spend the day going fishing with Josh Whiteland, a local Wadandi Custodian and tour guide, who takes visitors out on his Djiljit Coastal Fishing Experience from Feb to May. You'll hear stories, go for a swim, and fish off the coast for herring, salmon and bream. And, later, Whiteland will cook up your catch and show you how to forage for a salad. There are other cultural tours and experiences through the year, too.

koomaldreaming.com.au

FRASER GALLOP ESTATE

TASTE HIGH-QUALITY WINES IN LOW-STRESS SURROUNDS AT ONE OF THE REGION'S FINEST.

The Fraser Gallop cellar door is surprisingly low-key for such a prestigious winery. Though it's only been around 20 years or so – half the age of some of the bigger names – Fraser Gallop produces some of Margaret River's best wine, particularly when you consider the prices. That said, the cellar door here is a modest affair – just a small room where flights of wine samples will only set you back $10. That's great value, and it's very likely you'll redeem that cost against the purchase of a few bottles – particularly if you have some space at home to age wine. Fraser Gallop offers immersive tours of the vineyard and property, including samples of the latest vintages straight from the barrel, on Friday and Saturday for $95 per person.

frasergallopestate.com.au

LARRY CHERUBINO

THE WINE LIST HERE IS LONG, AND EVERYTHING IS GOOD.

You know you visit some wineries and everything you taste there is fairly good, but then there's one wine that really blows you away? Well, at Larry Cherubino, every wine is *that* wine. There is a huge range here to try, across pretty much every price point you can imagine, from entry-level $15 drops to top-of-the-line $175 specials, and the consistency is just incredible. Everything is good. Everything is made with care. Obviously, you should visit the Margaret River cellar door (there's one in downtown Perth as well), in the heart of Wilyabrup, to go through a basic tasting, or something themed, region-based, or step up to some of the exclusive releases. There's a lot to choose from. There's a restaurant on-site, too, called Frui Momento, doing set menus of high-end Mod-Oz cuisine, with options to add delights like oysters or caviar.

larrycherubino.com

Top Fraser Gallop Estate *Opposite* Leeuwin Estate

LEEUWIN ESTATE (14)

THE MAKERS OF AN ICONIC CHARDONNAY HAVE PLENTY MORE TO OFFER.

If you only taste one wine during your stay in Margaret River, make it the Leeuwin Estate Art Series Chardonnay, widely regarded as the best of its kind in Australia, rated in the prestigious *Langton's Classification of Australian Wine* as among Australia's five most exceptional wines. It's an absolute classic and it is not, as you have probably surmised, exactly cheap. Still, sign up for a range of different tasting options at the serpentine cellar door at Leeuwin Estate, and you will be able to swirl and sniff and taste chardonnay perfection. And then, figure how you can afford to take a bottle home. Leeuwin has been around since 1973, and its HQ is a big old building with a wide verandah perfect for long afternoons picking at delicious food, taking time to wander through the art gallery, explore the grounds, listen to the birds, and drink some more wine.

leeuwinestate.com.au

MARGARET RIVER DISTILLING CO (15)

FLEDGING DISTILLERY HAS SOMETHING FOR EVERY SPIRITS-LOVING VISITOR.

For a region that's so keen on food and drink, Margaret River has a surprising dearth of great distilleries, though a few are beginning to pop up – check out West Winds, Three Lily's and Dune – and Margaret River Distilling Co is up there with the best of them. Situated on the outskirts of Margaret River town, just near the banks of the waterway itself, the distilling company is a multi-tier operation that produces single-malt whisky under the Limeburners label, makes a series of gins called Ginversity, makes sour-mash bourbon-style whisky called Tiger Snake, and the team is even trying its hand at rum. At the Margaret River HQ there are tastings, a restaurant, gin-making classes at the Ginversity, and accommodation at Riverglen Chalets.

distillery.com.au

MIKI'S OPEN KITCHEN

LOCAL INSTITUTION APPLIES A JAPANESE MINDSET TO THE BEST LOCAL PRODUCE.

Ask pretty much any local in Margs where you should eat during your stay and they will mention Miki's. This is a much-loved stalwart of downtown Margaret River, that consists of a long, U-shaped bar surrounding the titular open kitchen, where Miki and his team create a series of dishes that are Japanese in inspiration, but totally local in the sourcing of produce. The serving style here is all set-menu degustation, though diners have the choice between seven or eight courses, and each can be paired with either matching wine, sake or a mix. There's even a kids' degustation, for diners aged 12 and under. In classic Japanese style, everything here has been considered and cared for, and the experience is superlative.

mikisopenkitchen.com.au

SETTLERS TAVERN (17)

NO-FRILLS PUB MAKES A WELCOME CHANGE FROM THE WINE-SUPPING SCENE.

When all of the wine-tasting and beer paddles and fancy food starts to become a bit much, make your way directly to Settlers Tavern, the laidback Margaret River pub that's usually packed with a mixed crowd of surfers, farmers, winemakers, and probably a fair few people who could claim to be all three. Settlers has a bistro serving pub-grub classics, and a bar with a heap of local beer on tap, and Margs wine by the glass. There's regular live music, too.

settlerstavern.com

SI VINTNERS (18)

THE WINES ARE NATURAL AND SO IS THE HOSPITALITY AT THIS CHARMING WINERY.

Si Vintners wears its nattie heart on its tattered, mud-stained sleeve, a fiercely minimal-intervention outfit where it's hands-off in both the vineyard and winery. The result, from winemaking pair Sarah Morris and Iwo Jakimowicz, is a range of wines with texture and character, recognisable grapes treated in unrecognisable ways, unique, individual and always interesting. The cellar door here reflects the natural approach, it's a friendly, low-key joint with a lovely outlook and knowledgeable, passionate staff. Be sure to book ahead.

sivintners.com

STELLA BELLA (19)

BRING THE KIDS AND THE DOG, AND PREPARE FOR A HIGH-QUALITY TASTING EXPERIENCE.

Stella Bella was once something of a punchline among the Margaret River crew, infamous for its dodgy rosé – those days, however, are long gone. Stella Bella is now a premium winery turning out a whole range of excellent wine, all the local classics like cab sav, chardonnay and sem-sav blanc, made with obvious skill. The cellar door here is open every day, and it's a laidback space where dogs and kids are always welcome, and you can take your time working through a tasting flight, or grabbing a glass of your favourite and enjoying a BYO picnic on the lawn.

stellabella.com.au

VASSE FELIX (20)

GREAT NEWS: THE MARGARET RIVER ORIGINAL IS STILL THE BEST.

It's not often the true original can still claim to be the best, but in the case of Vasse Felix that is 100 per cent legit. The first vines were planted here in 1967, when all the local farmers thought Perth doctor Tom Cullity was crazy for trying to make wine. These days Vasse Felix has four vineyards throughout the region, growing fruit that is used by winemaker Virginia Willcock to produce a dazzling range with top-notch cab sav, chardonnay, shiraz and more. Pay a visit to Vasse Felix, in a building overlooking Tom Cullity's original vineyard, and you can do a standard or 'Icon' tasting, take one of several different themed tours, have a glass of wine and a snack in the Wine Lounge (or on the lawn if the weather is good), or sit down on the verandah to some of the best food in Margaret River at the Vasse Felix restaurant.

vassefelix.com.au

Opposite **Voyager Estate**

VOYAGER ESTATE (21)
A SMALL SLICE OF SOUTH AFRICAN WINE COUNTRY GREETS GUESTS IN MARGARET RIVER.

If you've ever visited South Africa's wine country, around Stellenbosch and Franschhoek, with its white-washed Cape Dutch–style homesteads and gorgeous views, then you'll be having flashbacks as you come down the long driveway at Voyager Estate. The cellar door and restaurant here is set in a Cape Dutch replica, a beautiful building with views over the Stevens Valley, in which you can do wine tastings, eat a seasonal degustation lunch at the acclaimed restaurant, or take tours of the grounds. Voyager Estate's wine portfolio is a sprawling affair with all sorts of limited single-block releases and experimental projects, so it's worth putting aside plenty of time to experience everything you want to get your hands on. And, of course, enjoying the salubrious surrounds.

voyagerestate.com.au

WILD HOP BREWING (22)
YET ANOTHER DOWN-TO-EARTH BEER PURVEYOR DOING EVERYTHING RIGHT.

You have to love a Margaret River brewpub. No formality, no pretense. Just open spaces and big smiles, everyone welcome, space for kids, room for doggos, food ready to order, and plenty of beer on tap. Wild Hop Brewing follows that pleasing formula, with its big bar and restaurant overlooking a dam near surfie Yallingup, a place to relax on a big couch, chill on the lawn, sit outside on some big comfy chairs and just soak it all in. This is a family-run operation – of course it is – that doesn't put its beer in bottles or cans, so if you want to try it you'll have to visit the brewery, or find it at a local Margs pub. There are 11 beers on tap at the brewpub, and a kitchen churning out wood-fired meats served family-style with all the tasty sides.

wildhopbeer.com.au

The Perfect Day
MARGARET RIVER

Western Australia

10AM SI VINTNERS

Begin south of Margaret River town at the laidback cellar door of Si Vintners (see p.222), where you can sample lo-fi wines in their natural habitat.

11AM DORMILONA

Head towards Margs now, just 15min up the road from Si Vintners, to Dormilona (see p.219), another flag-bearer for minimal-intervention winemaking in an otherwise conservative region, and a label that is doing it impressively well.

12.30PM VASSE FELIX

Travel from the new-school to the old-school, to Vasse Felix (see p.222), the original Margaret River winery, for a tasting and then lunch at the excellent on-site restaurant.

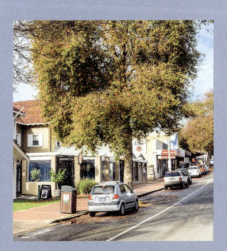

3PM DOMAINE NATURALISTE

It's only 10min up the road from Vasse Felix to visit Domaine Naturaliste (see p.218), one of the new stars of the region, where incredibly good wine is available at a very reasonable price.

4.30PM WILD HOP BREWING

Finish your day of touring and tasting in the north of the region, at Wild Hop Brewing (see p.223), where you can sip a delicious brew and enjoy the sunset.

7PM MIKI'S OPEN KITCHEN

For dinner tonight, head back to Margaret River town to enjoy a must-do gastronomic experience, a set-menu meal of Japanese-style goodness at Miki's Open Kitchen (see p.221).

Pemberton vineyards

PEMBERTON AND MANJIMUP

KANIYANG AND BIBBULMAN COUNTRY

There's only been wine in Pemberton and Manjimup, neighbouring regions just south and east of Margaret River, since 1977. Actually – that's just Pemberton. In Manjimup no one thought to plant vines until 1988. These are two relatively new wine regions, regions whose official borders were only drawn up in 2005, and where there is still only a smattering of wineries. The good news, however, is that the wineries here are incredibly good, making use of the Bordeaux-like conditions to make world-class chardonnay, sauvignon blanc, cabernet sauvignon and merlot. What this means is that these two regions are far more than just a stopover between Perth and Albany, and far more than a side hustle for the better-known Margaret River establishments.

Aside from wine, Pemberton and Manjimup are both famed for their trees. In particular, the towering karri forests around Pemberton, highlighted by the fire lookout trees – skyscrapers once used as lookout points, which these days can still be climbed for spectacular views. Gloucester Tree, for example, stands 61m tall, or about the same height as the Sydney Opera House. Meanwhile, an amazing 80 per cent of the entire Manjimup region is dedicated to forest and national parks, and this area is one of Australia's largest producers of black truffles. These are the lands of the Noongar Peoples, and they are deeply beautiful and moving.

10 CHAINS WINERY

LAIDBACK WINERY IN AMONGST BEAUTIFUL KARRI FORESTS.

Set in the shade of towering karri forests, surrounded by some of the region's most beautiful landscape, 10 Chains is one of Pemberton's friendliest wineries. It's a family-run operation, run by Kate and Shaun Woods, that produces lovely chardonnay, semillon, shiraz and more from estate-grown grapes. The winery is a no-frills sort of affair, where you can pat the dog, gaze at the views, and enjoy a relaxed run-through of the product. As it's such a small operation, be sure to make an appointment before arriving.

tenchains.com.au

AMPERSAND ESTATES

PEMBERTON'S OLDEST WINERY HAS MODERNISED, WITH WINE, SPIRITS, HAMPERS AND ROOMS.

The word 'ampersand' means the '&' symbol, meaning 'and', which is obviously fitting for Pemberton's oldest winery, Donnelly River Wines, which has been given a major recent makeover, including a new name. Ampersand is now a winery… *and* a 'gourmet picnic venue', *and* a wedding venue, *and* a distillery, *and* an accommodation site. Lots of 'ands', for a place that does lots of good things. The accommodation is spread across three private residences: the two-bedroom Settlers Cottage, the sprawling five-bedroom Homestead, and similarly expansive five-bed Vintners Residence. The cellar door is light and airy, the ideal spot to showcase wines that have benefited from the touch of Margaret River winemaker Bruce Dukes. The distillery, called Rainfall, is a boutique producer of vodka and gin. The picnics are gourmet hampers of local produce curated by the Ampersand team. And, the wedding venues are gorgeous. This place has it all.

ampersandestates.com.au

AUSTRALIAN TRUFFLE TRADERS ③

DIG UP SOME BLACK GOLD WITH A VISIT TO A WORKING TRUFFLE FARM.

If you should ever happen to find yourself dining on black Périgord truffles at a high-end European restaurant from around June to Sept in any year, there's a good chance those precious fungi will have come from Manjimup. This is one of the southern hemisphere's leading regions for truffle farming, and the product is shipped to some of the finest restaurants in the world, particularly when their own local truffles are out of season. To learn more about truffles, or to join a truffle hunt, to taste truffle, and maybe even to buy some truffles, be sure to call past Australian Truffle Traders, just outside Manjimup. Their truffle season runs for three months, from June to Aug, and the hunt is a blast.

australiantruffletraders.com

BELLARMINE WINES ④

DISCOVER JUST HOW GOOD RIESLING CAN BE WITH ACCESS TO BACK-VINTAGES.

Here's the thing about a lot of riesling: upon its release by the winemaker, usually when it's a year or two old, it's very nice. Very nice, but not amazing. Leave that riesling longer, however – put it in a cellar and forget about it for a decade or more – and very nice wine becomes nothing short of ambrosial. Though many of us don't have a cellar, or the patience with which to utilise one, there's good news, because Bellarmine Wines in Pemberton – which specialises in riesling – has back-vintages for sale, stretching back to 2008. Make an appointment for a tasting here, and you will be able to see just how good riesling can be when it's given a bit of time.

bellarmine.com.au

Top Black truffles at Australian Truffle Traders
Opposite Hidden River Estate

HIDDEN RIVER ESTATE ⑤

SAMPLE GREAT FOOD USING LOCAL PRODUCE BEFORE OR AFTER A TASTING.

Hidden River Estate's wines are lovely, but that's not the main reason to visit this Pemberton favourite. The real drawcard here is the restaurant, with its terrace overlooking rolling, vine-covered hills and forests, and its varied, though crowd-pleasing menu that makes the best of local produce, including plenty of options here for vegetarians and vegans, from pumpkin gnocchi to home-made falafel. There's a small pantry selling house-made spice blends, many of them traditional recipes from the Middle East. And, of course, there's wine – the Pemberton classics of chardonnay, sauvignon blanc and merlot.

hiddenriver.com.au

HILLBROOK WINES

FAMED WINEMAKER BRINGS HIS SKILLS TO THE PEMBERTON TERROIR.

If you know of and enjoy the wines at Castle Rock Estate (*see* p.237), a highly-awarded winery in the Great Southern region, and Duke's Vineyard (*see* p.237), a similar venture, then you're going to love Hillbrook – mostly because these wineries share the same winemaker, Rob Diletti. Here, Rob gets to work in the more Bordeaux-like climate of Pemberton, producing semillon-sauvignon blanc, chardonnay and merlot and getting rave reviews for it. Visits here are by appointment only, and the winery is about half an hour out of town.

hillbrookwines.com.au

JASPERS BAR

AN INSANELY LARGE WHISKY COLLECTION AND TOP-NOTCH FOOD IN THE HEART OF PEMBERTON.

You probably weren't expecting this: a fully-fledged whisky bar in the heart of Pemberton, a rocking place stocked with more whisky than you've seen in a long time, from classics to rarities and cellar-door exclusives, and from Scottish to Irish and Japanese to Australian. Jaspers is nuts, not what you would think to find here at all, and yet so, so welcome. It's not just a whisky bar either – it's also a restaurant, doing fine foods, steaks, burgers, char-grilled vegetables and seafood, that are designed to be paired with various whiskies. And it also has lovely cabins with king-sized beds, ensuite bathrooms, big couches and private decks. The highlight, though, is the whisky collection, which could keep any passionate drinker amused for months.

jasperspemberton.com

Top Peos Estate

PEOS ESTATE ⑧

FAMILY DYNASTY TURNS OUT BEAUTIFUL WINES AMONG THE SOUTHERN FORESTS.

The Peos story is a classic for this part of WA, a family of European migrants – in this case, from Macedonia – who set up shop south of Perth and created a dynasty from agricultural graft. The Peos have farmed everything from dairy cattle to beef and vegetables on their fertile property near Manjimup, and in 1996 the third generation of Peos in Australia decided to return to their roots, planting grapes and making wine in the style of their late grandfather, PY Peos. And the venture was a raging success. These days Peos Estate is picking up all sorts of awards for its excellent chardonnay, pinot noir and shiraz, still made using grapes tended by the Peos family. Their cellar door, among the towering Southern Forests, is open by appointment, and well worth booking ahead for.

peosestate.com.au

SILKWOOD ESTATE ⑨

HIGH-END WINERY ALSO HAS CLASSY FOOD AND SWISH ACCOMMODATION.

Silkwood is the full package; you don't need to go anywhere else (though, you still should). There's wine here, excellent wine, some of Pemberton's finest, high-quality riesling, chardonnay and cabernet sauvignon, among many others. The cellar door is a convivial space with a lovely outlook, ideal for swirling and sipping your way through an extensive list. It has one of the region's best winery restaurants, serving cuisine that is creative, delicious and locally sourced. And then you also have accommodation, in the form of four luxe chalets set among the forest, each with all the mod-cons, including a full kitchen and private balcony overlooking the lake.

silkwoodestate.com.au

TANGLETOE CIDERY AT MOUNTFORD WINERY ⑩

ENTERPRISING TEAM IS TURNING CLASSIC PRODUCE INTO DELICIOUS CIDER – AND THERE'S WINE TOO.

The fertile soils of the Pemberton region are good for growing many things: not just grapes, or truffles, or even the fresh vegetables you find being sold on the side of the road, but also apples. That's good news, because there are people here turning those apples into cider, including the team from Mountford Wines, who do a side hustle in fermented apple juice known as Tangletoe Cidery. It's all housed under one roof – actually a Swiss Family Robinson–style chalet – just north of Pemberton. Here you can taste the organic wines, which have been in production since 1987, and – even better – its range of ciders. The British-style scrumpy is a particular favourite.

mountfordwines.com.au

TREEHOUSE TAPAS AND WINE ⑪

SPANISH-STYLE EATERY FEATURES A HOST OF HARD-TO-FIND LOCAL WINES.

There's a small problem with the Pemberton and Manjimup regions: there are some sensational wineries around here, but not all of them are open to visitors. In fact, some of the best remain sadly closed, focused on the growing and pressing of grapes rather than the welcoming of gawkers. Sad. Still, there's a solution, and it comes in the form of Treehouse Tapas and Wine, a Pemberton eatery with a long and comprehensive list of local wines on offer, from the likes of Picardy, Below & Above, and Mazza Wines, none of which you will find on these pages, because they don't have cellar doors. Call into Treehouse, however, and order a bunch of small plates of Spanish-style share plates, and you can slurp their products to your boozy heart's content.

treehousewinebar.com.au

The Perfect Day
PEMBERTON AND MANJIMUP

Western Australia

10AM PEOS ESTATE

Begin your day out to the west of Manjimup, at one of the region's most-awarded wineries, Peos Estate (see p.231), for a private tasting by appointment.

11AM AUSTRALIAN TRUFFLE TRADERS

After Peos, it's only 20min over to Australian Truffle Traders (see p.229), where – if you arrive in winter – it's possible to join a hunt for black Périgord truffles.

1PM HIDDEN RIVER ESTATE

Head south now, down into the Pemberton region, for a sample of the lovely wines at Hidden River (see p.229), and then a leisurely lunch of local produce.

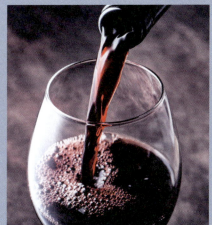

3.30PM HILLBROOK WINES

Go deeper, now, through the towering forests of Pemberton, to Hillbrook Wines (*see* p.230), where the Bordeaux-style drops are getting rave reviews.

7PM TREEHOUSE TAPAS AND WINE

Finish the day with dinner at Treehouse Tapas and Wine in Pemberton (*see* p.231), where many of the region's best wineries - some of which don't have cellar doors - are on the list.

Vines at Harewood Estate

GREAT SOUTHERN
MINANG COUNTRY

Here, once again, is a West Australian wine region that can boast some stupendous geographical gifts. Not just the soil and the climate and the hills that are perfect for cool-climate winemaking, but two ruggedly beautiful mountain ranges in Porongurup and Stirling in the north of the region. There's also one of Australia's best long-distance walking trails, the Bibbulmun Track, that cuts through its southern reaches, as well as some of the country's most striking beaches in the Denmark and Albany areas, and vast hectares of untouched karri forests throughout.

Though Great Southern is tucked at the bottom of WA, as far south as the state goes, it's still only a 4hr drive from Perth before you hit Mount Barker, the gateway to the region and one of five distinct sub-regions here, each with its own topography and climate, that make up this immense area that runs west to Frankland and Walpole, and east towards Bremer Bay.

Great Southern might be a large region, more than 1.5 million hectares, but it's one that's sparsely populated with cellar doors, which means there's a bit of driving involved, and it's certainly best to confine your daily wanderings to one sub-region – either Frankland River, Mount Barker, Porongurup, Denmark or Albany – rather than attempt to tick several off in a few short hours.

Both Denmark and Albany make excellent bases for exploration, not just for their access to wineries, but their proximity to spectacular beaches that are perfect for a quick dip (ah, in summer), plus some excellent restaurants, wine bars, and even a micro-brewery or two. The food around here is affordable and tasty, and the vibe across the board is a little more relaxed than the more well-known Margaret River to the north.

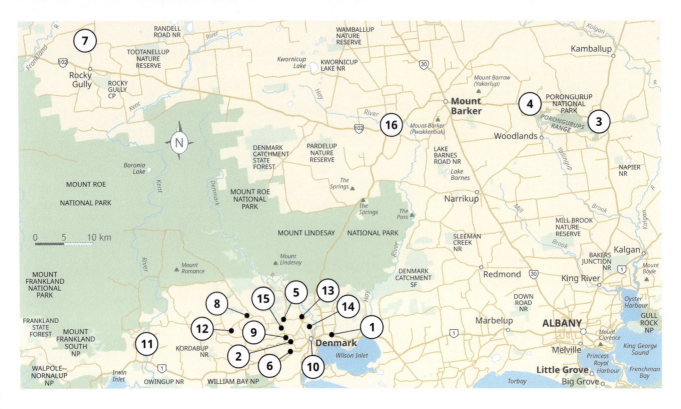

BOSTON BREWING CO. ①

LAIDBACK BREWPUB JUST HAPPENS TO DO A SIDE HUSTLE IN HIGH-QUALITY WINE.

Boston Brewing is interesting: this was one of the first breweries established in the Great Southern region, a Denmark estate with a big restaurant and dining area, a serious operation producing fantastic pale ales, wheat beers, IPAs, göses and more. People pile in on weekends to sit in the sun, skol a few ales and dine on a menu that's packed with local ingredients that have been given a crowd-friendly spin, with pizzas, burgers, risotto, pasta and more. So far, so normal. And yet, have a look around you as you gaze over grape vines, as far as the eye can see. Because Boston Brewing Co is the sister establishment of Willoughby Park, one of the best wineries in the region, a renowned producer of riesling, cab sav, shiraz and more. Willoughby Park has a standard cellar door, on the same site as Boston Brewing Co., where wine fans can do tasting flights. Alternatively, plenty of Willoughby wines are available by the glass at the brewery and restaurant. This really is the best of both worlds.

bostonbrewing.com.au

CASTELLI ESTATE ②

FAMILY WINERY TURNS OUT AN ASTONISHING LINE-UP OF VARIETIES AND STYLES.

Nothing is done by halves at Castelli Estate. Here is a boutique, family-run winery that produces a suite of more than 40 different wines across price points that range from $16 at the bottom end to $70 at the pinnacle. These wines are made with fruit grown in vineyards across the Great Southern region and even into Margaret River. They're divided into seven sub-labels, each with its own style and theme, from traditional sparkling wines to single-estate red blends, as well as experimental rare varietals and bargain-basement rosé. If you can't find something you like on the list here, then you just straight-up don't like wine. Call into the Denmark cellar door, which is a Tudor-style mansion (again, nothing by halves) and find out. Tastings are free, though it's $5 if you want to move into the top bracket. Share platters of local food are also available.

castelliestate.com.au

CASTLE ROCK ESTATE ③

PORONGURUP CELLAR DOOR SHOWS BEAUTIFUL WINE WITH A PERFECT BACKDROP.

Here's a little slice of everything that's good about the Great Southern. You have an intimate, friendly cellar door in Porongurup, a no-frills sort of space with wood panelling and a hand-scrawled blackboard for a menu. You have views that take in the splendour of the region, the vines lined up, row after row, with a shimmering backdrop of the Stirling Ranges. And then you have the wine, seriously high quality riesling, pinot noir and chardonnay that's as good as anything produced in the big-name regions of Australia. There are so many reasons to visit Castle Rock Estate, and so many reasons you'll want to stay.

castlerockestate.com.au

DUKE'S VINEYARD ④

THERE'S SOMETHING FAMILIAR ABOUT THE WINE AT THIS PORONGURUP CLASSIC.

If you liked the wines at Castle Rock, I've got good news: the winemaker there, Robert Diletti, also travels 10min down the road to make the wine at Duke's Vineyard. This winery is part of the Porongurup 'riesling belt', so you can expect superb riesling, as well as shiraz and cabernet sauvignon. And you can drink it at the beautiful Duke's cellar door, a modern building – designed by Hilde Ranson, who co-owns the operation with her husband Duke – with floor-to-ceiling windows that capture views out to the Stirling Ranges, and showcases the Great Southern in all its glory. This is a super-friendly spot where you will often find yourself being served by Duke himself, and visitors are more than welcome to BYO food for a picnic with a view.

dukesvineyard.com

ESTATE 807 ⑤

THE ANIMALS RUN THE SHOW AT THIS SWEET BOUTIQUE WINERY.

You get the feeling, very quickly, on arriving at Estate 807, that Stephen Junk and Ola Tylestam love their animals. Drive up to their cellar door just outside Denmark and you might spot an alpaca or two, a few sheep, maybe some ducks, some chickens, or one of four cocker spaniels that essentially run the place. And then you find out that Estate 807 has a Dog Range, a line of wines named after their dogs – and some of the other animals – and you realise that, oh yes, these guys definitely care for their furry and feathered friends. That care is extended to the wine produced in their name too, as well as the fancier Reserve Range, and it's also there in the welcome to guests at the cellar door, which has a deck overlooking the pinot noir vines. Settle in, and watch for the menagerie.

estate807.com.au

Top Boston Brewing Co.

Great Southern

FRANKLAND ESTATE (7)

RIESLING KINGS OFFER GREAT EXPERIENCES TO THOSE WHO MAKE THE EFFORT TO VISIT.

Here's another of the Great Southern big guns. Frankland Estate is in Frankland River, and it makes world-beating riesling, as well as excellent syrah, and even touriga nacional (a Portuguese grape becoming increasingly popular in Australia). Though this is a big operation, the cellar door is still a fairly intimate affair, probably due to its relative isolation, more than an hour from either Albany or Manjimup. Still, make the effort and you will be rewarded. You can do a standard tasting for $10, or shift up to $25 and get a tour of the vineyard from one of the winemakers, and then a guided sample of the Frankland range. There's even a chance to try a few wines straight from the barrel.

franklandestate.com.au

HAREWOOD ESTATE (8)

SAMPLE RIESLINGS FROM FOUR SEPARATE SUB-REGIONS FOR THE FULL SOUTHERN EXPERIENCE.

It's time for a crash course in Great Southern riesling, courtesy of one of its best producers. Visit the Harewood Estate cellar door near Denmark and you can taste some of the finest riesling from four of Great Southern's sub-regions: Porongurup, Mount Barker, Frankland River and Denmark. Harewood Estate has vineyards in all four, and from those vineyards it produces unique rieslings that each have something to say – for wine nerds at least – about the place they came from. For everyone else, they're just delicious. Harewood also makes excellent shiraz, pinot noir and cabernet, more than enough to see you through a tasting at its beautiful cellar door.

harewood.com.au

FOREST HILL VINEYARD (6)

CLASSY WINE MADE FROM OLD VINES PROVIDES HISTORY IN A GLASS.

Forest Hill's main vineyard was the first planted in the Great Southern region, and those vines, dating back to 1965, still produce fruit, which is still turned into sensational, award-snarfling wine. Situated just west of Denmark – though the estate's oldest vines are in Mount Barker – Forest Hill is most famous for its single-block range, particularly its rieslings and cabernet sauvignon, from vines planted in either 1965 or 1975. This is Great Southern history that you can swirl, sniff and slurp at Forest Hill's stylish cellar door. If you like what you're tasting, be sure to snap it up, as this stuff sells out each vintage.

foresthillwines.com.au

Top Harewood Estate *Opposite* The Lake House

THE LAKE HOUSE ⑨
GRAB A HUGE LUNCH PLATTER AND SETTLE IN HERE FOR THE LONG HAUL.

The Lake House is the ideal destination for drinkers and diners in the Great Southern region, particularly if you're basing yourself around Denmark. You'll always find something good here. There are wine tastings all day, samples of the Lake House's excellent riesling, cab sav, shiraz and chardonnay. Then there's a restaurant on-site too, doing huge platter-style lunches which, if you want, you can pair with a tasting. There's also a cafe doing morning and afternoon tea, and a shop, called Vinofoods, selling homemade sauces and other condiments. To top it all off, they sell their own skincare range called WineSpa. And there's the location itself, which is Great Southern perfection – lawns and bushland and that eponymous lake.

lakehousedenmark.com.au

MJS WINE BAR ⑩
FRIENDLY WINE BAR OFFERS A TOUR OF THE REGION, FROM THE COMFORT OF A COUCH.

MJ's is a pretty chill little spot in central Denmark. It's a tiny bar that's ideal for those who want to get their head around the local wine scene without schlepping out to every vineyard in the region. Grab a big couch or a chair and enjoy a great selection of local wines, while being surrounded by a great selection of locals. There are small plates of food too. Check its socials.

MOOMBAKI WINES ⑪
IT'S ALL DONE BY HAND AND IT'S ALL DONE WITH SKILL AT THIS FAMILY VENTURE.

There aren't too many lo-fi winemakers making a mark in the Great Southern region – it tends to be mostly traditional Australian winemaking here – though there are a few upstarts hoping to change all of that, and Moombaki is one of them. This family-run winery, near Denmark, has actually been in business more than 20 years, quietly producing a consistent and high-quality range of wines with minimal intervention. All of the fruit is grown on the estate, harvested by hand, and the wines are created with obvious love. Call in to see, as unlike many of the lo-fi producers in Great Southern, Moombaki has a cellar door, open five days a week, run by co-owner Melissa Boughey. If you're in the market for an interior refresh, her winemaker partner, David Britten, also makes and sells his own wooden furniture.

moombaki.com

RICKETY GATE ESTATE (12)

IMPRESSIVE WINERY AND CELLAR DOOR MAKES THE MOST OF ITS NATURAL GIFTS.

Rickety Gate Estate – named after its owner, John 'Ricketty' Ricketts – is an impressive property, both for the 'terroir' largely responsible for the excellent wines here, not to mention the scenic views, as well as the huge winery, barrel room, cellar door and restaurant overlooking the vines. Set just outside Denmark, this is a popular spot for weddings and other events, though if you just want to pop in and sample the cool-climate wines, all made on the estate, that is definitely an option. Come for the wine, stay for the views.

ricketygate.com.au

ROCKCLIFFE WINERY (13)

AWARD-WINNING WINERY IS KNOWN BETTER FOR ITS AUTHENTIC ITALIAN GELATI.

Rockcliffe might be a winery, and a distinguished one at that – its estate-grown cabernet sauvignon, chardonnay and shiraz are regarded as some of this region's finest – and yet the reason plenty of people flock here, just north of Denmark, has nothing to do with wine at all. It's gelato. Rockcliffe bills itself as a 'winery and gelateria', with Northern Italian and Sicilian-style gelati made on-site using local ingredients, as well as a few Italian imports. These artisanal ice-creams are cult favourites, and with good reason. Of course, you shouldn't miss the wine while you're here. The cellar door is a friendly, relaxed space offering tastings across the impressive Rockcliffe range, and there's a heap of space for a BYO picnic. But you'll probably want another scoop of gelato before you leave.

rockcliffe.com.au

SILVERSTREAM WINES (14)

MAKE A BOOKING TO EXPERIENCE THIS LOW-KEY BUT HIGH-QUALITY WINERY.

Here's another classic of the Denmark sub-region, a no-frills venture that just makes really, really good wine. Silverstream is only open to visitors by appointment, though it's worth making that effort because a visit here is a window into the Silverstream world, a winery that is moving towards biodynamic status, and a chance to taste the fruit of owners Tony and Felicity Ruse's labours. Plenty of Denmark's best wineries can be found along this stretch of Scotsdale Rd, so it's no surprise to find Silverstream enjoys optimal conditions to make its chardonnay, riesling, cabernet franc and pinot noir. Gorgeous spot too, among the forests with a whiff of sea breeze.

silverstreamwines.com

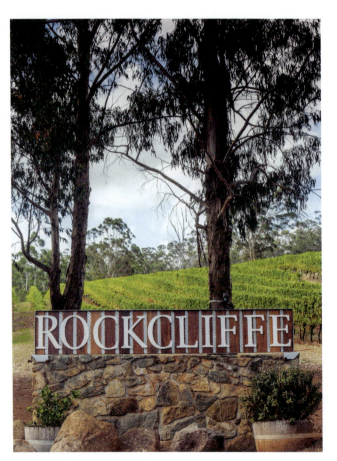

Rockcliffe Winery *Opposite* Singlefile Wines

SINGLEFILE (15)

EACH SUB-REGION GETS A CHANCE TO SHINE AT THIS GREAT SOUTHERN CLASSIC.

Move, in single file or otherwise, directly to Singlefile Wines, just outside Denmark, and get yourself ready for one seriously impressive tasting. Singlefile makes a lot of wine, with fruit sourced from throughout Great Southern's sub-regions, as well as Margaret River, and it's all very, very good. The winery is best known for its chardonnay, which is killer, though it also does riesling, shiraz and cab sav that will have you looking up your bank balance and tossing up how much you can spend. There's a lovely cellar door here too, with plenty of lawn space and lake views, areas to sit with a bottle or hang out with some snacks. Don't miss the Sense of Place private tasting too, if you're really keen: a snapshot of Great Southern's sub-regions, delivered via some of its finest wines.

singlefilewines.com

WEST CAPE HOWE WINES (16)

JOURNEY TO MOUNT BARKER – NOT WEST CAPE HOWE – TO SAMPLE SOME DELIGHTFUL WINE AND PIZZA.

Confusingly, West Cape Howe Wines is not in West Cape Howe. It's actually more than an hour north, near Mount Barker, but it's worth getting over that anomaly to visit one of Mount Barker's best winemakers. The site here is spectacular, with a tree-lined drive leading to a modern building with views to die for. Settle in for a generous tasting of an enviable range of wines, all the Great Southern classics, such as chardonnay, riesling, cab sav and shiraz. They also do pizzas here, which makes it an ideal pit-stop if you're on the road between Manjimup and Albany.

westcapehowewines.com.au

The Perfect Day
GREAT SOUTHERN

Western Australia

10AM HAREWOOD ESTATE

If you're based in Denmark or its surrounds, it's only 15min up the road to Harewood Estate (see p.238), where you can do a crash course in sub-regional variation via the winery's rieslings.

11.30AM SINGLEFILE

Just 10min from Harewood lies Singlefile (see p.241), a phenomenally good winery with a huge suite of wines to work your way through.

1PM THE LAKE HOUSE

By now you've got a hunger for lunch, and 5min south of Singlefile you will hit the Lake House (see p.239), home of what is probably the Great Southern's best winery restaurant, as well as some delicious wine.

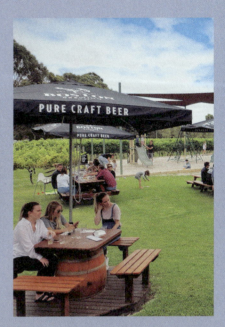

3PM ROCKCLIFFE WINERY

After lunch, it's only 10min north-east to get to Rockcliffe (see p.240), which is well known for its wines, though just as famous for its gelato - grab a few scoops and relax on the lawn.

6PM BOSTON BREWING CO.

Finish up today, maybe after a quick siesta in Denmark, at Boston Brewing Co. (see p.236), the region's best craft brewery, where there's a great menu of crowd-pleasing dishes.

Northern Territory

The Top End might not have wine, but it does have a rapidly growing craft beer scene, and a few artisanal distillers utilising unique native ingredients.

DARWIN AND ALICE SPRINGS

LARRAKIA COUNTRY (DARWIN/GARRAMILLA) AND ARRERNTE COUNTRY (ALICE SPRINGS/MPARNTWE)

You're right: the Northern Territory does not have any wine regions. It's far too hot (and in parts, rainy) up here to think about tending vines. In fact, it's often far too hot and rainy up here to think about much except a cold beverage, which goes some way to explaining the recent proliferation of craft breweries centred around Darwin/Garramilla, but also beginning to flourish in Alice Springs/Mparntwe. We're talking great beers served in friendly surrounds, the sort of places where you feel like a local before you've even polished off the first schooner.

We're also talking about artisanal distillers, which have begun cropping up in the Top End as well, and who are putting their own welcome spin on gin and other tasty spirits, often using native ingredients that you won't find anywhere else in the country.

There's so much more to experience in the NT too, from iconic attractions such as Uluṟu and Kata Tjuṯa, to the natural wonders of Kakadu, to the multi-faceted charms of laidback Darwin itself. First Nations cultures in the NT are strong, and easily accessible for visitors. The food scene is also coming on in leaps and bounds, taking influence from a huge range of global traditions that have found their place in the Top End.

There's all of this magic in Australia's north, all of this beauty – and now, if you find yourself in need of refreshment, there's always something good to drink.

Heli Pub Crawl *Previous* Enjoying a cold drink on Anzac Hill, Alice Springs

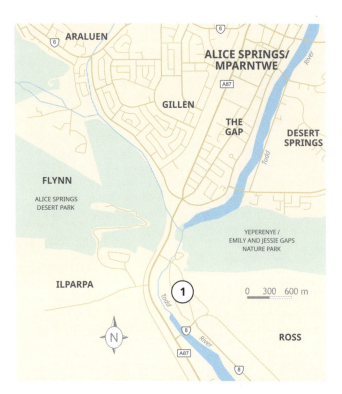

ALICE SPRINGS BREWING CO

LOCAL SUCCESS STORY BRINGS TASTY BREWS TO THE RED CENTRE.

Alice Springs, the team here admits, is a terrible place to brew beer. It's always too hot. It costs a lot to truck in supplies. And yet, they're doing it – and they're doing it extremely well. Alice Springs Brewing Co only opened in 2018, and it's been going absolutely gangbusters ever since, requiring more equipment and specialist expertise, with plans now to begin distribution interstate. These guys have taken everything in their stride, and their Red Centre brewpub is already a venerated local institution, a place where you'll find plenty of regulars crowding in for a range of hot-weather-friendly ales and lagers, paired with pizzas and wings.

alicespringsbrewingco.com.au

BEAVER BREWERY (2)

EASY-DRINKING BREWS MAKE THIS A POPULAR FRIDAY NIGHT STOPOVER.

If it's Friday night and you're in Darwin, there's good news: Beaver Brewery is open. This is a pretty small operation, family-owned and run, that only welcomes guests one night a week, but when they do, they do it properly. There's a different food truck parked here every week, churning out meals to go with the brews, which are designed to suit the Darwin climate. We're talking lager, pale ale, mango lager, and even a boozy lemonade, with plenty of seasonal offerings taking up the extra taps.

beaverbrewery.com.au

CHARLIE'S OF DARWIN (3)

IT'S ALL ABOUT LOCAL INGREDIENTS AT THIS GIN BAR AND DISTILLERY THAT IS BOTH CLASSY AND CASUAL.

Here's a great idea: a gin that is not just distinctly Territorian, but distinctly Darwin, a gin whose botanicals come from the local area, foraged from the local surroundings, native ingredients that you couldn't find anywhere else. And that's what Darwin Distilling Co has done, creating a signature gin using Kakadu plum, waterlilies and native lemongrass, and it's Darwin in a bottle. It's also on to taste or buy at Charlie's of Darwin, the swish gin bar and restaurant run by the same team, a speakeasy-style venue the likes of which you probably didn't think you would find in the Top End. Charlie's is a classy though friendly space, and the perfect spot to try unique Darwin gin. The distillery is in the same building, and offers gin-blending classes, from which you will walk away with your very own unique bottle.

charliesofdarwin.com.au

Opposite Alice Springs Brewing Co

Darwin and Alice Springs

HELI PUB CRAWL

GET HIGH ON THIS UNIQUE EXPERIENCE: A TOUR OF TOP END PUBS BY CHOPPER.

Strap yourself in – literally – for one amazing and truly memorable day, a tour of five Top End pubs in seven hours, with transport via helicopter. That's right, the team from Airborne Solutions will ferry you and a bunch of friends by air from Darwin to some absolute icons of the Top End scene, including the Lodge of Dundee, Crab Claw Island Resort, the Darwin River Tavern and Goat Island Lodge. Along the way, you'll be able to spot billabongs and creeks, long stretches of coastal splendour, endless forests and more, before making a rock star landing at a well-known boozer and calling in for a beer and a bite to eat. There's nothing else in the NT like this.

airbornesolutions.com.au

ONE MILE BREWERY

TWO FRIENDS BRING THEIR PASSION FOR GOOD ALE TO DARWIN'S OUTSKIRTS.

There's nothing too fancy about One Mile Brewery, which is exactly what people love about it. Set in an industrial estate just south of Darwin Airport, the One Mile brewpub has both indoor and outdoor spaces, relaxed areas designed for the casual sampling of the local product. That comes in the form of a highly smashable kolsch, as well as plenty of session-friendly ales, and boozy ginger beer and lemonade. This is a passion project for owners and brewers Stuart Brown and Bardy Bayram, a business that began in a shed and has bloomed into a fully-fledged Darwin institution. Call past and become part of the story.

onemilebrewery.com.au

PURPLE MANGO BREWERY (6)

COUNTRY CAFE IS ALL ABOUT SMALL BATCHES AND BIG FLAVOURS.

Marrakai is not in Darwin, but when you're heading to Kakadu, go past Coolalinga, about an hour down the road, and through Humpty Doo until you find the turn-off for the Purple Mango Cafe. And then you've arrived. This is an unlikely brewery in an unlikely location, a very small operation doing a great line of refreshing beers, available in schooner form, or lined up on a tasting paddle. There's pizza at the cafe, plus if you really like the look of the place (or you've overdone it on the schooies), you can camp out – the Purple Mango has powered and unpowered campsites.

purplemangocafe.com.au

SIX TANKS BREW PUB (7)

THERE ARE UP TO 26 TAP BEERS TO CHOOSE FROM AT THIS POPULAR BREWPUB.

Set in the heart of the Darwin CBD, Six Tanks is one schmick micro-brewery, featuring not just those eponymous six tanks, but a whopping 26 beer taps featuring the full local range, as well as cracking craft brews from around Australia. You could come back here every day and never get bored. Six Tanks also has a full restaurant serving perfect beer food, the likes of pizzas, burgers, salads and other classic dishes, as well as a menu for the little 'uns. This is a convivial, comfortable space, the perfect spot to down a few drinks and meet a few local characters.

sixtanks.com.au

WILLING DISTILLERY (8)

LOCAL GIN MERCHANTS DISH UP SOME OF DARWIN'S FINEST SPIRITS.

Willing Distillery wears its heart on its sleeve – and its label. Printed on every bottle in large letters, as big as the brand name itself, are the words 'Made in Darwin'. This is a proudly local operation, family owned and run, situated in the Winnellie industrial area near Darwin Airport. Willing is producing mostly gin at the moment, made using a suite of local NT botanicals with the standard juniper, though there's also vodka in the mix, and whisky on its way. Sample it all at the distillery and cellar door, a friendly space, big on community, where you can sip drinks – it's $13 to taste three different spirits, $9 to try two, plus there are several local craft brews on tap. You can snack on cheese boards, charcuterie platters, and … crocodile jerky. Because this is, after all, Darwin. Don't you forget it.

willingdistillery.com.au

Top Enjoying a beer on the Heli Pub Crawl
Opposite An enticiing cocktail at Willing Distillery

Queensland

*Check out one of Australia's craft beer hotspots
in the Sunshine Coast, before discovering a wide range of
under-the-radar wineries in Queensland's high country.*

THE GRANITE BELT
KAMBUWAL COUNTRY

Friends, it's true: Queensland, the state that used to be a quirky footnote to Australian wine guides, has begun to prove itself as a serious player on the national scene. There is some great wine coming out of the Sunshine State, in particular from the Granite Belt, the high-altitude region around the towns of Stanthorpe, Glen Aplin and Ballandean in the Darling Downs. The conditions up here, as winemakers have discovered, is similar to the south of France's Burgundy region, making it suitable for a wide range of grapes that local growers aren't afraid to experiment with. Here in the Granite Belt, you'll find everything from albariño to petit manseng to malbec to pinotage clinging to the wires.

As the name suggests, this region is mostly famous for its massive rock formations – huge granite outcrops that are particularly spectacular in Girraween National Park, just 15min south of Ballandean's cluster of wineries.

The Granite Belt is also known for its carpets of wildflowers – the name 'Girraween' means 'place of flowers' – as well as local produce like apples, and some of the state's finest beef. This is a laidback, agricultural area, a relatively new player on the wine scene, accessible via a 3hr drive south-west of Brisbane/Meanjin, or 3.5hr from the Gold Coast. There's some lovely country accommodation, a few breweries around, and the whole place has a knockabout charm to it.

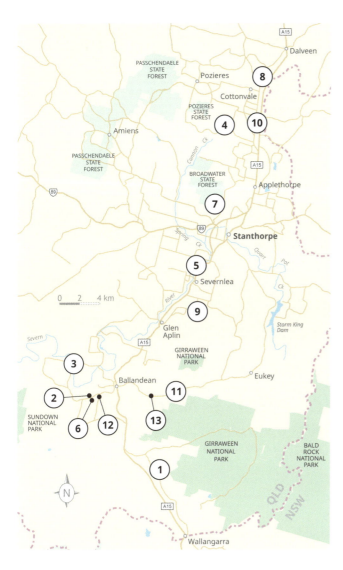

BALANCING HEART

EVERYTHING IS IN HARMONY AT ONE OF THE REGION'S MORE EXCITING NEW OUTFITS.

The heart in question here is made of stone: a rock formation in the centre of the shiraz vines, a natural landmark that has become the namesake of the winery. The hearts of those who work here, however, have plenty of passion, plenty of feeling that goes into everything, from the tending of vines, to the fermenting of grapes and the welcoming of customers in for a taste. Balancing Heart is a relatively new winery, having once been known as Balancing Rock, and these days is in the safe hands of Mick Hayes, Australian Winemaker of the Year in 2017. His wines all have a theme of balance – Essense & Bloom Verdelho, Mineralogy & Surreal Shiraz – and are all seriously good. Give them a sample at the friendly cellar door, a few minutes south of Ballandean. There are pizzas and a lunch menu available.

balancingheart.com.au

Top Vineyards in Ballandean *Opposite* Golden Grove Estate
Previous Ballandean Estate, Granite Belt

BALLANDEAN ESTATE ②

HISTORIC WINERY IS STILL IN TOUCH WITH ITS ITALIAN ROOTS.

There have been grapes in the ground at Ballandean Estate since 1932, though it wasn't until Angelo Puglisi took over from his parents in the late '60s that the table grapes were pulled out and shiraz vines planted, and the Granite Belt's wine industry began. Angelo, incredibly, still runs Ballandean Estate, and his winery is still producing great wine, though it's gone far beyond those original shiraz vines, and these days has malbec, nebbiolo, chardonnay, and even saperavi. As you would expect given the Italian heritage, the Ballandean cellar door is all about a warm welcome, something good to drink, and a big plate of food to devour. There are a range of tasting experiences on offer, plus picnic hampers to take out into the vines, and a restaurant set in the old barrel room, right next to the 150-year-old port barrels, which are still filled with Ballandean's fortified wines. Check out the gourmet pantry while you're here, too.

ballandeanestate.com

BENT ROAD/ LA PETITE MORT ③

YOUNG WINEMAKERS PUSHING THE BOUNDARIES AND CREATING SOMETHING AMAZING.

Walk into the Bent Road winery and check out the scattering of wide, circular openings in the ground, like manhole covers, and you'll realise something: this is not your average Granite Belt production. Those openings are the mouths of amphorae – large clay pots traditionally used for winemaking in Georgia, buried in the ground. The Bent Road team use them for a range of wines, allowing the juice to sit on skins for days or weeks at a time, for the company's edgy sub-label, La Petite Mort. This place is all about experimentation, in fact, using ancient techniques in new ways, pushing boundaries, taking risks. And the results are excellent: the sort of interesting, textural, unique wines you might expect to find in the Adelaide Hills, rather than southern Queensland. There's no cellar door at Bent Road, though they're more than happy to take visitors by appointment. Make sure you take them up on it.

bentroadwine.com.au

BOIREANN ④

RED-WINE SPECIALISTS ARE LEADING THE GRANITE BELT PACK.

Boireann is comfortably out in front when it comes to the quality of wine produced in the Granite Belt – this isn't the oldest winery, it's not the flashiest winery but, damn, it produces some seriously good stuff. We're talking cabernet sauvignon that can hold its own with Australia's big guns; shiraz blazing the trail for cool-climate regions; Italian varietals easily leading their fields this far north. No wonder Boireann is one of only two Queensland wineries awarded five red stars by reviewer James Halliday. For all that prestige, the cellar door, up in the far north of the region, is a pretty simple affair, offering basic tastings four days a week, with few airs and graces. It's refreshing, in fact, and indicative of the Granite Belt vibe. Fine wines, no messing around. And FYI, white wine fans need not apply: it's nothing but red at Boireann.

boireannwinery.com.au

BRASS MONKEY BREWHOUSE ⑤

ONE-MAN-BAND BRINGS DELICIOUS CRAFT BEER TO THE GRANITE BELT.

Ernie Butler is a man who loves his beer, so much so that he owns, operates and staffs Brass Monkey Brewhouse, in Severnlea, pretty much solo. That guy behind the bar, working the taps, telling people about the different beers available? That's Ernie. It brings a pleasant, family vibe to a Brass Monkey visit, where locals and tourists pack in on weekends, from Friday to Sunday, to try the beers – from pale ales to stouts to alcoholic ginger beer – eat the pizzas, and enjoy themselves.

brassmonkeybrewhouseptyltd.com

GOLDEN GROVE ESTATE ⑥

RARE ITALIAN VARIETALS BRING A TOUCH OF THE MEDITERRANEAN TO THE MOUNTAINS.

The Costanzo family were Italian migrants who moved into the Ballandean area in 1946, planting grapes to sell at the local market and to press into rough wine to sell to their fellow countrymen in the area. Skip forward 80 years or so, and Ray Costanzo is now a third-generation winemaker who is taking things forward, planting rare Italian varietals such as nero d'avola and vermentino to give Golden Grove Estate a point of difference. It works, too: the wine is seriously good, and the welcome at the cellar door here, with its beautiful leafy patio, is always warm.

goldengroveestate.com.au

Golden Grove Estate *Opposite* Ballandean Estate

GRANITE BELT BREWERY (7)

STANTHORPE STALWART CONTINUES TO TURN OUT HIGH-QUALITY BREWS.

Granite Belt Brewery is the real deal, an operation that has been cranking out tasty brews for more than a decade now, a much-loved Stanthorpe institution that should be on every curious drinker's itinerary. The team has a full bar and restaurant on-site at the brewery, serving bar snacks and bigger meals – nachos, burgers, pizzas – that pair well with a schooner of IPA, pale ale, or one of the regular rotation of seasonal special brews. There's accommodation on-site, too: 20 cedar-wood cabins set on 30 acres of natural bushland, a 5min drive out of Stanthorpe, and a four-bedroom house that can sleep 10 people. Some cabins are pet-friendly, and some have outdoor spas.

granitebeltretreat.com.au

HERITAGE ESTATE (8)

LEADING WINEMAKERS AREN'T AFRAID TO LEAN ON THEIR HERITAGE.

Very few wineries in this fledgling region are awarded the coveted five red stars by wine reviewer James Halliday and his team. In fact, there are only two: Boireann (*see* p.257) and Heritage Estate. Clearly this is a serious winemaking operation, with two vineyards, one in Cottonvale in the north, for growing white grapes, and one in Ballandean in the south, for red. The shiraz, tempranillo, fiano and pinot gris from Heritage Estate are justifiably famous around these parts. Call into the Heritage Estate cellar door, at the Cottonvale vineyard, and you can taste the full range while perched on rosewood and leather seats that date back to the 1800s. There's a restaurant here too, doing Vine+Dine lunch experiences (matching food with wine), plus accommodation in the form of a three-room cottage, built in 1864.

heritageestate.wine

SAVINA LANE (9)

DRINK AND LEARN AT THIS FORWARD-THINKING WINERY.

It's not so much a wine tasting at Savina Lane, in Severnlea, but more of a wine education. You might be here to drink, but you will also learn. There are two tasting experiences on offer. First is the Curious Wine Encounter, for $10, which takes about an hour, and includes a taste of all the Savina Lane wines, which are varieties you may not have heard of or tasted before. Alternatively, there's the Wine Decoded session, for $45, a 2hr experience that begins with a tasting in a black glass – try to figure out what you've just drunk – and includes food, which is used to demonstrate the way a wine's flavour can change depending on what you're eating. All up, this is something different, something interesting, and a welcome change-up experience. Make sure you book ahead.

savinalanewines.com.au

SUMMIT ESTATE (10)

RELAX WITH A PICNIC ON THE LAWN AT THE REGION'S MOST ENJOYABLE CELLAR DOOR.

Bring your four-legged friends to the Summit Estate cellar door, in Thulimbah: doggos are very much welcome here, both inside the tasting room and outside on the patio. This place is all about enjoyment, from the warm welcome, to the long trading hours (they're open till 7pm on Fri and Sat for Sunset Sessions, rare for a winery), to the fact visitors are encouraged to bring a picnic and some games and settle down on the lawn for the long-haul. The wine is great, too: Mediterranean and other European varieties that fit the Granite Belt's Strange Bird categorisation (varieties responsible for less that 1 per cent of Australia's harvest), and are delicious, particularly when consumed with friends with a cracking view of the sunset.

summitestate.com.au

SYMPHONY HILL (11)

BALLANDEAN WINERY MAKING A PLAY TO BE THE BEST IN THE GRANITE BELT.

Symphony Hill is swinging hard, as they say, really going for it with their wines, attempting to create world-class products in a region that hasn't always been known for them – and they've gone some way to succeeding. Set down in Ballandean, where it's perfect for red-grape growing, Symphony Hill has been picking up a swag of awards for its cabernet sauvignon and shiraz, as well as its petit verdot. White grapes are sourced from elsewhere in the region, so you have the best of both worlds here. The cellar door is a friendly space that's part of the winery, where the drops on offer change with the season, whatever is recently released and available, from wines you will know well to the rarer likes of lagrein, fiano and gewürztraminer.

symphonyhill.com.au

TOBIN WINES (12)

ULTIMATE SMALL-BATCH PRODUCERS GO FOR QUALITY OVER QUANTITY.

It's all about low yields and high quality at Tobin: production here is limited to between 100 and 160 cases of wine for each variety, which is absolutely tiny, even compared to other Granite Belt producers. It means there's a lot of care put into the likes of Tobin's chardonnay, semillon, merlot and shiraz. It also means there isn't much available to buy. Drop by the winery, in Ballandean, and see what's about – whatever is there will be worth a sample.

tobinwines.com

TWISTED GUM WINES (13)

QUINTESSENTIAL GRANITE BELT CELLAR DOOR IS THE PERFECT SPOT FOR A TASTING.

You know those tourism ads, with the slogan, 'Where else but Queensland?' You'll be thinking that as you hang out on the wraparound verandah of the old, 1920s Queenslander home that functions as a cellar door for Twisted Gum Wines. Where else but Queensland? Where else would you have these views from this house, where else would you be drinking these wines in such surrounds? Twisted Gum is a family-owned business where yields are low, and the cellar door does tend to close for the year once the product is sold out, so be sure to call ahead. If you can get in, you'll be treated to a generous tasting of small-batch reds and whites, with an atmosphere that couldn't be anywhere else.

twistedgum.com.au

Opposite Transporting grapes through the vineyard

The Perfect Day
THE GRANITE BELT

Queensland

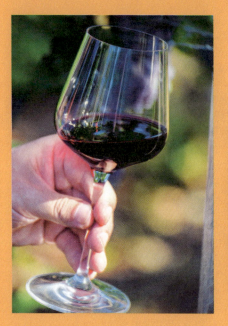

10AM BALANCING HEART

Begin the day bright and early at the southern end of the Granite Belt, at Balancing Heart (*see* p.255), to sample Mick Hayes's collection of thoughtful, experimental wines.

11AM BENT ROAD/LA PETITE MORT

Head back up the road, closer to Ballandean, to Bent Road/La Petite Mort (*see* p.256), where you get the best of both worlds, with beautiful, experimental wines across two different labels.

12.30PM GRANITE BELT BREWERY

Have lunch today up in Stanthorpe, about 25min away, where Granite Belt Brewery (*see* p.258) has paddles of local beer and plenty of great food options.

3PM BOIREANN

Continue on north to Boireann (*see* p.257), producer of arguably the finest wines in the Granite Belt, for a tasting with few airs and graces.

5PM SUMMIT ESTATE

Finish the day with a Sunset Session at Summit Estate (*see* p.259), where there's room to spread out with a picnic on the lawn, and to toast the end of the day with some more top-notch wine.

Aerial view of the Sunshine Coast Hinterland

SUNSHINE COAST

GUBBI GUBBI AND JINIBARA COUNTRY

It would be easy enough to visit the Sunshine Coast, to stay here for a few days or even a few weeks, and not even realise this is a wine region. And in fact, it's not, really: Queensland only has two officially designated wine regions, the Granite Belt and South Burnett, so there's no shame in having concentrated your previous Sunny Coast visits on more typical activities like beach-bumming, surfing, fishing, and dining at some of the region's excellent restaurants. The Sunshine Coast is home to the likes of Noosa, Maroochydore, Mooloolaba and Caloundra, hubs for beach culture, as well as the Glasshouse Mountains, natural wonders ripe for exploration on foot.

But ... there's wine here. There's beer, too – in fact, a burgeoning craft brew scene. Plenty of spirits as well. The wine is made up in the hinterland, around beautiful hill towns like Montville and Maleny, and many other producers of delicious things have huddled around those areas too, which makes exploration easy, not to mention spectacularly beautiful. Back down at sea level, meanwhile, there's a host of bars, breweries and other restaurants that provide access to the local spoils.

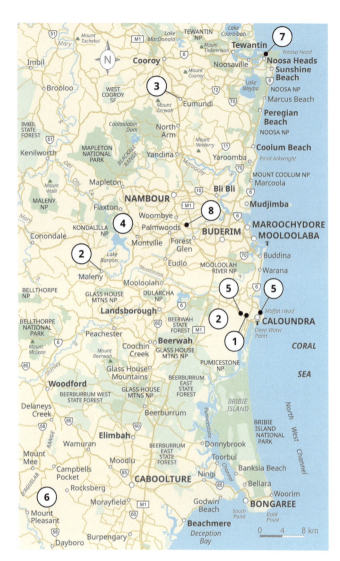

BEACHTREE DISTILLING CO. ①

NATIVE INGREDIENTS TAKE CENTRE STAGE AT THIS FLEDGLING CALOUNDRA DISTILLERY.

The gins and vodka produced by Beachtree, on the outskirts of Caloundra, are all about respect for Country: the base spirit is distilled from sugar cane, plenty of which you will find growing all over Queensland, and the botanicals for the gin are what you might call 'bush tucker' – native plants that have been utilised around here for millennia, something Kamilaroi man and master distiller Steve Grace is keenly aware of. (Of course there's a few juniper berries thrown in as well.) Beachtree has only been up and running since 2020; Steve and his partner Kirra have built something with heart, something with soul, and it shows. Drop by the distillery for a tour and a tasting.

beachtree.com.au

BROUHAHA ②

COME JOIN IN AT THE RESTAURANT OR BREWERY AT ONE OF THE SUNNY COAST'S FINEST.

The Sunshine Coast can boast an embarrassment of craft breweries these days, and Brouhaha is one of its best. This is a schmick operation with two outlets: a crowd-pleasing restaurant and bar in the company's original home, the hinterland at Maleny, and a new, more industrial brewery space – though still with plenty of spots to sit and nurse a few brews – near the coast in Baringa. At either venue you'll be able to taste the core range: Queensland-friendly easy-drinkers like lager, pale ale and sour, as well as more experimental, seasonal brews. There are food trucks at the Baringa brewery, and a full restaurant in Maleny, serving all the hits: burgers, steaks, pizzas and more. Vego and kids' options are available.

brouhahabrewery.com.au

Opposite Brouhaha Brewery

EUMUNDI BREWERY AT IMPERIAL HOTEL ③

AN ICONIC FACILITY IS REBORN AS A MUCH-LOVED CRAFT BEER HUB.

Back in the day – that is, the 1980s – Eumundi used to be well known for its local brewery, which churned out precisely one beer, Eumundi Lager, that was so popular major brewer CUB swooped in, bought it, and shifted its production off-site. And, then eventually, stopped making it. Skip forward to 2017, when local brewer Chris Sheehan was handed the keys to the old facility and tasked with bringing it to life again, and the modern iteration of Eumundi Brewery was born. These days, Eumundi produces a whole suite of craft brews that are ideal for the Queensland climate, from lager to pale ale to alcoholic lemonade, and ideal for the town too – a place of artisan makers and a famed market. The brews are served up at Eumundi's Imperial Hotel, where there's upscale pub grub to match it.

eumundibrewery.com.au

FLAME HILL VINEYARD ④

THE COAST'S LEADING WINEMAKER IS A DESTINATION ALL OF ITS OWN.

You can't talk about wine production in the Sunshine Coast without mentioning Flame Hill, the clear leader of the pack. Flame Hill is based up in Montville, an arty, boutique hinterland town 420m above sea level, where conditions are right to grow a whole range of grapes, from verdejo to sauvignon blanc to barbera to shiraz. Those grapes are turned into fine wine with skill by Frances Futter, and they're all on for tasting at the beautiful Flame Hill cellar door, overlooking vines and forest. The restaurant here does beautiful food, the full paddock-to-plate experience, utilising ingredients from the garden and the Flame Hill Angus beef farm, served on the deck. There's a more casual option too, on the terrace, where charcuterie platters can be paired with a bottle of wine. Oh, and Flame Hill has accommodation, in Sinclair Cottage and Symphony House, twin properties each with up to three bedrooms.

flamehill.com.au

MOFFAT BEACH BREWING CO (5)

LOCAL FAVOURITE MAKES THE MOST OF AN IDYLLIC BEACHSIDE LOCATION.

Moffat Beach Brewing Co is proper Sunshine Coast, a brewpub that looks out over the ocean, just 50m from the sand, where you can hear the waves crashing and taste the salt in the air. It's a pumping little spot that hosts live music and comedy nights and has plenty of great, beach-friendly food to pair with the likes of a summer ale, a pale ale or a mid. Nearby in Caloundra is the brewery proper, known as the Production House, where there are 20 rotating taps of the freshest beer around, plus a permanent food truck doing American-style barbecue. Choose a venue or visit both.

moffatbeachbrewingco.beer

OCEAN VIEW ESTATES (6)

FAMILY WINERY IS PUSHING THE BOUNDARIES OF QUEENSLAND'S VITICULTURAL POSSIBILITY.

Though it's a bit of a stretch to call Ocean View Estate part of the Sunshine Coast – it's all the way down in the town of Ocean View, about half an hour north of Brisbane's outskirts – this is still worthy of inclusion, given its accessibility from the Sunny Coast, and the quality of the visiting experience. Thomas and Kate Honnef first planted vines here in 1998, turned out their first wine vintage in 2002, and haven't looked back, despite their property really pushing the limits, climate-wise, of grape-growing possibility. These days, there's a cellar door for standard tastings, a restaurant doing Thai-leaning Mod-Oz cuisine, a wedding venue, a function room, and accommodation across the one-bedroom Cabernet Cottage, the two-bed Shiraz Cottage, and the sprawling five-bedroom Winemakers Cottage. If you're interested in how you go about making wine effectively on Brisbane's doorstep, Thomas and his daughter Hannah are usually around for a chat.

oceanviewestates.com.au

SAILS WINE BAR

PREPARE TO SPLASH OUT ON ONE OF QUEENSLAND'S LARGEST WINE COLLECTIONS.

Noosa is fancy as – this is where you'll find pretty much all of the Sunshine Coast's priciest restaurants, as well as the sort of people who patronise them – so it's no surprise to find that Sails (formerly Rumba) exists here. This is a classy wine bar set just back from the bustle of Hastings Street, Noosa's main drag, and its wine cellar houses one of the largest and most diverse collections in Queensland. We're talking everything from Henschke to Penfolds Grange, Chateau Margeaux to Domaine Romanee Conti. In other words, bring your credit cards.

sailsnoosa.com.au

Dining with water views in Noosa
Opposite Moffat Beach Brewing Co

SUNSHINE & SONS

LOCAL SPIRITS PRODUCERS ARE DOING BIG THINGS IN AN ICONIC LOCATION.

If you grew up in Queensland, or you ever passed through on a childhood road trip, you will know all about the Big Pineapple, one of Australia's iconic 'big things'. Though the attraction is now sadly closed, the pineapple remains, and it works as a signpost for a business just nearby: Sunshine & Sons distillery. This place is a team effort, run by a group of friends and passionate spirits drinkers, who are churning out a large and impressive range of gins and vodkas, with rum also on the way. The distillery is open for tastings and cocktails, and it also sits right next door to Diablo Co, a pop-up bar for yet another Sunny Coast craft distillery, making this the ideal spot for artisanal booze sampling.

sunshineandsons.com.au

The Perfect Day
SUNSHINE COAST

Queensland

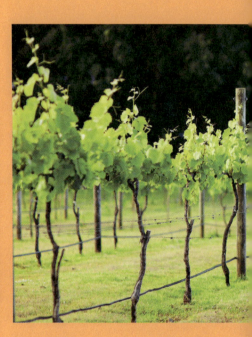

11AM – BEACHTREE DISTILLING CO.

Begin bright and early - at least as far as spirit-drinking goes - with a quick tour of the facilities and a sample of the products at Beachtree Distilling Co. (see p.264) in Caloundra.

12.30PM – BROUHAHA

Head half an hour west, into the beautiful Sunshine Coast hinterland, to stop in for a tasting paddle of beer and a cracking lunch at Brouhaha's Maleny outpost (see p.264).

2.30PM FLAME HILL VINEYARD

It's now a gorgeous 20min drive to Flame Hill Vineyard (see p.265), the premier producer of wine in the Sunshine Coast, for a tasting at the lovely cellar door.

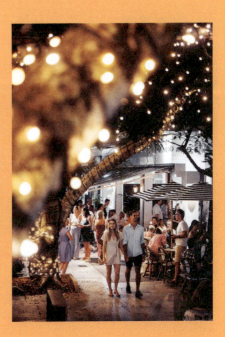

4PM EUMUNDI BREWERY AT IMPERIAL HOTEL

Head north now, about 40min up the road to the Imperial Hotel in Eumundi, where you can sample the tasty beers created by the Eumundi Brewery crew (see p.265).

6PM SAILS WINE BAR

Finish up your day on the fancy streets of Noosa, where you can duck into Sails (see p.267) and splash out on some seriously good wine from the bar's whopping cellar.

SOUTH BURNETT

WAKA WAKA COUNTRY

The area around Kingaroy, about a 3hr drive north-west of Brisbane/Meanjin, is something of a fruit bowl for Queensland, an agricultural zone known more for its orchards – as well as its cattle stations – than anything to do with viticulture. That is slowly changing, however, thanks to a band of winemakers who have been pressing grapes and making booze here since the early 1990s, and are starting to get noticed with their warm-climate, Mediterranean-style wines.

To visit here is to drive through bucolic countryside, skirting massive Bjelke-Petersen Dam – also known as Lake Barambah – calling in at quiet, friendly cellar doors to try the product and hang around for a chat. Nothing happens too quickly in this part of the world, which is more than fine.

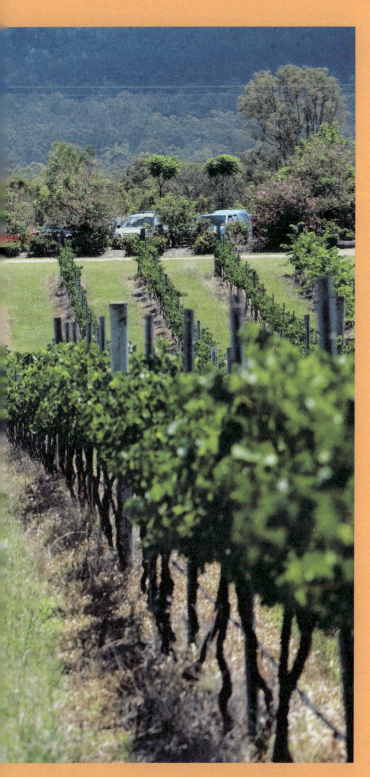

Dusty Hill

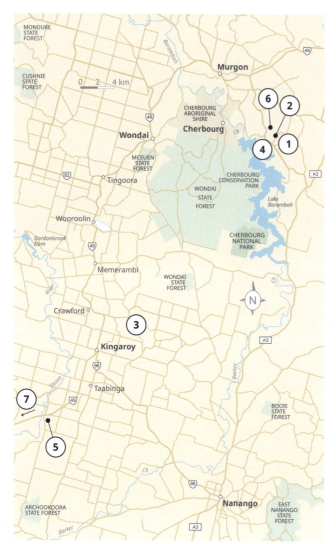

BARAMBAH CELLARS ①

FRIENDLY CO-OP OFFERS THE CHANCE TO SAMPLE THREE WINERIES' PRODUCTS.

Here's a great introduction to the boutique South Burnett scene – a co-operative of three local wine labels: Nuova Scuola, Lightning Tree and Hillsdale Estate. One or other of the winemakers are likely to be in pouring out the tastings too, which provides ample opportunity to learn all about this fledgling region. Barambah Cellars is actually on the vineyard at Nuova Scuola, where winemakers and owners Sarah Boyce and Stefano Radici also serve up share platters of local food, and run a B&B, a one-bedroom cottage that sleeps up to four people. This is a gorgeous spot run by lovely people, and well worth calling into.

nuovascuola.com.au

Top Grapes on the vine

CLOVELY ESTATE ②

ONE OF THE REGION'S LEADERS IS ALL ABOUT MAKING CONNECTIONS.

You have to love the Clovely Estate philosophy: to bring people together through good food and wine, to connect people to the land and to each other via the shared experience of a meal. Surely that's something everyone can get on board with, and what better place to do it than at Clovely Estate itself? This winery is one of the true leaders of the South Burnett pack, producing Mediterranean-style wines – moscato, semillon, shiraz, saperavi – that can hold their own with some of the bigger players on the Australian scene. Owners Brett Heading and Susan Mercer also produce an extensive range of olive oils, and you can stay on-site too, with a choice of three cottages overlooking the verdant South Burnett landscape. Call in, and connect.

clovely.com.au

CRANE WINES ③

SOUTH BURNETT'S ORIGINAL WINERY STILL HAS PLENTY TO OFFER.

Crane Wines is the South Burnett original: there were shiraz grapes planted on the property here in 1898, and that vineyard remained in production until 1970. That site was resurrected in the '90s, and these days Crane produces a large range of wines: sweet, dry, sparkling and fortified. A visit here is country hospitality at its finest, with plenty of product to taste, as well as a pantry full of homemade preserves to check out, plus there's a B&B taking up a whole wing of the old homestead, with a private verandah and views over rolling countryside. The perfect spot to settle in and enjoy the rural lifestyle.

cranewines.com.au

DUSTY HILL ④

COME FOR THE WINE, STAY FOR THE HEARTY IRISH PUB FOOD.

Dusty Hill isn't just a winery – it's a village. It's an Irish tavern and restaurant, a cellar door, a bottle shop, a gourmet food store, a wedding venue (in the old cooperage), a function space, and a B&B, with two cottages and a hotel to choose from. Situated on rolling hills with views over Lake Barambah, this is a lovely spot, where you can call in for lunch and a wander around, as well as taste the local wines, which are made on-site from estate-grown grapes. There's a lot of pride that goes into Dusty Hill – and it really shows.

dustyhill.com.au

KINGSLEY GROVE ⑤

TASTE WINE, TUCK INTO PIZZA OR PITCH A TENT AT THIS SPRAWLING FAMILY ESTATE.

You know you're among friends at Kingsley Grove. This is a family-run affair, having been founded by Michael and Patricia Berry in 1998, and now run by their son, Simon, who is head winemaker. You're likely to run into either Simon or his wife Jo if you call past the rustic cellar door for a tasting of their Bordeaux-style wines. And why not stay for lunch too, with great pizzas served, or even check-in for the long-haul: there are a heap of camping and caravan sites, and Kingsley functions as something of a meeting place for dedicated travellers calling through the area.

kingsleygrove.com

MOFFATDALE RIDGE

THE KINSELLA FAMILY HAVE THE FULL PACKAGE IN THE PERFECT LOCATION.

Moffatdale Ridge sits in the heart of South Burnett wine country, within 'cooee' of Clovely Estate (*see* p.273), Barambah Cellars (*see* p.272) and Dusty Hill (*see* p.273), and it's a beautiful, genial spot to sip your way through a few wines and enjoy a good lunch. The property has been in the Kinsella family for more than a century, and these days Jason and Susan are producing a tight but enjoyable list of reds, whites, fortifieds and liqueurs. They run a great restaurant too, called D'Vine, open six days, serving platters and hearty meals that pair perfectly with some very reasonably priced wine.

moffatdaleridge.com.au

SHACKLETON'S WHISKY BAR ⑦

AUSTRALIA'S HIGHEST WHISKY BAR BRINGS WEE DRAMS TO THE BUNYAS.

Here's an unexpected quirk of South Burnett culture: 'Australia's highest whisky bar', according to the owners, set up in the Bunya Mountains about an hour south of Kingaroy. Shackleton's Whisky Bar is part of the Bunya Mountains Tavern, which has accommodation and a restaurant, as well as this little spot set up by former South Burnett mayor, Wayne Kratzmann, who has a passion for a wee dram and isn't afraid to share it. If you're in the area and you love a whisky, be sure to call past.

thebunyas.com.au

Moffatdale Ridge

The Perfect Day
SOUTH BURNETT

12.30PM

11AM CLOVELY ESTATE

Begin your day with a sample of perhaps South Burnett's best wine, at Clovely Estate (*see* p.273), plus grab a few bottles of the local olive oil.

12.30PM MOFFATDALE RIDGE

Continue on to Moffatdale Ridge (*see* p.274), just a few minutes' away from Clovely, where you can run through a tasting of the local wine, plus enjoy a relaxed lunch at D'Vine restaurant.

2.30PM BARAMBAH CELLARS

End your Moffatdale exploration at nearby Barambah Cellars (*see* p.272), where you can taste wine from three boutique labels.

4PM KINGSLEY GROVE

Head south now, through Kingaroy and on to Kingsley Grove (*see* p.273), a family-run winery with plenty of space on-site to pitch a tent or park the caravan for the night, as well as sample a pizza for dinner.

Tasmania

Australia's smallest state packs one of its biggest punches, with a host of premium wineries, world-leading whisky distilleries, and high-quality produce available from the source.

THE TAMAR VALLEY AND PIPERS BROOK

PYEMMAIRRENER, TYERRERNOTEPANNER AND LAIRMAIRRENER COUNTRY

Sharp-eyed wine nuts will have picked up that the Tamar Valley is not, in fact, a designated wine region. Neither is Pipers Brook. They're both sub-regions of Tasmania, which in itself is a single, large wine region taking up the entire island and state. Of course, that's not too helpful when making holiday plans – you wouldn't stay in Launceston, near the Tamar Valley, and just call past a winery in the Derwent Valley, near Hobart – so for the purposes of this book, I have split the Tasmania wine region into manageable chunks: sub-regions that make sense as single holiday destinations, the sort of places you could stay for a good few days and cruise around and enjoy. You'll want to visit them all though: Tasmania is packed with gastronomic delights, from farm shops selling homemade goods to cutting-edge cuisine served in spectacular surrounds, as well as cooking schools, wineries, breweries, cideries, and world-leading distillers of fine whisky.

We begin with perhaps the most famous of Tassie's sub-regions, and indeed the area that produces the island's most famous and expensive wines: the Tamar Valley, and its neighbouring area, just across a ridgeline, Pipers Brook. Both regions make up one truly gorgeous part of an already lovely state, with vineyards that hug either side of the sparkling kanamaluka/ River Tamar, an area that's also dotted with great restaurants and independent food producers.

Base yourself in the historic city of Launceston, known fondly as Launnie or Lonnie – the spelling is hotly debated by the easygoing, friendly locals – and organise some transport to enjoy the region's spoils: from sparkling wine to rival those of Champagne, to top-quality chardonnay and pinot noir, and farm-fresh produce.

Clover Hill Wines

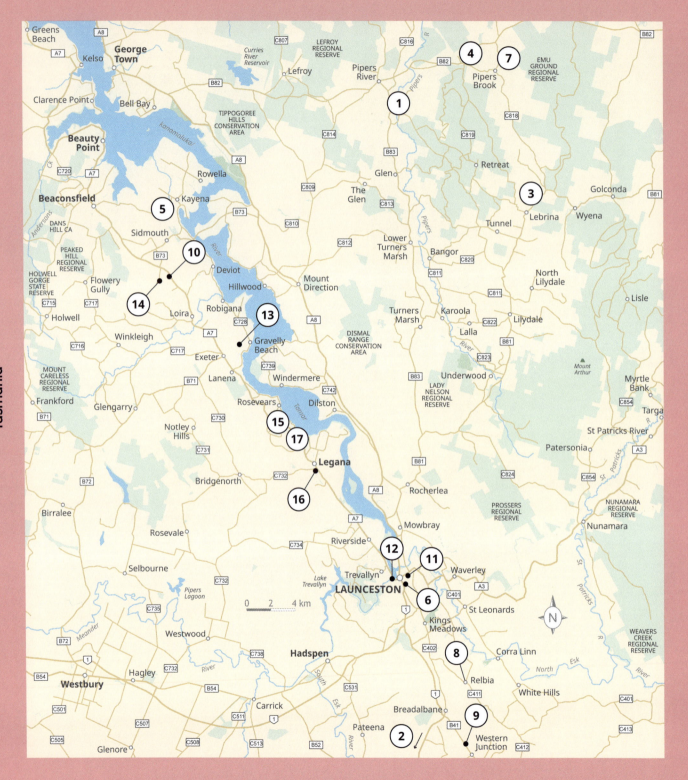

BAY OF FIRES

THREE FAMOUS BRANDS COME TOGETHER FOR A PERFECTLY ROUNDED EXPERIENCE.

Let's get the location straight first – this winery is not in the famed Bay of Fires area. It's in Pipers Brook, and it's an iconic cellar door that is actually three iconic cellar doors. Bay of Fires has three distinct labels, each offering something different: there's Bay of Fires itself, which is a full range of premium sparkling and table wines; Eddystone Point, a more affordable, approachable range of table wines; and House of Arras, which is solely premium sparkling wines that are among the finest in Australia. On a visit to this lovely, countryside cellar door, you can do a standard tasting that will take you through samples of all three labels; choose to focus purely on riesling, chardonnay or pinot noir in a Masterclass tasting; or really go for it with a Premium Arras Tasting, which is a deep-dive into the famous sparkling range. Leave plenty of time too, to check out the views, and pat the winery dog.

bayoffireswines.com.au

CALLINGTON MILL

SPARKLING NEW FACILITY IS AIMING TO TAKE OVER THE WHISKY WORLD.

Warning: this sprawling whisky distillery is not actually in the Tamar Valley or Pipers Brook. It's in the charming town of Oatlands, about an hour and a half south of Launceston. Still, it bears mentioning in here because this is one serious – and seriously amazing – whisky distillery, a hyper-modern facility with high ambitions to become the finest producer of wee drams in Australia. And it probably will. A visit here could take up a full afternoon – by the time you've checked out the historic mill and stables, taken a self-guided tour of the distillery, sampled the large range of Callington products, and then grabbed a meal at the excellent restaurant. Not to mention explored the historic town. Well worth the drive to experience.

callingtonmilldistillery.com

CLOVER HILL WINES

DIG INTO TASMANIA'S WINEMAKING PAST WITH A MUSEUM MASTERCLASS.

You could opt to do just a standard tasting at Clover Hill Wines, high up on a ridgeline in Pipers Brook. You could try a little of every wine in the current range of premium sparklings, made in the traditional method from Champagne, and walk away very happy. But why not go next-level, with a Wine Masterclass? My recommendation would be the Museum Masterclass, a tasting that lines up all of the current releases – the Blanc de Blancs, Rosé, Exceptionelle Vintage and more – against the same wine made 10 years previously, fished out of the Clover Hill cellar. This gives the perfect insight into the effect of bottle aging, as well as a look into the changing nature of Clover Hill winemaking over the years. Whatever your choice, however, this is one beautiful cellar door, a stunning building with views over vines to die for, and you will want to hang around for a good long time.

cloverhillwines.com.au

Top Clover Hill Wines

GOATY HILL ⑤

TASMANIA HAS NEVER LOOKED BETTER THAN UNDER A GUM TREE WITH A WINE IN HAND.

Life is good at Goaty Hill, where you get to relax out on the deck overlooking the vines, or grab a picnic table under the shade of a massive gum tree and gaze out over the bucolic Tasmanian countryside. Of course, it helps if you have a glass of wine in your hand, and that's no issue here. Grab several, in fact, in the form of a standard tasting range, plus a huge platter of local produce – deli meats, paté, cheeses, olives, pesto – or a cheese plate to help ease any hunger pangs. Goaty Hill makes very good wine, and they serve it in the perfect surrounds.

goatyhill.com

HAVILAH ⑥

WINE BAR, WINE LABEL, BOTTLE SHOP, RESTAURANT – IN OTHER WORDS, PERFECTION.

There's a lot going on at Havilah. First up, this is without doubt Launceston's best wine bar and bottle shop, a cosy, friendly space with the sort of drinks list any big-city establishment would be proud of. Havilah is also, however, a wine label, an experimental brand of lo-fi, natchie drops like pet nats and skin-contact whites. And then Havilah also has a sister wine label, Two Tonne Tasmania, a far more serious sibling that is making classical, premium riesling, chardonnay and pinot noir from fruit sourced from four sites in the Tamar sub-region, and a few based elsewhere. These disparate parts all come together every Sunday, when Havilah the bar acts as a cellar door for Havilah the label, and Two Tonne Tasmania. There are tastings of both labels' full suite of wines, plus drinks by the glass, or to take away, as well as Havilah's usual wine list and a la carte menu. Literally something for everyone.

havilahwine.com.au

DELAMERE VINEYARDS ④

COME FOR THE WINE, STAY FOR THE CHAT AT THIS LAIDBACK VINEYARD.

The Delamere cellar door is only open on weekends, so there's a reasonable chance winemaker Shane Holloway will call past to say hello. If he does, settle in for one of the most entertaining chats you will ever have at a cellar door. This guy has knowledge and he has opinions, and he will freely share either. Even without Shane around though, you're going to love Delamere – a laidback winery that produces serious wine. As this is the Tamar Valley, the sparklings here are excellent, but Delamere also produces a range of table wines, including excellent pinot noir and chardonnay, and an $80 rosé that is an absolute show-stopper. Take a seat outside on the patio, grab a selection of your favourite snacks from the fridge – cheese, charcuterie, premium Spanish tinned seafood, etcetera – and enjoy.

delamerevineyards.com.au

Top Jansz

JANSZ (7)

PROFESSIONAL OUTFIT IN PIPERS BROOK DOES EVERYTHING RIGHT.

Jansz is one of the proper big guns of the Tassie wine world, a name known around the world for the quality of its sparklings. A visit here is appropriately professional, in a lovely, airy room overlooking a lake and vines, where staff pour out curated tastings of the Jansz range, which goes from entry-level non-vintage to high-end vintage rosé (though still affordable) and late-disgorged sparkling. There are plenty of food platters too, from a cheese selection to a full-on gourmet picnic. Bookings are encouraged.

jansz.com.au

JOSEF CHROMY (8)

ENJOY A FEW UNIQUE ACTIVITIES – FROM YOGA TO FISHING – WITH YOUR WINE.

Here's another icon that needs little introduction, a well-known name in Australian wine that has a sprawling cellar door and restaurant just south of Launceston. The cellar door is set in the original 1880s homestead, surrounded by manicured gardens, with plenty of space to spread out. There are all sorts of experiences to enjoy here, from the standard sampling of four different wines, to a tasting, and then lunch at the on-site restaurant, which has held a chef's hat designation since 2017. You can go on a behind-the-scenes tour of the winery, have an introduction to fly fishing (which includes a cellar door visit, because obviously), and even join in Yoga in the Vines which, of course, concludes with a wine-tasting and lunch.

josefchromy.com.au

LAUNCESTON DISTILLERY (9)

BOOK A FLYING VISIT TO THIS CLASSIC LOCAL WHISKY PRODUCER.

Flying into Launceston? You'll barely need to touch down before you begin to sample the local product at Launceston Distillery, set in a disused aircraft hangar right next to the airport. It's not just convenience that's the attraction here, either: the distillery, up and running since 2015, produces an excellent range of single-malt whiskies in a variety of styles, finished in a range of casks – bourbon, tawny, sherry – some smoky and peated, some not. Whatever your preference, drop in for a tour, which takes place on the hour from 10am to 4pm, and sample the range.

launcestondistillery.com.au

LOIRA VINES (10)

FLEDGLING OUTFIT IS DOING EVERYTHING, AND DOING IT WELL.

If you happen to bump into Loira Vines' owners Adrian and Mirabai Carruthers – and this is a boutique operation, so there's a good chance you will – be sure to ask the story of how two NSW-based professionals came to be in possession of a Tasmanian vineyard and winery. It's a good yarn. Once you're through that, concentrate on the products in front of you: classic Tamar wines, the likes of pinot noir, chardonnay and shiraz; apple cider, made on-site from fruit grown on the farm; and even beer, made using hops grown right there in front of you. There's accommodation at Loira, too – a studio apartment with a kitchenette and views over vines.

loiravines.com.au

SAINT JOHN (11)

TAKE A CRASH COURSE IN TASSIE CRAFT BEER AT THIS UBER-POPULAR BAR.

The team at Saint John, a deceptively large bar in downtown Launceston, are serious about beer, but friendly enough to make you feel like there's no shame in not being able to match their knowledge. Trundle up to the bar, point at a tap and ask about it – they'll give you the full rundown, and in no time you'll be sitting up at a high table, sipping a cold glass of something delicious. Saint John has up to 17 taps of local and imported craft beer on at any one time; it also has a big fridge full of hard-to-find bottles and cans, plus the bar serves burgers and tacos (and other tasty things), and hosts functions and events in the private Barrel Room. If you're wondering where all of the city's beer nerds hang out, it's here.

saintjohncraftbeer.com.au

Top Delicious spread at Stillwater

STILLWATER (12)

RESTAURANT ICON IS ALSO A BOUTIQUE HOTEL, SET IN AN OLD MILL.

For the longest time, Stillwater in Launceston has been known for its food, for its fine-dining menu featuring local produce cooked with a slightly Japanese bent. The wine list has always been cracking too – a skillfully curated mix of Tamar favourites and a few others from around Australia and the world. The building, a 180-year-old flour mill by the mouth of the Cataract Gorge, was always a feature. Now, however, it's even more of a feature, because you can stay there. Stillwater the restaurant is also Stillwater Seven, a boutique hotel with seven rooms within the old mill, unique, beautifully designed and decked-out spaces that are an absolute pleasure to spend time in – particularly once you ease open the doors of the mini-bar and discover you have enough wine, beer, spirits, snacks and even fresh bread to keep you sated for weeks. Don't forget, however, to come downstairs for dinner.

stillwater.com.au

STONEY RISE ⑬
SURFERS BRING A LAIDBACK VIBE – AND GREAT WINE – TO ONE GORGEOUS TAMAR LOCATION.

If you know a bit about surfing, then you'll realise that Stony Rise is a popular break near the town of Robe in South Australia. That area is also the former home of winemaker Joe Holyman and his partner Lou, who upped stumps and moved to Tasmania when they found a gorgeous plot of land near the banks of kanamaluka/River Tamar, but opted to bring the name of their fledgling winery across the Tasman with them. Hence, a Tamar winery with a surfer on the label. The cellar door experience at Stoney Rise has a chilled vibe to it, too: it's run by Lou, who's charming and knowledgeable, it has a stunning view of the water, and it's an anything-goes sort of place. Here you can taste Stoney Rise's excellent suite of lo-fi wines, or crack open a bottle made by a cult producer who has influenced Holyman's techniques, plus snack on casual but tasty food. Whatever your choice, this place is an absolute pleasure.

stoneyrise.com

SWINGING GATE ⑭
THE WINE LIST IS LONG AND THE POURS ARE GENEROUS AT THIS ECCENTRIC TAMAR NEWBIE.

Doug Cox is a winemaker who just doesn't know when to stop. Check out the list of wines up for tasting at his ramshackle, anything-goes cellar door: a sprawling list of experimental, minimal-intervention drops, from pet nats to skin-contact whites, to reds that are a little more on the classical side. You've got pinot gris, frontignac, riesling, merlot, pinot noir, chardonnay and more. You've got a cellar door that's an old shed filled with bric-a-brac, tumbledown and friendly, and yet another insight into Doug's wandering mind. The tasting pours here are generous and the vibe is loose – fortunately, there's accommodation on-site in the form of a few glamping domes set up among the vines, so you can stay as long as you like to enjoy it.

swinginggatewines.com.au

TAMAR RIDGE ⑮
GO BACK TO THE VALLEY'S ROOTS WITH TASTINGS FROM TWO FAMOUS LABELS.

Here's your chance to experience the Tamar Valley's long winemaking history: some of the first vines in the area were planted at this vineyard, and at the Tamar Ridge cellar door visitors can sample the work of Tasmanian viticultural royalty in the shape of sparkling wine pioneer, Dr Andrew Pirie. This is essentially a cellar door for two labels: Tamar Ridge, which focuses its attention on premium pinot noir, and Pirie, which is all about fine sparkling wine. Roll up here, grab a table with a view, and you'll be taken through a selection of both labels, with Mediterranean-style snacks up for grabs on weekends. While you're here, wander next door (just a few metres away) to Turner Stillhouse for a tasting of high-quality gin and whisky.

tamarridge.com.au

TIMBRE ⑯
WOOD-FIRED MEATS ARE THE STAR AT THIS INNOVATIVE EATERY.

Timbre is deceptive in its complexity. Everything seems pretty easy-going and simplistic here, from the minimalist dining room to the friendly service. Even the menu doesn't give a lot away: it's more just a brief list of ingredients. So, it's a pleasant surprise when the dishes on the tasting menu begin arriving and you realise the skill and the elaborateness of the food in front of you. We're talking vegetables treated as stars, the humble likes of carrots and kohlrabi elevated to all new levels; and meats roasted to perfection in a wood-oven, served with rounds of sides that have each been considered and executed perfectly. That everything else is so low-key and laidback only adds to the impressive nature of the food. The Velo winery is also on-site, though the wine list at Timbre has hits from around Tassie and the rest of Australia.

timbrekitchen.com

A crash course in sparkling wine

The Tamar Valley, and in particular the Pipers Brook area, is prime sparkling wine territory, where grape-growing and wine-storage conditions are perfect for making a product that can hold its own with the best in the world - including Champagne. Given you're bound to be faced with numerous sparkling-wine labels during your time here, it's worth knowing what all the terms on those labels mean. Here are some common phrases to look for:

NV

Stands for Non Vintage. This wine will be made from a blend of grapes sourced over numerous vintages, or years, with the aim to make a consistent product that will taste the same every time you buy it.

VINTAGE

Vintage sparkling wine, meanwhile, is made from grapes sourced from a single year - which will be marked on the label - and indicates superior quality. Most wineries will only make a vintage sparkling on particularly good years.

GRAND VINTAGE

This is even better than a vintage sparkling, only made in the absolute best years. And usually priced accordingly.

BLANC DE BLANCS

This means 'white from white', and it indicates that only white grapes - usually chardonnay - were used to make the wine.

BLANC DE NOIR

Meaning 'white from black', this indicates that the wine is made purely from pinot noir. If the wine isn't labelled either Blanc de Blancs or Blanc de Noir, it will have been made from a mixture (some or all) of chardonnay, pinot noir, pinot meunier, pinot gris, pinot blanc, pinot meslier and arbane.

ROSÉ

Sparkling wine labelled rosé has been left on skins - that is, allowed to ferment with the red pinot noir skins for a few hours, thus imparting far more red colouring - and will have a pinker, rosier colour.

LATE DISGORGED

Okay, we're going to get techie here. To make sparkling wine, the grape juice is fermented in the usual way, and then bottled immediately, where more yeast and sugar is added, and the wine undergoes a second ferment in the bottle, creating fizz, and also 'lees', or dead yeast cells. These lees help to impart flavour, so sparkling wine is often left 'on lees' for periods of several years, sometimes up to a decade, with the bottles regularly rotated to stir the lees and increase the flavour. Once winemakers think the wine is ready, they will 'disgorge' it, which involves inverting the bottle, allowing the lees to gather in the neck, then freezing the neck, opening the bottle, and watching, no doubt with giddy joy, as the pressure inside shoots that frozen cap of lees out. Winemakers then add 'dosage', or more wine mixed with sugar to top the bottle up and adjust its sweetness to the desired level. The term 'late disgorged' means the wine has been left on lees for an extended period, longer than usual for that particular winemaker, which indicates superior quality, as well as more complex flavours: usually toasty, nutty, even honey notes.

Brut nature

The following phrases indicate the sweetness of the wine, and how much sugar has been added in the 'dosage'. Brut nature has no sugar added – it's the driest of the dry.

EXTRA BRUT

This is still very dry, with just a small amount of sugar added at dosage.

BRUT

The most popular and the most common, still dry, but with a hint of sweetness.

EXTRA DRY

Not as dry as brut, despite the name, and with a stronger hint of sweetness.

DRY

This is actually medium-sweet, with a significant amount of sugar added at dosage.

DEMI-SEC

Sweet sparkling wine, usually something you would have with dessert.

DOUX

The sweetest of the sweet, and could be a dessert on its own. Not something you will see very often in Australia.

UTZINGER ⑰

A LITTLE TOUCH OF THE SWISS ALPS COMES TO TASSIE, IN THE FORM OF EXCELLENT WINE.

The Utzinger story begins in Iran – because, of course it does. There, in the city of Esfahan, Swiss tourist Matthias met Australian tourist Lauren. Matthias was a winemaker, looking for a place to ply his trade. Lauren was a traveller, hoping to one day return home. The pair travelled together for a while, before eventually heading back to Tassie, where Matthias discovered conditions not totally dissimilar to his home in Switzerland. And so, Utzinger the wine label was established. Matthias and Lauren bought a plot of land on a hill overlooking the Tamar, planted vines, set up a Swiss-style barn, and started making a name for themselves. Their cellar door is spanking new and run by the family, a cosy space with an incredible view, the perfect location to sample the fruits of a beautiful love story. Don't miss the chardonnay and the pinot – both sensational.

utzingerwines.com

Top Utzinger

The Perfect Day
THE TAMAR VALLEY AND PIPERS BROOK

Tasmania

10AM CLOVER HILL WINES

Today's adventure is a wide loop beginning and ending in Launceston, taking in both sides of kanamaluka/River Tamar. You begin on the eastern side, with a sparkling flight and a view at Clover Hill (see p.281).

11.30AM DELAMERE VINEYARDS

Make your way north to Delamere (see p.282), a rustic spot where you can grab a table in the shade and sample some truly amazing wine.

1PM STONEY RISE

Have a low-key lunch at Stoney Rise (see p.285) - a toasted sandwich, some charcuterie - matched with a flight of excellent local wine, or something from a little further afield.

3PM UTZINGER

As you wind your way back down the western bank of the river, call in at Utzinger (*see* p.287), a friendly family-run winery that is one of the valley's new stars.

6PM SAINT JOHN

Back in Launceston, begin the evening's festivities with a beer and a chat at Saint John (*see* p.284), the craft beer bar you wish your home town had.

7PM STILLWATER

Dinner tonight is a Mod-Oz extravaganza from Stillwater (*see* p.284), also in Launceston, with food so delicious you'll just keep on eating until you have to be assisted up to your room for the night.

Darlington Vineyard

EAST COAST
PAREDARERME AND PYEMMAIRRENER COUNTRY

There's nothing done by halves on Tasmania's east coast. Nothing here is subtle. In fact, it's sublime. The coastline to the north of Hobart is as ruggedly beautiful as they come, with long stretches of white-sand beach, dotted with fishing villages and holiday homes, backed by hills and native bushland, encompassing a few of Tasmania's best-known coastal reserves in Freycinet and larapuna/Bay of Fires.

If you love the outdoors, you're going to love the East Coast. If you love fishing and scuba-diving, hiking and camping, climbing and kayaking, then you're going to love the East Coast. Oh, and if you're into wine and food as well? Then we have good news.

Tasmania's East Coast sub-region is a long, thin strip of verdant land that runs from Bream Creek in the south (just an hour from Hobart), to St Helens in the north, taking in the stunning beauty of Coles Bay, Freycinet and Wineglass Bay, the beachside glory of Bicheno, the windswept charm of Akaroa. The bulk of the wineries are huddled around Cranbrook, about halfway up the coast, and if you're planning to do a day skipping from tasting to tasting, that's the area you want to centre yourself. Otherwise, they're quite scattered, but that's fine: jump in the car and drive along the famed Great Eastern Drive, enjoying the sheer beauty of the coastline, calling into wineries, distilleries and farms along the way.

CRAIGIE KNOWE

FRIENDLY SPOT TURNS OUT WINE FLIGHTS, PASTRIES, CHOCOLATE AND EVEN HIGH TEAS.

This place is like being invited over to a friend's house – only, your friend lives on a farm in the Tassie countryside, and produces wine, bakes pastries, and stocks artisanal chocolates. In other words, this is the friend you've always wanted to have. Craigie Knowe is the oldest vineyard in the East Coast region, planted in 1979 by the side of a creek in Cranbrook, and it's still a small-batch, family-run affair with charm to burn. The team here do free tastings of their Bordeaux-style wines – which are all very reasonably priced, particularly for premium-only Tasmania – plus they can do chocolate pairings, platters of local produce, pastries and even high teas. There's plenty of space outside to relax, or if it's cold, huddle in the big barn and get to know your new friends.

craigieknowe.com.au

DARLINGTON VINEYARD

BOUTIQUE WINERY KEEPS THINGS SIMPLE, AND AFFORDABLE.

Your exploration of the East Coast has barely begun and already you're at Darlington Vineyard, in the holiday town of Orford, just over an hour's drive from Hobart. Orford is gorgeous, a beachy place at the mouth of the Prosser River, and Darlington Vineyard is just as lovely, a boutique winery that grows just four varieties – pinot noir, chardonnay, riesling and sauvignon blanc – and grows them well. It's all pretty laidback and low-key here, an intimate tasting experience at the modest cellar door. Though the wines are affordable, with pretty much everything under $30, they're pleasingly high quality.

darlingtonvineyard.com.au

DEVIL'S CORNER ③

MODERN, SPACIOUS WINERY BRINGS A LITTLE GLAMOUR TO THE EAST COAST.

You haven't even entered Devil's Corner, you haven't even sighted a bottle of wine, and already you're blown away. There's a tower at the entrance to the winery, a column with a staircase in the middle leading to a lookout up top, from where the true splendour of the East Coast is laid out before you: the Freycinet Peninsula, Moulting Lagoon, acre upon acre of rolling vineyards, and so much more. It's gorgeous, and it gives a fair impression of what lies ahead. In this region of small, modest cellar doors on boutique sites, Devil's Corner is something else – a slick operation with a modern, spacious tasting room making the most of those stupendous views. There are tasting paddles here, plus charcuterie platters, and two restaurants on-site: Tombolo, which does wood-fired pizzas; and Fisher of Freycinet, with local seafood, a perfect match for the cool-climate wines. You can't go wrong, whatever your choice.

devilscorner.com.au

FREYCINET WINERY ④

OLD-SCHOOL FAVOURITE IS STILL PRODUCING THE BEST WINE IN THE REGION.

Tasmania's East Coast is a relatively young region, filled with up-and-comers in the wine world, those still seeking to make their mark. And then there's Freycinet, which has well and truly arrived. If your preference is good wine, if you only want to taste the best, then head directly to Freycinet, just off the Tasman Highway north of Cranbrook. Freycinet is undoubtedly the leader of the East Coast pack, producing some of the Apple Isle's best riesling and pinot noir. Despite this formidable reputation, however, the cellar door is a pretty modest affair, where knowledgeable and passionate staff can walk you through a relaxed sample of Claudio Radenti and Lindy Bull's award-winning range. There's also homemade olive oil to try and buy.

freycinetvineyard.com.au

GALA ESTATE ⑤

ONE OF TASSIE'S OLDEST BUSINESSES NOW MAKES SOME OF ITS NICEST DROPS.

Another vineyard in the impressive Cranbrook cluster, Gala Estate has some serious history: it's part of the second oldest family business in Tasmania, a sheep station that has been in the Amos family since 1821. It wasn't until 2009 that someone had the bright idea to throw a few grape vines in the ground and, soon after, Gala Estate the wine label was born. These days, Kiwi Liam McElhinney is in charge of winemaking, and he makes an enviable range of chardonnay, pinot noir, sauvignon blanc and more. Stop into the farm for a sample at the cellar door, set in an old cottage and doing by-appointment-only tasting flights across three tiers: White Label, Black Label, or The Reds. Regardless of your choice, this is a great place to soak up the Amos family history and enjoy the fruits of their (new) labours.

galaestate.com.au

Top Devil's Corner Cellar Door *Opposite* Darlington Vineyard

East Coast

KATE'S BERRY FARM (7)

WHY HAVE LUNCH WHEN YOU CAN HAVE DESSERT – AND SOAK UP SWEEPING VIEWS.

Perched high above Swansea and overlooking the Freycinet Peninsula, Kate's is a cool-climate berry farm with a cafe serving artisan chocolates and delicious desserts. Once you've sampled the food here, choose from the range of homemade sauces, jams and fruit wines to create a picnic or stock your pantry. The rustic cafe has plenty of indoor seating, though on a sunny day it's hard to resist a spot outside to marvel at those views.

katesberryfarm.com

THE LOBSTER SHACK (6)

FEAST ON FRESH LOCAL SEAFOOD WITH ONE OF THE BEST VIEWS AROUND.

Bicheno is a gorgeous little holiday town just north of Freycinet, a place people come to surf, to fish and to feast on the ocean's bounty. If your priority is the latter, head directly to The Lobster Shack, a Bicheno institution dedicated to that most prized of crustaceans. This is a 'sea to supper' operation, something of a farmgate for dedicated lobster fishers who sell their wares on the waterfront in the form of lobster rolls, lobster platters, whole natural lobsters or even lobsters mornay. There's plain old fish and chips, too, if you're not pushing the boat out. Grab a glass of local wine, stare out over the Gulch waterway, and you're in heaven.

lobstershacktasmania.com.au

MILTON VINEYARD (8)

WHILE AWAY A LONG AFTERNOON WITH DELICIOUS WINE AND MATCHING SNACKS.

Here's another winery in the Cranbrook area, and another of extremely high quality in a gorgeous setting. Milton's cellar door is set on the banks of a dam, with views over vines, and it's a beautiful place to while away a few hours sipping wines and snacking on good food. The team here, helmed by owner Kerry Dunbabin, serve cheese platters to match the wine, and on weekends during summer there's a food truck doing more substantial meals. Mostly though, you're here for the wine, which takes in shiraz and pinot noir on the red side, and chardonnay, pinot gris and gewürztraminer in the whites. All are made with love on a farm that has been in operation since 1826.

miltonvineyard.com.au

Top Milton Vineyard *Opposite* Priory Ridge

PIERMONT ⑨

COUNTRY-LUXE RETREAT AND RESTAURANT CAPTURES THE EAST COAST'S BRILLIANCE.

Piermont is a special place, a slice of the wild Tasmanian East Coast that will stay with you forever. This is a retreat, first and foremost, a place to stay and soak up the peace of the surrounding wilderness on an extensive property, in rustic-chic accommodation that ranges from standard hotel-style suites to studio cottages and a three-bedroom residence overlooking the ocean. There's a restaurant at Piermont too, which is also very much of its place, a fine-diner serving five-course set menus featuring the best local produce, the likes of oysters, king prawns, crabs, lamb and wagyu sourced from the surrounding area, beautifully presented in Piermont's 180-year-old homestead. There's plenty of space too, to walk off (or kayak or even mountain-bike) any over-indulgence.

piermont.com.au

PRIORY RIDGE ⑩

TAKE A BREAK FROM SIGHTSEEING IN TASSIE'S NORTH TO SAMPLE A DRINK OR TWO.

Priory Ridge is as far north as north goes in terms of the East Coast sub-region: it's set on the northern outskirts of St Helens, a stone's throw from Binalong Bay and larapuna/Bay of Fires. It's sublime country up here, and Priory Ridge makes wine that is similarly impressive on its family-run vineyard. The selection is pretty compact – one pinot noir, one sauvignon blanc, a pinot gris and a chardonnay – but that small selection ensures everything is made with care. You're probably in this area for the scenery, for the outdoor attractions and the natural beauty, but you should definitely make time for the wine.

prioryridgewines.com

SPRING BAY DISTILLERY (11)

ENJOY OCEAN VIEWS AND WORLD-CLASS WHISKY JUST NORTH OF HOBART.

Sit at the bar in the tasting room at Spring Bay Distillery, and you can see one of the key ingredients that makes the single-malt whisky here so good: the ocean. With casks maturing in the room behind you, within sight of sea, it's no surprise to find a saline, maritime quality to the spirit here, something that infuses over years of maturation, that adds another dynamic to the interplay of standard whisky characteristics. It's also, of course, just a very pleasant thing to look at as you sip your way through a tasting here, of not just the whisky but Spring Bay's range of gin and vodka. The experience includes a tour of the distillery and the bond store (where those casks are kept), and of course a sample of the product. All this, and you're only an hour from Hobart.

springbaydistillery.com.au

SPRING VALE VINEYARD (12)

CONVICT HERITAGE CONVERGES WITH WINE CULTURE AT CRANBROOK ESTATE.

The cellar door at Spring Vale Vineyard, just south of Cranbrook, is a slice of history: it was built in 1842, using convict labour, like so many places in Tassie, and it's now heritage-listed, an absolutely lovely place to relax for an hour or so and sample the local product. The farm has been in the Lyne family since 1875, and there's been great wine produced here for almost 40 years. It's mostly about pinot noir, though there's also excellent chardonnay and pinot gris. There's a restaurant on-site too, called Mel's Kitchen, situated under a marquee among the vines, it's the perfect place to visit if you want to prolong your stay and drink some more of that wine.

springvalewines.com

TWAMLEY FARM (13)

BEGIN YOUR EAST COAST EXPLORATION WITH A HIT OF THE REGION'S HISTORY.

This idyllic spot sits at the base of the East Coast sub-region, only an hour or so outside Hobart and yet a whole world away from city life. The farm has been in the Turvey family since 1833, and though there's still plenty of agricultural business being done, this is also a great place to spend the night, staying in either a converted 1840s stable (with an outdoor cedar hot tub), the modern Farm Pod, or a glamping tent. Twamley also owns The Storekeeper's, a cottage in the town of Buckland, just nearby. While you're staying at the farm, there are cooking classes, hiking and mountain-biking trails, a target shooting range, and a host of historic buildings to explore.

twamleyfarm.com.au

Top Spring Vale Vineyard

VAN BONE (14)

FOODIE COUPLE HAVE CREATED TRUE DESTINATION DINING IN MARION BAY.

Picture a restaurant in Europe, or maybe Japan: a purpose-built eatery set far from civilisation, a destination in itself, a place of pilgrimage that gets whispered about by foodies in the know. A place where the greatest care is taken to utilise local ingredients and turn them into something of alchemical wonder, to coax out flavour and texture, to take diners on a three- or four-hour journey into another world. That's Van Bone, and it's not in Europe or Japan, it's in Tasmania, in Marion Bay, just an hour or so outside Hobart. Chef Tom Hardy and his partner, manager Lauren Stucken, have created an amazing experience here, one you will have to book in for well in advance – the restaurant only seats 20 people, and is only open for lunch four days a week – and one in which you will have to be surprised by the menu, given it changes almost daily. Still, you have to come here.

vanbone.com.au

The Perfect Day
EAST COAST

Tasmania

10AM SPRING BAY DISTILLERY

This isn't for the faint-hearted: it's 10am, and it's time for a whisky. Your day begins at the bottom of the East Coast sub-region, at Spring Bay Distillery (see p.296), for a quick tour and a wee dram.

12PM CRAIGIE KNOWE

Now it's time to head up to the East Coast proper, on a beautiful 1hr drive hugging the beaches towards Cranbrook. Make your next stop at Craigie Knowe (see p.292), the oldest vineyard in the area.

1PM DEVIL'S CORNER

It's only 10min up the road now from Craigie Knowe to Devil's Corner (see p.293), where you can climb the tower to the lookout, have a tasting of the wine, and then choose pizza or seafood for lunch.

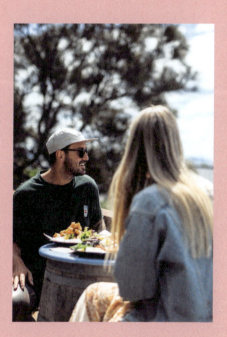

3PM FREYCINET WINERY

Stop in for a sample of the East Coast's best wine, served up with a friendly smile at the deceptively modest Freycinet cellar door (see p.293).

6PM THE LOBSTER SHACK

Finish off your day at The Lobster Shack (see p.294) with a feast of local crustaceans, eaten overlooking the sea, and paired with a local sauvignon blanc or pinot gris..

Meadowbank

THE DERWENT VALLEY AND HOBART

LAIRMAIRRENER AND NUENONNE COUNTRY

Hobart/nipaluna isn't just close to wine regions, it pretty much is a wine region, given there are plenty of vines in the ground on the Tasmanian capital's outskirts, and wine is being made on its CBD streets (*see* Glaetzer-Dixon, p.303). This is a city with an embarrassment of foodie and boozy riches, and you don't even have to jump in a car to experience them. Just wander the streets and you will find breweries, distilleries, wineries, restaurants, cafes, markets ... whatever your heart and stomach desire, essentially.

Though, you should venture a little out of Hobart, because you only have to make your way west along the banks of the River Derwent for a few minutes before you're in the Derwent Valley sub-region, a verdant and burgeoning area that just happens to be perfect for growing things: grapes, hops, vegetables and more. New Norfolk is the hub of the valley and a tucked-away town with plenty of highly regarded artisan and antique stores. Some of Tasmania's best wineries are nearby, some of its best breweries, and some of its best-known eateries. Block out a good few days for the Derwent – and you'll still feel you could have stayed for longer. Maybe, like so many of its residents, a lifetime.

AGRARIAN KITCHEN 1

TASMANIA'S FOODIE ICON IS STILL DISHING UP THE GOODS IN NEW NORFOLK.

Everything that's great about the Tasmanian food scene – the connection to the land, the love of local produce, the hands-on vibe, the do-it-yourself mentality – is encapsulated by the Agrarian Kitchen, a much-loved restaurant and cooking school in New Norfolk, just outside Hobart. Set up by foodie doyens Rodney Dunn and Séverine Demanet in 2008, the Agrarian Kitchen helped make the Tassie food scene what it is today, leading the locavore way, and it's still thriving. The restaurant is a light, airy space where the focus is on food grown and produced by the local community: some raw, some smoked, some fermented, some wood-fired. The cooking school helps interested visitors master these techniques, as well as take the locavore mentality on board. For those just calling through, there's a no-bookings kiosk open on weekends.

theagrariankitchen.com

DERWENT ESTATE 2

TASSIE CLASSICS SERVED WITH STYLE ON THE BANKS OF THE DERWENT.

There's such a rustic charm to the Derwent Estate cellar door, set in a heritage-listed 1820s cottage, that you forget you're only 20min outside a state capital. It's a short journey from Hobart to this vineyard on the banks of the Derwent, and well worth the effort, given the views and the history and the tasty, tasty wine. Derwent Estate focuses on the Tassie classics, chardonnay and pinot noir, though there's also some fantastic riesling and pinot gris to sample. The team here serve lunches too, pretty modest affairs that are delicious, and perfect with the wine.

derwentestate.com.au

Agrarian Kitchen *Opposite* Glaetzer-Dixon Urban Winery

EXPLORERS LODGE ③
GO FOR FULL DERWENT VALLEY IMMERSION AT THIS FRIENDLY, RAMBLING B&B.

You could very easily base yourself in Hobart for a daytrip to the Derwent Valley – still, there's something to be said for complete immersion in the Derwent lifestyle, and you can do that at Explorers Lodge, a lovely B&B in the town of New Norfolk, about half an hour outside the city. Set in a rambling Hamptons-style house, the lodge has personality to burn, with beautiful rooms, peaceful gardens, and easy access to amazing antique stores and the Agrarian Kitchen (*see* p.302), a 5min drive away.

explorerslodge.com.au

GLAETZER-DIXON FAMILY WINEMAKERS ④
URBAN WINERY DOES THINGS A LITTLE DIFFERENTLY ON THE STREETS OF HOBART.

Nick Glaetzer is something of a black sheep in his family. The Glaetzers have been making wine since 1888, and they've been doing it in the Barossa, where Glaetzer Wine is still well known and respected. And yet, after doing a few vintages in Germany and the US, Nick decided instead to head to Tasmania and set up shop – inspired by the urban wineries he'd seen in California – in Hobart itself, where he has a full winery in an old ice-making factory just outside the CBD. Call in here by appointment for a visit, either in the smart tasting room or among the barrels and fermentation tanks of the winery itself, and you'll be taken through the full range of Nick's high-quality drops, including a pinot noir that will knock your wine-loving socks off. And then, just walk back to your accommodation.

gdfwinemakers.com

INSTITUT POLAIRE

TAKE THE SPIRIT OF EXPLORATION WITH YOU INTO THIS MULTI-FACETED GIN BAR.

Just down the road from Institut Polaire, a mere roll of a wine barrel down a short hill, the big ice-breaking ships begin their journeys to Antarctica, to explore and research at the bottom of the world. Hence, Institut Polaire (the polar institute) the smart name for one of Hobart's smartest little bars, which is all decked out in ice-cool tones. Here you can taste the in-house gin, Sud Polaire, sample some of the cracking in-house wine, by Domaine Simha, and feast on imaginative, up-market snacks that will set you up for the evening. Institut Polaire is a hard place to pigeonhole, in fact, given these varied attractions: it's more than a wine bar, more than a cellar door, more than a restaurant, more than a social venue. The fact everyone who works here is so damn nice, and the booze so damn delicious, just adds to the attraction. Book ahead and ask for a spot at the bar.

institutpolaire.com.au

LARK DISTILLERY ⑥

THE ORIGINAL AND STILL THE BEST OFFERS A LITTLE SLICE OF TASMANIA WHISKY HISTORY.

Bill Lark is the godfather of the Tasmanian whisky industry, the first person to successfully apply for a distilling license since the practice was outlawed in Tassie in 1838, and certainly the first to demonstrate to the world that Tasmania is the perfect place to make this cherished spirit. These days there are plenty of distilleries on the island – more than 80 and counting – but Lark is the original and still the best. The distillery has four public venues in Hobart (as well as its new headquarters in Pontville, *see* p.313), from The Still, a swish bar and tasting room, to the Whisky Stall, a small display on the wharf, and even a gin bar, appropriately called Gin(bar). For first-timers, however, you can't beat the Lark Distillery Cellar Door, set in an original distillery and bond store by Constitution Dock. Settle in for a flight of tastings, and then decide which bottle you're going to take home.

larkdistillery.com

LAWRENNY ESTATE ⑦

HEAD TO THE FAR END OF THE DERWENT VALLEY FOR A MEMORABLE WHISKY TASTING.

You can't go much further in the Derwent Valley than Ouse – in fact, at more than an hour out of Hobart, you're technically already in the Central Highlands, despite the River Derwent continuing to flow nearby. Still, if you're into distilled spirits, Lawrenny Estate should be on your itinerary. The single-malt whisky here is absolutely top-notch, and Lawrenny also does an impressive line of high-end gin and vodka. Visit here and you can stroll the grounds of an absolutely stunning 1800s estate, snap a million photos of the riverside homestead, and then take a seat either on the lawn or inside the cellar door and work your way through a sample of everything on offer. The location is amazing, and the spirits, premium drops made 'paddock to bottle' on-site, are industry-leading. What more could you want?

lawrenny.com

LUCINDA WINE BAR ⑧
LOCAL FAVOURITE EATERY BRINGS LO-FI SENSIBILITY TO BOTH WINE AND FOOD.

There are plenty of great places to eat in Hobart – some listed in these pages, but too many to cover in full. However, if you're after both great food and great wine, both of which share a hands-off, lo-fi sensibility, then book yourself a spot at Lucinda. This is a cosy, classy little joint, one that keeps the food local, with ingredients sourced from as close to Hobart as possible, but allows the natural-leaning wine list to branch out across the world, taking in cult producers and sought-after labels from wine regions you didn't even know existed. Chat to the knowledgeable bar staff, tell them what you like, and they'll open something to suit.

lucindawine.com

Top Meadowbank *Opposite* Institut Polaire

MEADOWBANK ⑨
FAMILY WINERY HAS TAKEN ITS PRODUCT NEXT-LEVEL – PLUS, THEY DO MONTHLY LUNCHES.

Out in the far west of the Derwent Valley, at the end of a long dirt road, at the top of a hill, lies Meadowbank … and it's well worth making the effort to get here and experience it. There has been a vineyard here since 1976, but it's only in the last few years that Meadowbank has really started to make its mark, with a dynamic winemaker, Peter Dredge, using great materials to create something magical. Meadowbank doesn't have a cellar door as such, but it does welcome visitors; you just need to call well in advance to book an appointment for a tasting. The winery's owners, the Ellis family, also host a monthly Meadowbank Long Lunch – a friendly meal and chat – which includes a tour of the vineyard, an in-depth tasting, a few samples of wine from the Meadowbank cellar (which stretches back through 40 vintages) and a family-style feast at a long table. If you're in town at the right time, chuck this in your calendar.

meadowbank.com.au

The Derwent Valley and Hobart

MONA ⑩

HOBART'S PREMIER TOURIST ATTRACTION HAS A HUGE AMOUNT TO OFFER FOODIES.

What can you say about the Museum of Old and New Art that hasn't already been said, what superlatives can you use that haven't already been gushingly written? People love MONA, and with good reason. It's a sensational experience that begins with a fast ferry ride from central Hobart, and then takes in grand modern architecture, a sprawling and eclectic art collection, two fine-dining restaurants, a cellar door for two wineries, and another one for a craft brewery. There's accommodation on-site, of course. You may not love the art – that's the point apparently, to provoke reaction, whether positive or not – but you will absolutely love the experience. On-site Faro calls itself a 'revolving restaurant', given its theme and menu changes every three months. MONA is also home to Moorilla Estate (one of Tasmania's best wineries), and pours the excellent Domaine A range (*see* p.306), plus there's a dedicated wine bar, a cocktail bar called Void, a burger joint called Dubsy's, and a locavore fine-diner called The Source. This is Hobart's premier tourist attraction, and for good reason.

mona.net.au

NEW NORFOLK DISTILLERY ⑪

ARTISANAL RUM GETS A WELCOME SPIN AT THIS SMALL-BATCH DISTILLERY.

Given the Tassie obsession with whisky, and the proliferation of gin distilleries, it's nice to find someone doing something a little different. New Norfolk Distillery focuses on rum: high-quality, small-batch rum. It's probably best known for its spiced rum, though the distillery also turns out a few interesting bits and bobs, such as a Dutch Cookie Liqueur, and a Lamington Liqueur. There's no distillery door here – it's generally closed to the public – though if you book ahead on the website there are tours and tastings available for groups of two or more.

newnorfolkdistillery.com

SONNY (12)

JOIN THE QUEUE FOR ONE OF HOBART'S MOST POPULAR DINING EXPERIENCES.

The downside of Sonny: no bookings, so if you want to get into this wine-bar-cum-small-plates-diner, you'll have to either arrive early, or join the long queue out the front. Sonny, in downtown Hobart, is perennially popular, not just for its compact but high-quality menu of Mod-Oz food, but its extensive and impressive wine list, with something different open by the glass every night, and its relaxed but sophisticated vibe. This is a long, narrow room filled with like-minded souls, the perfect demonstration of just how frankly rad modern-day Hobart can be.

sonny.com.au

STEFANO LUBIANA (13)

WELCOME TO THE BIG ITALIAN FAMILY YOU NEVER KNEW YOU WERE A PART OF.

It's not Tuscany. It's not Sicily. It's not Umbria. It's ... Tasmania? The Stefano Lubiana cellar door is a little slice of Italy, with its terracotta tiles and its sunny patio draped in leafy vines. There's also a distinctly Mediterranean warmth to the welcome at this family-run and highly rated winery just outside Hobart, where the tastings are generous and the long lunches stretch well into the late afternoon. There's so much to love about Stefano Lubiana. To begin with, the wine here, all biodynamic, is incredibly good, the full range from chardonnay to pinot gris to riesling to pinot noir. Stefano also makes a mean range of Italian-style spirits, the likes of amaro and grappa, and he's even working on a Japanese-style umeshu. To visit the winery is to be welcomed into the family, to enjoy big platters of Italian-style food, drink beautiful wine, enjoy the views and the company and feel like you're in Europe again. This place is a must.

slw.com.au

Opposite **MONA**

T-BONE BREWING CO (14)

GOOD TIMES ARE HAD BY ALL AT THIS CRACKING NORTH HOBART BREWERY.

The titular T-Bone here is Tom Bignell, son of whisky maker Peter Bignell, who's the ultimate DIY enthusiast, someone who produces a range of award-winning spirits using a homemade still and a few old spare parts on his farm up near Kempton (*see* Belgrove Distillery, p.312). Tom, meanwhile, makes his own beer, in slightly more salubrious surrounds on the slopes of North Hobart. The brew pub here is all about having a good time, whether that's by nursing one of the freaken great T-Bone beers – standards such as the choc-milk stout, pale and golden ales, or seasonal brews like the red IPA, or a stout aged in one of Peter's old rye whisky barrels – playing a few old-school board games or pinball machines, or feasting on T-Bone's snacks or outside food that you're more than welcome to bring in and enjoy.

tbonebrewing.com.au

TWO METRE TALL BREWERY (15)

SOUR FARM ALES HAVE HIT THE BIG TIME, THANKS TO THIS UNIQUE PROJECT.

Brewer Ashley Huntington jokingly refers to his passion project as 'the worst brewery in Tasmania', given the reviews his sour, barrel-aged farmhouse ales used to get when he first launched them in the early 2000s. Whether Huntington's skills have improved or the Tassie tastes have matured is anyone's guess – maybe a little of both – but this is now one of the most respected and loved craft breweries in the state, a producer of unique, idiosyncratic ales made with hops grown on-site at his Derwent Valley farm. The cellar door here is a pretty laidback affair, just a shed on the farm with a couple of hand-pumped beer taps and a few bottles in the fridge. Visitors are welcome to bring their own food, take a seat at the bar or on the lawn and enjoy a sample of the best worst beer in Tasmania.

2mt.com.au

The Perfect Day

THE DERWENT VALLEY AND HOBART

10.30AM TWO METRE TALL BREWERY

Kick the day off with a visit to the western end of the Derwent Valley, to Two Metre Tall (see p.307), a friendly farmhouse brewery doing serious beer.

12PM STEFANO LUBIANA

It's about 25min east from Two Metre Tall Brewery to Stefano Lubiana (see p.307), probably the best winery in the Derwent Valley, where there's time for a tasting and a long, lazy Italian-style lunch.

3PM MONA

You have two hours now before Hobart's premier tourist attraction (see p.306) closes - utilise that time with art viewing, or wine-tasting, or cocktail-supping, or snacking, or all of the above.

6PM LARK DISTILLERY

Back in Hobart, make time for a quick whisky tasting at Lark Distillery (*see* p.304), the original and best, down by the docks.

7.30PM LUCINDA WINE BAR

Finish off the evening with dinner at Lucinda (*see* p.305), which couldn't be more Hobart if it tried, with a locavore menu and an unpretentious crowd.

COAL RIVER VALLEY

PAREDARERME COUNTRY

As soon as Hobart disappears in your rearview mirror, you're in another world: the Coal River Valley, just 25min or so from the Tassie capital, a place of rolling hills, historic little towns, and so many good things to eat and drink.

The Coal River Valley sub-region begins just north-east of Hobart, around the town of Cambridge, and stretches up north through charming Richmond, to sleepy Campania and beyond. Throughout, you have verdant farmlands, with plenty of roadside stalls to look out for, selling all manner of locally grown produce.

The southern section of the Coal River Valley is all about wine, though none of the sparklings that are made so successfully up north; here it's more about high-quality riesling and pinot noir, though with plenty of chardonnay and a few other interesting grapes thrown in. The north, meanwhile, is prime whisky country, where you will find some of the Apple Isle's best distilleries.

Regardless of where you choose, this is a quiet and charming place to spend time, a sub-region you could easily explore from a base in Hobart, and just as happily choose to spend a few nights enjoying.

BARILLA BAY OYSTER FARM ①

GET YOUR BIVALVES DIRECT FROM THE SOURCE, JUST OUTSIDE HOBART.

You're in oyster country: you might as well go to the source. Set on the banks of the Pitt Water Nature Reserve, and right by the airport, Barilla Bay is an oyster farm, restaurant and function venue, and an attractive place to be if you're a fan of bivalves. There are tours of the farm, which include a tasting of local ginger beer and six freshly shucked oysters, and plenty of great food at the restaurant, which overlooks the water, with kunanyi/Mount Wellington looming ever-present in the background. Take some advice: go hard on the oysters, pair them with a bottle of local sauvignon blanc, and you're on your way.

barillabay.com.au

Top Fresh oysters at Barilla Bay Oyster Farm
Opposite Coal River Valley farmland

Coal River Valley

BELGROVE DISTILLERY (2)

ENIGMATIC FARMER TURNS WHISKY-MAKER (AND ARTIST) – AND IT'S A HUGE SUCCESS.

Peter Bignell is an enigma, the sort of person you think you have pegged – but then you realise you really, really don't. Peter is a farmer who found himself with a surfeit of rye one year, after a sale gone wrong, and so decided to make some whisky. He built a still, refashioned an old laundromat dryer into a malting station, rejigged an old gas bottle into a peat smoker, and away he went. The whisky was such a hit that Belgrove Distillery was born, and it's gone from strength to strength ever since – though it's still based on Peter's farm, just outside Kempton to the north of the valley, and it's still very much a DIY outfit. Call in for a tour of the facilities, and a tasting of the vast Belgrove range at the makeshift bar in Peter's old horse stables. And then look at some of the photos and realise that Peter Bignell, Tassie farmer and whisky maker, also does ice sculptures and sand sculptures and is something of an artist. Huh.

belgrovedistillery.com.au

COAL RIVER FARM (3)

CHEESY ENJOYMENT FOR THE WHOLE FAMILY, PLUS SOME FRUIT TO PICK.

Travelling with kids? Take them to the farm. In fact, even if you aren't travelling with tiny humans, you will want to call past Coal River Farm for a sample of the local produce. Depending on the time of year, you can pick your own berries and fruit from the orchard, watch as chocolatiers and cheesemakers do their thing, sample their finished products, and even have breakfast or lunch at the restaurant. The farm – which will actually surprise you with its architectural edge, its black cubes and floor-to-ceiling windows with a view – also does 'High Cheese', which is essentially a cheesy afternoon tea, as well as cheese boards with up to five cheeses. Cheese.

coalriverfarm.com.au

DOMAINE A (4)

AS YOU WOULD EXPECT, DAVID WALSH'S 'OTHER' WINERY IS DOING THINGS DIFFERENTLY.

Domaine A goes its own way. In this land of pinot noir and chardonnay, where growing conditions are similar to those in Burgundy, in the east of France, Domaine A seeks to make wine in the style of Bordeaux, from France's far south. That means cabernet sauvignon, big and heavy, and sauvignon blanc, aged in oak, textural and savoury. Many said it couldn't be done, but happily, they were wrong. Domaine A makes incredibly good Bordeaux-style wine in the land of what should be Burgundy, with price tags to suit (though see the Stoney Vineyard range for more affordable options). The winery is now owned by David Walsh, he of MONA and Moorilla Estate (*see* p.306) fame, so it's a slick operation, and a visit to the cellar door here is a pleasure from start to finish. While the cabernet is obviously the star, don't miss Lady A, the winery's sauvignon blanc, which is treated with a respect this maligned – and sometimes frankly terrible – grape is not often afforded.

domaine-a.com.au

EVERY MAN & HIS DOG ⑤

JOIN THE FAMILY, PAT THE DOG, AND ENJOY SOME OF THE BEST WINE AROUND.

The hospitality at Every Man & His Dog has a distinctly country vibe: this is a family-run operation in which visitors are welcomed like extended members of that family, sat down on the patio, treated to a relaxed tasting, plied with cheese and other snacks, and asked to keep an eye on the dog. The whole thing is thoroughly charming, so much so that you almost forget to appreciate the quality of the small-batch wine, which is super-high. No one who visits has a bad word to say about this place – they're already one of the family.

everymanandhisdogvineyard.com

FROGMORE CREEK ⑥

CELLAR DOOR AND RESTAURANT HAS THE GOODS FOR THOSE WHO'D LIKE TO SETTLE IN FOR THE DAY.

Life is good at Frogmore Creek: out on the patio in the sun, overlooking the vines and glittering expanse of the Pitt Water Nature Reserve and sipping a glass of wine; on the covered verandah, with those same leafy views and enjoying something good to eat; inside at the tasting room, chatting to the friendly staff and working your way through the Frogmore range. Yep, life really is good here, and you're only 20min out of Hobart. Frogmore Creek is a large operation with plenty to recommend it, not least the amiable, knowledgeable staff and the multitude of options for enjoying yourself on-site. The wine here is excellent, featuring a few grapes you may not have seen much of – check out the gamay, or petit verdot – plus the food is fantastic Mod-Taswegian, and the views are just outright gorgeous. If you have time, head on up to the mezzanine level and check out the story of Tasmanian wine.

frogmorecreek.com.au

Opposite **Domaine A**

KILLARA DISTILLERY ⑦

THE LARK DYNASTY CONTINUES, IN THE FORM OF THIS BOUTIQUE OPERATION.

Kristy Booth-Lark has some serious pedigree: she's the daughter of Bill Lark, godfather of Australian-made whisky (*see* Lark Distillery, p.304), and she has inherited her father's love of and skill at making distilled spirits. Kristy owns and runs Killara Distillery, deep in the Coal River Valley, and it's her you are likely to meet when you call into the boutique distillery for a tasting of whisky, gin or liqueur. All are excellent, though the gin is probably the highlight, made using botanicals grown on Kristy's property. In fact, someday soon, pretty much everything will be grown here: Kristy is working at planting more botanicals, putting in a field of barley to make whisky, and even growing oak trees to use in her own barrels. The future of Tassie distilling is in good hands.

killaradistillery.com

LARK AT PONTVILLE ⑧

TASSIE'S MOST FAMOUS WHISKY PRODUCER HAS A FLASH NEW HEADQUARTERS.

This isn't a whisky distillery – according to Lark, it's a 'whisky village'. Tasmania's oldest producer of single-malts has recently acquired a fancy new headquarters (adding to its Hobart venues, *see* p.304), taking over a historic homestead and stables in Pontville, about half an hour north of Hobart, and transforming it into a whopping 130,000-litre distillery and bond store. Visitors to Lark at Pontville can take a tour of the facility (3pm every Sat and Sun, $99 per person), sample a few of the products at the cellar door, or really push the boat out with 'Fuse', an experience in which a Lark whisky expert will guide you through the finest casks in the store and allow you to create your own blend. That costs $499 per person, and needs to be booked in advance.

larkdistillery.com

Coal River Valley

OLD KEMPTON DISTILLERY ⑨

TAKE A PEEK AT THE WORLD OF DISTILLING OBSESSIVES AT THIS FRIENDLY SPOT.

You can feel the passion at Old Kempton Distillery when you chat to any of the staff here, though in particular to the distilling team. They love what they do, and they're very good at it. To find out just how good, book yourself a spot at the cellar door, housed in an 1840s colonial-era inn in the sleepy town of Kempton, about a half hour north of Coal River Valley proper. If it's a sunny day, take a seat out in the courtyard and work your way through a paddle of four spirits: maybe whisky, or gin, or liqueur, or some of everything. There are group tours of the distillery run every day at 1.30pm. There's also a cafe and shop on-site, serving excellent, locally sourced cuisine. Grab a platter to take with you to the courtyard.

oldkemptondistillery.com.au

Old Kempton Distillery

POOLEY WINES ⑩

ONE OF THE VALLEY'S OLDEST WINERIES PROVIDES ITS MOST ENJOYABLE EXPERIENCE.

Anna Pooley's grandparents, Denis and Margaret, needed something to do in their retirement from the Hobart auto industry back in 1985, so they decided to plant a few vines in Cooinda Vale, in the Coal River Valley, and make some wine. Fast forward to the present day, and Anna is now in charge of a family legacy that has grown into one of the most important in Tasmania: Pooley Wines is exceptional, with incredibly good riesling, shiraz and merlot, and you have to pay a visit here to sample the product. Though the cellar door, just outside historic Richmond, is set next to the family home, a gorgeous 1830s mansion, there's nothing stuffy about the place. The welcome is friendly and relaxed, there's a big garden with plenty of spots to hang out with a drink or two, and there are wood-fired pizzas for lunch from Fri to Sun. Sit, sip, and soak up the history.

pooleywines.com.au

PRESSING MATTERS ⑪

GREAT NAME, EXCELLENT WINE – AND THAT'S WHAT REALLY MATTERS.

As an English nerd and a lover of puns, I'm pretty obsessed with Pressing Matters as a name. You know, pressing grapes, pressing matters, the pressing really matters ... it works on many levels and I love it. Anyway. Even if you don't share my love for punnery, there's also very, very good wine to be had at Pressing Matters, which is what really, um, matters. This winery specialises in pinot noir and riesling, with a wide range of both that you will find popping up on restaurant lists throughout Tasmania as you journey around. Make an appointment and go to the source, however, and you'll enjoy a personal and relaxed visit here, with the chance to sample some excellent product, including what must be Tassie's best sweet riesling.

pressingmatters.com.au

PROSPECT HOUSE (12)

IMMERSE YOURSELF IN COAL RIVER HISTORY WITH A STAY AT THIS MANOR HOUSE.

Though you could easily transit daily between Hobart and the Coal River Valley, why not stay overnight and soak up a bit of its heritage? Prospect House is a boutique hotel and restaurant set in an 1830s manor just outside lovely Richmond town. It's also right across the road from Pooley Wines (*see* p.314), only one of the finest winemakers in Tasmania, so if you're ever thirsty, just wander on over. Prospect House has 11 rooms – 10 standard, one suite occupying most of the top level in the main house – as well as a fine-dining restaurant that serves five-course set-menu degustation meals (book in, even if you're not staying here). Everything oozes class for the perfect weekend break.

prospecthouseprivatehotel.com.au

PUDDLEDUCK (13)

NOTHING IS TAKEN TOO SERIOUSLY HERE, AND IT'S ALL THE BETTER FOR IT.

Puddleduck is super-chill, the sort of place you visit when you just want to hang out and relax, to drink nice wine, snack on tasty food, and while away a few hours. You can even bring your own food, in fact; Puddleduck serves its own Pecking Menu of simple plates, but if you want to bring something fancier along to enjoy either on the covered, adults-only balcony, or in the open, family-friendly Green Zone, you're more than welcome to do that. In between snacks, take a tour of the vineyard, do a wine tasting at the bar, or grab a generously poured tasting paddle to carry back to the table. Nothing is taken too seriously here – though the wine is still very high quality.

puddleduckvineyard.com.au

STARGAZER (14)

LOW-KEY WINERY SHOWS OFF THE BEST OF LO-FI COAL RIVER WINEMAKING.

'Sing out if you're ever in Tasmania,' says winemaker Samantha Connew, not to a close friend or to a particular acquaintance, but to everyone who takes the time to click through to her website and read about her passion. Sing out if you're ever in Tasmania – as in, book an appointment and come on past the winery for a visit. You'll be glad you did, too: Sam's wines are so good, the perfect example of what can be done when you take skill and talent and a lo-fi approach to winemaking and apply it to the best Coal River Valley fruit. You get premium chardonnay, riesling and pinot noir that sells out every year, and that has helped build Sam a reputation as one of the island's real talents. Sing out, if you're ever in Tasmania.

stargazerwine.com.au

SULLIVANS COVE DISTILLERY (15)

TASTE THE 'BEST WHISKY IN THE WORLD' AT THIS NOW-FAMOUS DISTILLERY.

There are two seriously big names in Tasmanian whisky: Lark, the original (*see* p.304), and Sullivans Cove, which many would say is the best. Those 'many' include the judges from the World Whiskies Awards, who awarded the title of Best Single Malt Whisky in the World to Sullivans Cove in 2014. So yes, this is serious stuff, and it's also incredibly good. The Sullivans Cove distillery is in Cambridge, just outside Hobart, at the foot of the Coal River Valley. There are tours of the distillery run daily, though if you're not that keen on looking at various metal columns, you can head straight to a tasting: $30 for three whiskies; $65 for three special release or old whiskies; or $20 for a brandy flight. Whatever your choice, the tour and tasting slots book up well in advance, so be sure to jump in there early.

sullivanscove.com

The Perfect Day
COAL RIVER VALLEY

Tasmania

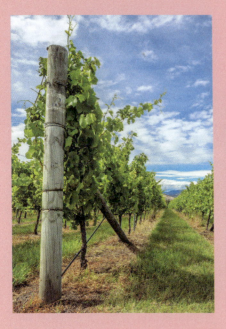

10AM FROGMORE CREEK

Begin at the southern end of the valley with an extensive wine slurping at Frogmore Creek (*see* p.313), the picturesque winery just 20min outside Hobart.

11AM COAL RIVER FARM

Head north, oh, about 1min from Frogmore, and you've arrived at Coal River Farm (*see* p.312), where there's plenty of time to pick some fruit, sample some cheese, and relax a little.

12PM POOLEY WINES

It's just another quick jaunt up the road from Coal River Farm to Pooley Wines (*see* p.314), where you can work your way through some of Tassie's finest riesling and shiraz while tucking into a wood-fired pizza for lunch.

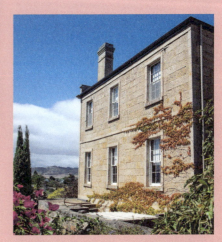

2PM DOMAINE A

Continue north from Pooley, about 10min or so, almost to Campania, where you'll find Domaine A (*see* p.312), expert makers of Bordeaux-style wines in cold-climate conditions, and a pleasure to visit.

3.30PM KILLARA DISTILLERY

Head back down towards Richmond now and call in at Killara (*see* p.313), the distillery run by Kristy Booth-Lark, for a laidback sample of her ultra-local gins and whiskies.

7PM PROSPECT HOUSE

Enjoy a sumptuous degustation-style dinner at your accommodation for tonight, Prospect House (*see* p.315), after a sunset walk through historic Richmond.

Farmhouse Kitchen

THE HUON VALLEY AND BRUNY ISLAND

NUENONNE COUNTRY

There's not much of Australia left once you go south of Hobart: just 100km or so, really, until the land drops away and there's nothing but rolling ocean until you hit Antarctica. That's amazing to think about, and also impossible to picture as you leave the Tasmanian capital and almost immediately find yourself in the Huon Valley, the bucolic food bowl of the state, the home of apple orchards and forest-covered hills and a burgeoning culture of really, really good food.

The Huon Valley oozes charm, with character-filled villages, a creative spirit of artists and makers, and amazing views at every turn. Though it's still quite rural, it boasts an ever-growing population of dynamic growers and artisans who are making the most of the incredibly good produce on hand to make cider, wine, beer, whisky and so much more. And then you throw in nearby Bruny Island/lunawanna-alonnah, windswept and interesting, with its embarrassment of artisans making good things to eat and drink, and you have a region that you most definitely want to spend a good amount of time in. You could attempt a daytrip from Hobart but this is somewhere you want to meander around.

BRUNY ISLAND CHEESE CO. ①

TRY THE CHEESE AND DRINK THE BEER AT THIS BRUNY ISLAND STALWART.

This is Bruny Island, you have to understand, so it shouldn't be a surprise that the cheese joint also makes beer, and that the beer the cheese joint makes is also very, very good. Bruny Island is probably better known for its dairy than its ales, and that's fine, because the cheese here is lovely. Bruny Island Cheese Co. also does a nice line of jarred condiments, sauces and cheese accompaniments, which it sells on-site. And, of course, it makes beer, craft beer that it has been producing since 2016 using local ingredients, such as Tassie-grown hops, Bruny Island honey, and Bruny Island water. The brews here are flavoursome and unique, the likes of open-fermented farm ales, a malty red ale, and a delicious dark ale called Bruny Black that is absolute sensational on a cold, windswept island day. Particularly when paired with a good cheese. Bruny Island Cheese Co. also owns Glen Huon Dairy, over the channel in the Huon Valley, a dairy farm that offers tours for interested visitors.

brunyislandcheese.com.au

Top Browsing at Bruny Island Cheese Co.
Opposite Bruny Island Premium Wines

BRUNY ISLAND HOUSE OF WHISKY ②

COMPACT BAR OFFERS THE LARGEST RANGE OF TASSIE SINGLE MALTS ON EARTH.

Whisky fans: this is exactly what you need. The Bruny Island House of Whisky has the most extensive collection of single-malt Tasmanian whiskies in the world, more than 150 different bottles from all over the state, including rare and limited-edition releases. All are available for tasting too, so rather than schlep from distillery to distillery on the main island of Tasmania, having no real way to directly compare and contrast the products, you can stop into this great little Bruny Island bar and sample to your whisky-loving heart's content. There's whisky produced on-site here too, a single-malt called Trapper's Hut, plus gin, called Seclusion, available in three limited releases.

tasmanianhouseofwhisky.com.au

BRUNY ISLAND PREMIUM WINES ③

FAMILY OUTFIT DOES A LITTLE OF EVERYTHING, AND IT DOES THEM ALL WELL.

By now it should be no surprise to find that, yes, here's a Bruny Island producer with Bruny Island in its name (they're a proud bunch), and also that here's a Bruny Island producer doing several things and doing them well. As the name suggests, the main business here is wine, a passion project for Richard and Bernice Woolley, who are making top-notch chardonnay, sav blanc, pinot noir and cabernet merlot on an island that doesn't always make things easy for winemakers. The company also makes cider, crafted with love by Bernice and her son, Joseph, and it is also, unsurprisingly, excellent. The cellar door does lunch, as well as tastings of everything made here, and it's a pleasure from start to finish.

brunyislandwine.com

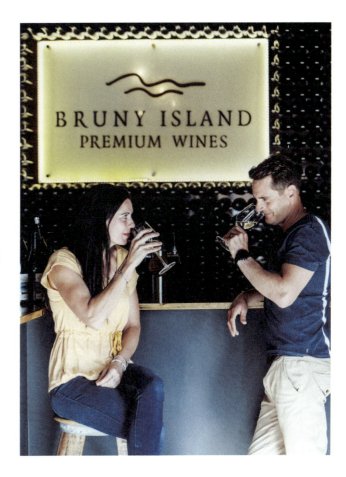

COAST HOUSE ④

TAKE IN THE OCEAN VIEWS FROM ONE OF THE HUON'S BEST ACCOMMODATION OPTIONS.

It's very easy to access the Huon Valley direct from Hobart – drive 40min and you're already into the action – but it's even better to stay here for a few nights and lap up the rural idle. Do that at Coast House, a stunning property on the banks of the Huon River, with expansive views out to the ocean. This is a luxurious, adults-only house with two queen bedrooms, a long verandah, and a full kitchen, with gourmet meals in the freezer and wine included. Sit in front of the wood fire, gaze across the water with a glass of something good in hand, and enjoy.

coasthousetasmania.com

FARMHOUSE KITCHEN ⑤

ENJOY ITALIAN HOSPITALITY AT ITS FINEST AT THIS FRIENDLY COOKING SCHOOL.

There's a beautiful warmth to the Farmhouse Kitchen experience, even if the weather outside is anything but. Giuliana White is the daughter of Italian migrants, a couple from Puglia who moved to Hobart in search of a better life. Giuliana has inherited much from her parents, not least a love for the cuisine of southern Italy, and skill in its preparation, as well as a naturally hospitable nature that has made her Huon Valley cooking school understandably popular. Giuliana runs classes in Italian cookery with her daughter Genevieve, either 4hr masterclasses on the likes of pasta making, vegetarian cookery, Italian bread and pizza, meat, and rice, and 2.5hr mini classes on particular classic dishes, including tagliatelle con sugo di carne (pasta with meat sauce), tiramisu, and gnocchi with tomatoes. Masterclass students are invited to have lunch with Giuliana and Genevieve after their course is finished, which is an experience you don't want to miss.

thefarmhousekitchen-tas.com

FAT PIG FARM

BE INSPIRED WITH A PADDOCK-TO-PLATE FEAST HOSTED BY A FAMOUS FARMER.

Matthew Evans is surely one of the ultimate tree-changers, a former Sydney restaurant critic who went the whole hog, so to speak, and moved to rural Tasmania with his wife Sadie, to run a pig farm. Their Huon Valley operation, Fat Pig Farm, has morphed over the years to become the consummate 'paddock to plate' experience, hosting cooking classes, spreading the small-farm gospel via workshops in sustainable farming practices and design, as well as hosting weekly Friday Feasts – long lunches that show off the seasonal produce derived from the farm, from vegetables and fruits grown in the garden, to those titular pigs roasted whole and served with all the trimmings (and a little local pinot noir). These events are social occasions that often run well into the evening, hosted by Matthew and Sadie on the property, and surrounded by the Huon Valley's rural splendour. When you make a booking, they'll provide you with their location. No doubt many a guest has begun planning their own tree change.

fatpig.farm

FRANK'S CIDER HOUSE ⑥

THE HUON'S SIGNATURE FRUIT IS MADE INTO ITS SIGNATURE BEVERAGE.

You're on the Apple Isle, and the Huon Valley is responsible for 80 per cent of Tasmania's apple production, so it makes perfect sense that here you will also find producers of fine apple cider. Frank's is one of an impressive cohort of Huon Valley cider-makers (also *see* p.324 and p.325), run by Naomie Clark-Port, the fifth generation of Clarks to grow apples on this Franklin farm, though the first to turn them into cider. She's been highly successful in that endeavour, and now has a ciderhouse and cafe too, in the centre of the historic, quaint town of Franklin, where there are free tastings of Frank's cider, plus platters of fresh produce and seasonal lunch dishes. Orchard tours are also run occasionally; check the website for details.

frankscider.com.au

HARTSHORN DISTILLERY ⑦

UNIQUE OPERATION IS 'WHEY' OUT THERE WHEN IT COMES TO SPIRITS.

Hartshorn Distillery, you'll think – never heard of it. And then you will see one of the bottles of spirits here, with its distinctive all-black label scrawled by hand with white text, and realise – ah yep – know it well. Hartshorn has been making waves around Australia with its Sheep Whey Vodka, a spirit distilled using leftover whey from Grandvewe Cheeses, a cheesemaker on the same property. Utilising something that would normally just be tossed out, Hartshorn has now released a whole range of whey spirits, from vodka to gin to liqueurs to a peated spirit close to whisky. Drop by the distillery in Birchs Bay, with its views over Bruny Island, for a standard tasting, or maybe take a gin creation workshop, or a class on churning your own butter.

hartshorndistillery.com.au

HOME HILL WINERY ⑧

THE HUON VALLEY'S PREMIER WINERY DOES NOT DISAPPOINT.

If you do nothing else on your visit to Home Hill, try the Kelly's Reserve Pinot Noir. That's the wine that has made this boutique operation famous, the one that has put the Huon Valley on the map, in some ways, as a wine-making sub-region. Though all of the pinot noirs at Home Hill are excellent – in fact, all of the wines full-stop – the Kelly's Reserve is the real show-stopper. Happily, too, a bottle of it will go very nicely with the food served at the on-site restaurant, which takes high-quality local ingredients and treats them with a little Italian pizazz to create a beautiful, memorable experience. Everyone will tell you to visit Home Hill, in the heart of the valley at Ranelagh, and with good reason.

homehillwines.com.au

KATE HILL WINES ⑨

CULT WINERY PROVIDES AT INTIMATE ATMOSPHERE FOR TASTING AND RELAXING.

Great thing about Kate Hill Wines: if you visit, and go for a tasting at the cellar door, there's a good chance you will run into Kate herself. She's usually around when it's not harvest time, and is always generous with her time, as well as her expertise, pouring out wines, having a chat. That's what makes this place special, really. It's intimate. It's familiar. Of course, it helps that the winery is absolutely beautiful, with a cellar door set in a heritage-listed 1880s cottage that overlooks water and vines. Hill makes the classic Taswegian varietals, chardonnay, pinot noir and shiraz, with a minimal-intervention approach that lets the winery and the region speak. And they have great things to say.

katehillwines.com.au

Top Vodka at Hartshorn Distillery *Opposite* Frank's Cider House

MASAAKI SUSHI

HIGH-END SUSHI IN SMALL-TOWN GEEVESTON? IT'S A THING.

The town of Geeveston, population 616, really should not be home to the best little sushi restaurant you have ever been to. And yet, why not? It sits near the banks of the Huon River, right by the seafood-rich D'Entrecasteaux Channel, and it's also the home of Masaaki Koyama, an insanely talented sushi chef who decided to shift his life from Wakayama, Japan, to small-town Tasmania. Masaaki now plies his trade for the lucky residents of Geeveston – as well as the many people who make the trek down here just to eat – doing takeaway sushi platters, as well as dine-in meals, that make the most of the local produce, both from in the sea and on the land.

masaaki.com.au

Masaaki Sushi *Opposite* Willie Smiths Apple Shed

MEWSTONE

BROTHERS RUN THE GAMUT FROM CLASSIC TO NATCHIE IN LOVELY FLOWERPOT.

If Flowerpot isn't just the sweetest name for a little town you've ever heard, I would like to know what is. That's not the only reason to come here though, just to say you've been to Flowerpot. It's also to visit Mewstone, a relatively new winery that is making a splash with a whole slew of wines that offer something for everyone, from classic, single-estate wines under the Mewstone label, to more experimental and diverse drops under the Hughes & Hughes banner, to a zero-sulphur, low-fi seasonal range called Hughes & Hughes Living Wines. That might sound like a lot, but everything made here by brothers, Matthew and Jonny Hughes, is supremely high-quality, and impressive. The smart, wood-panelled cellar door is on-site at the winery, in pretty Flowerpot, and for $25 the team will run you through a mixed selection of eight wines from across the Mewstone spectrum.

mewstonewines.com.au

PAGAN CIDER

THE FULL BREADTH OF CYGNET FRUIT IS USED TO MAKE THESE TASTY CIDERS.

Pagan does plain old apple cider, if that's what you're into. And it's super-tasty. But don't limit yourself to that one offering, because there are so many different types of fruit that grow down here in Cygnet, and much of it is utilised at Pagan to make ciders that speak of their heritage, ciders that speak of their surroundings, ciders that sing. Call into the Pagan Shed, a small tasting room with a large outdoor area, and you can enjoy a free tasting of the full range that's available on the day (some seasonal ciders won't be around): we're talking pear cider, cherry cider, cider with quince, cider with blueberry, cider with apricot and even peach. It's all delicious, and there's no doubt you'll want to hang around for a few full glasses.

pagancider.com.au

PORT CYGNET CANNERY ⑬

CREATIVE EATERY MAKES THE BEST OF LOCAL PRODUCE IN A REVOLVING MENU.

There is no shortage of great places to eat in the Huon Valley, as you will soon discover, though this is perhaps the most impressive of the lot. Port Cygnet Cannery is, as the name suggests, a former apple canning factory that has been magicked into a hub of high-end food and beverage. There's a restaurant, which we will get to in a second, but there's also a takeaway pizza joint, a coffee roaster and espresso bar, and even a South African-style biltong maker. But the star of the show is the eponymous restaurant, which sources much of its produce from the Cannery's farm nearby, as well as a select group of local growers and artisans, to turn out a varied menu that roams in territory from wood-fired pizza to set-menu lunches to vegetarian feasts. Check it to see what will be happening on the day and time you arrive. Whatever it is, it will be delicious.

portcygnetcannery.com

SAILOR SEEKS HORSE ⑭

SAMPLE PERFECT PINOT NOIR CREATED BY A COUPLE OF ADVENTUROUS SOULS.

Behold, the owners of one of the best winery names in the business: Gilli and Paul Lipscombe, British expat winemakers who were inspired by a 'wanted' ad they once saw in their local Cygnet cafe, from an adventurer looking to procure transport for a trek around Tasmania. The pair recognised a kindred spirit, and the name stuck: Sailor Seeks Horse. The Lipscombes have a passion not just for adventure but also pinot noir, which is what they specialise in down here on 'the edge of viticultural possibility', as they say of their southern vineyard. This is a very small operation, and it's open by appointment only.

sailorseekshorse.com.au

WILLIE SMITHS APPLE SHED ⑮

THERE'S AMPLE SPACE FOR SIPPING AND RELAXING AT THIS CLASSIC CIDER PRODUCER.

The 'shed' at Willie Smiths is more like a giant barn, and inside it lies a rambling space of tables and couches and chairs, along with a bar and kitchen that utilises all the Tasmanian goodies (there's a heap of space outside too). What everyone is here for, mostly, is the cider, made from apples farmed organically by the Smiths, who have been doing this for four generations (so, yes, there's definitely a Granny Smith or two in the family). The Willie range is all apple cider, from traditional to 'bone dry', as well as a seasonal Heritage Blend that you have to try if you get the chance. There's food at the shed too – share platters and heartier meals – plus regular live music, and a weekly artisan and produce market.

williesmiths.com.au

The Perfect Day
THE HUON VALLEY AND BRUNY ISLAND

Tasmania

11AM HOME HILL WINERY

Begin today at the leisurely time of 11am with a tasting at Home Hill Wines (see p.323), in Ranelagh, where the pinot noir alone makes this cellar door worthy of a visit.

12PM KATE HILL WINES

Just a few minutes away from Home Hill lies another of the classic Huon Valley wineries, Kate Hill Wines (see p.323), where there's a good chance of running into Kate herself as you enjoy a leisurely tasting.

1.30PM WILLIE SMITHS APPLE SHED

For lunch, head a little further up the road to Willie Smiths (see p.325), where there's a menu of easily approachable food, plus excellent cider, and the chance of some live music.

4PM HARTSHORN DISTILLERY

Hartshorn Distillery (see p.323) sits half an hour from Willie Smiths, on the coast, near friendly Birchs Bay. Have a tasting of the unique sheep's whey spirits.

6PM PORT CYGNET CANNERY

Continue on a large loop to the town of Cygnet for tonight's dinner destination, Port Cygnet Cannery (see p.325). There's always something different happening here, though a good chance of a wood-fired pizza.

Bruny Island Cheese Co., Tas

INDEX

10 Chains Winery 228
23rd Street Distillery 204
919 Wines 205

A
Adelaide Hills SA 178-87
Adelaide Zone SA 198
Agrarian Kitchen 302
Alexandra Hotel 149
Alice Springs NT 247-51
Alice Springs Brewing Co 248
All Saints Estate 136
Alpha Box and Dice 168, 177
Alpine Valleys Vic. 128-9
Ambleside Distillers 179
Amelia Park 216
Amherst Winery 147
Ampersand Estate 228
Animus Distillery 98, 104
Apex Bakery 155, 164
Arrente Country 247
Artemis 47, 51
Artisans of Barossa 155
Ashton Hills Vineyard 179
Audrey Wilkinson 5, 14
Australian prosecco 138
Australian Truffle Traders 229, 232
Avani 75, 84

B
Backwoods Distilling Co 130
Badlands Brewery 17
Baie Wines 87
Baker Williams Distillery 28
Balancing Heart 255, 260
Balgownie Estate 141
Ballandean Estate 256
Ballarat Vic. 140
Bannockburn Vineyards 87
Bar Rochford 36, 45
Barambah Cellars 272, 275
Barfold Estate 120
Barilla Bay Oyster Farm 311
Baringo Food and Wine Co 98
Barking Owl Distilling Co 130
Barossa Distilling Co. 155

Barossa Gin School/Durand Distillery 156
Barossa Valley SA 153-65
Barossa wine, history 157
Barwon Heads Winestore 88
Basils Farm 88
Bass & Flinders Distillery 76
Bay of Fires 281
Beachtree Distilling Co. 264, 268
Beaver Brewery 249
Beechworth Vic. 130-5
Beerfarm 217
Bekkers 169, 176
Belgrove Distillery 312
Bellarine Distillery/The Whiskery 88
Bellarmine Wines 229
Bendigo Vic. 141-2
Bendooley Estate 47
Bent Road/La Petite Mort 256, 260
Bentspoke Brewing Co. 36, 45
Best's Wines 143
Bibbulman Country 227
Bidawal Country 106
Big Tree Distillery 98
Billson's Brewery 131
Billy Button Wines 128
biodynamic wine 183
Birdie Noshery 17
Blackjack Wines 141
Blackman's Brewery and Pizza Bar 89
Bleasdale Vineyards 199
Blind Corner 217
Bloodwood 18, 24
Blue Pyrenees Estate 147
Boireann 257, 260
Bondar 169
Boon Wurrung Country 73, 106
Boston Brewing Co. 236, 243
Brae 89
Brand's Laira 202
Brass Monkey Brewhouse 257
Brave Goose Vineyard 116
Bress 142
Brewicolo Brewing Co. 90
Bridge Road Brewers 131, 134
Brockenchack Wines 156
Brokenwood 5

Brookside Vineyard 209
Brouhaha 264, 268
Brown Brothers 138
Bruny Island Tas. 319-27
Bruny Island Cheese Co. 320
Bruny Island House of Whisky 321
Bruny Island Premium Wines 321
Bungandidj Country 202
Burrwang Village Hotel 48

C
Calabria Family Wines 56
Callington Mill 281
Canberra ACT 35-45
Cannibal Creek 107
Cape Jaffa Wines 202
Carmel Cider Co 209
Casa La Viña 6
Castelli Estate 236
Castle Rock Estate 237
Cellars at Heathcote II, The 120, 124
Centennial Vineyards 48, 51
Chalou Wines 18
Charlie's of Darwin 249
Charlotte Dalton Wines 200
Charred Kitchen Bar & Restaurant 18, 25
Chauncy 121, 125
Cheeky Monkey Brewing Co./ Caves Road Brewpub 217
Cirillo Estate 156
Clare Valley Distillery 190
Clare Valley SA 189-97
Clonakilla 37, 44
Clovely Estate 273, 275
Clover Hill Wines 281, 288
Clyde Park 90, 95
Coal River Farm 312, 316
Coal River Valley Tas. 310-17
Coast House 321
Cobaw Ridge/Joshua Cooper 99, 104
Coldstream Brewery 62, 71
Collector Wines 37
Colonial Brewing 218
Comyns & Co 6
Contentious Character 37

Coonawarra SA 202-3
Core Cider House 210, 213
Coriole 169
Corymbia 210
Courabyra Wines 52
Craigie Knowe 292, 298
Craiglee Vineyard 97
Crane Wines 273
Crank Handle Brewery 128
Crawford River 146
Crittenden Estate 75
Crowne Plaza Hunter Valley 6
Cullen Wines 218
Cupitt's Estate 55
Curlewis Winery 90
Curly Flat 99
Currant Shed, The 170

D
Dal Zotto 139
Dalwhinnie 147
d'Arenberg 170, 176
Darlington Vineyard 292
Darwin NT 247-51
David Franz 157
De Bortoli Wines 57
De Iuliis 7
De Salis 19
Delamere Vineyards 282, 288
Delatite Winery 149
Derwent Estate 302
Derwent Valley, The Tas. 301-9
Devil's Corner 293, 298
Dhaba at the Mill 100
Dharawal Country 46, 55
Dirt Candy 7
Dirty Three Wines 108, 113
Djab Wurrung Country 143, 146, 147
Dja Dja Wurrung Country 98, 141
Dobson's Distillery 53
Dogrock Winery 148
Domaine A 312, 317
Domaine Naturaliste 218, 225
Dormilono 219, 224
Duke's Vineyard 237
Dusty Hill 273

E
Eagle Bay Brewing 219
East Coast Tas. 291-9
Eastern Peake/Latto Vino 140
Eden Brewery 49, 51
Eden Road Wines 38
Eighteen Sixty 116, 119
Eldorado Road 131
Elton's Bar + Bites 28
Estate 807 237
Eumundi Brewery at Imperial Hotel 265, 269
Every Man & His Dog 313
Exp. 7
Explorers Lodge 303

F
Fallen Giants 143
Farmhouse Kitchen 322
Fat Pig Farm 322
Fermoy Estate 219
Fino 157, 165
Fish by Moonlite 91
Flame Hill Vineyard 265, 268
Fleurieu Distillery 200
Flying Brick Cider Co. 91
Forest Hill Vineyard 238
Four Pillars Gin 62, 70
Four Winds Vineyard 38
Fowles Wine 116, 119
Foxeys Hangout 75, 85
Frankland Estate 238
Frank's Cider House 322
Fraser Gallop Estate 220
Freycinet Winery 293, 299
Frogmore Creek 313, 316
Funk 2.0 210

G
Gaffney's Bakery 121, 125
Gala Estate 293
Garbin Estate 211
Geelong and the Bellarine Peninsula Vic. 86-95
Giant Steps 63, 70
Gilbert Family Wines 29, 32
Gippsland Vic. 106-13
Gisborne Peak Winery 100
Glaetzer-Dixon Family Winemakers 303
Goaty Hill 282
Golden Grove Estate 257
Goodieson Brewery 170, 177
Goona Warra Vineyard 97
Goulburn Valley, The Vic. 114-19
Grampians, The/Gariwerd Vic. 143-5
Grampians Ale Works 143
Grampians Estate 144
Grand Ridge Brewery 108, 113
Granite Belt, The, Qld 254-61
Granite Belt Brewery 258, 260
Granite Hills 100
Grazing 38
Great Hops Brewery 53
Great Southern WA 235-43
Greenock Brewers 158
Grosset 190
Gubbi Gubbi Country 263
Gunaikurnai Country 106
Gunditjmara Country 146
Gundungurra Country 46
Gurneys Cider 109, 113

H
Habitat Artisan Precinct, Dromana Vic. 76-7
Hahndorf Hill 180
Hanging Rock 101
Harewood Estate 238, 242
Harman Wines 109
Hartshorn Distillery 323, 327
Harvest Kitchen 158
Havilah 282
Hayes Family Wines 159
Healesville Grand Hotel 63
Heartswood 64
Heathcote Juniper Lounge 121
Heathcote Vic. 114-15, 120-5
Heifer Station Wines 19
Heli Pub Crawl 250
Helm Wines 39, 44
Henschke 159
Hentley Farm 159
Henty Vic. 146
Heritage Estate 258
Hidden River Estate 229, 232
High Country Vic. 127-39
Hillbrook Wines 230, 233
Hobart Tas. 301-9
Hochkirch Wines 146
Hoggett Kitchen 110, 113
Holgate Brewhouse 101, 105
Home Hill Winery 323, 326
Hoosegg 19

Hunter Valley NSW 3–15
Huntington Estate 29, 33
Huon Valley, The Tas. 319–27

I

Institut Polaire 304
Ironbark Hill Brewhouse 9
Islander Estate, The 200

J

Jaara Jaara Country 120
Jack Rabbit 91, 95
Jackalope 75
Jamsheed 64
Jansz 283
Jardwadjali Country 143, 146, 147
Jasper Hill 121
Jaspers Bar 230
Jauma Organic 180
Jayden Ong 64, 70
Jetty Road Brewery 76
Jim Barry Wines 191
JimmyRum Distillery 77
Jinibara Country 263
Joadja Distillery 49
Jones Winery & Vineyard 136
Josef Chromy 283

K

Kambuwal/Ngaraba Country 254
Kamilaroi Country 53
Kangaroo Island SA 201–2
Kangaroo Island Brewery 201
Kangaroo Island Spirits 201
Kaniyang Country 227
Kate Hill Wines 323, 326
Kate's Berry Farm 294
Kaurna Country 153, 167, 178, 189, 198, 200
Keith Tulloch Wine 9
Kilikanoon 191
Killara Distillery 313, 317
King River Brewing 139
King Valley Vic. 138–9
Kinglake Whisky 65
Kingsley Grove 273, 275
Kitchen & Butcher 65
Knappstein Enterprise Winery 192
Koerner Wine 180, 192
Koomal Dreaming 220

L

Lairmairrener Country 279, 301
Lake Breeze Wines 199
Lake George Winery 39
Lake House, The 239, 242
Lake's Folly 9
Lane Vineyard, The 181, 187
Langhorne Creek SA 199
Lark at Pontville 313
Lark Distillery 304, 309
Lark Hill Winery 40
Larrakia Country 247
Larry Cherubino 220
Launceston Distillery 283
Lawrenny Estate 304
Le Bouchon 78
Leeuwin Estate 221
Lerida Estate 40
Lethbridge Wines & Hat Rock Vineyard 92, 95
Leura Park Estate 92
Lightfoot and Sons 110
Little Rebel Coffee Roastery 77
Little Rickshaw 171
Lobethal Bierhaus 181
Lobster Shack, The 294, 299
Logan Wines 29, 32
Loira Vines 283
Lost in a Forest 181, 187
Lot.100 182, 186
Lowe Family Wine Co. 29
Lucinda Wine Bar 305, 309
Lyons Will 102

M

M Chapoutier 122
Macedon Ranges Vic. 96–7, 98–105
McLaren Vale SA 167–77
McWilliam's Wines 57
Main Ridge Estate 78
Mallaluka 41
Manjimup WA 227–33
Margan 10
Margaret River Distilling Co 221
Margaret River WA 215–25
Masaaki Sushi 324
Meadowbank 305
Medhurst 65
Merilba Estate Wines 53
Meru Country 204
Mewstone 324
Michael Hall Wines 160, 165
Miki's Open Kitchen 221, 225
Millbrook Winery 211, 213
Millers Bread Kitchen 77
Milton Vineyard 294
Minang Country 235
Minya Winery 92
Mitchell Harris Wines 140
Mitchelton Wines 117, 119
MJs Wine Bar 239
Moffat Beach Brewing Co 266
Moffatdale Ridge 274, 275
MONA 306, 308
Monichino Wines 117
Montalto 78
Montara 144
Moombaki Wines 239
Moon 117
Moonah Restaurant 92
Moorooduc Estate 79
Mornington Peninsula Vic. 73–85
Mount Avoca 148
Mount Benson SA 202
Mount Horrocks 193, 196
Mount Langi Ghiran 144
Mount Monument 102, 105
Mount Pleasant 10
Mount Towrong 102, 104
Mountford Winery 231
Mr Little Cider 77
Mrs Baker's Still House 148
Mudgee Brewing Company 30
Mudgee NSW 27–33
Murchison Wines 118
Murdoch Hill 182, 186
Muse 10, 15

N

Nagambie Brewing and Distillery 118
Napoleone Cider 65
Narkoojee 110
Nashdale Lane Wines 20
natural wine 8
New England Brewing 54
New England NSW 53–4
New Norfolk Distillery 306
Ngadjuri Country 153, 189
Ngambri/Ngunngawal Country 35
Nganyaywana Country 53

Ngarrindjeri Country 199, 200
Ngeringa 183
Nicholson River Winery 111
Nira-Balluk Country 120
Noongar People 227
Nuenonne Country 301, 319

O
Oakdene Vineyards 93, 95
Oakover Grounds 211
Oakridge Wines 66, 71
Ocean Eight 79
Ocean View Estates 266
Old Kempton Distillery 314
O'Leary Walker Wines 193
Oliver's Taranga 171
One Mile Brewery 250
Orange NSW 16-25
Ovolo Nishi 41

P
Pagan Cider 324
Pago Middleton 201
Palling Bros Brewery 122
Paper Scissors Rock Brew Co 144
Paredarerme Country 291, 310
Parrot Distilling Co 20
Passing Clouds 103
Paste 49, 51
Paxton Wines 171
Pemberton WA 227-33
Penfolds Magill Estate 198
Peninsula Fresh Seafood 77
Penny's Hill 172
Pennyweight Winery 131, 134
Peos Estate 231, 232
Pepper Tree Wines 11
Peramangk Country 153, 178, 200
Peregrine Ridge 122, 124
Perry Street Hotel 30
Perth Hills WA 208-13
Petaluma 183
Petersons Wines 54
Pfeiffer Wines 137
Philip Shaw 20, 25
Pialligo Estate 41
Piermont 295
Pierrepoint Estate 146
Pikes 193, 197
Pimpernel Vineyards 66

Pioneer Brewing 21
Pipers Brook Tas. 279-89
Pizzini 139
Poachers Pantry Smokehouse 42, 44
Pokolbin Distillery 11
Polperro 80
Pomonal Estate 145
Pooley Wines 314, 316
Poonawatta 160
Port Cygnet Cannery 325, 327
Port Phillip Estate/Kooyong 80, 85
Portarlington Grand Hotel 93
Portsea Hotel 80
Prancing Pony Brewery 184
Pressing Matters 314
Primo Estate 172
Printhie Wines 21, 24
Priory Ridge 295
Prospect House 315, 317
Provenance (Beechworth) 132, 135
Provenance (Geelong) 94
Pt. Leo Estate 79, 85
Puddleduck 315
Purple Mango Brewery 251
Pyemmairrener Country 279, 291
Pyrenees, The Vic. 147-8

Q
Quealy Winemakers 81
Queenscliff Brewhouse 94, 95

R
Racine Bakery 21, 24
Radis Estate 203
Ravensworth 42
Red Hill Brewery 81, 84
Reed & Co Distillery 129
Rehn Bier 160
Renzaglia Wines 22
Restaurant Botanica 11
Rhino Tiger Bear Wines 77
Rickety Gate Estate 240
Rieslingfreak 160, 165
Ringer Reef 129
Ripplebrook Winery 111, 113
Riverina NSW 56-7
Riverland SA 204-5
Robert Stein 30, 32
Rockcliffe Winery 240, 243
Rosby Wines 31, 33

Roth's Wine Bar + Cellar 31
Royal Mail Hotel Dunkeld 145
Rutherglen Vic. 136-7

S
Sailor Seeks Horse 325
Sailors Grave Brewing 112
Sails Wine Bar 267, 269
St Andrews Beach Brewery 82
Saint John 284, 289
St. Ronan's Cider 66
Samuel's Gorge 172
Sandalford Winery 212, 213
Sanguine Estate 122
Savaterre 132, 134
Savina Lane 258
SC Pannell 173, 176
Scorpo Wines 82
Scotchmans Hill 94
Seed 194, 197
Seppelt 145
Seppeltsfield Road Distillers 161, 164
Serafino 173
Settlers Tavern 222
Sevenhill 194, 196
Seville Estate 67
Shackleton's Whisky Bar 274
Shaw + Smith 184, 187
Shaw Wines 42
Shifty Lizard Brewing Co. 173
Shoalhaven Coast NSW 55
Si Vintners 222, 224
Silkwood Estate 231
Silverstream Wines 240
Simon Tolley Wines 184
Singlefile 241, 242
Sittella Wines 212, 213
Six Tanks Brew Pub 251
Skillogalee 195, 196
Small Acres Cyder 22
Sonny 307
Soumah of Yarra Valley 67
South Burnett Qld 271-5
Southern Fleurieu/Kangaroo
  Island SA 201-2
Southern Highlands Brewing
  and Taphouse 50
Southern Highlands NSW 46-51
sparkling wine terminology 286-7
Spring Bay Distillery 296, 298

Spring Vale Vineyard 296
Standish Wine Company, The 161
Star of Greece 174, 177
Star Lane 132
Stargazer 315
Station Lane Distillery 50
Stefano Lubiana 307, 308
Stella Bella 222
Stillwater 284, 289
Stoney Rise 285, 288
Sullivans Cove Distillery 315
Summertown Aristologist, The 185, 187
Summit Estate 259, 260
Sunbury Vic. 96–7
Sunshine & Sons 267
Sunshine Coast Qld 263–9
Sutton Grange 142
Swan Valley WA 208–13
Swell Taphouse 174
Swiftcrest Distillery 149
Swinging Bridge 22, 25
Swinging Gate 285
Symphony Hill 259

T
T-Bone Brewing Co 307
Tahbilk 118, 119
Tallangandra Hill 43
Taltarni 148
Tamar Ridge 285
Tamar Valley, Tas. 279–89
Tamburlaine 23
Tangletoe Cidery at Mountford Winery 231
Tapanappa 185
TarraWarra Estate 68
Taungurung Country 98, 115, 120, 149
Taylors 195
Tedesca Osteria 82, 84
Tellurian Wines 123, 124
Ten Minutes by Tractor 83
Tertini 50, 51
The Cellars at Heathcote II 120, 124
The Currant Shed 170
The Derwent Valley 301–9
The Goulburn Valley Vic. 114–19
The Grampians/Gariwerd Vic. 143–5
The Granite Belt, Qld 254–61
The Huon Valley Tas. 319–27
The Islander Estate 200

The Lake House 239, 242
The Lobster Shack 294, 299
The Lane Vineyard 181, 187
The Pyrenees Vic. 147–8
The Standish Wine Company 161
The Summertown Aristologist 185, 187
The Vegan Dairy 77
The Vineyard Retreat 175
The Vinter's Daughter 43, 45
The Wine Farm 112
The Wine House 13, 14
The Wine Hub 123
Thick as Thieves 68
Thomas Wines 11
Thousand Pound 137
Three Tails Brewery 31, 33
Timbre 285
Tobin Wines 259
Tom's Cap Vineyard 112
Tonic 23
Traviarti and Nature of the Beast 133
Treehouse Tapas and Wine 231, 233
Tscharke 162, 164
Tumbarumba NSW 52
Tumut River Brewing Co. 52
Turkey Flat 162
Twamley Farm 297
Twisted Gum Wines 259
Two Metre Tall Brewery 307, 308
TWØBAYS Brewing Co 77
Tyerrenotepanner Country 279
Tyler's Vineyard 212
Tyrrell's 12, 14

U
Unico Zelo 185
Upper Goulburn Vic. 149
Usher Tinkler 12
Utzinger 287, 289

V
Van Bone 297
Vasse Felix 222, 224
Vegan Dairy, The 77
Vignerons Schmolzer and Brown 133, 135
Vinden Wines 13, 15
Vinea Marson 123, 125
Vineyard Retreat, The 175

Vinter's Daughter, The 43, 45
Vintners Bar & Grill 162, 165
Voyager Estate 223

W
Wadandi Country 215
Waka Waka Country 271
Wathaurung Country 86, 140
Watts River Brewing 68
Waveroo Country 128, 130, 136, 138
Weathercraft 133
Welder's Dog Brewery 54
West Cape Howe Wines 241
Western Ridge Brewing 162
Whadjuk Noongar Country 208
Whistling Kite 205
Wild 142
Wild Hop Brewing 223, 225
Willie Smiths Apple Shed 325, 326
Willing Distillery 251
Wine Farm, The 112
Wine House, The 13, 14
Wine Hub, The 123
Wines by KT 195
Wiradjuri Country 16, 27, 52, 56
Wirra Wirra 175
Woiwurrung Country 97, 98, 106
Wonnarua Country 3
Woodend Wine Store 103, 105
Wowee Zowee 83
Wurundjeri Country 61
Wynns Coonawarra Estate 203

Y
Yabby Lake 83
Yack Creek Distillery 133
Yaithmathang Country 128
Yalumba 163
Yalumba Menzies Retreat 203
Yangarra Estate 175
Yarra Valley Vic. 61–71
Yarra Yering 69
Yellow Billy 13
Yering Station 69, 71
Yuin Country 55
Yuki in the Hills 185

Z
Z Wine 163

JimmyRum, Vic

ABOUT THE AUTHOR

Ben Groundwater gets to travel and drink for a living, and it doesn't get much better than that. He's a Sydney-based writer who specialises in travel and food; he's a columnist for *The Sydney Morning Herald* and *The Age*, a widely published feature writer, the host of the popular travel podcast 'Flight of Fancy', and the author of four books. Ben has twice been named the Australian Society of Travel Writers' 'Travel Writer of the Year'. In a previous life he has also been a travelling cook for a European tour company, a farmhand in northern Scotland, and a short-order cook at a US ski resort. These days he prefers swanning around wine country.

ACKNOWLEDGEMENTS

I would like to start by acknowledging the Cammeraygal People, Traditional Custodians of the land on which I live, as well as the Traditional Owners of the lands of all the Australian wine regions I've been lucky enough to visit in researching this book, and pay my respects to their Elders past and present.

I'm eternally grateful for the help I've received from a huge range of people while researching and writing this book. To my in-house sommeliers and wine snobs, Bridget Raffal and Harry Hunter, thank you so much for the knowledge, and the chicken. To James Halliday and his team of reviewers for the Wine Companion, you have indeed been my companions throughout this experience, sitting on my desk watching over all I do, and
I owe you a debt of gratitude.

To all of the state and regional tourism boards who have assisted with travel and information in the research phase of this book – in particular Sherene Somerville from Tassie, and Taryn Wills in the Barossa – a huge thank you as well.

And of course, a special shout-out to all the people I've drunk with or been drunk with or shared food with in various wine regions around the world over the years: you're the reason I love this stuff. Here's to another round.

A big thanks, too, to the team from Hardie Grant, to Melissa Kayser, Megan Cuthbert and Alice Barker, who have been the driving force behind this project, for their support and their confidence and for helping to make this book the absolute best it could be. And thank you to Hardie Grant's First Nations consultant, Kirsten Hausia, for your invaluable assistance, and to Kate Kiely for proofreading, Hannah Schubert for typesetting, and Andy Warren for designing.

Most of all, however, I would like to thank my partner in life and in food consumption and wine drinking – and their assessment – Jess, who does the hard yards while I'm travelling, who looks after our kids while I get to be away, who does the unsung work that is by far the hardest (as well as doing the very important work of her real job). So much of the knowledge in this book is hers; so many of the opinions expressed here are the products of long conversations between the two of us over beverages of varying quality.

Jess, this book literally would not be possible without you. Thank you. I love you. Now please take that trip to Tasmania.

Photo credits

Front cover: Duy Dash

Back cover: iStock Photo

Pages iv, xviii, 36, 41, 42, 44 (left), 45 (middle and right) 150, 155, 172, 173, 176 (middle and right), 181, 182, 184, 186 (middle and right), 188, 191, 192, 193, 197 (left), 198, 200, 201, 212, 216, 219, 220, 244, 248, 299 (right), 328 Tourism Australia; vi, xiv, 31, 33 (middle) Three Tails Brewery; ix, 274, 275 Moffatdale Ridge; xiii, 18 ChaLou Wines; xvii, 206, 214, 218, 225 (left) Domaine Naturaliste; 88 Basil's Farm/Angela Carrasco; xx, 49, 51 (top right), Ryan Cuerden/Eden Brewery; xxii, 5, 7, 9, 14 (left and middle), 19, 20, 21, 22, 23, 24 (left and middle), 25, 26, 30, 32, 33 (right), 35, 37, 39, 44 (middle and right), 48, 50, 51 (bottom left), 52, 54, 55, 56, 57 Destination NSW; 2, 12 Cessnock City Council; 6 Mjk Creative; 10, 15 (right) Nikki To; 13, 15 (left) Stef Mileski, Motel Picture Co./Vinden Wines; 14 (right) The Wine House; 16 Amy Barrington; 24 (right) Kristen Cunningham; 33 (left) Huntington Estate; 38 Tim Clark Photography @timclark1; 40 Nic Gossage; 43, 45 (left) Erin Dando/The Vintner's Daughter; 46 Kramer Photography, www.kramer.photography; 47, 51 (top left) Artemis Wines; 51 (bottom right) Paste Australia; 58, 60, 66, 67, 68, 69, 70 (left and right), 71 (left and middle), 72, 78, 80, 81, 82, 83, 84 (right), 89, 90, 94, 95 (top left, bottom left and right), 96, 99, 100, 101, 102, 103, 104 (right), 105 (middle and right), 106, 108, 110, 111, 113 (top left, bottom left and right), 114, 115, 116, 117, 118, 119 (top left and right, bottom left), 120, 123, 124, 125 (middle), 126, 129, 132, 134 (middle and right), 135 (left), 136, 137, 139, 140, 141, 142, 145, 147 Visit Victoria; 63, 71 (right) Andrew Paoli at Paoli Smith; 64, 70 (middle) Lauren Bertacchini, Red Fish Blue Fish; 76, 335 Chris McConville/JimmyRum Distillery; 79, 85 (right) Visit Victoria/Anson Smart; 84 (left) Avani Wines; 84 (middle) James Broadway Photography; 85 (left) Mornington Peninsula Regional Tourism; 85 (middle) Michelle Williams; 86 Visit Victoria/Chris McConville; 91 Visit Victoria / Melbourne Convention Bureau; 93, 95 (top right) Oakdene/Pete James; 104 (middle), 125 (left), 224 (middle), 226, 233 (left), 243 (left), 260 (left), 268 (left), 272, 310, 316 (middle) Shutterstock; 105 (left) Mount Monument; 107 Cannibal Creek; 109, 113 (top right) Gurneys Cider; 112 Visit Victoria/Jessica Shapiro; 119 (bottom right) Nils Versemann / Shutterstock.com; 125 (right) Grace Seow; 130 Barking Owl Distilling Co; 134 (left), 149, 168, 177 (left), 180, 187 (left), 208, 211, 217, 232 (right), 240, 255, 258, 261 (right), 269 (left) Alamy; 134 (right) James Broadway/Savaterre; 135 (right) Melany Wimpee; 152, 163 Yalumba; 156, 165 (left) Seppeltsfield; 158, 174, 178, 187 (middle and right), 196, 203, 204 South Australian Tourism Commission; 159 Thomas Rosenzweig / Shutterstock.com; 164 (left) Apex Bakery; 164 (middle) Tscharke; 164 (right) Ben McMahon; 165 (middle) Michael Hall Wines; 165 (right) Vintner's Bar and Grill/South Australian Tourism Commission; 166, 169, 176 (left) Bekkers; 170, 177 (middle) Goodieson Brewery; 171 d'Arenberg; 177 (right) Josie Withers/SATC; 186 (left) Adelaide Hills Wine Region/South Australian Tourism Commission; 195 Lewi Potter/Seed; 197 (right) Duy Dash/Seed; 199 John Montessi; 205 Italo Vardaro; 210 Funk 2.0 / Caitlin Ruth Photography; 213 Cavan Images / Alamy Stock Photo; 221 Leeuwin Estate; 223 Voyager Estate; 224 (right) Vasse Felix; 224 (middle) Wild Hop Brewing Co; 224 (right) Jason Knott / Alamy Stock Photo; 228 Hidden River Estate; 229 Sarah Hewer/Australian Truffle Traders; 230, 232 (left) Peos Estate; 232 (middle) Craig Kinder/Australian Truffle Traders; 233 (right) becauz gao / Shutterstock.com; 234, 238, 242 (left) Harewood Estate; 237, 243 (right) Boston Brewing Co; 239 Frances Andrijich/The Lake House; 241 Singlefile Wines; 242 (right) The Lake House; 246, 251, 325, 326 (right) Liam Neal; 250 Willing Distillery; 252, 254, 256, 257, 260 (right), 261 (left), 262, 265, 266, 268 (middle), 269 (right), 271 Tourism and Events Queensland; 260 (middle) Bent Road; 268 (right) Tourism Australia/ Tourism and Events Queensland; 276, 293, 298 (right), 314, 317 (middle) Lusy Productions; 278, 281, 288 (left) Andrew Wilson; 282, 288 (middle), 300, 303, 305, 320, 321 Adam Gibson; 284, 288 (right), 289 (right) Nat Mendham; 287, 289 (left) Utzinger; 289 (middle) Saige Dingemanse; 290, 292 Pete Harmsen; 294, 295, 296, 299 (left), 323, 324, 327 (left) Tourism Tasmania and Rob Burnett; 298 (left) Spring Bay Distillery; 298 (middle) Leisa Tyler/Alamy Stock Photo; 302 Jarrad Seng; 304 Supplied Courtesy of Institut Polaire; 306, 307 (right), 312, 317 (left) MONA and Jesse Hunniford; 307 (left) Tow Metre Tall Brewery; 307 (middle) Jess Curtin/Stefano Lubiana Wines; 308 (left) Tourism Tasmania & Kathryn Leahy; 308 (right) Osborne Images; 311, 316 (right) Tourism Tasmania & Nick Osborne; 316 (left) Benny Marty/Alamy Stock Photo; 317 (right) David South/Alamy Stock Photo; 319 Clément Aubert; 322, 326 (middle) Chris Phelps; 326 (left) Home Hill Winery; 327 (right) Port Cygnet Cannery.

Published in 2022 by Hardie Grant Explore,
an imprint of Hardie Grant Publishing

Hardie Grant Explore (Melbourne)
Wurundjeri Country
Building 1, 658 Church Street
Richmond, Victoria 3121

Hardie Grant Explore (Sydney)
Gadigal Country
Level 7, 45 Jones Street
Ultimo, NSW 2007

www.hardiegrant.com/au/explore

All rights reserved. No part of this publication may be reproduced, stored in a retrieval system or transmitted in any form by any means, electronic, mechanical, photocopying, recording or otherwise, without the prior written permission of the publishers and copyright holders.

The moral rights of the author have been asserted.

Copyright text © Ben Groundwater 2022
Copyright concept, maps and design © Hardie Grant Publishing 2022

In palawa kani, the language of Tasmanian Aboriginal People, with thanks to the Tasmanian Aboriginal Centre.

The maps in this publication incorporate data © Commonwealth of Australia (Geoscience Australia), 2006. Geoscience Australia has not evaluated the data as altered and incorporated within this publication, and therefore gives no warranty regarding accuracy, completeness, currency or suitability for any particular purpose.

Incorporates or developed using [Roads Nov 2020, Hydrology Nov 2012] © Geoscape Australia for Copyright and Disclaimer Notice see geoscape.com.au/legal/data-copyright-and-disclaimer

Maps contain parks and reserves data which is owned by and copyright of the relevant state and territory government authorities. © Australian Capital Territory. www.ACTmapi.act.gov.au Creative Commons Attribution 4.0 International (CC BY 4.0) © State of New South Wales (Department of Planning, Industry and Environment) Creative Commons Attribution 4.0 International (CC BY 4.0)

© State of New South Wales (Department of Primary Industries) Creative Commons Attribution 4.0 International (CC BY 4.0)
© State of Victoria (Department of Environment, Land, Water and Planning) Creative Commons Attribution 4.0 international (CC BY 4.0) © State of South Australia (Department for Environment and Water) Creative Commons Attribution 4.0 Australia (CC BY 4.0) © State of Western Australia (Department of Biodiversity, Conservation and Attractions) Creative Commons Attribution 3.0 Australia (CC BY 3.0 AU) © Northern Territory Government of Australia (Department of Environment, Parks and Water Security) Creative Commons Attribution 4.0 International (CC BY 4.0)
© The State of Queensland (Department of Environment and Science) Creative Commons Attribution 4.0 International (CC BY 4.0) © Commonwealth of Australia (Great Barrier Reef Marine Park Authority) Creative Commons Attribution 4.0 International (CC BY 4.0) © State of Tasmania (Department of Primary Industries, Parks, Water and Environment) Creative Commons Attribution 3.0 Australia (CC BY 3.0 AU)

A catalogue record for this book is available from the National Library of Australia

Hardie Grant acknowledges the Traditional Owners of the Country on which we work, the Wurundjeri People of the Kulin Nation and the Gadigal People of the Eora Nation, and recognises their continuing connection to the land, waters and culture. We pay our respects to their Elders past and present.

Ultimate Food & Drink: Australia
ISBN 9781741178005

10 9 8 7 6 5 4 3 2 1

Publisher Melissa Kayser
Project editor Megan Cuthbert
Editor Alice Barker
Proofreader Kate Kiely
Trainee editor Gemma Taylor
Content consultant Kirsten Hausia
Cartographer Emily Maffei and Claire Johnston
Production coordinator Jessica Harvie
Design Andy Warren
Typesetting Hannah Schubert
Index Max McMaster

Colour reproduction by Hannah Schubert and Splitting Image Colour Studio

Printed and bound in China by LEO Paper Products LTD.

The paper this book is printed on is certified against the Forest Stewardship Council® Standards and other sources. FSC® promotes environmentally responsible, socially beneficial and economically viable management of the world's forests.

Disclaimer: While every care is taken to ensure the accuracy of the data within this product, the owners of the data (including the state, territory and Commonwealth governments of Australia) do not make any representations or warranties about its accuracy, reliability, completeness or suitability for any particular purpose and, to the extent permitted by law, the owners of the data disclaim all responsibility and all liability (including without limitation, liability in negligence) for all expenses, losses, damages (including indirect or consequential damages) and costs which might be incurred as a result of the data being inaccurate or incomplete in any way and for any reason.

Publisher's Disclaimers: The publisher cannot accept responsibility for any errors or omissions. The representation on the maps of any road or track is not necessarily evidence of public right of way. The publisher cannot be held responsible for any injury, loss or damage incurred during travel. It is vital to research any proposed trip thoroughly and seek the advice of relevant state and travel organisations before you leave.

Publisher's Note: Every effort has been made to ensure that the information in this book is accurate at the time of going to press. The publisher welcomes information and suggestions for correction or improvement.